The Vital Message

The Vital Message

Continuing Education and the University of Cambridge 1945–2010

by
Mark Freeman

First UK edition, published in Great Britain in 2023 by Regents Court Press

An imprint of Regents Court Press Ltd, St Albans, Hertfordshire, UK

ISBN: 978 1 9163084 8 0

British Library Cataloguing-in-Publication Data

A catalogue record for this book is available from the British Library

Typeset by Regents Court Press Ltd

Cover design by Lily Wielar

Cover image: book-boxes that were sent to local centres in the Cambridge extramural region until the 2000s, discovered by the author in the Stuart Room at Madingley Hall.

For Laura, Kara and Millie

Contents

List of tables

Foreword
by James Gazzard

As I sit in a beige airport departure lounge on a piercingly bright autumnal Californian late afternoon, awaiting an inevitably delayed flight home, it's possible to mindlessly browse thousands of higher education courses offered by universities cast around the globe. Many of the courses are open to all, assuming an internet connection and, more often than not, competency in the English language. In some cases, whole curricula can be accessed free of charge: 'click now to enrol'. Rich learning materials, videos and interactive quizzes scroll down the screen. Knowledge democratised. Learning for all. To a point, perhaps.

It is possible to trace the arc of progress from today back through 150-years to a churchyard in the English East Midlands. A young academic from the University of Cambridge called T .O. Harding prepared to deliver his introductory remarks, in October 1873, on a 12-week course entitled 'Force and Motion'. Unremarkable, really. Except when you stop to consider the location of the teaching and the makeup of the audience. The venue was not a university campus and the audience neither exclusively young, male, privileged nor vetted for previous qualifications. The modest group gathered in Harding's class were men *and* women – factory workers, office clerks, school teachers and the like – ordinary people, accessing a Cambridge quality education in a dimly lit room in Derby's city centre.

Harding's class were actually 'cohort 1' in an experiment in what was to go on to become a global university-led extension education movement. The first students to fall under an officially sanctioned programme of extramural education; the University of Cambridge's Local Lectures Syndicate, today known as the Institute of Continuing Education. A faint sketch of a blueprint for an open university – beyond the walls of a campus – had moved from drawing board to reality. A door opened to a different type of university.

These extramural communities of learning had a profound impact on many; particularly informing citizens to articulate their thoughts in order to secure more meaningful work, educate their children or campaign for greater societal fairness. The educational networks spread across England. Groups of peripatetic tutors began to teach in new ways to respond to the needs of their audiences; and in several cities they led the formation of university colleges, a number of which now sit within the Russell Group of research-driven highly selective institutions. It is interesting to reflect, perhaps, that universities often tend to hunger for the status of research intensity and selectivity, even when originally formed as teaching-intensive open-access centres of education.

This tendency might explain some of the challenges faced by most English university-led departments of continuing education over the years. Often poorly understood and positioned on the periphery of university activities, and seldom backed and boosted by government policy, the experience of most departments has been one characterised by turbulence, change and precarity. In more recent times, as half of younger people in England enrolled on campuses as full-time students, as part of Tony Blair's 'education, education, education' revolution, the support for lifelong learning was greatly reduced and as demand fell many departments of continuing education closed. Those that persevered were forced to innovate, give birth to new academic disciplines and experiment as early adopters with new modes of delivery, including fully online teaching and important new approaches to authentic student-led curriculum design. Adult learners would often progress from novice to expert; with students progressing to become the teachers and further proliferating the work.

Mark Freeman's book, *The Vital Message*, captures a choppy seven-decade period from 1945 to 2010 through the eyes of key stakeholders directing, delivering and consuming lifelong education at Cambridge. It builds on the books published at our jubilee in 1923 and centenary in 1973. As we mark our sesquicentennial anniversary in 2023, this new publication is a genuine reflective exploration of the influential innovation originated at the extramural department at Cambridge: of mistakes made, of opportunities missed, of the constant drive to change and adapt just to survive, and of the perennial tension in which a research-led selective entity such as Cambridge works to both help and hinder a teaching-intensive open university such as the Institute of Continuing Education.

As things stand today, looking out to a plethora of specialist professional schools in fields ranging from business and leadership to sustainability to AI, challenger 'start-up' universities offering education to all and the aforementioned online marketplaces, it is my belief that

Professor Freeman's book places a spotlight on, and captures the value of, multidisciplinary, open-access and affordable departments of continuing education housed within leading universities.

The value they present lies, of course, in the communities of learning they curate, educate and sustain, and the voice this gives to adults irrespective of whether they left school with a bucketload of qualifications or none, whether they joined the class aged 25 or 85, and whether they are learning for personal interest or professional advancement – or both.

In closing, as my flight begins to board, it is interesting to reflect that when you browse online storefronts of the new online platforms for courses, there is not much of substance to be found which considers the history of the university extension education movement, its role in shaping the worldwide higher education sector, and the important contributions of professionals in the field or its impact on adult learners. Consequently, I hope this book will inform policy-makers, continuing education professionals and lifelong learners about Cambridge's story, and enable them all to imagine how the next chapters of extension education will be shaped at their organisations and in their communities around the world in the name of enabling *all* adults to equitably access exceptional learning opportunities throughout their lives.

James Gazzard BSc (Hons) PhD MBA PGCert MA FHEA
Director of Continuing Education
University of Cambridge Institute of Continuing Education

Preface

This book was commissioned by the Institute of Continuing Education, University of Cambridge (ICE), to mark the sesquicentenary of the the first Cambridge university extension lectures, which took place in October 1873. Jubilee and centenary histories were published in 1923 and 1973 respectively, so I am conscious that the history of continuing education – or extramural studies – at Cambridge is being repeatedly rewritten, and that this will continue to happen in the future. I should also acknowledge that, although commissioned to write the book, I have no other connection with ICE or with the University of Cambridge; whether this is an advantage or otherwise may be open to debate. In any case, writing the book has been a challenge, particularly because its focus is on the period after the Second World War: as one historian has commented, '[w]riting the history of university adult education after 1945 is considerably more difficult than for any preceding period'.[1] In support of this, I am grateful to James Gazzard, director of ICE, for commissioning the book and for supporting me throughout the long process of writing it.

As Joanna Bourke has recognised in a bicentenary history of Birkbeck, University of London – also published this year – institutional history has 'many perils', and it is impossible to 'please everyone'.[2] I am sure that I will not do so with this book. It is very difficult to write about the most recent period in the life of any institution, and I have taken the decision to end the account in 2010 rather than trying to bring it right down to the present day. With only a handful of exceptions, I have largely avoided mentioning any current members of staff or students at ICE, and have attempted to treat all periods with some historical detachment.

Nevertheless, and despite its length, the book's coverage is admittedly uneven. I have given the greatest prominence to what was known as the 'regional programme', later the 'extension programme', and more recently the 'public programmes' – that aspect of ICE's diverse work that grew out of the emergence of university adult education in the late nineteenth and early twentieth centuries, and formed the largest single part of its activity until quite recently. Other publications have appeared to mark the eightieth and ninetieth anniversaries and – again this year – the centenary of ICE's International Summer Programmes, although these do form a part of the narrative in this book. Even in the long sections of each chapter on the regional programme, though, I have tended to focus more on some issues than others; another author would have written a very different account of ICE's history.

The book is based on two main sources: archival material held in Cambridge University Library and in ICE's current home at Madingley Hall, and a small sample of around 25 interviews with former (and a handful of current) members of staff and students. The archival material would support a much longer study, or series of studies, and it is particularly rich for the history of the public programmes. I have drawn heavily on material in the public domain – particularly ICE's annual reports, of which there is a complete set at Madingley Hall – but the archival material has added richness and detail, particularly for the earlier periods covered by the book.

Interviewees could go 'on the record' or contribute anonymously, and all have had the opportunity to review anything that is attributed them in the text. In this context it is particularly important to emphasise the debt that I owe to Christopher Padfield, who died shortly after we met in February 2023. It was a great pleasure to discuss with him, and with Dame Polly Courtice, the history of the Cambridge Programme for Industry, whose history is entwined with ICE's for some of the period covered by this book. I am honoured to have had the opportunity to incorporate his insights into the relevant sections of *The Vital Message*. I am immensely grateful, too, to all my other interviewees, and particularly to those who subsequently made many helpful corrections of the text and suggestions for improvement. Michael Allen, David Davies, Dame Polly Courtice, Sarah Ormrod and Richard Taylor, in particular, have read large sections of the book in draft form. Of course, I remain responsible for any errors of fact or interpretation in the book.

The title of the book, *The Vital Message*, comes a quotation in chapter 7 from one of ICE's annual reports (see page 204). The phrase nicely captures the sense of purpose – the missionary spirit, perhaps – that has sometimes been associated with university adult education. The word 'movement' has often been used in connection with adult education, and certainly many of those who have worked in it have seen their activities in this way.

I have incurred many other debts in writing the book. The teaching, domestic and professional staff at Madingley Hall have been unfailingly helpful and courteous throughout the time I have spent writing the book. It is invidious to single out individuals, but – along with James Gazzard, who is mentioned above – I am particularly grateful to Donna Johnson, Rebecca Barnes, Richard Stuckey, Christine Kinally, Richard Gant, Louisa Kennedy and Gilly Walker and to the many members of the reception, garden, catering and bar staff who have made my many visits to the Hall so enjoyable and productive. I am also grateful to Cambridge University Library, especially the Department of Manuscripts and University Archives, and to other libraries including my own university library at UCL, as well as the British Library and – for different, but no less important, reasons – the landlords and staff of the Three Horseshoes in Madingley. As well as all my interviewees, I have benefited from conversations with Sharon Clancy, Peter Cunningham, Lottie Hoare, John Holford and Bill Jones, and with delegates at the Universities Association for Lifelong Learning conference at Madingley in 2023, which was held alongside the Standing Conference on University Teaching and Research in the Education of Adults. I would also have liked to have the chance to discuss the project, as I did others, with the late Malcolm Chase, who was an inspiration in many ways, and whose publications on the history of university adult education stimulated much of my thinking on the subject.

Some of the preparatory work for the book has been shared at conferences of the International Centre for Historical Research in Education at UCL, at the History of Education Society and at the International Forum for Young Scholars in Education at East China Normal University. All the organisers of these conferences have helped with the development of this project, and I am likewise grateful to them. I would also like to thank Diana Munby for her support, and for sharing her memories of Lionel Munby, as well as lending me some fascinating documents from his long working life in Cambridge. David Davies has also given me access to documents from the 1990s. I have also had fruitful discussions about writing institutional history with Sam Blaxland, Joanna Bourke, Georgina Brewis and Tom Woodin, among others.

I have also benefited from the support of my two UCL Education, Practice and Society Undergraduate Research Fellows, Yixuan (Alice) Wang and Jianuo (Vivian) Yang. They have made a substantial contribution to the book, providing research support as well as much-needed encouragement. It has been a pleasure working with them, and with Lily Wieler who designed the cover.

Finally, I am grateful to all those, too many to name, who have encouraged me through the interesting but sometimes arduous process of writing this book. The past three years have presented unexpected challenges, and I am grateful to the many who have supported me through them. As always, I am sustained by times spent in the company of my family and friends. This book is dedicated to Laura, Kara and Millie, with affection and gratitude.

Chapter 1
The mustard left on dinner-plates: Cambridge and extramural studies before 1945

This book is about the extramural activities of a single university, and an atypical university at that. As one former member of staff at Cambridge – Adrian Barlow – has explained, the word 'extramural' is 'now out of favour', but in many respects 'apt and reasonably accurate' as a description of what this book will explore.[1] As a residential and collegiate university, Cambridge has mainly concerned itself, throughout the many centuries of its history, with full-time students who spend a concentrated period of time 'within the walls'. Despite the emergence of new 'redbrick' universities in the nineteenth and early twentieth centuries, and the wave of purpose-built campus universities after the Second World War – not to mention other institutional developments in higher education or the alternative models available elsewhere, particularly in Scotland – the dominant image of what we now call the 'student experience' is of a young person spending three years in the more or less rarified environment of a residential university. The standard histories of higher education, and of individual universities, rarely focus on what was happening 'extramurally' – beyond the walls – although it is widely acknowledged that some new institutions themselves emerged from the extramural activities of others.[2] Many excellent institutional histories have only a brief mention of extramural teaching, or none at all.[3] Even the 1981 history of the University of Liverpool, by former director of extramural studies Thomas Kelly – author of one of the standard histories of adult education in Britain – has only a few pages on 'fringe activities', including extramural education.[4] For most of its history, university extramural activity has been pursued in separate departments, often with separate sources of funding, and has been outside the mainstream of subject-based teaching and research.

Partly for this reason, university adult education – the most institutionally distinctive aspect of extramural activity, at least for most of the twentieth century – developed a somewhat separate tradition of writing historically about itself. There is a large body of historical research, much of it now quite old, on the 'tradition' – a word that is repeatedly used – of university extramural education. This is often presented in terms of the marginal status of extramural departments, a theme pursued in a number of studies and summarised by

Malcolm Chase: '[a]dult education, perceiving itself to be marginal, has felt the need frequently to seek both the validation and inspiration of history'.[5] From the 1950s in particular, university extramural departments and their spokesmen self-consciously placed themselves within a 'Great Tradition' (Chase noted that 'the capitals, it would seem are now obligatory'), and the result was a series of historical accounts that presented university adult education as embattled, taking a defensive perspective and a self-justifying tone.[6] This in turn, some argued, weakened the influence that the extramural departments of universities could wield in wider educational policy and politics; and it could result in 'self-absorption and prevarication' as well as an uncertain position within university hierarchies and governance.[7] It is certainly possible, as this book will show, to find examples of these tendencies at Cambridge, although one of the virtues of an institutional history is that a wider range of activities and perspectives can be explored in more depth, and some of the internal debates and changes of direction can be uncovered.

The terminology of extramural education has evolved over time, not always without controversy. The sub-title of this book, for example, refers to 'continuing education', a term that would be unknown to the pioneers of extramural studies at Cambridge in the nineteenth century, but which came to dominate the field of university adult education in the late twentieth. In part, this reflects ongoing changes of mission, as universities enter new fields of activity and discard old ones, but it also relates to the marginal status, and perhaps also the self-perception, of those who work in the field. As Barlow notes,

> Extension lectures, extramural studies, lifelong learning, continuing education: the labels change over time. Partly, this is because the very concept of extramural studies keeps evolving; partly it is because each earlier label carries connotations later thought to be unfortunate. In some corners of every university, the very idea of extramural studies is treated with condescension: how do part-time adult learners, studying for personal fulfilment or for professional development, really fit into the modern world of the research intensive university?[8]

The language in this book will reflect the changing terminology of the field, and I acknowledge that this can seem clumsy. I have in places used 'university adult education' as a catch-all term for the subject-matter of the book, though this term, too, is rather imprecise, given that almost *all* students at universities are in fact adults, at least legally. Ultimately, the range of terminology reflects the complexity of the topic, and it is difficult to avoid this when writing about university adult education and its many branches.

The purpose of this first chapter is to outline briefly the history of extramural studies at Cambridge before 1945, to set the scene for its subsequent rapid expansion and development. There are much fuller accounts of the period before the Second World War in two previous anniversary histories. One of these, *University Extension* by W. H. Draper, is mentioned in the text below. The other is the centenary history of Cambridge extramural education, *The Peripatetic University* by Edwin Welch, published in 1973.[9] I have drawn quite heavily in places on Welch's book, which has a strong focus on the late nineteenth and early twentieth centuries, and was based on a large body of archival material that is now mostly in Cambridge University Library.

*

Any history of 'continuing education' must first consider the emergence of 'university extension'. There were many early forms of university extension, not least the establishment of new universities and colleges in the mid-nineteenth century, in London and in the industrial towns of the north and midlands. What is usually meant by the term, though, is 'the extension of facilities for part-time university education', and there were ad hoc attempts to do this in the mid-nineteenth century, sometimes by individual academics in association with locally organised societies in various parts of the country.[10] One example was Adam Sedgwick, professor of geology at Cambridge, who lectured to 'townspeople' as well as his own students; his audiences included women, who were not able to study at Cambridge during the five decades that he occupied his chair. Sedgwick 'gave vivid and widely reported lectures throughout the country'.[11] Another popular lecturer was James Stuart, a fellow of Trinity College and mathematics graduate, who in 1867 gave a series of lectures in four cities – Leeds, Liverpool, Sheffield and Manchester – on the history of science to audiences brought together by the North of England Council for Promoting the Higher Education of Women. Stuart also lectured to railway workers at Crewe, and to members of the co-operative society at Rochdale; and developed the idea of what he called 'a peripatetic university the professors of which would circulate among the big towns'.[12] It was Stuart's strong belief that the 'permeating influence' of the university could and should be spread to constituencies that it did not already reach; and it was clear that both women and 'working men' were potential audiences for the popular lectures that he and others gave.

University extension 'formally arrived' in 1873, when the University of Cambridge Local Lectures Syndicate was established, with Stuart himself as the secretary. The Syndicate was created by, and reported to, the Council of the Senate, which it and its successors would continue to do for well over a century.[13] The nearest precedent within the university was the Local Examinations Syndicate, but whereas this venture – established in 1858 – had become 'entirely self-supporting', this would not be the case for 'local lectures'.[14] Indeed, from 1878 the organisational arrangements were changed, with a Local Lectures Committee operating under a Syndicate that covered both lectures and local examinations.[15] Nevertheless, the local lectures gathered impetus right from the start. The first lectures were in Derby, Nottingham and Leicester in the autumn of 1873, and by 1875-6 there were 128 courses of lectures, each lasting for a term. This number was not matched again for some time, but the new educational movement was reaching impressive numbers of people: in 1878-9, there were 56 lecture courses with a total attendance of 4,920.[16] They took place in 'local centres' across the country, and were delivered by a range of lecturers from the Cambridge 'list', some of whom were successful enough to make a living through university extension for many years. The Shakespeare and biblical scholar Richard Green Moulton, for example, was one of a number of 'professional' extension lecturers in the late nineteenth century, teaching across the country and basing some of his books on the lectures that he gave.[17] The local centres themselves were often 'extension societies', attached to an existing educational institution.

James Stuart himself, whose name was – and would remain – indelibly associated with the establishment of university extension, retained some involvement and much influence after his appointment in 1875 as Cambridge professor of mechanism and applied mechanics. He was elected to parliament – as a Liberal – in 1884 and would sit as an MP for most of the rest of his life, although he never held ministerial office. In 1890 he married Laura Elizabeth Colman, daughter of the mustard manufacturer Jeremiah Colman of Norwich, who was also a Liberal MP. Stuart himself led the mustard company for some years after Colman's death in 1898, and died himself in 1913.[18] When Laura Stuart died in 1920, she left £5,000 (worth more than £180,000 in today's values) to endow extramural studies at Cambridge.[19]

From an early date, the Universities of Oxford and London, and others too, began to develop their own extension programmes, and by 1893-4 it has been estimated that more than 60,000 people were attending lectures. For Cambridge lectures, the number in that academic year was 10,452 across 133 courses, and it was not unusual for 200 to be in attendance at a single lecture, with numbers sometimes getting up to 800 or even 1,000.[20] The standard length became a course of 10 to 12 lectures, running over a single term, and the subjects of study were varied: in the early 1890s, across the Cambridge, Oxford and London programmes, there were 457 extension courses, of which 191 were on the natural sciences and 159 on 'history or political economy', with a further 104 on literature.[21] The format of courses evolved 'almost accidentally' to involve three key features. One was the circulation of a printed syllabus, which outlined the contents of the lectures and contained a reading list and questions for students to consider. This could be a long document: one of Moulton's, for an 11-week course, consisted of 63 pages.[22] The second feature was the expectation that students would do written work, often in advance of the class, generally answering a series of questions set by the lecturer. Some students would then sit an examination, answering set questions in a more formal way and potentially receiving a university award: at Cambridge, this was the Vice-Chancellor's Certificate, first awarded in 1879, which required successful completion of examinations at the end of a three-year series of extension courses.[23] The numbers entering extension course examinations could be quite impressive in the late nineteenth century: in 1893-4, for example, 1,415 students entered, comprising more than a tenth of those attending the Cambridge lectures.[24] From 1894 'sessional certificates' were also issued for students who had passed an examination at the end of a single year.[25]

The third key feature of university extension was the separation of the lecture from a subsequent 'discussion' or 'class' period. This reflected what became the two distinct purposes of the courses: on the one hand, 'to awaken and stimulate a general interest amongst a wide circle of people in certain subjects', but also 'to encourage some of the audience to undertake systematic study of such subjects'.[26] This meant that each extension course meeting would have a lecture of around an hour followed by a discussion lasting about as long, but the latter would be attended only by those aiming at 'systematic study'. Clearly those intending to enter the examination would be among them, but many others went to the discussion sessions too: in 1893-4 they were attended by 4,219 students, a little under half of those who went to the lectures.[27] This meant, in turn, that the discussion period cannot always have functioned very effectively – it would not be unusual to have at least 50 or 60 students present – and this in turn undermined the 'standards' that the universities were already consciously trying to impose on the extension movement. As the two distinct aims of the courses suggest, there was a 'fundamental ambivalence of purpose' about university extension: was it 'general cultural education' or was it primarily aimed at more focused, serious students?[28] The tension between these two objectives – the latter of which might seem particularly the province of universities, the former perhaps achievable by many other agencies too – would underlie many subsequent debates on the nature and purpose of university adult education.

By the early twentieth century, the university extension movement was shrinking somewhat; if it was not quite running out of steam, it was certainly facing new educational movements and trying to meet emerging demands. The number of students attending lectures declined, from around perhaps 50,000 at the start of the century to around 30,000 on the eve of the First World War; and on courses run by Cambridge, although attendances remained high, the numbers attending the discussion period declined, while those taking the examinations fell quite precipitately. In 1912-13 there were 80 courses across 71 separate 'local centres', with 11,488 students attending lectures, 2,260 (around a fifth of the total) going on to the discussions, and just 268 sitting the examinations.[29] If the movement had ever aimed to reach a working-class student constituency, it was failing to do this, although there is no doubt that it was serving other equally important groups. Around two-thirds of the students were women – often school teachers or pupil-teachers – and it has been estimated that the working-class component of the student body was around a fifth to a quarter.[30] There had been some successes in embedding the culture of university education in places without any other higher education institutions, and indeed some universities – Sheffield, Nottingham and Exeter are examples – grew in part out of university extension activity, in each of these cases involving Cambridge.[31] Despite this, though, it was quite clear in the early twentieth century that university extension itself 'was providing very little continuous and systematic teaching of a university standard'.[32]

One substantial impetus towards change came from the establishment, in 1903, of the Workers' Educational Association (WEA), led by Albert Mansbridge. The role and impact of the WEA has been much debated in the literature on adult education, and this will not be addressed here, but the partnerships that initially developed between universities and the WEA in the years before the First World War would powerfully influence the development of adult education for most of the twentieth century. The organisation grew quickly – it had 110 branches and 7,000 individual members by 1912[33] – and embodied a sense of educational idealism that, in its broadest conception, sought to support individuals in working-class social movements to (in Mansbridge's words) 'lift themselves up through higher knowledge to higher works and higher pleasures, which, if responded to, will inevitably bring about right and sound action upon Municipal, National and Imperial affairs'.[34] The universities, particularly Oxford, took notice of this development, and a widely cited report in 1908 on *Oxford and Working-Class Education* led to the establishment of a national joint advisory committee bringing together universities and the WEA. This new organisation had access to a so-called 'golden stream' of funding from central government and local authorities, and it strongly pushed for the provision of a new kind of three-year course of study, the tutorial class.[35] This kind of class is described in more detail below, but it represented a significant departure from the shorter term-long extension courses, and required a more sustained commitment from students to a period of study that was of equivalent length to the university undergraduate degree. Cambridge started running tutorial classes in 1909, at its local centres in Leicester, Portsmouth and Wellingborough.[36]

Tutorial classes seem to have attracted much the same kind of students – albeit probably more serious and committed – as the older extension courses. Depending on the location, they were attended by 'the teachers, the insurance agents, the railway clerks and the post office clerks in their "villas"', by 'skilled artisans and managers living in recently-built houses', and at Leicester in particular by 'the owners of a bookshop and a dairy, an insurance superintendent and the secretary of the Charity Organisation Society'.[37] As with extension courses, tutorial classes were not necessarily cheap to attend at this time, and this would remain the case even after the 'golden stream' flowed more generously after the First World War. Nevertheless, it was clear by 1913 that tutorial classes would be 'a permanent part of the Syndicate's work', and this expectation was not confounded by the disruptions of the war itself.[38] The war reduced the amount of extramural work quite considerably – the number of extension courses provided by the Cambridge Syndicate halved, and the number of students fell similarly, while the numbers entering for examinations was no more than a trickle – but a few tutorial classes continued to run.

By this time university extension was already being seen as an educational tradition, and demonstrating a strong interest in its own history. Even in the late nineteenth century, historical accounts of it were being published, and in 1923 there was a jubilee history covering Cambridge and other universities. William H. Draper's *University Extension: A Survey of Fifty Years 1873-1923*, published by Cambridge University Press, told a detailed story of the emergence of university extramural teaching in Cambridge, Oxford and London, with additional material on other universities that had followed Stuart's lead in the early twentieth century. Draper emphasised the role of the three-year tutorial class,[39] and in 1921-2 there were 342 tutorial classes across the university extension movement, with a total of 7,783 students, who were expected to attend 24 class meetings each year and produce written work – which in some cases, notably at the University of London, could be assessed, and students could achieve a certificate.[40]

Draper was writing on the cusp of a significant change, which would extend and strengthen the universities' role in adult education. In 1919 the report of the Adult Education Committee of the Ministry of Reconstruction – often referred to in adult education circles simply as the '1919 Report' – had strongly endorsed the role of universities and voluntary organisations in non-vocational education; and, stimulated by the climate of optimism that this engendered and by expectations of funding being available to support their work, many universities established extramural departments for the first time. University College Nottingham led the way in 1920, and was followed by Exeter in 1922, Bristol in 1923, Newcastle in 1926, and then Hull, Southampton, Birmingham and Leicester later in the 1920s.[41] In 1924 new adult education regulations issued by the Board of Education established 'Responsible Bodies' that were eligible for central government grants to support activity ranging from tutorial classes to the 'shorter and less demanding' university extension lecture courses.[42] Universities, the WEA and other organisations could be Responsible Bodies, and it has been argued that the willingness of the state to fund shorter courses undermined the distinctiveness of what universities did in adult education, as well as potentially 'widening the gap between extramural and intramural work' and ensuring that the new departments, or indeed older ones, were marginalised from the core activities of their parent universities.[43] Certainly the receipt of government grants exposed university adult education to the oversight of HM Inspectors, which was not the case for most other parts of the university sector; however, the relationship between extramural departments and the inspectorate seems mostly to have been good.[44] In brief, what the new regulations fostered was a period of 'new extension', in which a more structured pattern of provision would gradually emerge.[45]

At Cambridge, the new funding arrangements resulted in organisational changes to the administration of the extramural activities of the university. The central change was the formation of a Board of Extra-Mural Studies to replace the Local Lectures Syndicate, allowing for stronger external representation on the central decision-making body. The new Board consisted of 21 members: the vice-chancellor was an *ex officio* member (at this point the vice-chancellor's job was usually held for one, two or three years by the head of one of the colleges), and there were 10 nominated by the university's Senate, five by the WEA and five by the Local Centres Union, the body that represented the local extension centres in their relationship with Cambridge.[46] The Board had a full-time secretary, an assistant secretary and two members of clerical staff, and in 1927 it would move into a new building, Stuart House on Mill Lane, which replaced the previous 'cramped' headquarters. Stuart House had a library, which also served as a common room for the small number of mature students who were studying as Cambridge undergraduates; and from this library book-boxes were sent out across the network of local centres for their students, who were often at a great distance from any university or other library, to use.[47] Book-boxes dated back to the early years of university extension: the first were sent out by Oxford in 1885.[48]

The secretary to the Board, on its establishment in 1924, was D. H. S. (Somerset) Cranage, a former Anglican curate who had been the Local Lectures secretary from 1902 and held a number of other roles across education and the Church of England, becoming dean of Norwich in 1928.[49] Cranage lectured on church history and architecture, and as secretary oversaw Cambridge's involvement in courses taught with the WEA. His assistant secretary was the mountaineer George Mallory, whose death on Everest alongside Andrew Irvine in 1924 created a vacancy.[50] Mallory's replacement was a Cambridge history graduate, Geoffrey Hickson, who – when Cranage moved to Norwich – took over as Board secretary. Hickson would hold the position for almost four decades, retiring in 1967; he was remembered for his 'distinctive contribution to the pattern of adult education in England'. Among other things an 'accomplished violinist', he was a man of 'versatility and liberality of interest', and in his leadership role was highly trusted by those who worked for him, the number of whom would increase significantly after the Second World War.[51]

As one colleague wrote of Hickson on his retirement, he 'made possible significant developments because he has left his staff alone while supporting them in whatever they achieved'.[52] Hickson did some teaching, though other duties limited his contributions in this respect, and he also served two terms as mayor of Cambridge after the Second World War.[53]

When Hickson died in 1978, the Board noted that '[h]e was the last of the Secretaries whose parish was the whole of England', organising classes as far afield as Devon, Yorkshire and Northumberland.[54] During the first decade of his leadership, the provision of courses was increasingly concentrated within the East Anglian region: although some more remote centres continued to provide Cambridge courses, the growth of other university extramural departments meant that, increasingly, each university was responsible for its own fairly well-defined extramural region. Some geographical anomalies remained, and the process of regional consolidation took time: in 1935-6, for example, Cambridge was still running extension courses in Hastings, Portsmouth, Paignton, Barnstaple, Southport and Grantham, although courses run with the WEA were more likely to be in its 'own' region, which at this time included Rugby, in Warwickshire, where a tutorial class was running.[55] There had already been a process of negotiation, and often competition, between universities for the right to run extramural activities in particular places, and the competitive side of this may have intensified as more meaningful funding was made available for the work. Cranage had already complained about new universities 'encroaching' into some Cambridge centres, and Hickson had to deal with territorial changes through the 1930s: the Hull local centre, for example, transferred from Cambridge to its own city's university in 1933.[56] It has been argued that what emerged from this process was a network of 'extramural empires', often jealously guarded by the universities, in which their own self-interest was pursued as much as the greater goal of expanding adult education opportunities to the wider population; one observer called the universities 'predatory' in this respect.[57]

As the universities carved up their own 'extramural empires', strong attempts were made to build up more local centres within them: a process of internal colonisation, to stretch the metaphor. In the Cambridge region – comprising Cambridgeshire, Northamptonshire, Norfolk, Suffolk, Essex, Hertfordshire and Bedfordshire, with a few outlying centres – there were some large centres of population in which courses of various kinds were provided, but there were also large tracts of countryside in which real efforts were made to spread university adult education. Working initially with the WEA in Bedfordshire from 1927, the Board established a Rural Areas Committee, collaborating with local authorities and obtaining grants from educational charities such as the Cassel Trust.[58] The provision ranged from short courses to three-year tutorial classes, and continued into the Second World War, laying the ground for subsequent expansion the late 1940s and early 1950s. A whole series of 'pioneer' activity established new local centres and uncovered new demands for educational opportunities among the population of the region, and cemented the relationships both with the centres themselves and with the WEA. The local activity was supplemented with residential courses, organised with the National Council for Social Service, for the unemployed during the depression of the 1930s; and students from the rural areas were able to attend Saturday schools in Cambridge, an 'experiment' that proved popular throughout the decade.[59] By 1937-8 the Board was running a total of 31 tutorial classes and two 'preparatory' classes that it hoped might become tutorial classes, with a total of 651 enrolments, and 50 one-term extension courses with 3,585 attending the lectures.[60]

The subjects of courses evolved over time in response to student demand. In the early 1930s, literature was the most popular subject, comprising 33% of all courses taught by the Board, with history and art/architecture both at 17%, music at 14%, science at 8% and 'economics, social and political theory' – a catch-all category – standing at 11%.[61] With the international situation deteriorating in the 1930s, 'international affairs' became increasingly popular with students. As the Board noted in 1938,

> Attention may be drawn to the large proportion in recent years of courses dealing with international affairs: these have attracted consistently good attendance and have been accompanied by excellent discussions and a wide use of the books provided. The Board believe that much valuable work has been done and that by providing a forum for instruction in the discussion of this subject of wide-spread topical interest they have made a real contribution to education in citizenship.[62]

By the middle of the Second World War – throughout which the Board managed to run its courses, with almost double the number in 1942-3 than in 1932-3 – the 'economics, social and political theory' category (which included international affairs) accounted for 48% of the courses, with literature falling to

19%, science to just 1%, music to 4% and history to 9%. Art and architecture sustained their popularity, with 19% of courses in that year.[63]

In order to qualify the Board to receive grants in respect of courses, students needed to be 'effective': in other words, they needed to attend at least two-thirds of the meetings and to produce written work. This could be a stiff requirement, and many students did not become 'effective': for example, of the 651 who enrolled in tutorial and preparatory classes in 1937-8, only 439 (just over two-thirds) satisfied the requirements.[64] The production of written work, and a sustained effort at reading, were more usual in tutorial classes than elsewhere, and on the shorter 'extension' courses it was a minority activity, though sometimes the students did produce good work. On these courses, students could also sit an examination, which was even less common, but one tutor recalled how these assessed activities could benefit a wide range of students from very different backgrounds:

> the average number of weekly papers for my courses ranged from one to eight .... Examination entries were very small, as could be expected at this time, rarely rising above three. The examinations were, of course, set and examined independently, though they took into account the lecturer's estimate of the candidate. None of my students failed, and several passed with distinction, among them [a] future Professor of Physics and a young woman at Southport who had few educational opportunities but responded to help and encouragement to such an extent that her papers improved week by week: she gained a distinction .... If there were not many students of this kind, they were the most rewarding of all[.] ... [I] was engaged in a worthwhile, if unusual, educational enterprise.[65]

The standards of work produced by extramural students varied somewhat, and it is not always clear whether or in what ways it was comparable to that of internal full-time students. This was not, though, the main point. As a report on university adult education explained some years later, 'however successful the extra-mural student may be, comparison with intra-mural students is pointless and misleading'.[66] As the WEA and other bodies emphasised, examinations were not the central purpose of the adult student's engagement with university education: '[m]uch of what he learns – new interests, a new attitude to knowledge, and a new tolerance and understanding in dealing with other people's opinions – is in any case not examinable'.[67]

*

In total, there were four main types of course. Tutorial classes were generally, though not always, organised in collaboration with the WEA, and stood at the apex of all the Board's activities, though student numbers were comparatively small. Described by Hickson as 'the highest standard sought in the Adult Education movement in this country – or in any other', a tutorial class was expected to meet 24 times a year in each of the three years, for two hours each time, and to have between 18 and 30 members.[68] It would study a single subject, ideally with a single tutor, across the whole three years, and would involve substantial student effort in terms of both class participation and the production of written work. Although there were no formal awards given to tutorial class members, they were expected to reach high standards in their work, and to participate in a community of learners that would evolve over time. For the WEA, a tutorial class was

> much more than a group of students listening to a lecture. It is an exercise in self-government, a joint enterprise .... The students choose their own subject of study. They express a preference for the tutor under whom they wish to work. They co-operate with him in the preparation of the syllabus, or master plan, of the three year course. They appoint their own class secretary and librarian.[69]

The high ideals may not always have been attainable:

> [a tutorial class] is a true fellowship; a community of friends with different attitudes towards life but common interest in an absorbing, challenging and exciting education[al] experience. It provides great opportunity for the development of individuals, and through their activities – should they so choose – for improving the quality of social life. No eloquence should be necessary to stimulate all social-minded men and women to seize it.[70]

In practice, many students could not cope with the demands of a tutorial class, and the number becoming 'effective' may have been between a half and two-thirds of the initial enrolments; however, the courses remained the gold standard for university adult education for several decades to come. There were around

30 tutorial classes under Cambridge auspices each year in the late 1930s, falling to 11 in the last academic year of the war.[71]

'Sessional' classes were larger in number by the mid-1940s, and lasted one year rather than three, though they were still considered 'longer and more systematic' than extension courses or other shorter programmes of study.[72] Many 'sessionals' grew out of the Rural Areas Committee work in the 1930s, and they would become a major area of activity after the war. As with a tutorial class, there would be meetings over two terms – sometimes 20 but ideally 24 – lasting two hours each, and regular attendance and written work was required for a student to become 'effective'. After the twelfth meeting of a sessional class, it could apply to become a tutorial class.[73] Alongside sessionals were terminal classes, which had been very important in the 'pioneer' work of the Rural Areas Committee but would be supplanted by sessionals in the 1950s. Half the length of a sessional, a 10- or 12-meeting terminal class still required attendance and written work, but it was recognised that the duration of a course would not enable students to explore a subject in the kind of depth that a longer venture would allow. There were some 'short terminals' with just six meetings; these were often, again, 'pioneer' activities that tested the demand for university adult education in a particular local centre.

The final type of course – and the largest in terms of student numbers right through the 1950s – was the well-established university extension or 'local lecture' course, whose history was traced back to 1873 and James Stuart, and which would persist as a distinct category of provision into the 1970s. Although its educational value had been in doubt for a long time – it had been heavily criticised in the 1908 Oxford report, for example – it continued as a popular activity through the interwar period, albeit not on the scale of its late nineteenth-century peak. Around 4,000 students were attending an average of between 40 and 50 courses each year in the 1930s, but with only a handful entering for the examinations.[74] This was, though, the only element of the Board's teaching for which successful students could obtain any kind of award: the Vice-Chancellor's Certificates were a form of accreditation that may have been – according to Geoffrey Hickson – 'of little real value', but they lasted into the interwar years.[75] By the late 1920s these certificates entitled students to exemption from the 'Previous Examination' – the main instrument governing admission to undergraduate study at the university – and from a year's residence in Cambridge.[76]

*

The interwar period saw a significant expansion of the Board's provision of residential courses, both for its own students at local centres and for the broader national and international community. The numbers involved, at this stage, were small compared to the regional programme of tutorial, sessional, terminal and extension courses, and compared to what would come after the Second World War, but the developments were significant, and made Cambridge – along with Oxford and, perhaps to an extent, London – unusual among university extramural departments. In the late nineteenth century, there were 'summer meetings' for university extension students, with several hundred in attendance in some years: the 'first real' one in 1893 took extension students from both Cambridge centres and those from other universities to colleges and lodgings in the city and to a range of educational activities. Running in subsequent years alternately with a summer meeting in Oxford, this became a regular part of the Board's educational work, and even attracted overseas visitors, who numbered 69 of the total attendance of 467 in 1896; the number and proportion increased significantly over the next two decades.[77] The summer meetings continued, each year with a theme: in 1920 it was 'Spain', in 1922 'Medieval and Modern Italy', in 1924 'Egypt' and in 1926 'India', while in the 1930s students had 'Tudor England' (1936) and 'The British Empire, with Special Reference to Modern Problems' (1938). In 1930, the meeting ran for three weeks, on 'Some Aspects of the Twentieth Century', with extension students charged £1 10s. 6d. to attend (the equivalent of around £80 today), and others £2 2s., although 'working men and women' could be admitted half-price.[78] As the WEA developed in the early twentieth century, its own summer schools were held for tutorial class students, and Cambridge was the venue for the early ones, though for much of the 1920s and 1930s the YMCA college at Cheshunt was used instead.[79]

In 1923 the Board organised its first 'Vacation Course for Foreign Students', with 122 students in attendance over a 19-day period, and there were 240 – from 21 countries – at the second in 1925.[80] During the remainder of the interwar years the course was held in alternate years in Cambridge and Oxford, usually on the same theme: 'Contemporary England: Its Language, Literature, Institutions and Music'.[81] The influx of students was noticed by the local press in Cambridge, and it was easy to draw parallels with contemporaneous developments in international affairs: one local newspaper noted in 1925 that '[f]or the past three weeks Cambridge has been giving, unconsciously, an excellent practical demonstration of a miniature League of Nations at work'.[82] The vacation course featured a series of plenary lectures to support the regular theme, more focused classes on specific subjects, a series of excursions near Cambridge and to London, and sometimes debates on particular topics such as 'a woman's sphere is in the home', 'nationalism is only a phase in the progress of mankind', or 'the world is a better place than it used to be'. One contributor to these courses, the science fiction author and mystic Aelfrida Tillyard, described the vacation course scene as

> hectic .... There were hundreds of people swelling and eddying about the various rooms of the Arts' School, all looking very purposeful and most of them happy and elated. I have a very interesting class .... Two Czech girls, an Italian girl, ditto man, an Egyptian who had studied law in Paris, a Pole and the rest German men.[83]

The constituency served by this course was clearly very different to that of the regional extension programme. The number of students attending it expanded through the interwar years, peaking in 1937, but of course it went into abeyance during the Second World War.

*

Most of the extramural teaching was done by members of the university or by people appointed from outside for the purpose. By the 1930s some well-known names were involved, such as the child psychologist C. W. Kimmins, the composer Ernest Markham Lee, Leonard Southern – of Emmanuel College, author of *An Outline of Physics* – and the geologist and mountaineer Noel Odell, of Clare College. Odell was a member of Mallory and Irvine's expedition in 1924 – he was the last person to see them alive – and in 1936, with H. W. Tilman, made the first successful ascent of Nanda Devi, the highest mountain yet climbed at that time.[84] He taught university extension courses on 'Modern Exploration', 'Rivers and Lakes and Their Services to Man' and other topics, and would remain as a part-time tutor for the Board into the 1970s.[85] Cécile Matheson, a former suffragist and long-serving member of trade boards and various official inquiries into social conditions in Britain and abroad, taught both for the Cambridge Board and its Oxford equivalent – the Extra-Mural

Delegacy – and was well known for her publications including a textbook for study circles entitled *Citizenship: An Introductory Handbook* (1917).[86] These lecturers were mostly based in Cambridge, London or nearby, but others lived at a greater distance, serving what remained of Cambridge's national remit in university adult education. For example, Edgar Allison Peers, a pioneer of language learning and professor of Spanish at the University of Liverpool, was available for extension courses 'within reach of Liverpool or occasionally of London'.[87] For all the part-time tutors, the conditions of work were 'very uncertain', with 'no guarantee of regular employment'.[88]

Apart from Hickson, the Board did not have any full-time staff on either the administrative or teaching side until the 1930s, although Hickson worked with full-time WEA organising secretaries where these existed in the Cambridge region. However, in 1931 a full-time lecturer and two full-time tutors were appointed: David Hardman was responsible for 'local lectures', and Frank Lee and William Pearson Baker became resident tutors in Northamptonshire and Cambridgeshire respectively. Hardman had been the first socialist president of Cambridge University Union during his time as a student at Christ's College in the 1920s, and Lee taught economics and politics. Baker was a rural sociologist, and largely responsible for the work of the Rural Areas Committee in stimulating demand for adult education in the region; he would remain at the Board into the 1940s. His courses in the 1930s included 'History and Civilization in Britain' at Bury St Edmunds (tutorial class), 'Cambridgeshire, Past and Present' at Isleham (terminal), and an extension course at Wethersfield on 'Country Life, Past and Present'.[89]

In 1934-5 Hardman became Hickson's assistant secretary, and was joined in that role by George Pateman, who had been secretary of the WEA Eastern District; meanwhile, Harold Plaskitt became resident tutor in Bedfordshire.[90] A specialist in history and politics, Plaskitt wrote several textbooks, including a collaboration with Harold Shearman, who worked in Bedfordshire as the WEA's organising secretary.[91] Shearman himself would become a member of the London County Council, and in due course the first chair of the Greater London Council and briefly of the Inner London Education Authority.[92] A 'staff tutor' – H. H. Daisley, who had taught philosophy on a part-time basis since 1927 – was appointed in 1935, and two more resident tutors in 1937: these were A. E. Douglas-Smith in Essex and John Hampden Jackson in Norfolk. Douglas-Smith would remain through the 1940s, and Hampden Jackson until his death in 1967: he taught national and international history and politics, for the Oxford

Extra-Mural Delegacy as well as the Cambridge Board.[93] Hampden Jackson was well-known as a 'socialist writer on contemporary history', publishing a whole series of books on both British and European topics, as well as *Marx, Proudhon and Contemporary Socialism* in 1957.[94] According to one recollection, Hampden Jackson was 'an inspired teacher of adults who … was … accustomed to giving trenchant expression to his views'.[95] It is clear, then, that there was a strong socialist orientation to the full-time staff of the Board, unsurprising given the importance of collaborative work with the WEA and the wider traditions of working-class adult education in the interwar period. The staff complement, though, remained small, and at the end of the Second World War there were just six full-time members of the teaching staff at the Board of Extra-Mural Studies.

One of these was Maurice Bruce, who was appointed as a 'James Stuart Lecturer' in 1937, with funding that came from the endowment given by Stuart's widow in 1920. As Bruce put it, 'the endowment may be said to derive, as the old jest has it, from the mustard left on dinner-plates'.[96] Bruce's job was mainly concerned with university extension courses, and he worked right across the country, sometimes travelling 1,000 miles in a week to do his teaching: he later recalled that 'there were times when I felt that I was living in trains'.[97] These commitments continued into the war years. Bruce taught a huge range of courses on history and literature, and to large audiences.[98] Like other tutors in the late 1930s and into the war years, Bruce found himself teaching more courses on 'international affairs'. In the 1930s that subject was also taught for the Board by Frank Darvall, a former president of the National Union of Students and later a diplomat and director of the English-Speaking Union, and by Barbara Ward, a freelance lecturer and journalist, author of various books and articles on the international situation and later known for her work on economics and the environment.[99] Bruce himself, the son of a postman who later became director of extra-mural studies at the University of Sheffield, 'combined a rigorous approach to scholarship with a commitment to working class education', and later wrote a substantial and much-reprinted history of the modern welfare state.[100]

Alongside its teaching, the Board was responsible for the provision of a small number of bursaries, established just before the First World War to ensure that 'a proportion of the working-class students in each [tutorial] class may pass regularly and easily' to the University of Cambridge itself.[101] Initially this was for just one year, and then two, but it became increasingly clear that what these students wanted was to spend three years in Cambridge reading for a degree, and from 1928 this became generally the case, once the university agreed to exempt bursary holders from the Previous Examination.[102] Generally two were awarded each year, meaning that six adult students with Board funding would be in residence at any time. Women were occasionally among the recipients. Competition was intense – in 1937-8, for example, there were 71 applicants for the two awards available – but some of the recipients, at least, did well at Cambridge and ended up with jobs in adult education. For example, H. E. Poole, a former bursary holder, was appointed as the WEA organising-secretary in Norfolk in 1937.[103] The bursaries reached only a very small proportion of those who attended tutorial classes, but they were taken seriously as a responsibility of the Board, and represented a small ladder of educational opportunity at a time before local authority grants became widely available to students.

*

At the end of the Second World War university extension in Cambridge had been going on for 72 years and was an established, if still somewhat precarious, area of activity for the university. The Board of Extra-Mural Studies had a substantial programme of teaching within its region, running 14 tutorial classes, 59 sessionals, 77 terminal classes and 69 extension lecture courses in the first full academic year after the war (see table 2.1). It was also looking forward to restarting its summer courses for international students, and most importantly to appointing a larger full-time staff to allow it to become a more secure and effective element of the university's profile in the wider community. The Rural Areas Committee was wound down at the end of the war, and the Board reconstituted to face the post-war years. It was not clear what these years would look like: there had already been various changes to the grant regulations for university extramural courses in the 1930s, and more would follow in 1946, but the basic pattern of activity on the regional programme would follow the lines set out in this chapter. The next chapter explores the post-war expansion of university adult education and the new elements that would be added to it in both war and peace.

Chapter 2
Expanding frontiers: the 1940s and 1950s

The post-war period was a time of expansion and change for university adult education, in the context of the other educational changes of the period. The introduction of compulsory full-time secondary education, the development of new and existing universities themselves – which would accelerate in the 1960s – and further changes in 1946 to the funding available for Responsible Bodies in extramural education all created a climate in which the expansion of university adult education was seen as both possible and desirable. Some new extramural departments were established in universities that did not already have them; the total number of grant-aided courses expanded from 1,374 in 1937-8 to 3,441 in 1948-9; and full-time staff numbers increased from 116 in 1939 to 199 in 1949.[1] Pre-war 'extramural empires' were solidified and sometimes fought over, and the maintenance of a separate stream of funding from the Ministry of Education (the Board of Education had been promoted to a ministerial department) allowed extramural departments a considerable measure of independence from their parent universities, which were funded by the University Grants Committee.[2] Other providers were entering the field of adult education, too: the 1944 Education Act had made the provision of further education a statutory duty of local education authorities (LEAs), although this was not effectively funded or staffed.[3] In 1953 the Ashby Report on adult education endorsed the Responsible Body arrangements, involving partnerships between universities, the WEA and other voluntary organisations; and although there were real-terms reductions in the funding available for university adult education in the 1950s, most universities were able to operate on a much larger scale than before the Second World War. With some fluctuations, the number of grant-aided courses continued to increase, reaching 5,000 by the early 1960s.[4]

The expansion of university adult education led to considerable debate in the 1950s about its purpose and priorities, often centred on what 'university standards' should mean. What was it that universities, as distinct from other educational agencies, should bring to the field? Sidney Raybould, Professor of Adult Education and Extramural Studies at the University of Leeds, argued in 1951 that, 'in certain fields of study' adult students could do university-level work in courses that were sufficiently long and rigorous, but that in practice a lot of extramural courses were 'too elementary … to justify university provision'.[5] It was in the three-year tutorial class that the aims of university adult education could be best achieved, and this was what universities should be concentrating on. They 'should engage in adult education only when it can be carried on at a university level, and not otherwise', declared Raybould.[6] He argued that post-war extramural departments were providing too many short courses and not enough longer ones, and 'a shifting of emphasis from quantity to quality' was needed.[7]

Similar themes were taken up in 1956 by Harold Wiltshire, director of extramural studies at the University of Nottingham, who defended what he called the 'Great Tradition' of tutorial and sessional classes, offered in partnership with the WEA, against a marked tendency in extramural departments to offer shorter, specialist and often residential courses for specific groups of professionals and technical workers; this undercut the 'traditional' mission of the university to provide courses that supported 'education for its own sake'.[8] The tensions between these approaches to university adult education would be quite apparent in the Cambridge context during the 1940s and 1950s. One historian has argued that, in this period, extramural departments 'became very skewed towards satisfying the intellectual hunger of the educated middle-class for greater self-fulfilment': this judgement is difficult to substantiate completely for the activities at Cambridge, not least because there is little data on who the students actually were, but it is certainly true that the Board was serving many students who had already gone through secondary or even higher education.[9] For Wiltshire and others, it was not clear that universities should be in the business of vocational education, but others felt that there was an opportunity to 'liberalise technical education', or at least to play a part in that process.[10]

At the end of the war the Board was offering its courses in what was now a fairly stable extramural region, centred on the eastern counties: Cambridgeshire itself, Essex, Suffolk, Norfolk, Hertfordshire, Bedfordshire and – at this stage – Northamptonshire were the focus of its activities, although there was a handful of more distant local centres that continued to have a relationship with Cambridge. The most notable was Southport, in Lancashire, where extension courses took place though the 1950s, and there was also ongoing provision in Derby, where the first extension lecture had taken place in 1873.[11] These were exceptions, though, and efforts were overwhelmingly concentrated on the eastern region. The complex pattern of tutorial, sessional, terminal and extension courses made for a rather cumbersome administrative machinery: there were two sub-committees, one of which organised provision alongside the WEA, and another that dealt directly with the local centres.[12] Overseeing the WEA's Eastern District was the powerful figure of Frank Jacques, a former railway clerk and Labour parliamentary candidate, who had become secretary of the district in 1936 and would remain until the 1980s. Jacques has been described as 'an English graduate, socialist, an always genial, rather craggy encourager of young teachers ready to carry the word out into the wet and windswept Fens'.[13] He was a strong advocate of the 'Great Tradition' in the 1950s, and the relationship between the Board and Eastern District remained important: the WEA summer schools, for example, ran successfully again after the war, and into the 1960s and beyond.

*

In the 1940s and 1950s the Board itself was a large body, consisting of 25 or more members representing both the university and its partner organisations. The chair and ten additional members were nominated by the Council of the Senate; the WEA sent two representatives from its national organisation and three more from its Eastern District; and the local centres were represented through the Cambridge Local Centres Union, a body that tried to represent the interests of the centres to the Board itself, though it was not always particularly effective.[14] The Board was chaired by Frank Salter, a fellow of Magdalene College (he became its president in 1951) and popular tutor, as well as the author of two 'slight books' on Karl Marx and Sir Thomas Gresham before the war.[15] Salter had been a member of the Board from its inception in 1924, and oversaw the substantial transition in its work and structure after the war. As well as Geoffrey Hickson, his assistants and the teaching staff, there was a small group of administrators, most notably Bernard Green, who had started work as an 'office boy' in 1917, becoming 'second clerk' in 1924 and chief clerk in 1935.[16]

Like other extramural departments, the Board expanded its full-time teaching staff considerably after the war. The situation of those who worked for it could be somewhat precarious. Staff in the 1930s enjoyed modest salaries and only short-term appointments, and in 1937 Hickson considered their position – along with those of the resident tutor for Bedfordshire (appointed in 1935), and the two assistant secretaries David Hardman (1931) and George Pateman

(1935) – with some sympathy. He was concerned to give them 'some security of tenure', but did not expect this to last for a lifetime:

> it cannot be suggested at the present time that men of ability and comparative youth, such as hold these posts now, can expect to find in them a complete life's career. Unless there is to be some radical development in adult education with a corresponding increase in resources, it is only natural that these men may sooner or later seek other employment which may offer not only better prospects of remuneration but also a wider field for their talents.[17]

The unanticipated 'radical development' did, in fact, materialise: the expansion of resources for university adult education after the Second World War transformed the landscape and resulted in a considerable expansion of the Board's full-time staff in the initial post-war years. By this time, though, David Hardman had already left the Board's employment: he was elected as the Labour MP for Darlington in the general election of 1945, going on to serve as Parliamentary Secretary to the Minister of Education.[18]

With Pateman remaining as one of the two assistant secretaries, Hardman was replaced by Frank Bell, a Cambridge graduate – in French and Spanish – who had for three years been a Japanese prisoner of war, two of them spent in the Batu Lintang Camp. There, Bell had organised the so-called 'Kuching University', teaching and running classes in various subjects, under conditions of repression and often extreme secrecy, for the others in the camp.[19] Nicknamed, for obvious reasons, 'Tinker', Bell was a 'meticulous methodical person', who even created makeshift 'diplomas' for those he taught at Batu Lintang, replacing these with printed versions after the war.[20] One of his fellow prisoners of war remembered how he made books from scrap paper, cardboard and cloth, kept notes of his teaching and his students' 'progress and marks' – 'quite an incredible undertaking' in the circumstances of a Japanese camp.[21] The impact of these experiences on Bell was quite profound, and shaped his future approach to life and education. In 1946 he wrote:

> If I can learn to build my life in the best that those years brought; if I can practise the wide tolerance and sympathy which it needed three years of captivity to wring unwillingly from me; if I can go forward through the years that remain to me, when so many of my friends have been so

> suddenly cut off, our struggles and our sufferings will not have been in vain.[22]

According to Bell, it was during this time that he 'began to see something of the good that can be brought about by adult education', and he was 'most encouraged' on his repatriation 'to find that there is widespread interest in this vital aspect of our planning for the future'.[23] Bell spent the first ten years after the war as an assistant secretary, leaving in 1955 to establish the Bell School of Languages in Cambridge, having failed to achieve his aim of establishing a department for English as a foreign language in the university itself.[24] Among his early post-war activities was the organisation of courses for German prisoners of war, some of whom remained in Britain until at least 1948.[25]

The expansion of activity in the early post-war years led to the appointment of a third assistant secretary in 1950. This was John Andrew, a specialist in English literature who would, in due course, succeed Geoffrey Hickson as secretary to the Board.[26] Andrew's degree was in English, from post-war Cambridge, following wartime service in the Royal Navy, during which he had come under the influence of the WEA. His degree studies at St Catharine's College had been under the Board's 'direction', though he had not received one of its own bursaries for mature students.[27] Andrew became a committed adult educator, describing his English literature courses as being 'among the happiest things to which I was able to contribute' during his long service with the Board, which in total would last 27 years.[28] On the departure of both Pateman and Bell in 1955, Andrew was designated deputy secretary, at which point two new assistant secretaries were appointed.[29]

Teaching staff fell into two categories: resident tutors and staff tutors. Resident tutors had two key roles: to teach in their subject, mainly in the county in which they were based, and to do the 'organising' work, that is to promote the Board's courses in local centres, often alongside the increasing number of resident WEA 'tutor-organisers'.[30] There was a small reduction of the expected amount of teaching to allow for these additional duties. Staff tutors were employed to teach in a particular subject, though they would often range well beyond their specialism, and over a period of time new interests and subjects could emerge. There was not, in practice, any significant difference between the terms, conditions and duties of those who were designated resident tutors and those who were staff tutors, but the resident tutor's job was often a difficult and lonely one. All staff, but particularly resident tutors, were expected to liaise closely with the local centres at which they taught and to oversee the teaching in their particular county. The specific strand of work centred on 'rural areas' had come to an end during the Second World War, and resident tutors were expected to play a 'pioneering' role in developing new local centres and identifying new areas of demand, particularly for tutorial and sessional classes. The usefulness of resident tutors, as distinct from staff tutors, would become an area of contention in the 1950s, as members of the Board and its staff argued whether the specific positions were necessary at all.

The new post-war funding arrangements allowed for a substantial expansion of the Board's full-time teaching staff, which quickly grew from six to 16. Despite Hickson's doubts as to whether university adult education could provide a 'life-time career', some of those appointed in the 1940s were to stay with the Board for the rest of their working lives; they were members of the post-war generation of adult educators who shaped the emerging extramural world and, in many cases, made substantial contributions to the development of their own disciplines. This was the case among both resident and staff tutors. Among the former was Leslie Wayper, who was appointed as resident tutor for Bedfordshire in 1946 and, like Andrew, would eventually become secretary to the Board, in his case in the late 1970s. In his early thirties at the time of appointment, Wayper had taught on a part-time basis for the Board and WEA since 1935, and had served in the Royal Army Educational Corps (RAEC) during the Second World War.[31] The war had interrupted his University of Cambridge doctoral research on Anglo-Austrian relations, and after the war he taught European history, international affairs and other subjects, mainly in tutorial and sessional classes; he also wrote a 'Teach Yourself' book, *Political Thought*, published in 1954.[32] Wayper left Bedfordshire in 1949 to become a staff tutor.[33]

While Wayper was in Bedfordshire, a new post of resident tutor for the neighbouring county of Hertfordshire was created in 1947: the appointee was Vivian Ramsbottom, a pre-war Cambridge geography graduate who had taught for the WEA and in secondary schools, and had served in the Friends Ambulance Unit during the Second World War.[34] Ramsbottom's teaching focused on economics and politics, with some forays into political thought and ideas: for example, he led a terminal course on 'Conservatism, Communism and Socialism' at Letchworth in 1950-1.[35] In 1955, when the two assistant secretaries left the Board, he was moved from Hertfordshire to replace one of them. (The other new assistant secretary, Dennis Raymond, was appointed from outside the Board, and stayed for just three years.) There were also new resident tutors. In Essex there was Reginald Barrett, a former school teacher and WEA tutor, who focused on sociology and political theory, and in Norfolk John Hampden Jackson, who had been in his position since before the war.

In Suffolk the resident tutor was Henry Clement, a Cambridge history graduate and, again, former WEA tutor and school teacher, who could teach a '[w]ide range of historical subjects', including European and world history, as well as social and economic history.[36] Clement would publish widely during his twenty years working for the Board. His accessible accounts of both ancient and modern history reached large audiences, and some were reprinted numerous times.[37] They were aimed at student audiences, often containing essay titles and class exercises.[38] Meanwhile, the pre-war resident tutorship in Northamptonshire was retained, but Frank Lee did not stay in that job; he became a staff tutor instead. He was replaced in Northamptonshire by Colin Griffiths, a historian with experience of WEA and Army education, who stayed in the Board's employment until 1981; and in Cambridgeshire and the Isle of Ely a new resident tutor was appointed to replace W. P. Baker: this was James R. Mitchell, also a historian who had completed his degree in 1946 and had worked for the Army Bureau of Current Affairs during the war. Mitchell would remain until the 1980s, and taught modern British history, American history and Russian history, among other things.[39] Griffiths taught colonial history and various courses on current and international affairs.[40]

Most members of the expanded staff were not resident tutors, but designated as staff tutors in a particular topic, and could often be expected to work across large parts of the extramural region. Some of the staff tutors had started work before or during the Second World War: these were W. P. Baker (history and politics, formerly resident tutor in Cambridgeshire), H. H. Daisley (philosophy), A. E. Douglas-Smith (English and history, formerly resident tutor in Essex), Frank Lee (economics and politics) and Maurice Bruce, who left in 1947.[41] These men were augmented by a new group of staff tutors after the war, including two women: Marion Springall, a former history teacher who had worked as a part-time tutor in Norfolk during the war and was known for her 1936 book *Labouring Life in Norfolk Villages 1834-1914* (based on her University of London doctoral research); and Helen Lowenthal, who worked for the Board after the war, leaving in 1950 and subsequently becoming education officer at the Victoria and Albert Museum and in due course the first vice-president of the National Association of Decorative and Fine Arts

Societies.[42] Lowenthal 'established an exceptional reputation for her contribution to the growth and quality of extra-mural arts education', and prior to Cambridge had worked for the BBC and the Council for the Encouragement of Music and the Arts during the war, as well as in Army education.[43] Lowenthal taught art and art history classes, while Springall was an important participant in the early post-war growth of local history, which is discussed in more detail below. Also, to meet a flurry of post-war demand for new courses and lecturers, three women – and one man – were given short-term staff tutor positions in 1946.[44]

In two of those four cases, the appointments were repeatedly renewed. One was G. S. Zair, whose position lasted into the 1950s and who also taught international affairs, as well as modern European history; he was moved to be resident tutor in Essex in 1948, replacing Reginald Barrett, and left himself in 1954.[45] The other was Rachel Young, a pre-war history graduate from Oxford who had worked in school teaching in Nottingham and as an organiser of clubs for the unemployed in the Potteries, and spent the Second World War in the Land Army, among other things.[46] Beginning her work for the Board with classes in local government, Young moved on to social history and then, alongside Springall, taught a series of local history courses in Norfolk, where she was based – she became resident tutor there in 1954.[47] By the mid-1950s Young was the only woman on the full-time teaching staff (Springall had left in 1953), and indeed in 1955-6 only seven courses – in addition to Young's six – were taught by women, a considerable reduction from the wartime and early post-war years, when women covered a large component of the regional programme.[48] A new staff tutor, Eileen Andrews, was appointed in 1956 to teach biology – an Oxford zoology graduate, Andrews was already teaching sessional classes for the Board[49] – but she left six years later to become an HM Inspector for Schools.[50] Young herself, meanwhile, had left in 1961, to become Keeper of Strangers' Hall Museum of Domestic Life in Norwich, and thereafter worked until her retirement in museums and museum education, although she retained a lifelong association with the WEA.[51]

The other staff tutors appointed in 1946 – in addition to those mentioned above – were Christopher Lee (no relation of Frank), Montagu Clifford and Lionel Munby, all of whom would have long careers at the Board. Lee was an Oxford-educated historian and former WEA tutor who was temporarily editing the journal produced by the British Institute of Adult Education when he took up his work at Cambridge.[52] He taught history, English literature and sometimes the history of art; he was a flexible staff tutor who could turn his hand to topics as varied as 'The Spirit of the Age', local history and 'English Landscape Discovered', as well as art history, Shakespeare and poetry.[53] Clifford was, in the late 1940s and early 1950s, the only scientist on the full-time staff: a biologist with a 1938 PhD from Cambridge, he had taught on the Board's courses for some years prior to becoming a staff tutor.[54] Clifford offered courses ranging from 'The Biology of Sex' to 'The Social Relations of Science' and 'Science, Philosophy and Religion'.[55] Just as Hampden Jackson, Clement and Wayper had made their subjects accessible through publications aimed at wider non-academic audiences, so Clifford was a member of the four-man editorial board for the 1956 *Pictorial Encyclopedia of Scientific Knowledge*, which declared itself to be 'the first book to attempt to explain the whole of elementary scientific knowledge purely in terms of pictures'.[56] Both Clifford and Lee worked for the Board until the late 1970s.

Lionel Munby was an Oxford history student in the 1930s, when he had joined the Communist Party; he served in Italy during the Second World War, and also contributed to Army education.[57] Most of Munby's teaching was in Hertfordshire, on local history: this eventually resulted in his book *The Hertfordshire Landscape*, published in 1977 in Hodder and Stoughton's 'Making of the English Landscape' series.[58] Like many of his colleagues, Munby was an active researcher as well as teacher, contributing articles to journals including *History* (the Historical Association's academic journal), the *Cambridge Review* and *Adult Education*.[59] From 1955 he was editor of the *Amateur Historian*, later the *Local Historian*, serving in that capacity for 20 years. Munby lived in Cambridge – unusually, perhaps, he never lived in the county for which he was best known as a local historian – but travelled extensively for his teaching.[60] He was active in the Communist Party through the 1950s and 1960s, serving on its National Cultural Committee, and he 'remained a Communist' until the 1970s.[61] He was a member of the Communist Party Historians' Group, rubbing shoulders with Eric Hobsbawm and others, and contribuing in various ways to its work.[62]

More new members of teaching staff arrived at the Board in the late 1940s and early 1950s. In 1948-9 C. H. Macgregor, who taught economics and related subjects, was appointed as the new resident tutor in Norfolk, when John Hampden Jackson returned to standard staff tutor duties; Macgregor stayed for six years until he left to seek ordination in the Church of England.[63] In 1949 yet another historian, Leslie James, was appointed to replace Wayper as resident tutor for Bedfordshire; James, too, stayed for a few years before becoming a non-resident staff tutor in the mid-1950s.[64] James was another who could teach international affairs, as well as geography and history; he sometimes ran courses focused specifically on the Middle East.[65] Meanwhile, in 1951 A. E. Douglas-Smith left to work at the University of the West Indies; he was replaced by a new staff tutor in English literature, Leo Salingar, a Shakespeare scholar who had been a school teacher in Liverpool and Newcastle, and whose ambitious doctoral research on 'English drama in its relations to social history and the history of philosophical thought in the seventeenth century' was left uncompleted due to war service in the RAEC.[66] Salingar was a staff tutor for more than a decade, during which time he contributed to the *Pelican Guide to English Literature*; and after leaving in 1962 for a university lectureship and fellowship at Trinity he published two important books on Shakespeare and his contemporaries.[67] Like many other university adult educators, Salingar was skilled at 'making great literary works – and his own great learning – accessible'; and also like many others in the field, he was a 'traditional leftie'. Adult education, for Salingar as for others, had a clear and explicit social purpose.[68] Meanwhile, the long-serving Frank Lee, who had been one of the Board's first full-time teaching appointments in 1931, died suddenly in 1955.[69]

Staff tutors, and even new assistant secretaries, remained in a somewhat precarious position even after the war and well into the 1950s. Most were appointed initially for either two or three years; this could turn into a five-year appointment that was not renewed, although more often it was followed by *another* appointment for five years. Eight staff tutors were reappointed in this way at a single Board meeting in 1954, and another four in December 1955, while another was given just two years.[70] Staff tutors were at the mercy of demand for their subjects, and to extent for themselves as tutors, although local centres did generally prefer a staff tutor to one of the Board's many part-timers. Some had to change the focus of their teaching in order to meet student demand. Lionel Munby, for example, was appointed with the expectation that a large part of his teaching would be on trade union history, among other things, but found that 'trade unionists did not queue up to study their past or even their current problems', and he had to move in different directions in order to maintain his position.[71] Even his courses on social history, world history and 'The Changing Face of England' in 1947-8 did not attract large numbers, and he embarked instead on teaching local history, mainly in Hertfordshire, which proved a durable and innovative area of work (see below).[72] Yet for Munby and others, job security remained an issue of concern through the 1950s. As late as 1955 Hickson repeated his point of 1937: '[t]he Board have always been rather doubtful whether extra-mural teaching, as conceived hitherto, offers a satisfactory life-time career, but the desire of the Staff for greater security is natural, especially in view of national tendencies'.[73] Thus when H. H. Daisley retired in 1958, having begun working for the Board as a part-time tutor in 1927 and been appointed as a staff tutor in 1935, he had spent 31 years either in precarious year-on-year employment or on short-term, albeit full-time, contracts.[74] Not until the same year, 1958, did the Board agree to reappoint those aged 40 and over, and with at least ten years' service, until the age of 60.[75]

Workload was another concern. Staff tutors were expected to teach on four or five evenings a week during the 24 weeks of teaching, and occasionally at weekends or on day schools; resident tutors taught four evenings a week. In the summer it was expected that tutors 'should have opportunity for reading and for preparation of courses', but many also had teaching duties at the Board's summer schools.[76] Teaching in the region often involved substantial amounts of travel: in 1947-8 Munby was teaching a tutorial class in Luton and a sessional class at Knebworth for both teaching terms; in Michaelmas Term he was also going to Bedford, Hatfield and Welwyn Garden City, and in Lent Term to King's Langley and, again, Welwyn Garden City for terminal classes. Meanwhile, Montagu Clifford taught four tutorial classes in the same year – in Cambridge, Kettering, Norwich and Welwyn Garden City – *and* a sessional class at Tittleshall in Norfolk.[77] All this required transport, generally by car given the need to carry book-boxes, and cars were not cheap or easily available in the early post-war years. Munby did not have his own car at this point, and remembered that 'a great deal of shared transport was common in post-war extramural work'.[78] For those who did have cars, the mileage allowance was a common feature of discussion at staff meetings, and it became a significant element of the Board's expenditure, too.[79] By 1956-7 total travel expenses (including for part-time tutors) amounted to £4,491 for the academic year (the equivalent of almost £100,000 today), compared with the total of £5,839 that was spent on part-time tutors' fees and £15,372 on salaries for the full-time teaching staff.[80]

The status of teaching staff, in relation to the Board itself and to the university as a whole, was also a matter of debate and some resentment in the 1940s and 1950s. It was only in 1947 that agreement – in principle – was reached to allow staff tutors who were not Cambridge graduates to be full borrowing members of the university library, along with 'internal' members of the university staff; and few of them had a college affiliation at this time.[81] When two members of staff were 'incorporated' into colleges in 1951, John Hampden Jackson hoped that this 'might lead to a general improvement in the status of all' colleagues, but it remained a concern for most of them.[82] In 1952 a staff meeting formally reminded the Board 'of their strong desire to have status equal to that of internal University teachers', and asked it to 'expedite the negotiations to that end'.[83] However, in 1957 the staff were still complaining that their salary scales did not yet 'approximate to' those of lecturers in the rest of the university, and even those would be lower than what was offered 'in the more generous provincial universities'.[84] Some had already left to work in other universities: Maurice Bruce was one, and W. P. Baker had moved to the University of Leeds in 1948, while others such as Young, Andrews and Macgregor left the staff to work outside the university sector.

At the Board itself, there were some tensions between the management and the paid staff. As the Board was not a university department as such, disputes over governance and representation could be complex and in some ways unusual; some arose in the early post-war years as a result of the rapid expansion of the teaching staff, which had been so small before 1945. As early as 1946, Hickson recognised that the 'informal' staff meetings should be replaced with a more 'regularised' arrangement, and this was done; but the staff wanted more. They pressed for representation on the various committees that undertook the Board's work; for the right to present reports for consideration at the Board's own meetings; and, most importantly, for direct representation on the Board itself. Except for the last, these were gradually conceded, but the teaching staff continued to press for Board representation; at this stage only Hickson and the assistant secretaries attended the Board meetings.[85] Only from 1957 did a sole representative of the full-time teaching staff attend Board meetings, and even then not as a voting member.[86]

For part-time tutors, the situation could be even more precarious and poorly remunerated. For some, with established positions and careers within or beyond the university, this may not have been a problem: Robert Rattray, for example, taught extension courses in literature, philosophy, drama and other subjects for the Board from 1945. Rattray had been the first principal of University College Leicester, from 1921 to 1931, then a Unitarian minister in Cambridge, and from 1951 to 1954 was president of Manchester College Oxford.[87] Others were members of the full-time staff in faculties, such as Edward Miller, a university lecturer in constitutional history and fellow of St John's, who would later become Professor of Medieval History at the University of Sheffield.[88] (He was also the brother-in-law of Leo Salingar, whose sister he had married in 1941.)[89] Miller's services as a WEA tutor were 'much in demand', attributed to his 'rare capacity for clarifying material without simplifying it', and he played a significant role in debates on the direction of extramural work in the late 1950s.[90] He was himself, from the early 1950s, a member of the Board. For staff within the university, teaching could provide useful extra income, but there was some uncertainty as to whether a ban on internal university lecturers from undertaking external teaching for payment during term-time applied to extramural classes. In the event there was a gentleman's agreement on this issue, provided that the teaching was not excessive, but in any case it was difficult to persuade full-time members of the teaching staff to travel to remote local centres in addition to their normal duties at the university.[91] Sometimes courses were cancelled because no tutor could be found.[92] For those without a car, an overnight stay was often required; and travel costs were reimbursed, but until 1959 part-time tutors could only claim second-class rail fares, whereas other members of staff could travel first-class.[93] In the same year – following another set of challenges in recruiting tutors – there was a proposal to pay part-time staff for time spent travelling, as was the practice in at least two other universities. This, though, was dismissed on the grounds that it would not solve the recruitment problem: 'potential tutors tend to be deterred more by the time involved than by any other considerations'.[94]

Some part-time tutors, though, did rely financially on work for the Board. Payment was 'rather modest', as Geoffrey Hickson admitted in 1955: at this time the fee ranged from £3 to £5 per class meeting (about £65 to £110 in today's figures), depending on experience and qualifications, and had hardly changed since the end of the *First*, let alone the Second, World War.[95] Payment increased a little by the end of the 1950s, ranging from £3 10s. to £5 10s. (though this amounted to very little in real terms), with a few tutors paid as much as £7; and there was a standard rate of £5 for classes taught on residential courses.[96] Part-time tutors were also more directly affected by the vagaries of student demand than were staff tutors: if a course was cancelled half-way through, or did not run at all, then they suffered 'both from loss of anticipated income and of possible alternative employment'.[97] Some one-off payments were made to tutors in these circumstances, but these were at the discretion of the Board and Hickson admitted that the situation was 'unsatisfactory'.[98] It is perhaps not surprising that some tutors 'did not always report the failure of classes to work at an appropriate level during the course of a session', given that their own income could depend on there being enough 'effective' students in a tutorial or sessional class.[99] In the event, part-time tutors were more likely to teach extension courses, with staff tutors concentrating on tutorial, sessional and terminal classes, although the distinction was by no means hard-and-fast. By the mid-1950s, 20 of the 32 tutorial classes and 19 of the 21 terminal classes were run by full-time staff of the Board. Part-timers still taught a small majority – 20 out of 38 – of the sessional classes, but generally in subjects that could not be covered by the staff tutors and assistant secretaries, particularly theology and religious studies, music and some areas of historical study such as American or Chinese history, as well as the emerging subject of archaeology. Meanwhile, of 48 extension classes, just 14 were led by staff tutors.[100] The proportions remained similar at the end of the decade.[101]

This division of labour – though never absolute – was partly a function of the need to maintain 'standards' in the face of both funding restrictions and the insistence of the Board itself on the importance of extramural classes doing university-level work. A heavy emphasis was laid on the quality of teaching, particularly in terms of tutors' understanding of the distinctiveness of adult classes. The supply of good part-time tutors was a perennial problem, and in the late 1940s training was considered inadequate. At Oxford, there was an 'apprentice-tutor' system, where new tutors shadowed more experienced ones, but at Cambridge the training was limited to a two-week course, generally run alongside the WEA summer school.[102] This was used both for its ostensible purpose and to identify potential tutors to add to the Cambridge list. Led in the 1940s by W. P. Baker and John Hampden Jackson, and later by various members of the full-time staff, it had three elements: general training on preparation, presentation, 'University standards', assessing written work, promoting discussion and practicalities such as filling out the class register; a series of 'general talks' on the organisation of adult education; and, for each participant, two 'practice talks' to an audience comprising the other members of the course and some WEA students. Guest lectures were given by Hickson, Frank Jacques, Frank Salter and even Sidney Raybould from Leeds, and there were detailed reports on each student's performance.[103]

*

Funding for most of the Board's courses was based on the number of 'effective' students: not only were students expected to enrol, but also to attend at least two-thirds of the meetings and to produce written work to the satisfaction of the tutor. In practice the standards of written work varied considerably, but staff were heavily invested in the promotion and maintenance of 'university standards': it was not simply a bugbear of Sidney Raybould's, but of most of who worked in university adult education, and certainly at Cambridge. Tutorial classes were held up as the apex of what the Board was doing, and 'satisfaction' was often expressed when their number increased.[104] It expanded quickly after the war, and stabilised between 30 and 36 per year in the 1950s (see table 2.1), with total student numbers usually above 500 and 'effective' students above 350. The number of one-year sessional classes also remained steady, although terminal classes declined. This was in part a matter of policy: terminal classes were intended as 'pioneer' activities that could support the development of longer, more rigorous courses, and Cambridge shared Raybould's doubts about their value. In fact, table 2.1 shows that a higher proportion of students on terminals were 'effective' than was the case on any other type of course, but this perhaps said more about the level and length of the course than about the quality of student work itself. Meanwhile, demand for extension lecture courses fluctuated, and only a handful of students ever submitted written work for these.

The quality of written work was repeatedly discussed and sometimes agonised over. For Vivian Ramsbottom, it was a 'bogey', and for all staff tutors it seemed that 'the work of many Classes … depend[ed] on a hard core of serious students'.[105] This was perhaps a little harsh: table 2.1 shows that around two-thirds of students on tutorial classes in the 1950s were 'effective', although the proportion on sessionals was below 60% and sometimes as low as 50%. As for extension courses, some doubted the value of bothering with them at all: John Hampden Jackson, surveying the whole range of the teaching programme in 1948, argued that 'it should not be considered a proper part of the University's duty to provide lectures for groups of listeners unless these are likely at some time to become students and to do some work'.[106] Similarly, when the English Folk Dance and Song Society sought the Board's help with a course in 1950, it was cautiously agreed to participate, 'provided that … the course was of educational value and not merely an entertainment'.[107] The importance of 'effective' students, as well as minimum numbers, extended to the continuance of courses that had already started: tutorials and sessionals could be deemed 'borderline' if students were not working to the expected standard, although, conversely, a terminal could be promoted to a sessional, and a sessional to a tutorial, if student engagement and performance were good.[108] It was emphasised that students should be writing 'continuously throughout a course', perhaps using the mechanism of the WEA 'class log', to which all students contributed in turn, and which was a good 'resistance-breaker' for those who were reluctant to write.[109]

Of course, it was recognised that writing – and indeed participation in class discussion – was not easy for many of the students in the Board's classes:

> Our students vary in their ability, and in their experience of studying. So that inevitably there will be great differences in the quality of work submitted: the Tutor must make allowance for this. Students are often reluctant to put pen to paper. This reluctance is understandable: some students are afraid of revealing their ignorance, particularly in so permanent a form as the written word; others fear inadequacies in their spelling or grammar; with yet others the physical labour of writing is considerable – though they may be able to talk quite freely. The home circumstances of some students may make it difficult for them to work on their own in reasonable quietness.[110]

Hence, as Raybould had emphasised, the need for longer, more sustained and rigorous study, supporting the development of students through a tutorial class and giving them the best chance to produce work of a 'university standard'.[111] There was also the challenge of reading: students in a tutorial or sessional class were expected to read at home between class meetings, as directed by the tutor, and they varied in their ability and willingness to do this. Books were despatched to local centres from the Stuart House library in book-boxes; the books were

> chosen by the tutor who was giving the the course, and they were always open at the front of the room when you arrived to give your lecture .... Some of these places were still quite remote from the library service and if the tutor could put some key texts in there, that tided them over.[112]

The boxes would remain at the centre for the duration of a course. In some places a student would be given responsibility for issuing the books; elsewhere this duty might fall to the tutor. Some centres did not have much room in which

Table 2.1
Regional programme statistics, 1945 to 1960

Year	Tutorial classes			Sessional classes		
	Classes	Enrolled students	Effective students	Classes	Enrolled students	Effective students
1945-6	14	274	171	59	1235	631
1946-7	14	310	179	60	1258	563
1947-8	14	251	166	42	853	510
1948-9	18	223	214	48	989	519
1949-50	18	310	203	51	948	574
1950-1	32	531	360	67	1206	658
1951-2	32	534	373	39	678	341
1952-3	35	517	353	36	655	377
1953-4	36	535	365	36	631	367
1954-5	32	536	359	35	609	361
1955-6	32	534	354	38	658	367
1956-7	35	574	384	38	678	371
1957-8	35	585	375	39	674	332
1958-9	31	451	286	37	758	393
1959-60	33	543	386	35	725	396

Year	Terminal classes			University extension lectures		
	Classes	Enrolled students	Effective students	Classes	Average lecture attendance	Number submitting papers
1945-6	77	1522	859	69	2810	163
1946-7	96	1851	1254	84	3043	84
1947-8	93	1762	1290	75	2976	131
1948-9	61	1136	826	74	2574	155
1949-50	60	953	804	75	2665	107
1950-1	46	639	433	55	2248	91

1951-2	48	727	553	51	1723	83
1952-3	40	617	474	46	1745	96
1953-4	33	500	376	43	1621	57
1954-5	29	393	300	40	1537	59
1955-6	21	322	228	48	2007	33
1956-7	20	296	246	53	2291	49
1957-8	20	309	223	57	2086	21
1958-9	26	409	312	53	1846	58
1959-60	33	474	353	44	1687	40

Notes: effective students include those attending at least two-thirds of the class meetings *and* submitting written work; from 1950-1, enrolled student numbers include original enrolments *plus* students subsequently added to the register. Source: annual reports.

to store the boxes, which meant that – if several different courses were running – they would be placed on top of each other, meaning that each week a tutor was likely to find their box at the bottom of a heavy pile.[113] Some students, though not all, would make good use of the books: a survey of loans from the boxes to tutorial and sessional class students in 1950-1 found that the number issued ranged from 0.6 to 5.2 per class member.[114]

*

Although university extension had been pioneered by a professor of mechanism and applied mechanics, and featured various popular science subjects presented to large audiences in local centres, the 'Great Tradition' of adult education tended to focus on 'liberal' and humane subjects, as well as subjects of social and contemporary significance such as economic history, international relations and politics. In the early post-war years this resulted in a preponderance of courses on the social sciences and humanities: table 2.2 shows, in descending order the approximate proportions of courses in each subject in 1947-8, although some courses would have overlapped across more than one category. The study of literature and history were longstanding staples of extramural teaching, and 'international affairs' remained popular into the early 1950s. It was taught by several members of the full-time staff – Henry Clement, Leslie

James, Leslie Wayper, James Mitchell, John Hampden Jackson and others – as well as a number of part-time tutors and lecturers. Different tutors gave the subject different emphases. Mitchell, for example, in a tutorial class at Peterborough, spent the first year on the USA, the second on the USSR and the third on Britain, with particular reference to its relations with the two great powers during the Second World War.[115] Wayper adopted a chronological approach that – in one year – spanned the French Revolution and the League of Nations, and much in between.[116] Whatever the focus, though, the content of an international affairs course could take account of recent political developments, and even things that happened as the course was being taught. In the context of a three-year tutorial class, with its traditions of self-government and collaborative curriculum planning, the subject was highly adaptable to the particular interests of both tutor and students.[117]

Table 2.2
Subjects of courses, 1947-8 (percentage of all courses taught)

History (including local history)	16
Literature	16
International affairs	15
Politics	11
Economics	9
Science	9
Music	6
Psychology	6
Philosophy	5
Art (including art history)	4
Law and justice	3

Note: these figures do not differentiate between types or length of course, and seem to include extension lecture courses and terminal classes.

Source: 'The Changing Demand for Subjects', paper for staff meeting, in Board papers for 23 May 1956: Madingley Hall archives.

Sociology and related subjects were taught in some local centres, though often to quite small numbers of students. Reginald Barrett and Lionel Munby co-taught a tutorial class in sociology at Braintree starting in 1946-7, but Munby's lectures on 'sociology' were essentially historical, demonstrating to students the foundations of contemporary social issues rather than analysing them from a theoretical standpoint.[118] W. P. Baker taught courses on 'Living in a Village', 'Present Problems of Rural Life' and 'Country Life: Past and Present', all of which drew on the work he was doing for his book *The English Village*, published in 1953.[119] There may have been some expectation of expanded demand for sociology after the war, as in the 1940s the largest set of acquisitions for the Stuart House library was made under that heading. More than 300 books were acquired – albeit some of which might better be catalogued as 'history' – in the five years after the war, but teaching in the subject did not take off until somewhat later.[120] Barrett taught 'Social Science', and there was also a course on 'The Family and Social Change', as well as a sessional anthropology course focusing on race and racial classification, and dealing with contemporary prejudices, while still focusing mainly on Africa.[121] Social history featured heavily, usually the social history of England; again, teaching responsibilities here were widely spread across the full- and part-time staff.

As table 2.2 shows, music and art were fairly low on the list of most popular topics in the 1940s, and music in particular would struggle to maintain its profile through the 1950s. There were always some courses, taught by part-time tutors in all cases, as there was no music specialist on the full-time staff. There were real challenges in teaching music, or even the appreciation of music, to extramural classes: it was difficult, given the need for some prior musical literacy, to recruit the minimum number of students; many local centres were not equipped with suitable pianos or gramophones; and the requirement for students to submit 'written work' did not sit easily with the ways in which the subject was taught.[122] Moreover, the Board had no proper record library or collection of musical books and scores, much to the chagrin of the most prominent of its part-time tutors, Hans Redlich, an Austrian emigré who lived in Letchworth and taught extramural courses for both Cambridge and Birmingham before eventually becoming Professor of Music at the University of Manchester.[123] Music did not thrive in the Cambridge region in the 1950s: in 1947-8 there had been three extension courses – at Newmarket, Welwyn Garden City and Hitchin – with a total of 121 students (eight of whom submitted work), and a further five sessional classes in various aspects of music and the appreciation of music, with 49 effective students between them. By 1955-6, however, there was just one extension course, on 'Music 1850-1950' at Towcester, and two sessional courses, at Colchester and Harpenden, with 11 and 9 effective students respectively.[124] Art and art history and appreciation were also minor subjects at this time, despite the efforts of Helen Lowenthal, who reported 'difficulties' in establishing the subject. She did succeed with some classes, and even organised international visits for art students, notably to Florence, but the subject remained a minority interest, and as with music there were challenges for students in meeting the 'written' work requirements.[125]

One of the features of extramural university teaching was the wide disciplinary range covered by many students in the local centres, and also by the teaching staff. Students in local extension societies – and on other courses such as the WEA summer schools – could return repeatedly for years, and in some cases decades, to study often very different things; and as such they were exposed to a much broader range of tutors and lecturers, and of subjects, than an intramural undergraduate would ever study. Over a career in extramural teaching, historians and teachers of English literature could expect to range over different periods, and others were required to teach more widely than might have been expected of their counterparts within subject-based university departments. More than this, few staff tutors remained within a single disciplinary area at any time, and certainly not across a whole teaching career. It was from extramural education that new interdisciplinary areas of study – most notably cultural studies – emerged during the post-war period, a development personified by staff tutors such as Raymond Williams (University of Oxford) and Richard Hoggart (University of Hull), and the growth of social history was also partly an outcome of post-war university adult education.[126] The same could be said for international affairs, with its mixture of politics, international relations, economics and, in some cases, political thought.[127]

Summer schools provided a good opportunity to experiment with multidisciplinary and team-taught courses. As Frank Bell explained in 1952, at WEA summer schools '[s]ome emphasis is now laid on a "synoptic" course of study in which a specified period is considered from the historical, literary, artistic and philosophical standpoints, thus breaking down the rather rigid barriers between academic subjects, less essential to extra-mural than to internal teaching'.[128] This practice had commenced in 1949, with a 'composite' course – soon rephrased as 'synoptic' – on 'Regency England', taught by Christopher Lee, Helen Lowenthal and Lionel Munby.[129] This was an 'experiment', for which students were 'carefully selected' – 'a balance of age and sex and class' was ensured, though with priority to students from the WEA Eastern District – and took historical, literary and art historical perspectives on the Regency period, reflecting the specialisms of the course leaders.[130] Lectures were on the economics of war and peace, the Prince Regent himself, architecture, landscape in the painting and literature of the period, the Romantic movement, technological and scientific 'advance', political ideas, government policy and 'The Reading Public and Public Opinion'. The course would be better described as multidisciplinary than interdisciplinary – there were separate reading lists for the three areas of study, as well as some 'general' texts – but it was clear to both staff and students that it entailed something new and challenging.[131] Lee, Lowenthal and Munby explained that it

> really seemed to give students and to bring out of them something they neither get nor give in winter [i.e. local centre] courses .... In this respect there is no comparison with the results of the older tradition [at summer schools] of separate subject courses, which could not provide the same kind of stimulus.[132]

Students' written work, too, managed to meet the demands of the two-week course: despite concerns, it 'did progress from an interest in specialities towards a grappling with the age as a whole'. Students did not find this easy, but it worked in the end: one who took the 'Regency England' course was initially 'intimidated by the mix-up of subjects and was a[t] first confused, failing to see what the course was about; but then ... came to see how it all hangs together and makes sense'.[133]

In the following year, the 'synoptic' course was on 'Edwardian England' – featuring literature, 'domestic' history and the history of international relations – and others followed: the practice was continued throughout the 1950s and into the 1960s.[134] There were courses on 'The England of William and Mary' (in 'heavy demand', with an unusually large group of 36 students), 'The Age of Shakespeare', 'The Age of Chaucer' and 'The Age of Dickens', among others.[135] For 'The Age of Dickens', in 1957, students were asked to read a historical outline, two novels and Tennyson's *In Memoriam* in advance of the course, and again the 'synoptic' elements were emphasised, although the essay titles were mostly quite discipline-specific: 'was Sir Robert Peel a traitor to his party in 1846?' and 'how far does Browning succeed in creating characters in his poetry?', for example.[136] The pioneers of these courses were content to discover that

> The idea of taking a reasonably short and carefully selected period out of Britain's past and studying it from as many aspects as possible, breaking outside even the expanding frontiers of formal history, proved neither impossible to achieve in practice nor a mere dilettante attraction.[137]

They made it clear, though, that 'the period to be treated must be brief … [and] cannot be chosen purely on economic-political or literary-artistic grounds. The available staff and their capabilities have to be carefully considered.'[138] The topic also had to be reasonably accessible to students. Problems occurred, for example, when 'The Age of Pericles' was chosen as the theme: the first such course dealing with non-British material and with ancient history, this was 'disappointing'. There was no classicist on the Board's staff, and the course was led by Rachel Young, Christopher Lee and Leo Salingar. They had the assistance of more specialist part-time tutors, but although the latter did a good job,

> Discussion, both in lecture and seminar, was full and lively, but because of the unfamiliarity of the subject it was more concerned with fact finding than with formulating ideas. It was more difficult than usual to discern any underlying theme or pattern in the fortnight's work.[139]

In 1961, the synoptic course took a modern theme, 'Ibsen and his Times', and by 1964 it had returned to the age of Shakespeare.[140] Where there was a coherent and tightly-focused period, the courses were generally 'satisfactory': for 'The Age of Dickens', for example, '[t]he period chosen worked out well, the history and literature being so closely connected'.[141]

On the regional programme, multidisciplinary courses were less common: each class had only one tutor, and there was an established pattern of demand for courses in history, literature, psychology and philosophy. However, moves in a multidisciplinary direction were being made by Montagu Clifford, who was faced with the challenge of providing courses for local centres where scientific subjects were rarely in heavy demand. Moreover, almost no local centres were in a position to provide facilities for teaching laboratory-based sciences, and – as with music – many scientific subjects would require prior knowledge that extramural students were less likely to have. Clifford, therefore, infused his teaching with sociological approaches, running tutorial classes in the 'Social Relations of Science', for example (at Desborough, in Northamptonshire, starting in 1948), 'Science and Society' (Linton, Cambridgeshire, also starting in 1948) and 'Science and Social Problems' (at Wellingborough, starting in 1950).[142] Even these were relatively small classes, barely meeting the minimum numbers of students required, and Clifford branched out in other directions, teaching – for example – 'The Story of Fenland' to a sessional class (at Isleham, in Cambridgeshire) in 1950-1 and tutorial classes on the 'Natural History of the Eastern Counties' at Knebworth (Hertfordshire) and King's Lynn from 1953.[143] The regional focus was an attraction to students in the local centres, and allowed for field trips and practical observations. By 1959, Clifford was running courses on 'The Natural History of East Anglia', which drew on geology, natural history and archaeology:

> This course is concerned to tell of those things that may be encountered, but not understood, by the ordinary rambler in East Anglia. It consists chiefly of a series of excursions to range the length and breadth of East Anglia in search of the natural evidence of its origin and development .... The course includes talks on the rocks and soils, plant life, scenery and prehistoric antiquities of the district. Guide books customarily regard a countryside as the scene in which are set historic buildings and places of natural beauty. In this course, however, an attempt is made to indicate how such buildings and vistas develop out of the basic fabric of the countryside, the rock and soil that underlie all superstructures, whether these be man-made or are the more immediate consequences of natural forces. In this way there emerges a picture of the present countryside of East Anglia as the current edition of a landscape that has been gradually changing throughout an immensely long past, with man as one of the latecomers who has done more than any other single influence to modify its form.[144]

Such a course could be seen, in some ways, as a precursor of the enduring and popular courses on landscape history that would become a mainstay of the Board's regional teaching in later decades.

There were also changing disciplinary demands from local centres in the 1950s, and these affected the shape of the teaching programme. History remained popular, but there was a gradual fall-off in demand for philosophy and psychology, as well as politics, and an 'abrupt decline' in demand for economics, as well as a diminishing interest in international affairs.[145] At the same time, however, a new demand arose for archaeology, influenced by the popularity of the subject on television: Mortimer Wheeler, in particular, was becoming a well-known figure on the screen in the mid-1950s, bringing the subject to new audiences.[146] The demand resulted in the appointment of a new staff tutor: John Alexander, a post-war Cambridge history graduate who was studying for a PhD at Cambridge – on the European Iron Age – alongside his work for the Board. Alexander was publishing work on Yugoslavian archaeology while teaching in Cambridge, and would move to the University of London in 1964 before returning to work in Cambridge's Department of Archaeology in 1970.[147] Under Alexander's influence, field archaeology would become a mainstay of WEA summer schools, featuring practical excavation work at the Roman settlement site at Castle Hill, to the north-west of Cambridge.[148] For Alexander, field archaeology 'cannot be learned through lectures ... [and] the study of Archaeology itself is incomplete without knowledge of the way in which an excavation is conducted'.[149] He presented the results of the excavation as an outcome of the teaching that he had done: 'these discoveries may be regarded as the by-product of the training programme' run by the Board.[150] By the end of the 1950s, there were six tutorial classes in archaeology across the Cambridge region, a sessional class and two terminals, mostly with high enrolments, although some students seem to have struggled with the written work. It was harder to teach practical archaeology in local centres on a weekly basis, but some of the courses were badged simply as 'Archaeology', while others focused on a particular topic such as 'The Archaeology of Early Civilization' or 'History and Archaeology of Roman Britain'.[151]

Perhaps the most significant subject to extend its reach in the post-war period, though, was local history. It was taught until 1953 by Marion Springall, throughout the period by Rachel Young in Norfolk, Lionel Munby in Hertfordshire and several part-time tutors across the region; and, from 1957 in Suffolk, by Henry Clement.[152] It had appeared on the regional programme before the war, at least as early 1934-5; there were two or three courses in it each year in the mid-1930s and around six by 1938-9, but in the early post-war period the number expanded to around 14 a year, peaking at 17 in 1950-1.[153] (These figures were calculated by Munby, counting extension and terminal courses as half a course each.) Moreover, the subject became a staple of tutorial and sessional classes – 14 of the 17 local history courses in 1950-1 were in one of these two categories – and in the years 1952-64 the average number of local history courses each year was around 11, with four of them being tutorial classes.[154] This heavy demand had not been anticipated, and nor was it welcome in some quarters: Frank Jacques, for example, considered local history 'escapist'.[155] Nevertheless, it was what students in the region wanted, and it became another example of a subject that, in Munby's words, 'developed as an academic discipline partly through its teaching in adult classes'.[156] It required tutors to have a mastery of different periods and areas of history, and an ability to apply their teaching techniques in a range of locations, as students in each town or village naturally wanted to study their own local history. It also required engagement with other disciplines: Munby instanced archaeology, geography and sociology, but other examples might be architecture, geology and even natural history. Indeed, Munby taught a tutorial class on 'Local History' at Swavesey together with Montagu Clifford and two other tutors, with Clifford leading the sessions on natural history and human settlement in the East Anglian region.[157]

Local history was an ideal subject for a tutorial class because of the opportunity it gave for students to do practical work with historical primary sources. Local record offices were emerging in many counties after the Second World War, making sources more easily – if not always *very* easily – available. Most local centres were at a distance from record offices, and Munby and others often found themselves transcribing material to use at classes, though photocopying would in time made this task less arduous.[158] In the 1950s, too, the first 'really useful' guides to local history research were published, while demand for extramural teaching was further stimulated by the emergence of specialist local societies and by the Standing Conference for Local History in 1948.[159] Local history remained 'a frontier subject', lacking academic respectability in most internal university history departments, but for Munby and others it was the epitome of what could be done extramurally:

> Adult students learn history with a more mature critical sense when they work on documents to discover some truth that is not yet known. The discovery may be a relatively trivial one, but the process of learning is not only more valuable, it is also more enjoyable than simply listening to lectures and writing essays, for students are, in part, choosing their own field of enquiry and asking their own questions.[160]

The potential of local history was endorsed in a 1955 report on the East Anglian region by HM Inspectorate, which declared that 'the subject of local history can inspire a group, however heterogeneous in character and unskilled in the techniques of study, to pursue a plan of work with much zeal and satisfaction'.[161] Although some local history courses were described in the report as 'lifeless and unenterprising', this did not apply to Munby and Young, who were 'at the height of their powers'.[162] Munby's classes, in particular, often worked with the tutor to produce a history of their town or village: one example was *Knebworth: The Story of Our Village*, first published in 1953.[163] Local history, under Munby's leadership, would continue to thrive into the 1960s and beyond.

*

A key development in post-war adult education was the expansion of residential provision, and Cambridge would follow – albeit slowly at first – in this direction. The early twentieth century had seen the establishment of a number of 'long-term residential colleges' for adult education. Some of these, most notably Ruskin College in Oxford (founded in 1899), were associated with universities, whereas others – such as Coleg Harlech in north Wales – had some university involvement.[164] Other adult education movements had established colleges of various kinds offering both long- and short-term residential opportunities for adult students. The post-war years, though, saw a 'mushrooming' of short-term adult education colleges, many of which were founded directly by – or had a strong involvement with – local universities and colleges.[165] Perhaps the most significant was Holly Royde, a residential centre for the University of Manchester, with roots in earlier initiatives in the 1930s; Holly Royde was taken under the management of Manchester's extramural studies department in 1949.[166] Others grew out of armed forces education during and after the war, and some emerged from private philanthropic activity.[167] The WEA, YMCA and – above all – LEAs were involved in the establishment, funding and running of others, and there were 24 short-term residential colleges in England by the start of the 1950s.[168] These developments were discussed by the Board and its staff, with a view to taking its own steps in the same direction.[169] Some wanted a residential college 'within the walls' of

Cambridge; space constraints made this clearly impractical, but the Board considered several sites in its extramural region in the early post-war years.[170]

A potential opportunity arose when the University of Cambridge acquired Madingley Hall – three miles west of the city – in 1948. This large sixteenth-century house, bought for £50,000, was considered a suitable site for residential courses, although it did not open until the 1951-2 academic year, and even then 'was only partially completed and the limited accommodation entailed some measure of improvisation in planning'.[171] In any case, extramural education did not have sole use of Madingley Hall: during term-time it was mainly a postgraduate hall of residence, with the residential college function adopted in vacations only.[172] Nevertheless, the Hall's early publicity advertised it as a 'residential college for adult education', although this terminology was used sparingly, if at all, after the early 1950s.[173] As with most such colleges – and many non-residential educational establishments too – there was a resident warden, initially Canon Charles Raven, former Regius Professor of Divinity and Master of Christ's College, and from 1954 Frank Salter, who remained chairman of the Board itself.[174] The premises were small, with a maximum of 50 in residence at any one time, but there were many advantages to running short-term courses at the Hall: unlike a remote local centre, it allowed for 'close contact' – albeit at three miles' distance from Cambridge – with the university itself, and for more use of internal teaching staff, rather than just the Board's full- and part-time employees.[175] Moreover,

> A Residential College offers certain opportunities for adult education that are not provided by Tutorial and Sessional Classes. Study is continuous and free from the normal distractions of daily life. The best and keenest students of a subject may be selected and the work carried on at a level which, perhaps, only two or three students in a normal class would be interested.[176]

The element of selection mentioned here was potentially controversial – the non-selective entry to extramural courses was a key feature of the 'Great Tradition' and of the Board's own regional programme – and this may have been one reason why, apparently, the WEA Eastern District displayed a 'disappointing attitude' to courses staged there.[177] Some of the Board's own tutors, too, were concerned that residential teaching might be developed at the expense of 'orthodox teaching in the field', and these issues would become more apparent later in the 1950s, as residential courses became an area of some contention among the staff.[178]

Strong supporters of residential courses, though, like assistant secretary Frank Bell, urged their benefits from the outset. Bell argued that '[e]ven within a week-end it is possible to plan an intensive programme which in actual teaching hours may be equivalent to one-third of a term', and that such courses offered staff and students a 'freedom from "caretakeritis"':

> There is none of the hurried atmosphere of so many classes in which either the caretaker is hovering like a bird of prey over the class or the tutor has continually to look at his watch to make sure he does not miss the bus. One could with difficulty imagine a greater contrast to this than the conditions at Madingley.[179]

The teaching staff agreed, up to a point. Many felt that a weekend course was too short, and would be little different from those offered at other residential colleges, where weekend or week-long courses were offered at a 'low standard'. Madingley Hall, by contrast, should have courses lasting at least two weeks, and ideally a month, and thereby 'gain a reputation for high standards, hard work, and long courses' – all supported by a resident tutor, who should work alongside the warden.[180] The emphasis on high standards echoed the ongoing debates about the value of tutorial and sessional classes and the importance of students studying at a high level and producing written work, and was epitomised in 1952 by a two-week course on English literature for students from local centres taught by the new staff tutor Leo Salingar.[181]

Madingley Hall continued to be developed and enhanced through the 1950s: some books from Stuart House were moved to its library; two hard tennis courts were installed in 1955; and the Board was quite 'satisfied' with the Hall's 'suitability' for its courses.[182] A college-like atmosphere was maintained there, and there was a licensed bar, though in 1956 it was felt that this was in urgent need of 'furnishing'.[183] A 'rising bell' was rung at 8.30am, half an hour before breakfast, and a 'dinner bell' at 7.25pm to summon students for dinner in the impressive dining hall.[184] The Hall was popular with the students who lived there and with those who attended residential courses: when one contributor to the *Cambridge Review* denigrated it as a 'hotel' and suggested that its dual purpose as a graduate student residence and a venue for extramural studies made it a 'white elephant', a group of residents protested angrily, praising its atmosphere and amenities.[185]

Residential courses had been an important feature of the Board's teaching long before the Second World War, not least in the 'summer meetings' of the university extension programme, the WEA summer schools and the four-week vacation courses for 'foreign students'.[186] Following a wartime hiatus, the latter were restarted in 1947, and have been held annually since then. The 1947 course attracted 157 students from 16 countries, and numbers expanded thereafter, stabilising at between 300 and 400 a year through the 1950s.[187] The course was publicised through the British Council and other agencies, and students applied to join it. In 1952, while 327 applications were accepted, a further 171 were rejected by the Board. Frank Bell, who was mainly responsible for organising the course in the early 1950s, explained that

> The student demand would, therefore, enable the Board immediately to increase the size of the Course by at least fifty per cent. This would, I believe, be a great mistake. It is not easy to preserve a feeling of intimacy and friendliness even with 300. With greater numbers it would be impossible.[188]

There were also practical difficulties in terms of both staffing and accommodation: one suggestion was to split the course and run it twice, but this would run into the same problems.[189] Some of the students were acccommodated in colleges, and others in university lodging houses or – in some cases – with families. The lodging houses, in particular, were not always suitable, and attracted complaints.[190] The course was expensive to attend: in 1957 the fee was £14, and college accommodation £7 10s. a week, making a total of £44 (the equivalent of almost £900 today) in addition to travel and other expenses; accommodation was somewhat cheaper in lodging houses, but excursions and some other events were paid for in addition to the basic fees.[191]

The format of the course changed little over time. It was centred on 'Contemporary England: Its Literature and Institutions', aiming 'to present a wide and varied picture of England and English life to-day'.[192] Students attended two lectures each morning and one on most evenings, given by staff tutors and external speakers and featuring a wide range of topics including contemporary politics, English music, literature, the National Health Service, town planning and the empire. In the afternoons, there were language classes, taught in small groups of around eight students, overseen by Frank Bell. There was a whole series of optional extra excursions – to Oxford, Ely and elsewhere in 1948, for example – and social events including, in that year, a reception hosted by Geoffrey Hickson in his capacity as mayor of Cambridge.[193] By 1957 the title of the course had changed to 'Contemporary *Britain*: Its Literature and Institutions', but the content was much the same. The usual range of lectures and language classes was augmented that year by a day trip to Stratford to see a production of *As You Like It*, and there were dances, tours of colleges and other excursions too.[194] Hickson's wife was the 'designated' hostess for the vacation course, spending most mornings in the 'reception room' and trying to ensure that students 'receive[d] invitations to meet English people'.[195]

There were some concerns about the level of work done on the vacation courses, partly due to the range of social and cultural activities that could impinge on students' academic efforts. Although active class participation and some written work were expected, it was felt that not all students were intent on 'serious study'. Young undergraduates who travelled to Cambridge may well have had other things, beyond academic work, on their minds. Nevertheless, as Bell explained,

> Each year the proportion of the more serious and rather older students is greater. This is sometimes not realised by observers in Cambridge .... This trend should continue, but without eliminating entirely the younger student who lays more emphasis on the first word of 'Vacation Course'.[196]

To support the development of more 'serious study', specialist seminar courses were offered alongside the main programme from 1952, in English literature and 'English institutions'. They were led, respectively, by John Andrew and Lionel Munby, both of whom 'testified to the quality of their students'.[197] By 1958 there was an additional seminar on international relations, and students seemed on the whole to be 'rather more serious' than before.[198]

Alongside the main vacation course, other opportunities for 'foreign students' were provided in the 1940s and 1950s. From the 1940s onwards, a parallel course was run in alternate years for 'foreign lawyers', introducing them to aspects of English law and legal practice. This featured a lot of visiting lecturers, specialists from Cambridge's law faculty and elsewhere, and – like the 'foreign students' – those who took part were mostly young. The average age of the 56 lawyers and law students who took part in 1948 was about 27, and it was considered that the younger students benefited more than the older participants.[199] A similar course for 'foreign theologians' was publicised in 1949, but did not attract sufficient interest to run.[200] Other regular ventures included an annual summer school for Swedish students, taking around 40 to Cambridge for three weeks, and from 1952 a special three-week study of 'English Literature for British and Foreign Students' – again with about 40 in attendance – led by staff tutor Christopher Lee and run in collaboration with the British Council.[201] By the mid-1950s, across the whole programme of residential courses, of which the international vacation courses made up the majority, more than 2,500 student-weeks were being spent in Cambridge under the Board's oversight every year.[202]

*

A key related development in the 1950s – on a small scale at first, but very important in light of subsequent developments – was the introduction of courses, mostly residential, for specific groups of selected students, often catering in some way for those students' 'vocational interests'.[203] This was happening across the range of extramural departments in the 1950s: one example was the University of Liverpool, where managers could study 'Problems of Business Organization' and probation officers 'An Introduction to Criminology', and where from 1956 onwards there was growing provision of courses for groups including 'teachers, social workers, doctors, lawyers and engineers'.[204] There, a 'demand' was also identified from 'child care officers, health workers, hospital administrators, youth leaders and voluntary social workers' – in other words, mostly 'trained employees of the State'.[205] At Manchester, too, there were courses for employees of both local and national government, including 'policemen, lay magistrates and magistrates' clerks, social workers, parish clerks and probation officers', and for middle managers and foremen from industrial companies, often using the residential facilities at Holly Royde.[206] Cambridge, of course, already had the 'foreign lawyers' course, and other moves were being made in a more vocational direction.[207] At a local level, Frank Lee led a course for child welfare officers at Wellingborough in 1950, and from 1950 onwards an annual summer school on 'Programme Design for Automatic Digital Computing Machines' was run, in collaboration with the Cambridge Mathematical Laboratory; attendance at this could reach 100.[208] There was also a long series of 'refresher' courses for school teachers and for some who worked in technical colleges: these covered mathematics, physics, chemistry, English literature and – for those working in technical colleges – 'liberal studies'.[209]

These emerging interventions in 'vocational' education were augmented by a series of bespoke courses for 'managers', 'supervisors' and industrial apprentices from 1953 onwards.[210] The managers' courses lasted four weeks, and as many as 42 students might attend; the apprentices' courses were shorter, at two weeks, but still attracted high numbers.[211] For the managers' courses, led by Leslie James, the aim was

> to give to men who have successful experience of management (and may be destined for higher responsibility) an opportunity of widening their knowledge of national and international problems that are relevant to their normal work, of discussing and reflecting upon them away from the distractions of ordinary life, and of developing their powers of critical analysis.[212]

In practical terms, the course had several elements. First, the students attended 'selected' university lectures, in economics, politics and history, and some in English; then there were specially provided courses in economics, international relations (taught by James himself, with some guest lecturers) and on 'contemporary problems of the Middle East' (again taught by James). In addition, there were various one-off lectures, and students had the opportunity to attend talks staged by university student societies, as well as to get support for essay writing. They stayed at Madingley and, apparently, 'fitted very well into the … community'.[213] Apprentices, meanwhile, who were drawn from the engineering industry, had four courses of lectures: 'The History of Science' by Charles Raven, 'The History of Engineering' by the versatile Lionel Munby and some guest contributors, 'The Use of English' by Frank Bell, and 'The Development of Our Social and Economic System' by course director Vivian Ramsbottom.[214] Each student chose an essay topic at the start of the course, and based their reading during the two weeks on that topic; Ramsbottom had two individual supervisions with each student (a heavy workload, given that there were 29 of them in 1956), describing the course as 'about the most exciting piece of teaching I have undertaken'.[215]

Meanwhile, the first residential course for members of a specific trade union – the National Union of General and Municipal Workers – was held in 1954, regarded by course leader Frank Lee as 'an important experiment'. Given the same title – 'The Social and Economic Background to Industry' – as the courses both for managers and apprentices, it covered issues relevant to trade union activity such as taxation, benefits and income differentials, but also included lectures on the history of trade unionism, and – like the apprentices – on 'The Evolution of Our Economic and Social System', as well as on various one-off topics. Students were taken on a tour of the 'wool' villages nearby, particularly Lavenham, and the course lasted a fortnight in total.[216] As with the course for managers, there was a selection process for this one: this was left to the union to organise, which seemed to Lee a 'chancy process', but it seemed to work well. These courses can be seen as an example of how the Board was beginning to grapple with the 'problem of how to liberalise technical education' in a period when – as Harold Wiltshire had noted – it was relatively easy to organise bespoke 'vocational' courses compared with sustaining the 'Great Tradition'.[217] Cambridge made fewer strides in this direction than some other extramural departments in the 1950s, but the 'experiment' with bespoke courses of this kind – if not with 'technical education' as such – highlighted some of the trends that might be followed in the future.

The content of courses for managers, supervisors, apprentices and trade unions evolved over time. Originally – as the range of subject-matter reflected, and as Geoffrey Hickson himself explained – 'the programme was planned and directed by a team of four', comprising 'a lawyer, an economist, an engineer, and a psychologist', and 'one objective was to try out a mixture of University disciplines'.[218] This reflected the emergent trends at the WEA summer school, but in the case of these courses for industrial personnel the 'synoptic' aims were less successful, and the emphasis moved towards economics as the courses developed during the 1950s. For Hickson, this offset the decline of that subject in the regional programme, and was therefore an appropriate direction in which to move:

> the common factor has been the study of economics: the back-bone of most of these courses has been a survey of recent economic history leading up to the consideration of various economic and social problems of today. Earlier in this century the study of economics and economic history was prominent in the extra-mural work of all Universities .... In recent years the demand in that field has markedly waned, and it is of interest that they

> are now proving to be such suitable and acceptable subjects in these residential courses.[219]

In any case, by the late 1950s the courses were an established element of the Board's vacation work; and similar courses were also being run by the University of Oxford's Extra-Mural Delegacy, having likewise commenced in 1953.[220]

Not everyone at the Board was happy with this direction. When a 'seminar' for managers was proposed in 1957, there was 'considerable discussion [as to] whether this Seminar represented work that the Board could appropriately undertake'.[221] Hickson, though, disagreed: not only were the courses resurrecting demand for economics, but they were also – in a wider sense – giving new energy to the tradition of 'liberal' education for which the Board stood. 'Fundamentally', he argued, 'this represents the kind of liberal education of adults which Universities have always sought to provide through their extra-mural work.'[222] Thus, although the students – referred to as 'members' – on the courses were sent by their employers on the understanding that there would be a vocational purpose to the experience, they were not being directly 'trained' to do their jobs, or indeed any other jobs. This was what made the *university* contribution to this kind of education distinctive. Thus in 1959, at the seventh running of the course for managers – attended by 39 men from 34 companies – it was emphasised that the purpose was *not* to teach practical aspects of management, and that both the staff and 'members' agreed that this was 'the correct emphasis in a course run by the University'. One student wrote in response to this course that

> The avoidance of attempting to teach management subjects was, to my mind, the fundamental strength of the course. The tutors were dealing with subjects in which they were quite at home and, as a result, I never had the feeling that we were wasting any time on theoretical treatments of essentially practical 'shop-floor' subjects. It has been our experience that where Universities, in similar courses, attempt to put over such subjects they fail, sometimes very miserably.[223]

This is *not* to say that there was *no* vocational dimension to the course: indeed, its leaders insisted that '[e]very effort was made to give members practice in the art of management'. The students chaired meetings with external speakers, and they were organised into self-managing 'syndicates' – project groups tasked with producing detailed reports on their discussions.[224] In this sense, again, elements of the self-governing nature of the tutorial class were grafted onto the residential course, which could be identified by its supporters as being part of a longer tradition of liberal adult education.

*

During the Second World War the Board – along with other university extra-mural departments – had quickly become involved in the provision of adult education for members of the armed forces, initially under the auspices of a Central Advisory Council (CAC), established in 1940. Independent of the services themselves, this body included representatives of voluntary adult education providers including the WEA and YMCA. There were 23 regional committees, of which one was responsible for an area broadly corresponding to the Cambridge extramural region.[225] This provided mainly one-off lectures or short series, which were easier to organise than longer courses in the context of rapid and unpredictable troop movements, although servicemen were also 'encouraged' to attend the ongoing courses run by the Board in the region.[226] This new element of the Board's activity was overseen by a new assistant secretary, Norman Scarlyn Wilson, a linguist and occasional playwright who had written articles for *The Times* in the early weeks of the war.[227] Scarlyn Wilson taught elsewhere for the Board in the post-war period, for example extension classes on 'Modern British Playwrights' at Newmarket and 'France' at Wellingborough in 1948.[228] The CAC lectures were viewed with suspicion in some quarters within the armed forces, and this suspicion was reciprocated when the Army established its own educational initiative – the Army Bureau of Current Affairs – which was seen as an attempt to 'undermine the growing civilian adult education schemes … organised by the CAC regional committees'.[229] There was suspicion at the local level, too: when assistant secretary David Hardman went to Southend to give a lecture to servicemen, the commanding officer grudgingly accepted his presence, but reminded him that he was lecturing only because 'the bloody War Office says you can'. The Army also objected to the presence of two pacifists who were lecturing on the Board's behalf.[230]

Mutual suspicion was in evidence after the war, too, as more collaborative ventures were established with the forces, particularly to offer educational opportunities to men doing National Service. The CAC was dissolved in 1948, and replaced with a Central Committee for Adult Education in HM Forces, which involved both adult education providers and the services themselves. However, the two sides had different priorities. As one participant in CAC explained just after the war,

> To maintain a democratic way of life was one of the primary objectives for which we went to war. Yet it might seem that training for war could not be democratic and must be authoritarian, and that we could not hope to fight successfully without some sacrifice of the very values for which we were fighting. Military efficiency is usually held to entail instantaneous and unquestioning obedience … and a ruthless concentration on winning the war to the exclusion of all other objectives. In adult education, on the other hand, it is ordinarily axiomatic that attendance should be genuinely voluntary, that each group of students should choose the subject of study, that all opinions are open to question and discussion and that bias and propaganda are 'taboo'.[231]

The 'inevitable friction' that arose from this conflict was highlighted in 1949, when one member of the full-time teaching staff of the Board was refused permission to teach on courses for the armed services on 'general security grounds'.[232] Geoffrey Hickson was frustrated by this, and made it clear that continued refusal without a satisfactory reason 'might seem to infringe academic freedom and therefore might prejudice the Board's contined co-operation in the present scheme'.[233] Hickson continued to pursue the matter well into the following year, but was unable to get any further information.[234]

In the event, the Board *did* continue to 'co-operate', and provided more than 1,000 lectures in some years, increasingly for the Royal Air Force (RAF) rather than the Army (only a minimal amount of teaching was done for the Royal Navy). Scarlyn Wilson remained, on a part-time basis, to co-ordinate the work; meanwhile, he also published a long account of the history of the CAC shortly after the war.[235] Some of the teaching related to the examinations taken by offers under the RAF's promotion schemes, including lectures on international affairs and 'imperial geography', but much was under the wider heading of 'Education for Citizenship', and included a range of current affairs, as well as music, drama and local history.[236] By 1952, the content of the promotion examinations had changed, and the Board was contributing more lectures for general RAF and

Army audiences; by this time there were 42 lecturers on its armed forces panel.[237] By this time, though, Hickson doubted whether the Board should be doing this kind of work. In the case of Army lectures, those on current affairs and 'citizenship' were useful, but one-off lectures on various topics 'cannot be regarded as having any great educational value, [and] it is difficult to suggest any alternative other than to suspend the work altogether'.[238] Two years earlier, at a meeting of the Board's teaching staff, 'some doubt was expressed as to whether it was worthwhile to continue education with the services',[239] and Hickson was increasingly sceptical, specifically in relation to the audiences for lectures to the RAF. 'The principal difficulty remains', he averred, 'that the bulk of these lectures are given to audiences that have been compulsorily paraded and such work can hardly be called liberal education.'[240] There may have been some value in lecturing to National Servicemen in the first year of their two-year stint – 'because it re-establishes an educational interest that has often been lost during the interval between leaving school and entering the services' – but other agencies, rather than universities, could have done this to much the same effect.[241]

During the 1950s the Board significantly reduced its contribution to education in the armed forces, a development accelerated by the ending of National Service in 1957. From more than 1,000 lectures a year in the early 1950s, the number fell to 785 in 1956-7, 629 the following year, 519 in 1958-9 and then just 388 in 1961-2.[242] Some of the teaching continued to relate to the RAF's promotion examinations, but other demands of the services were not so easily met. As early as 1950, the RAF had asked the Board to teach elocution to its officers, but this was quickly dismissed by Hickson as being the province of an LEA rather than a university.[243] It was increasingly clear that there was little congruence between the educational aims of the Board and the needs of the armed forces, although the range of lectures that *were* provided demonstrated the potential coverage of this work, and the ability of the Board's staff to teach across areas of both general and immediate contemporary significance. Among the lectures delivered in 1961-2, '[t]wo of the most commonly recurring subjects were Africa and the Common Market; other subjects included juvenile delinquency, glaciation, abstract art, the growth of cities, and ballistic missile guidance systems'.[244]

While the provision of lectures to the armed forces was in decline, this was partially offset by the use of Madingley Hall for residential courses specifically aimed at men in the services. In 1955-6 there were eight week-long courses –

five on 'International Affairs', two on 'The Middle East' and one on 'Europe since 1945' – with 214 students from the Army, RAF and US Air Force at Madingley.[245] In 1960-1 there were five residential courses at Madingley and four more in Cambridge, with a total of 242 officers from the RAF, US Air Force, Army Staff College and RAEC in attendance. The Madingley courses were generally on specialist topics, for example 'Sources of International Tension' and 'Problems and Policies of the Powers in Asia' for the US Air Force, and 'Britain and the Wider World' for the RAF.[246] For the Board, there were clear advantages to this: as with the industrial enterprises that used the Hall, the armed forces paid the full cost for courses, whereas when extramural students themselves attended, they had to be offered accommodation at a subsidised rate.[247]

The focus on international affairs, in which there was substantial expertise among the teaching and administrative staff, and which was now declining in popularity on the regional programme, demonstrated the advantages of redeploying resources in the direction of armed forces education. In 1959, for example, a week-long international affairs course for RAF officers featured seminars led by Henry Clement (on NATO and on Africa), John Hampden Jackson (the USSR, French North Africa and France itself), Vivian Ramsbottom (the USA, Communism and 'International Economic Problems') and Leslie Wayper (China, India and Malaya).[248] Students were required to write essays on such topics as 'why did the French Fourth Republic fall?' (this had happened less than a year earlier) and 'what changes can you discern in the foreign policy of Soviet Russia since the death of Stalin [in 1953]?'[249] Other courses were specifically tied to the RAF's promotion structure. In 1960, for example, 'The Commonwealth' was taught by Ramsbottom, Wayper, James Mitchell and Colin Griffiths, among others, in support of the Staff College Qualifying Examination; the attendance consisted of 30 officers, mostly Flight Lieutenants and a handful of Squadron Leaders.[250] Overall, these courses formed only a small proportion of the Board's work, but the residential component of teaching for the armed forces ensured that it had much more purpose and academic value than the one-off lectures that had predominated in the early post-war years. It also laid the foundation for continued development into the 1960s and 1970s.

*

By the late 1950s, if not earlier, the rapidly evolving context and shape of the Board's operations had uncovered differences of policy and outlook among its members and staff. These involved disagreements about approaches to the regional programme of extension, tutorial and sessional courses, and about the role of different categories of staff within it; about the extent to which the Board should involve itself in bespoke vocational courses; about the role of residential courses, especially at Madingley Hall, which was the 'most urgent question' of all; and ultimately about the nature and purpose of university adult education itself.[251] In 1958 an 'educational advisory committee' was formed 'to consider matters of educational policy' and to report back to the Board. Its members included Geoffrey Hickson himself and deputy secretary John Andrew, as well as staff tutors John Hampden Jackson, Leslie James, Lionel Munby, Leslie Wayper and Rachel Young.[252] The committee reviewed the whole history of extramural work in Cambridge, and its deliberations revealed clearly some of the faultlines that were opening up.

The gauntlet was thrown down by Hickson, who drew on his 30 years of experience as secretary to the Board of Extra-Mural Studies in a memorandum on 'The Work of the Board' that took as its starting point Harold Wiltshire's 1956 article on the 'Great Tradition'. Wiltshire had identified five key characteristics of this tradition: its emphasis on humane or 'liberal' studies; within this, a particular focus on social studies; its non-vocational nature and lack of examinations or awards; its openness to all; and its use of the tutorial or discussion model ('the Socratic method', in Wiltshire's words), rather than the extension-type lecture, as the centrepiece of its teaching method.[253] To these Hickson added a sixth feature: a particular focus on working-class students as its key constituency. He acknowledged the 'Great Tradition' and claimed to place a high value upon it, but argued that other traditions also existed within university adult education, and indeed that the older university extension movement itself – which had originated from Cambridge – differed in many respects from the very tradition that both Wiltshire and Sidney Raybould had placed at the centre of their analyses.[254] University extension, Hickson reminded the committee, did *not* focus solely or mainly on working-class students; it embraced the natural sciences as well as 'liberal' subjects (James Stuart himself was an obvious example of this); it *did* award certificates to students; and it used lectures and *not* mainly tutorials and discussion, although this may have been for 'financial reasons' rather than any pedagogical preference.[255] Moreover, the extension movement had evolved over time to meet changing conditions; and indeed the 'Great Tradition' itself 'was built on what had gone before to a greater extent than has often been realised or acknowledged and … in laying emphasis on certain aspects only of the preceding tradition, it led to a somewhat narrower conception of the functions of Universities in adult education'.[256]

Hickson argued that developments since the start of the 1950s had undermined the 'Great Tradition', though not quite in the ways and with the implications set out by Wiltshire. It was clear that there had been a decline of this kind of teaching in some, though not all, areas of the country, and that in this sense the supply of the 'Great Tradition' had 'outrun demand' for it. The rapid expansion of the post-war university adult education full-time workforce had met what demand there was, and some university extramural departments were now doing very different kinds of teaching under the label of 'university extension'.[257] In any case, universities could certainly not rely on a continued 'steady expansion' of this kind of work, demand for which had been at a 'standstill' for some time; and the implication of this was that – while partnership with the WEA remained valuable – university adult education could seek new opportunities elsewhere too.[258] For Cambridge, one such opportunity was the ongoing expansion of residential course provision: itself sustained by a long tradition of summer schools – initially for extension students, then with the WEA, and then the vacation courses for overseas students – these courses had become 'major activities' of the Board since the Second World War.[259] Residential courses like these had the advantage of being 'national, and even international, in their scope and appeal', whereas the bulk of the teaching programme was now centred on the East Anglian region.[260]

For Hickson, the 'standstill' of demand called into doubt the value of residential tutors, whose appointment had been a key element in constructing Cambridge's 'extramural empire' in the 1930s and 1940s, and into the 1950s. Writing in an earlier memorandum, Hickson argued that resident tutors were by this time of less value to the Board, and to the promotion of adult education more generally, compared with the pre-war period, when they were 'almost the only persons in their respective areas concerned with the promotion of adult education'.[261] By the 1950s there were LEA education officers and WEA tutor-organisers in the region as well, and in fact the Board had already reduced its resident tutor numbers by converting some appointments into staff tutor posts. For Hickson and others, restricting tutors to a specific part of the region made the staff less able to respond to changing demands for teaching in specific subjects.[262] The matter had come to a head when Vivian Ramsbottom left Hertfordshire to become an assistant secretary to the Board, and there had been disagreements as to whether a replacement should be appointed.

Finally, and perhaps most controversially – but, again, reflecting actual developments at Cambridge and beyond in the 1950s – Hickson called into question the dominance of the non-vocational focus of the 'Great Tradition', one of the elements on which Wiltshire had insisted. Hickson anticipated later (and echoed some older) arguments about the artificiality of the distinction between vocational and non-vocational adult education with some careful comments based on recent experience. He insisted that *all* university teaching, extramural or otherwise, should 'be a form of liberal education', but, '[p]rovided that this is the case, there is no reason why it should always be non-vocational and why a vocational purpose should not be indirectly served'.[263] The key point was that extramural teaching 'should meet some real educational need of the day which can be met by a University, at any rate for the time being, both appropriately and better than by any other agency'.[264] On one interpretation, this could be viewed as a fairly uncontroversial view, but it challenged both the elevated status of the tutorial class and, perhaps more significantly, the fourth of Wiltshire's elements in the 'Great Tradition' – its openness to all.

It is not surprising, then, that some members of staff took up Hickson's challenge and advanced a defence of the traditional activities of the Board, as least as they saw them. Rachel Young and John Hampden Jackson, supported by Board member Edward Miller, restated what they believed was the core aim of 'liberal adult education', that is 'to equip ordinary men and women for active citizenship in a democratic community', especially in the complex modern world.[265] This aim was not *only* an aim, though, but also a '*responsibility*': the Board should not just be waiting on demand for its courses, but should 'seek both to create and satisfy it'.[266] In this respect the role of resident tutors was critical, and the withdrawal of some of them had 'left a serious gap', weakening the discharge of this responsibility in the extramural region. Thus Young, Hampden Jackson and Miller not only supported the appointment of a resident tutor in Hertfordshire, but also argued for new ones in Bedfordshire and the Cambridgeshire Fenland, not least because of the opportunities and needs arising from the new towns and housing estates that had sprung up in the years since the war. The large and growing town of Luton, too, had been 'the scene of so many failures', and, closer to Cambridge, there was considerable scope for the development of extramural teaching in Trumpington.[267] Others also contributed to this debate: Lionel Munby, for example, felt that resident tutors were important in stimulating demand and co-ordinating the work of local centres, although he thought it unlikely that many staff tutors would welcome redeployment to a specific county.[268]

A different perspective was offered by Leslie James and Leslie Wayper, who agreed with Hickson on the need to 'adapt … to the changing conditions and needs of the whole society today'.[269] They were even more forceful than Hickson on the importance of residential courses, whether or not they were aimed at specific groups of people. Developing this side of the teaching would not necessarily mean cutting back on work in the local centres, but James and Wayper argued that the Board should not 'devote its main resources to a single section of the community which is, perhaps wrongly, still thought of as being educationally un[der]privileged'.[270] For Young, Miller and Hampden Jackson, this reflected a misconception about tutorial classes, in particular. They advanced a familiar argument about the social impact of tutorial classes – the 'students are commonly men and women actively engaged in the life of their local community; and through them the influence of the class extends to the whole of that community' – and reminded the committee that these classes also had value in bringing members of different social groups together, for an extended period, in the classroom.[271] These staff tutors insisted that openness to all was particularly important, because the responsibilities of extramural teaching were 'to the community at large and not to specially selected groups within the community' – and indeed few people would have the time or resources to attend residential courses anyway.[272] James and Wayper, though, were convinced that 'the most significant contribution that the Board can make to the needs of our present Society is to bring men and women from all walks of life into the atmosphere of a residential University', as was now happening at Madingley Hall.[273]

There were some elements of agreement across these different perspectives. It is clear that all the tutors agreed on the value of the educational community, whether this was in a tutorial class or a residential college environment; and none conceived – at least at this point – of a substantial reduction of the regional programme of extramural teaching. Even Young, Miller and Hampden Jackson, while urging a concern for 'the field of "liberal adult education" as distinguished from the vocational field', acknowledged that '[a] rigid line of demarcation, of course, is not easy to draw', and saw no problem with such initiatives as refresher courses for teachers or work with the Mathematical Laboratory.[274] They also urged more work in both technical and teacher training colleges, feeling that in these settings the Board could provide 'a liberal infusion to vocational training'; and this may not have been too far from Hickson's point that all university teaching should be 'liberal' in some sense, and that there could be indirect vocational benefits from something that was outwardly 'non-vocational'.[275] In any case, it was fairly clear that some change would happen – as indeed Wiltshire felt that it already had – and that in time this could be quite profound. Some of the Board's staff, including Munby, were keen to avoid a 'wrangle' over the issues; but, as he made forcefully clear, changing conditions would have an impact, whether the Board and its staff liked it or not; and he advised that '[r]esistance to new developments, merely on conservative, traditionalist grounds, will not help the existing adult education movement'.[276]

Wiltshire's third element of the 'Great Tradition' was the absence of examinations or awards – despite the importance of written work in tutorial and sessional classes, which was so often emphasised by the WEA and the Board itself. Hickson did not pursue the issue in his long memorandum, but he had considered it elsewhere, and it had a bearing on the debates surrounding vocationalism, in particular. At Cambridge, there was in fact a long tradition, dating back to 1883, of awarding Vice-Chancellor's Certificates to students, as well as sessional certificates to those who had completed extension courses; and the latter persisted into the 1950s: in 1950-1, for example, two students had received them: Alice Holland and Eileen Spafford (the latter with 'merit'), both members of a class on 'The Victorian Age' at the Southport local centre.[277] Some other universities awarded similar certificates or diplomas, though at this point in time only at the University of London was it a regular practice. Writing from the Cambridge perspective in 1951, Hickson noted that

> The number of such awards has been very small in the last 10 years [but] I have been reluctant to recommend the entire abolition of such awards, because it has seemed to me hitherto a pity not to retain a certain slight incentive to serious study through University Extension Courses.[278]

For Hickson, the question of certificates also fed into emerging debates about vocationalism:

> In my opinion the offer of certificates would not necessarily alter the character of the Board's teaching. I suggest that all teaching within the University is a mixture of liberal education and vocational training. Doubtless the Board would wish their teaching to remain a form of liberal education, but to my mind this does not mean that it must be confined to meeting demands that are non-vocational in character: such teaching without any essential alteration in its character might equally well meet demands that contain a bigger element of vocational purpose than is at present the case.[279]

At this point the suggestion of certification was relevant only to extension courses: the WEA had 'set its face' against such thing for tutorial classes, and this was again emphasised in the wake of Hickson raising the issue.[280] Most staff tutors, though, were not completely opposed to the idea: only Hampden Jackson 'made a strong plea that there should be no introduction of a Certificate on the grounds of adult education being the last stronghold of pure education without any incentives and without the limiting factor of examinations'.[281]

The discussion of certification pre-dated the deliberations of the educational advisory committee, but it was part of the wider re-evaluation of the purpose and priorities of extramural education that Cambridge and other universities were undertaking in the 1950s, and which was coming to a head at the end of the decade. Some universities – Leeds, for example – were beginning to experiment with certification in the mid-1950s, and although at Cambridge at least one staff tutor was pressing for 'some form of experiment' along these lines as early as 1952, none would be made until the 1960s.[282] Another proposal, to support a three-year Certificate in English Literature at the North Hertfordshire Technical College, Stevenage, was rebuffed in 1959, partly due to concerns about the control that the Board would be able to exercise over the syllabus and staffing.[283] The 'demand' for certification would later take on a fresh impetus, but in the 1950s Hickson and others at Cambridge adopted a more cautious approach.

*

The changes that resulted from these debates were at most incremental. Whether the Board wanted it or not – and, by the end of the 1950s, a majority of its members did – they were not to be given the sole use of Madingley Hall, which was a necessary first step towards a significant expansion of residential courses. By this time, the teaching staff were fairly evenly split on the question, though most were content for some additional use to be made of the Hall when it was available.[284] Matters were brought to a head by a suggestion in 1958 from British Petroleum (BP) for the long-term 'joint use' of the Hall by itself and the Board, with the company's own courses being run there – albeit with a 'director of studies' appointed by the Board.[285] The proposal, which could involve an initial arrangement lasting three to five years, was fiercely opposed by both Frank Salter and Edward Miller, who did not see the Board's role as providing 'closed' courses for employees of a single company – although BP tried to play down this element of it.[286] In the event, fuller consideration of the idea was delayed well into 1959, and then dropped entirely in 1960, but it set the scene for subsequent developments in the 1960s and beyond.[287] Meanwhile, after the long discussion about resident tutors, a new one was appointed in 1958 for Hertfordshire, as a belated replacement for Vivian Ramsbottom: this was Ray Pahl, a Cambridge geography graduate who would later become a professor at the University of Kent and a well-known sociologist of work, as well as the author of important studies on the sociology of friendship.[288]

In the 15 years since the end of the Second World War much had changed at the Board of Extra-Mural Studies, and in university adult education more widely. With the 'Great Tradition' under apparent threat – although the Board's own statistics would suggest otherwise, at least in its own extra-mural region – new priorities were emerging. Yet the 'tradition' still had a strong sentimental and rhetorical appeal, not least for Geoffrey Hickson himself, who had been its main representative in the University of Cambridge for more than 30 years by the end of the 1950s. The teaching staff felt it too: as early as 1953, when most had been employed in extramural teaching for less than a decade, they declared themselves, as a group, 'more than ever convinced of the value of … the Board's traditional work in the field'. Indeed, the fundamental structure of the regional teaching programme remained in place, albeit with some outlying areas of the Cambridge territory being 'lost' to other universities (Southport was finally taken over by the University of Liverpool in 1960);[289] the importance of 'university standards' was still a constant feature of internal discussions about the Board's priorities; the relatively unusual involvement of Cambridge, along with Oxford, in the provision of summer teaching for overseas students retained its profile within the overall structure of the Board's activity; and, perhaps above all, a sense of marginality from the mainstream of the Board's parent university persisted among many of those who were associated with it. Indeed, it has been suggested that – because, on the one hand, universities themselves were expanding significantly with a secure stream of funding and, on the other, the extramural departments were relatively confident of *their* mission and finance – 'it was in the 1950s and 1960s … that the extramural departments seemed to become most keenly aware of their marginal position'.[290] This was evident in particular to the Board's teaching staff, most of whom were struggling for recognition within the university and whose academic identities were bound up with the 'Great Tradition' as it was epitomised in the regional programme of classes. Despite the many concerns that were expressed in the 1950s for the future of this tradition in university adult education, the regional programme would continue to flourish in the 1960s, albeit in some new ways.

Chapter 3
Tested in the soil: the 1960s

The 1960s were a time of higher education expansion: new universities were being established, older ones were growing, some institutions were obtaining university status, and in the middle of the decade the arrival of polytechnics reshaped the whole landscape of post-18 learning. All this would have significant implications for university adult education, though at the start of the decade – and, arguably, at the end – it was not clear quite what these would be. The Robbins committee, which carried out one of the landmark inquiries into higher education, had the remit 'to review the pattern of *full-time* higher education in Great Britain', and extramural departments did not figure heavily in its 1963 report, although it did have a section on 'The Education of Adults' that expressed the expectation that such work would remain a function of most universities.[1] Robbins had nothing explicit to say about the separate stream of funding that had long sustained university adult education, although as it happened this remained in place for the 1960s and for a long time afterwards. It had, arguably, benefited extramural departments, which for all the concerns expressed in various quarters during the 1950s had in fact expanded considerably. Whereas there were 199 full-time tutors in extramural departments in 1949, the number had increased to 265 by the early 1960s, and the total annual Responsible Body grant across the sector had grown from £243,000 to £496,000, a real-terms increase of some 38% (inflation averaged 4% a year in the 1950s).[2] And yet, as one historian has commented, there remained 'a sense of insecurity, of not quite belonging to academia, and of the constant danger of being disowned by the parent university'.[3] By this time, if not earlier, some heads of extramural departments wanted the separate funding arrangements to end, arguing that this would draw them closer to their universities, although at Cambridge Geoffrey Hickson hoped that the government would 'let sleeping dogs lie'.[4]

University expansion presented two specific challenges to adult education departments. One of these was that they made older institutions vulnerable to competition from new ones: once a new university had started to offer adult education, it would quite reasonably want to establish its own 'extramural empire'. This was beginning to happen – the new 'plateglass' universities at Kent and Sussex took over provision in their regions from the University of Oxford, for example, and Warwick took some of Birmingham's local centres, while Surrey made a bid for some of the territory occupied by the University of London.[5] In the Cambridge region, new universities were being established at Colchester and Norwich, which in due course – although not as quickly as Kent, Sussex or Warwick – would develop extramural programmes in Essex and Norfolk, two of the counties in which Cambridge had a long-term presence. Then in 1968 came the Open University, with its part-time degrees for mature students and flexible patterns of study: Hickson expected that this would 'have to draw heavily on the resources of extra-mural departments', although in practice this did not happen to a great extent, and nor would it pose a significant challenge to what was happening at Cambridge in the medium term.[6]

More widely, expanding participation in full-time higher education, and the availability of part-time degrees for students at some universities – and, with time, the growing participation of women – had the potential in the longer term to undermine or change 'traditional' demands for extramural education, certainly when added to the impact of universal secondary education since the Second World War. Robbins had recognised that '[e]very increase of educational opportunity at one level leads almost at once to a demand for more opportunity at a higher level .... [T]he appetite grows by what it feeds on.'[7] There were already signs that different types of student were taking university extramural courses. Sidney Raybould commented in 1964 that

> almost everywhere extramural classes of the 'traditional' kind are tending to be provided more and more for students who have had an extended secondary education and in many cases full-time higher education as well, and less and less for students whose full-time education was confined to the elementary or secondary modern school or to the years of compulsory school attendance.[8]

This was even true on courses organised with the WEA, and seemed likely to continue, and to require a reconsideration of what universities, including Cambridge, should be doing. The vocabulary of adult education was changing, too: LEAs were moving towards a broader conception of 'continuing education', and universities – very tentatively at first – were moving in the same direction.[9] The phrase 'continuing education', comparatively rare in 1959, had become widespread by 1970.[10]

This added new dimensions to the question of what was distinctive about the university contribution to adult education, and what 'university standards' meant. The WEA and Universities Council for Adult Education attempted to clarify the role of universities in relation to adult education provision for specific groups in 1967. In a statement, the two organisations declared that universities should aim to 'help individuals acquire skills in the assimilation and assessment of new knowledge, and also skills in social action'; to raise awareness of 'social responsibilities'; and to 'transmit and interpret the facts, research findings and theoretical constraints relating to Britain's industrial life and to promote a critical evaluation of these'.[11] Work with these aims was explicitly labelled as 'liberal adult education', but for many of the thousands who came into contact with the Board's teaching during the 1960s, it had a clear vocational dimension too. As the last chapter showed, this was not new; and in the event, during the 1960s the Board continued doing the same things as it had done before, albeit rather more of them. The number of 'effective' students on the regional programme had declined in the 1950s, but recovered somewhat by the early 1960s, and increased rapidly in the second half of the decade; the popular and longstanding vacation courses continued to flourish, giving some financial ballast in a time of uncertainty; and there would also be a steady increase in the provision of non-grant-earning – but likewise profitable – courses, often on a residential basis, to the specific professional and other groups for which the Board was beginning to cater in the 1950s.

*

One casualty of the changing circumstances was the pre-war bursary scheme, which had allowed a small number of mature entrants to study for degrees at Cambridge, and which had been 'successfully revived' after the war. It had attracted very large numbers of applications: there were 178 in 1947, partly accounted for by pent-up wartime demand, and 139 in 1950.[12] A fairly substantial proportion of these were from women, 35 of whom applied in 1950, though none was successful on that occasion.[13] With only two bursaries awarded each year, competition was fierce, particularly given that increased allowances were by this time available for dependents.[14] Most bursaries, too, were supplemented by income from other sources, including residential colleges and LEAs, and holders could 'lead the normal life of a Cambridge student and ... partake in the various university activities, both educational and social'. They could also use the Stuart House library, which functioned as an additional common room for these students.[15] Most of them came from tutorial and extension classes, though with an increasing proportion in the post-war years having also spent time at a residential college such as Coleg Harlech, and there were no stipulations as to what students should do after graduation.[16] 'Some', the Board noted, 'may wish to return to their former occupations; others may prefer to fit themselves for fresh service in the [adult education] movement from which they have come.'[17] Neither of these directions proved easy to follow. For the first, as one pre-war student had put it, 'no sane person would re-enter a Coal Pit as an employee if he could avoid it'; and, moreover, 'locals would have regarded [this] as a sign of failure'.[18] As for the second, although the post-war expansion of adult education did provide some opportunities, it was still difficult for these former bursary holders to get a job: the Board itself did not employ them as staff tutors, and other areas of adult education were no less competitive, precarious and poorly remunerated than university extramural teaching.[19]

The students were mostly under the age of 30; they 'came from all over England and Wales and ranged from civil servants and managers to coalminers and tram conductors'.[20] In 1950, for example, one of the successful candidates was a 25-year-old newsagent's assistant from Bradford, who had studied in tutorial classes organised by the University of Leeds, and who went on to read Moral Science at Peterhouse; the other was a 29-year-old clerk in the Ministry of Food who was in a University of London tutorial class and also studied Moral Science, in his case at St John's.[21] In 1962, both the successful applicants had been at Coleg Harlech for the previous two years: one was a former miner and one had been a railway clerk.[22] In the post-war years other scholarships existed, too, and the Board administered some of these, taking oversight of the students to whom they were awarded; sometimes unsuccessful candidates for its own scholarships were also nominated for support elsewhere.[23] It was not always easy to find colleges to take the students,[24] but some were supportive, and at the peak of the bursary scheme, in 1952-3, there were 16 students across the three years of degree study.[25] Over time, though, as other funding opportunities became available, and especially following the introduction of LEA grants for students from the early 1960s, the bursary scheme struggled to attract applicants and eventually fell into disuse. There were only eight students by 1959-60, and at the end of the 1960s no bursaries were being awarded at all in some years.[26]

*

There was a substantial turnover of staff at the Board in the 1960s, although many of those appointed in the post-war years continued in their leadership and teaching roles. Montagu Clifford, Colin Griffiths, Leslie James, Christopher Lee, James Mitchell and Lionel Munby all served as staff tutors throughout the 1960s and beyond, giving continuity to the teaching programme; but Rachel Young left in 1961, Eileen Andrews in 1962 (she died the following year) and Leo Salingar in the same year. Salingar was briefly replaced by Francis Warner, a former vicar who had been education secretary of the Church of England Moral Welfare Council. Warner, an 'assistant tutor' rather than a staff tutor, was a poet and playwright; he left Cambridge in 1965 for a fellowship at St Peter's College, Oxford, where he remained for the rest of his career.[27] John Alexander departed in 1964, Ray Pahl in 1965, and Edward Miller – who was by this time warden of Madingley Hall – in the same year; Miller was replaced at Madingley by Robert Howland, a former Olympic athlete and by this time professor of classics at St John's College. The sociologist Ioan Davies worked at the Board for three years, as resident tutor in Norfolk, from 1962 to 1965, before leaving for a position at the new University of Essex. Meanwhile, Henry Clement died in service in 1964 and John Hampden Jackson in 1967.

Also in 1967, Geoffrey Hickson retired after almost four decades as secretary to the Board, and was replaced by his deputy John Andrew. According to the Board's annual report, under Andrew's leadership Cambridge would become 'more a national than a regional university in the world of adult education', and this comment reflected the accelerated shift towards an emphasis on 'continuing education' that would happen in

Andrew's decade as secretary to the Board.[28] Not least, he would in due course oversee one of the most significant developments in the second half of the twentieth century: the Board's move to Madingley Hall (see chapter 4).[29] To replace Andrew, one of the assistant secretaries, Vivian Ramsbottom, was promoted to the position of deputy secretary. The other assistant secretary, who had been with the Board since 1958, was Alan Stripp, a Cambridge graduate in Japanese, Chinese and Oriental history who had served with distinction during the Second World War, breaking Japanese codes at Bletchley Park and elsewhere. Stripp would later write memoirs of his wartime experiences, and lectured for the Board on both cryptography and music.[30] After Hickson's departure, Michael Allen became the junior assistant secretary in 1967. A former pupil of Bedford School and a graduate of St Catharine's College, Allen had taught English at King Edward's School in Bath before taking up the post; he had himself attended residential courses for teachers at Madingley Hall in the early 1960s.[31] As well as teaching English literature and ornithology on the regional programme, Allen was responsible for liaison with local centres across the region. In 1969 an additional assistant secretary, Elizabeth Harrison, joined the Board's staff, reflecting the increasing complexity of its provision; she was the first woman in a teaching or secretarial role since Eileen Andrews's departure some years earlier.

Six new staff tutors who were appointed in the mid-1960s would go on to long careers with the Board. Jack Herbert had a PhD from Cambridge on William Blake, and also specialised in German literature, later publishing books on Goethe, Jung and Rilke, and on W. B. Yeats.[32] He had worked in both Japan and Germany, and taught courses on British, European and American literature, Japanese drama and fine art, and European drama. Graham Howes taught sociology and theology, and was also, from 1967, a fellow of Trinity Hall, where he taught social and political sciences. His courses for the Board included the sociology of contemporary Britain, as well as the sociology of religion, in which he was developing a strong specialism.[33] Also in the mid-1960s, the psychologist Anthony Storey joined the staff. A former professional Rugby League player, Storey was the brother of novelist and playwright David Storey, author of *This Sporting Life* (1960), and Anthony also became a well-known writer: his novel *Brothers Keepers* (1975) features a thinly-disguised Cambridge psychologist and his playwright brother. Storey had been working as a senior educational psychologist for the West Suffolk Education Committee prior to his appointment at the Board, where he quickly became a 'much in demand' tutor.[34] Another popular tutor was David Trump, an 'eccentric archaeologist' who had spent five years as curator at the National Museum of Archaeology in Malta and would continue working on excavations in the Mediterranean throughout his three decades working for the Board.[35] He published the results of his excavations of the megalithic temples at Skorba in 1966,[36] and also continued some of John Alexander's work near Cambridge.

There were two new staff tutors working in local history, but they were not appointed until three years after Young's departure, which had left a 'serious gap'.[37] David Dymond – an accomplished local historian who had worked for the Royal Commission on Historical Monuments – was appointed to replace Clement as resident tutor in Suffolk. He would work for the Board for thirty years, based in Bury St Edmunds. Like most staff tutors at this time, Dymond did not have a doctorate – he eventually gained a Cambridge PhD in 2000 – but was highly active in local history research and would in due course succeed Lionel Munby as editor of the *Local Historian*, serving from 1976 to 1983.[38] Dymond wrote a string of books, including both specialist studies and local history textbooks, and had a particular interest in ecclesiastical history.[39] Another historian, Chris Barringer, joined in the same year as Dymond, in his case as resident tutor in Norfolk. Barringer had taught at Lancaster Royal Grammar School before moving to Hethersett, just outside Norwich, and like Dymond wrote a number of books on local history as well as supporting countless local historians with their own research.[40] He taught courses on geology, meteorology and and the English landscape, as well as – for university extension lectures – turning his hand to Africa, Latin America and the physical and human geography of Scandinavia. Barringer worked for the Board until 1991, when the Norfolk local centres were eventually transferred to the University of East Anglia.[41]

The position of the teaching staff was more secure than it had been in the early post-war years, but there were still some anomalies in relation to internal university teachers. All tutors had to serve a three-year probationary period, which could be waived in the case of appointments to university departments, but not for the Board. Most importantly, perhaps, staff tutors at Cambridge could not be promoted to senior lecturer or the equivalent, although the salary scales were harmonised in 1965.[42] ‘Assistant tutors’ could only be appointed on short-term contracts, and would have to leave at the end of their three years unless promoted to a staff tutor position – and if they were, then would have to serve another three years on probation. Only in 1966 were existing and future staff appointments, following the probationary period, made to the normal university retiring age – that is, 67 – rather than to age 60.[43] Meanwhile, the Board was finding it difficult to recruit suitable part-time staff in some subjects, particularly the physical sciences, and an extra assistant tutor, J. T. B. Marshall, was appointed to cover this area in 1967.[44] Workloads were still high, and the distances travelled still often long: in 1962 even experienced staff tutors were complaining of the challenges faced by having to teach four or five different courses in a week.[45] It was now standard for full-time tutors to have cars, and the mileage allowances remained a regular agenda item at staff meetings.[46] In 1965, with the cost of full-time teaching staff salaries amounting to £32,202 (in today’s figures, around £500,000), travel expenses across the Board’s work amounted to £6,501 (just over £100,000).[47] Occasionally tutors were injured in car accidents while driving to or from their classes.[48]

The Board itself was reconfigured in 1964, reducing in size from an unwieldy 30 members to a more manageable 18, with its teaching staff represented for the first time. From then onwards, it comprised five – including the chairman – appointed by the Council of the Senate; Geoffrey Hickson and the warden of Madingley Hall as *ex officio* members; three representatives of the teaching staff; and eight co-optees, who were generally from the WEA, the Local Centres Union, other universities, and sometimes from industry.[49] The Board was chaired until this point by Noel Annan, provost of King’s College; he was replaced by Eric Ashby, master of Clare, whose 1953 report on adult education was still a key reference point for universities. Ashby’s subject was botany, and he had been vice-chancellor of Queen’s University, Belfast, in the 1950s, and would continue to chair the Board until 1967 when he took the vice-chancellor’s job at Cambridge.[50] He was in turn succeeded by Geoffrey Lampe, professor of divinity and fellow of Gonville and Caius. Lampe would chair the Board through most of the 1970s, and was praised for ‘his wise and sturdy leadership, his great concern, … his wide sympathy with and his ready help in all [the Board] sought to do’.[51] The administrative machinery of the Board remained largely unchanged through the 1960s, and the WEA remained a vital partner in the regional programme. Its summer schools, too, persisted as an element of the residential programme throughout the decade and beyond: the fiftieth was held in 1964. District secretary Frank Jacques continued as a vital personal and administrative link between the Board and the WEA; and in 1965 he was co-opted as a member of the Board itself.[52]

The Board also had a small but growing body of administrative staff, some of whom had been associated with it for a long time: chief clerk Bernard Green was awarded an honorary MA degree on his retirement in 1969 after 52 years of service to the University.[53] Another long-serving administrator was Joan Sudbury, who had joined the Board during the Second World War and had been secretary to Geoffrey Hickson. When Hickson retired she took over as accounts clerk, along with W. J. Graves, who had himself worked with the Board since the 1920s. Sudbury also had the significant responsibility of finding accommodation for the large numbers of students who attended the Board's courses. She retired, with Graves, in 1977 and died in the following year, remembered as 'unfailingly efficient', and as having made 'a great contribution to making Stuart House the happy place it was'.[54] These long-serving administrators, alongside the small body of fixed academic staff, strengthened the sense of 'tradition' that pervaded adult education work at Cambridge, and provided some continuity during the changes of the 1960s and 1970s.

*

The regional teaching programme retained its appeal throughout the 1960s, and student numbers were increasing in particular on sessional courses, which offset a decline in attendance on extension lecture courses (see table 3.1). The proportions of 'effective' students remained similar to those in the 1950s: around two-thirds in some years in tutorial classes, around half in the sessionals and usually more than three-quarters in terminals. Written work by students on extension courses had died out completely by 1962, and there were some concerns about the lower proportions completing the written work on the growing number of sessional classes. Given the dependence of these classes on Responsible Body funding given in respect of 'effective' students, the teaching staff

Table 3.1
Regional programme statistics, 1960-1 to 1970-1

Year	Tutorial classes			Sessional classes		
	Classes	Enrolled students	Effective students	Classes	Enrolled students	Effective students
1960-1	31	558	355	44	759	399
1961-2	35	584	392	38	698	347
1962-3	32	544	358	40	787	382
1963-4	26	437	272	44	925	479
1964-5	24	421	269	40	783	421
1965-6	22	393	202	35	708	340
1966-7	30	523	331	44	855	449
1967-8	33	612	381	64	1208	731
1968-9	25	430	289	79	1467	752
1969-70	27	462	299	78	1459	827
1970-1	26	450	279	78	1614	942

Year	Terminal and miscellaneous classes			University extension lectures	
	Classes	Enrolled students	Effective students	Classes	Average lecture attendance
1960-1	39	602	490	43	1723
1961-2	33	620	497	39	1755
1962-3	44	606	217	41	1611

1963-4	33	507	361	32	1261
1964-5	32	416	324	29	1212
1965-6	39	602	489	36	1343
1966-7	38	582	458	34	1075
1967-8	43	572	455	43	1422
1968-9	32	447	396	43	1488
1969-70	34	528	420	42	1247
1970-1	37	470	379	39	1166

Notes: effective students include those attending at least two-thirds of the class meetings *and* submitting written work; enrolled student numbers include original enrolments *plus* students subsequently added to the register. The year 1970-1 is included here because the following year the pattern of recording certain types of course changed. Source: annual reports.

could get frustrated by the unwillingness of many of those who enrolled to do the written work and thereby become 'effective'. In 1960, 'it was recognized that if the members of a Sessional Class refuse to do the written work required by their tutor then there was no alternative but to close the class'.[55] Tutorial classes remained the gold standard for extramural education, and were particularly important to the WEA, as in previous years. Staff emphasised the strong commitment required from tutor and students in a tutorial class, and a sessional was often 'upgraded' to a tutorial if the quality of the work and students' interest in the subject justified it. The popularity of sessionals by the end of the 1960s – with more than three times the number of enrolments and 'effective' students as could be mustered on tutorial classes – suggests that a majority were not willing to make the three-year commitment required for the highest level of study. Nevertheless, its advocates were at pains to present the tutorial class as the epitome of the democratic conception of learning that extramural education, at its best, could embody:

> membership of a Tutorial Class can become a rare and most exciting experience. In the enlarged scope which it offers to students and tutor, they can boldly work out together the range and the order of the topics in which they are especially interested. It is a method which is flexible in allowing ample play for the special interests of a particular group of students, and the larger time-span also ensures room for a progressive and structured plan enabling students and tutor to follow through their subject in considerable depth. The intimacy which develops in the group enlivens discussion, and the fellowship of a deepened common interest speeds the growth of knowledge.[56]

There was also a practical advantage to students, in that course fees were 'tapered', with reductions in the later years of study, an arrangement that to an extent offset the unavoidable falling-off in attendance that could happen over such a long programme.[57]

Most students, though, were attending shorter courses, and it was sessional classes that enjoyed a boom in the second half of the 1960s, a trend that would continue into the following decade. Students were recruited in the traditional ways, though local centres and the WEA, but from 1967 the Board issued its own publicity, in the form of a consolidated list of courses: 5,000 copies of a fairly basic 'handbill' were circulated that year, with details of all the courses taught across the region.[58] Students were attracted by the range of subjects and the low fees. In 1969, Iris Free of Hauxton in Cambridgeshire told the local press that she had been attending the Board's courses 'for several years', and appreciated the chance to study at very low cost: '[i]t's open to anyone .... That's the ridiculous part about it. For 23s. for two terms ... you can have this kind of thing.'[59] (This student's fees were the equivalent of about £20 today, thanks to Responsible Body funding.)

The Cambridge extramural region was now concentrated on Cambridgeshire and its adjacent counties, with the exception of the local centre at Derby, which continued to run extension courses, though usually only one each year, until the early 1970s.[60] There was a change in Northamptonshire, where the University of Leicester was willing and able to take responsibility for the Cambridge centres. This was duly agreed in 1962, but three centres – Kettering, Towcester and Wellingborough –

'protested vigorously' against the planned transfer.[61] At Wellingborough, the protest was led by the centre secretary Avies M. Platt, a retired art teacher from Wellingborough County High School who was strongly invested in the traditions of university extension and emotionally attached to Cambridge itself. (In 1957 she had 'enquired whether lecturers should not be asked to wear academic dress when giving University Extension Lectures'.[62]) Platt refused to countenance Leicester: she insisted that the 'University of Cambridge Extension Society in Wellingborough … is what we are, and if we are killed off we shall just be dead, and not rise as something else'.[63] Cambridge had been providing courses at Wellingborough since the 1890s, and Platt claimed that her protest was *not* 'a snobbish matter of not wanting Red Brick …. It has always been Cambridge, and even Oxford won't do.'[64] In due course, a stay of execution – as Platt would see it – for the three centres was agreed, and while the rest of Northamptonshire became part of Leicester's extramural region, responsibility for Wellingborough, Kettering and Towcester stayed with Cambridge for the rest of the 1960s.

At the same time conscious attempts were made to develop new local centres, to breath new life into those which were struggling to keep going, and to identify new subjects and areas of interest. In Cambridgeshire, particular efforts were made with the village colleges, established by the LEA from the 1930s by the county's chief education officer Henry Morris. Village colleges were intended as community schools for 11-to-16-year-olds and to provide adult education, and the Board worked with the LEA, running popular sessional classes, in particular, in the colleges at Sawston and Melbourn, and tutorial classes at Melbourn, Impington and Cottenham. Michael Allen worked hard to maintain these courses and to provide them at the standard the LEA wanted, and recalls that 'the village college was a rather romantic idea … which lent itself to the sort of enthusiasm that the [Board's] staff had'.[65] The Board was represented on the governing bodies of the village colleges, a duty that fell mainly on the teaching staff.[66] Elsewhere, resident tutors did their best to stimulate demand, often in rural areas as well as growing towns such as Thetford, where there was no adult education centre but where some interest was prompted by courses on local history.[67] Repeated attempts were made in Luton, one of the largest centres of population in the Cambridge region, but 'little progress' was made there, as had been the case in the 1950s.[68]

In other places, though, flourishing local centres regularly managed to run the Board's courses, often alongside those from other providers: one example was the Letchworth Settlement, whose 'warden' from 1963 was Roy Evans. The Settlement had been running Cambridge courses since its inception in 1920, and Evans was an active member of the Local Centres Union, staying in close contact with the Board and its staff.[69]

The balance of subjects taught on the regional programme had changed by the early 1960s, with notable expansion in some areas and contraction, at least in relative terms, in others. Table 3.2 shows the proportion of courses on the regional programme in each subject area, and can be compared – though the categories are not always identical – with the figures for 1947-8 in table 2.2. History, including local history, had further strengthened its position – even before Dymond and Barringer joined the staff to add strength in local history – accounting for more than one-fifth of all courses, while international affairs had fallen away a little more, along with politics and economics. Philosophy, psychology and music retained a small but abiding presence, as did the sciences, while archaeology had been a new arrival in the 1950s. 'Language and literature', with 9% of courses, had declined somewhat since the 1940s, when it had shared the leading place on the programme with history. The two major growth areas were 'visual arts' and 'social studies'.

'Social studies' was increasingly taught through the means of sociology, under the influence of Ray Pahl, resident tutor in Hertfordshire, Ioan Davies in Norfolk, and subsequently Graham Howes as a staff tutor. Sociology was not a degree subject at Cambridge until 1969, when it became part of the 'social and political sciences' Tripos: Pahl later recalled that 'there'd been big debates in Cambridge about whether there should be sociology, and it was thought to be a slightly subversive, dangerous subject'.[70] Pahl himself had had no formal sociological traning, but his teaching met a heavy student demand for the subject. Moreover, through his teaching he developed the research projects that would make his name in the discipline: he was studying for a PhD at the London School of Economics while he was employed, examining the impact of population change in Hertfordshire, particularly on the 'rural-urban fringe'.[71] Hertfordshire's population had grown more than that of any other county in England during both the 1930s and 1950s, and it was the site of four of the designated post-war 'New Towns' – Stevenage, Hatfield, Hemel

Table 3.2
Subjects of courses on the regional programme, 1963-4 (percentage of all courses taught; n = 107)

History (including local history)	21
Social studies	14
Visual arts	13
International affairs	10
Language and literature	9
Science	7
Music	6
Archaeology	5
Philosophy	5
Psychology	5
Other	5
Politics/government	0

Notes: these figures include a small number of courses that were cancelled; they do not distinguish between length of course, and include tutorial, sessional, terminal and extension courses.
Source: 'Summary and Analysis of Courses and Classes, 1963-4', paper for Board meeting, 29 October 1963.

Hempstead and Welwyn Garden City – in which Pahl was simultaneously working to promote Cambridge extramural courses.[72] Lionel Munby had already had much success with local history classes in Hertfordshire, but this was generally in smaller centres of population. Pahl's first class, on 'local historical geography' in 1959, had been in a village – the students included 'the local gardener', a research scientist and the writer Alan Sillitoe – and led him into new areas of both teaching and research:

> Almost without guidance from me the courses ended up with a consideration of the neighbouring New Town's impact on surrounding villages. But the problems of present-day Hertfordshire could not be taught from books and, as classes could so easily denegerate into rambling chit-chat, I was obliged to probe, as

> vigorously and systematically as I could, into a limited aspect of the changing social and geographical pattern.[73]

Under Pahl's influence, Welwyn, Hatfield and Stevenage would all become 'fruitful centres' for extramural teaching in sociology, and not only in the sociology of Hertfordshire; both he and Leslie James taught courses on 'Africa' for students in the local centres of the county.[74] Local subject matter was always in demand, too: for Pahl, 'The Changing Face of Hertfordshire' proved a popular topic throughout the county, though he did not manage to persuade local centres to take tutorial classes in this or most other sociological topics.[75] One exception was 'Race and Colour at Home and Abroad', at Bishop's Stortford from 1961, reflecting contemporaneous developments in race relations.[76] 'There is certainly something of a narcissistic element in many people's interest' in sociology, Pahl noted, 'and it is still easy to frighten many away with a tough-minded lecture on "Class"', but he identified a strong emergent demand for the subject, particularly among the housewives aged between 25 and 35 who often formed the bulk of his students. Importantly, too, unlike other subjects in other places this demand was largely unrelated to any WEA activity in the county.[77] Thus he told the Board that

> Young housewives came to hear about social change in Africa and the sociology of Town and Country Planning; their children crawled round my feet untying my shoe laces and putting jam on my trousers .... Helped by the magazine sections of 'The Observer' and 'Sunday Times' pop sociology became fashionable.[78]

These were very different circumstances from those faced in Norfolk by Ioan Davies, who was responsible for some fairly effective provision in Norwich and a few other places, but who was also faced with local centres in villages that struggled to attract enough students. Pahl's approach would probably not have worked in a place like Gunthorpe, with a population of little more than 300. Such centres, Davies reported,

> have a high proportion of subjects which are often (from the point of view of the students) classed as entertainments (astronomy, antiques, local architecture, introduction to painting, local natural history,

> 'great religions of the world', some forms of local history), and several of [them] that have closed have done so under the stress of studying modern social problems and international affairs.[79]

Davies found himself teaching topics such as 'Where is Britain Going?' and 'Education and Social Change' to terminal classes in Norfolk, failing to attract large numbers in most local centres, although he did manage to run a tutorial class on 'Race Relations' in the small town of Watton from 1962 onwards.[80]

If interest in sociology had, in Pahl's view, been stimulated by the Sunday supplements, art and art history had – like archaeology in the 1950s – benefited from a high profile on the small screen. Kenneth Clark's series *Is Art Necessary?* had led the way in 1958, and the emergence of colour television allowed for much better representation of the visual arts. Clark continued to broadcast on the topic through the 1960s, eventually culminating in the classic series *Civilisation* (1969).[81] Art and art history became a popular subject for tutorial classes, such as Christopher Lee's 'Language of Painting' (at Bedford and Welwyn Garden City) and 'Foundations of Modern Art' (Chelmsford), and featured in sessionals taught by Lee and others, and terminal classes led by, among others, Graham Howes.[82] As Helen Lowenthal had done in the early 1950s, Lee identified various challenges in teaching in this area. Works of art were distributed all around the world, and 'facsimiles [were] of limited use', while presenting them through representations on slides could 'mis-represent a picture and … kill all sense of physical scale'.[83] Essay writing, he found, often did not work well in adult classes; rather, he felt that '[t]he best written work I receive is almost without exception the work they can be persuaded to do by themselves in a gallery'.[84]

'Language and literature' was primarily the study of literature: modern and ancient languages were not yet making an impact on extramural teaching. Modern literature, including drama, featured most prominently. Psychology was stimulated by the appointment of Anthony Storey, and retired staff tutor H. H. Daisley continued to teach philosophy on the regional programme into the 1960s. Music, meanwhile, gained some strength from the involvement of assistant secretary Alan Stripp. Like Hans Redlich in the 1940s and 1950s, Stripp was insistent on the importance of being able to play gramophone records to students, and aware of the particular challenges involved in teaching the subject in the extramural context, where there were barriers to participation:

> Very few [students] can play an instrument or read music. Most feel guiltily ignorant (as if music were intended for an exclusively professional audience) and are reluctant to expose themselves by asking questions. They are, however, very ready to seize opportunities for discovery.

Therefore, he explained, 'our purpose is to extend enjoyment and understanding, to widen repertoire, to study major questions of form, style and historical development, and to increase insight into the background of music'.[85] Science faced similar challenges, particularly the physical sciences: the Board recognised that teaching in this area – where many students lacked the necessary background knowledge to support university-level study – 'is not likely to be very specialised and it is probable that in such classes it would be a matter of interpreting the physical sciences to the layman'.[86]

Local history remained a key feature of the regional programme, reinforced by new staff and by enhanced facilities, especially for reproducing primary sources to use in classroom settings. Lionel Munby encouraged students to work directly with 'original documents', and believed that the use of primary sources among adult students was much more advanced than in traditional university history teaching: palaeography, for example, was taught to extramural students but not Cambridge undergraduates.[87] In the mid-1960s Munby would often teach 'a class of students working in pairs or small groups on Xerograph copies of documents, with the tutor moving from group to group answering questions, assisting with palaeographical problems, and suggesting new questions to which the student may seek answers'.[88] Teaching then, was not a tutor-centred didactic activity, but rather a research-led enterprise that often evolved into a writing partnership. This was by no means unusual in local history teaching, especially where the WEA was involved, but Munby was a particularly successful exponent of it.[89] As he had done in the 1950s, he continued to mentor students in his tutorial classes through the creation of their own local histories, many of which were published.[90] The most ambitious of these was a thirteen-volume study *Hatfield and Its*

People, arising from courses taught jointly with the WEA and published from 1959 to 1964.[91]

Other subjects were moving away from a 'lecture and discussion' model, too; Munby explained that this approach had its place, but that it carried a 'danger' of 'becoming entertainment as an end in itself'.[92] In any event, if formal lecturing was done, it should be done well, as Munby had learned in Army education during the war, trying to engage tired soldiers with his material: 'by continually modulating your voice, changing the tone, volume and pace, you make it difficult for people to sleep'.[93] Like Munby, other staff tutors increasingly used more active pedagogical techniques: in the sciences, for example, investigation and experimentation featured as often as possible, though the facilities at local centres were not always able to accommodate them.[94] In English literature, the 'close reading' of texts was increasingly at the centre of extramural teaching, as it was in the internal English department at Cambridge, while sociology involved students in compiling questionnaires and carrying out surveys.[95] In the 1960s the Board worked with the university's Department of Physical Chemistry to provide in-service teacher training to support the development of the Nuffield Science Project, a scheme that aimed to introduce into schools what was – according to one account – 'already "old hat" in adult education'.[96] When the Humanities Curriculum Project followed a little later, some adult educators congratulated themselves that the Project's 'major premises' were already well embedded into extra-mural practice.[97] These 'premises' centred on structured class discussion under the direction of an 'impartial' tutor. At Cambridge, John Andrew had certainly endorsed this for a long time, arguing – along with Munby – that such 'teaching techniques' would become increasingly important in the future.[98]

Not all made use of these evolving approaches: the quality of teaching varied, as might be expected given the size of the panel of part-time tutors. The long-term success of many local centres in attracting students year after year to Cambridge courses can be viewed as a sign of satisfaction with the teaching, but some did express concerns about it from time to time. When lecturers were relying on a didactic method of presentation, the qualities of personality and delivery were clearly of great importance, and these were not always to everyone's satisfaction. Writing in the late 1960s or early 1970s, one centre leader complained that '[f]or some years now, for every good lecturer … we seem to have had two bad lecturers … in between. It is these bad lecturers which [*sic*] cause attendances to fall off and undo all the good work which the good lecturers do'.[99] This correspondent outlined the weaknesses at some length:

> The bad lecturers are mainly young men who seem to have no idea of the job. They have nervous mannerisms – walking backwards and forwards, not looking at the audience. They repeat themselves so that we have to hear all they have to say twice and three times over …. By that means we are kept for an hour and a half listening to something which could have been said, quite interestingly, in half an hour. It is probably not intentional but it is sheer padding; they have not enough facts to give us.[100]

These criticisms were not aimed at the staff tutors, many of whom by this time could hardly be described as 'young men', but the correspondent hit on a point that was under consideration by the Board at this time, the need for better staff development among the panel tutors:

> Another fault … is the impromptu talker who has not really prepared his stuff and doesn't always remember what he told you last time. It is always a great relief to me when I see the wad of papers laid on the desk; even if he does not read direct from them we do know that the ground has been prepared and not thrown together. Is it possible to lay down any principles for these lecturers, or to give them some training in talking to adult, lay, but not dim-witted, audiences?[101]

The Board continued to run its tutors' training course through the 1960s, using it both to train adult educators and to identify tutors who might lead its own courses. It was attended by Cambridge postgraduate and undergraduate students, as well as some from further afield, and as on earlier iterations of the course the judgements on individual students varied considerably. Heavy emphasis, though, was placed on prospective tutors' ability to sustain student interest and participation, whatever the material on which their 'practice talks' were based.[102]

*

The overwhelming majority of courses offered in university adult education did not lead to certification; and although this had been floated as a possibility in the late 1950s it was not taken forward at the time. A few extension certificates were still being awarded, the last in 1962 to a small group of students from Great Yarmouth.[103] However, the emergence of new universities, and above all the Open University at the end of the decade, helped to generate demand from students for certification of their academic attainment. This had always been anathema to the WEA, but there was a groundswell of demand at a local level during the 1960s for extramural classes to award something more than simply a certificate of attendance. Ray Pahl had discovered this in Hertfordshire: during his seven-year tenure of the resident tutorship there, five new further education colleges had been established, with 'liberal studies' departments, and some were teaching towards the University of London Diploma in Social Studies. The students on his own courses often had vocational motivations for studying sociology – '[p]art-time social work has become the dream occupation for radical middle class housewives when their children grow up' – and Pahl argued that '[t]he demand for diplomas and certificates is real, needs investigation, and must not be allowed to be dissipated through lack of interest and action from Responsible Bodies'.[104]

In the event, the only significant move in this direction during the 1960s was in local history; a Certificate programme in the subject was launched in 1968, at the local centres in Great Yarmouth, Norwich and Ipswich. Demand for these courses was, to an extent, vocational: David Dymond explained that it was 'planned primarily for teachers, and it was known that local authority archivists would give full support' to a Certificate in the subject.[105] It was a four-year programme of study, and did not last beyond a year in Great Yarmouth, but the first successful students in the other centres were awarded their Certificates in 1972.[106] The programme had some implications for the open tradition of university adult education: as the Board's staff noted, 'all students admitted [to a certificated course] should be required to satisfy rigorous conditions of class membership whether or not they proposed to take the examination'.[107] This insistence aroused some disquiet from the WEA, as a result of which the 'rigorous conditions of class membership' were not insisted upon, and the classes were 'open to the general public' as well as to those who wanted to sit the examinations. Students who aimed at the qualification would prepare a 'folder of work' for each year of study, and would have an oral examination, with two external examiners.[108] The awards were a minority interest – across seven classes in the region in the first ten years, only 46 students were awarded a Certificate – but the principle of certification had been reintroduced to the practice of the Board, and the possibility of further such developments was clearly placed before both staff and students. Geoffrey Hickson, in his final year as Board secretary, raised the possibility of inter-university co-operation on extramural certificates, but the proposal was not taken up by Cambridge at this stage.[109] John Andrew, though, was aware by the end of the 1960s of 'the increasing pressure for specific tokens of personal achievement in the form of diplomas, certificates and part-time degrees', and expected this to continue into the future.[110]

Local history also drove the development of 'local studies', which became a feature of the teaching programme in the 1960s, building on some of the developments in multidisciplinary courses in the previous decade. An early use of the phrase 'local studies' was in the title of a residential course in 1954, led by Montagu Clifford, Rachel Young and Lionel Munby, but Munby placed the development in a longer tradition stretching back to W. P. Baker, the Board's first full-time tutor in the 1930s. In the 1960s, then, he was able to see new collaborations as 'continuing and ... developing a worthwhile tradition'.[111] There was 'continuing demand' for local studies in the late 1950s, and Ray Pahl's arrival as staff tutor specialising in sociology gave what had been a largely historical topic a new and potentially fruitful contemporary dimension; this was followed up by Graham Howes after Pahl left the staff.[112] By the late 1960s an annual residential course on 'teaching local studies', running for a week at Madingley Hall and aimed at 'teachers and other students' was attracting between 20 and 30 participants – including some from as far away as Wales and Scotland – and there was also a weekend residential course at Belstead in Suffolk.[113] These courses promoted the study of local areas through multidisciplinary lenses, and according to Munby and John Andrew epitomised what university adult education could achieve: '[s]ubjects developed across the normal divisions of academic disciplines, e.g. Local Studies, have an uncanny habit of developing the depth and precision of a new discipline when tested in the soil of extra-mural education'.[114]

They also enabled staff tutors and others to link research and teaching in new ways. Pahl had recognised this, using his New Town classes to gather data on which he based some subsequent publications, though he insisted that his findings should be seen as 'the joint work of tutor and students'.[115] As with the research disseminated by local history groups, Andrew and Munby noted that students were publishing 'contemporary sociological studies': '[t]hese are deliberately written for a local public to interest and inform them; they do not claim to be post-graduate research, but it is nevertheless true that they have contributed in many small ways to the advancement of knowledge'.[116] Members of staff also collaborated on research that addressed the local studies agenda: in 1968 a volume of essays was published, dedicated to the retiring Geoffrey Hickson and edited by Munby, on *East Anglian Studies*. This included chapters by John Alexander, Chris Barringer, David Dymond, Pahl and Munby himself, as well as two part-time tutors (Arthur Brown and J. R. Ravensdale) and Peter Eden, a former colleague of Dymond's at the Royal Commission on Historical Monuments who had recently been appointed to a post with the Department of English Local History at the University of Leicester.[117] The essays covered the geology, landscape, place-names, deserted villages, post-medieval houses, early modern politics and religion and eighteenth-century urban history of the region, with Pahl's chapter considering 'newcomers' in Hertfordshire New Towns, commuter villages and outer London suburbs.

Local studies did not quite take off as it might have done in the 1970s, but it may have helped to prepare the ground further for future developments, for example in landscape history, which became one of the most important subjects taught on the regional programme in the 1970s and 1980s. As Andrew and Munby explained in 1966, the English landscape 'has been looked at as a geological, archaeological, and historical phenomenon, and the human community has been studied historically and sociologically .... Study of a local community is an ideal way to learn the inter-relationship and relevance of many academic disciplines.'[118] This inter-relationship was also appreciated by students focusing on different areas of study: Iris Free, for example, realised that '[a]ny single subject inter-relates with others', adding that '[i]f you are interested in the arts generally, I don't think you are any good with one unless you have a fair knowledge, and find out as much as you can about the rest'.[119] Studying the range of subjects available, year after year, at local centres was an ideal way of doing this, and of being exposed to a range of tutors and perspectives that would be harder to experience as a discipline-focused undergraduate student inside the University of Cambridge, or indeed most other English universities.

*

For John Andrew, it was mainly residential adult education that had promoted 'a substantial growth of interdisciplinary studies', and the 1960s certainly saw a continued expansion of residential course provision by the Board.[120] The university had been urging this from the early 1960s, arguing – in line with Geoffrey Hickson's carefully articulated suggestions of the late 1950s – that

> in the changing circumstances Cambridge can again become a pioneer, and ... it could serve a new and growing need if its extra-mural activities were devoted more and more to students recruited on a national rather than a regional basis. This end could be achieved if the main activity of the Board were to be the organization in Cambridge of residential courses for students drawn from all over the country instead of ... courses for the benefit of local audiences in various parts of East Anglia.[121]

There was a gradual expansion of residential courses in the 1960s (see table 3.3), though the Board remained hampered by restrictions on the term-time use of Madingley Hall, and indeed the availability of accommodation elsewhere in Cambridge. Many of the initiatives taken in the 1950s lasted through the 1960s: one example was a course for English literature teachers, started by Leo Salingar in 1955, which continued a decade later to attract not only teachers, but also students who were reading for external degrees at other universities, and some who attended out of nothing more than a general interest in the subject.[122] By 1967-8 there were courses for mathematics and geography teachers, for students taking the University of London external BSc degree in

Table 3.3
Student numbers on selected residential courses, 1946 to 1970

Year	'Foreign Students'	Madingley Hall	Elsewhere
1946-7	157	-	-
1947-8	284	-	-
1948-9	273	-	-
1949-50	282	-	-
1950-1	306	-	-
1951-2	237	128	-
1952-3	380	478	-
1953-4	376	494	-
1954-5	390	517	-
1955-6	352	564	-
1956-7	325	493	-
1957-8	307	491	296
1958-9	344	499	417
1959-60	331	584	325
1960-1	353	623	320
1961-2	359	750	357
1962-3	368	614	645
1963-4	288	584	686
1964-5	301	563	410
1965-6	291	448	601
1966-7	325	587	769
1967-8	349	597	898
1968-9	338	581	870
1969-70	338	559	1085

Notes: not including summer courses on 'Linguistics and the English Language' and for 'Foreign Lawyers'; it is likely that other courses are also missing from this data, as they are from Welch, *Peripatetic University*, appendices.

economics, for archaeology students on the Board's regional programme to take part in excavations, for specific professional and industrial groups, and for many others. As with the English course, many of these stemmed from the 1950s, but were undertaken more often, and on a larger scale, as accommodation became available in new colleges such as Churchill and Fitzwilliam, and in Hughes Hall, during the 1960s.[123]

The largest residential course was still the 'Vacation Course for Foreign Students', running for four weeks and focusing on 'Modern Britain: Its Institutions and Literature'. This attracted a steady stream of applications, and most members of the Board's full-time teaching staff contributed, with some leading specialist seminars as they had done in the 1950s, and on the same topics: international relations, English literature and 'British institutions'. The latter, in 1963, considered the legal system, political parties, the economy, the welfare state, local government, the press and television, and the increasingly significant topic of 'Britain and Europe'.[124] Sometimes restrictions on space limited the number of students who could be accommodated, but in most years the course ran with more than 300 students (see table 3.3). Most were from western Europe: of the 132 men and 236 women who attended in 1963, the leading countries were France (66 students, almost a fifth of the total), Sweden (32), Czechoslovakia (28), Norway (26) and Germany, Switzerland and the USA (25 each). This was five years before the 'Prague spring', and apart from Czechoslovakia there was no significant representation from countries in eastern Europe: there were four from Hungary and one from Poland, but these were exceptions.[125] Despite the strong Swedish representation on the list for the vacation course, the separate summer school for Swedish students also continued to run each year, and the biennial course for 'foreign lawyers' and law students lasted through the decade and beyond, again attracting students mostly from continental Europe. Michael Allen recalls that this course was 'very much valued in Europe, which of course had quite different legal systems to ours. These young people from European countries needed to know about our law, and so there was a market there, which we exploited.'[126]

Running alongside the main summer course, each year from 1964, was another four-week programme in 'Linguistics and the English Language', aimed at existing or aspiring teachers of English. It had grown out of an emerging interest in 'English as a Foreign Language' and similar courses in 1950s and 1960s, and was directed by John Trim, a phonetics lecturer at Selwyn College who had been a key figure in the establishment of the university's Department of Linguistics in the 1960s. A post-war graduate in German, Trim was an advocate for the teaching of languages as an aspect of 'communication and cross-cultural understanding', rather than as 'purely … an accomplishment', and this was reflected in his longstanding role, throughout the 1970s and beyond, in the Council of Europe's 'modern languages project', which had a profound influence on the teaching of languages across the continent.[127] In this respect Trim was an ideal leader of a course that made a significant contribution to both the profile and the income of the Board of Extra-Mural Studies, and reflected its growing emphasis, particularly under John Andrew's leadership, on collaboration with other university departments and faculties. The course had 51 students in its first year, and was recruiting more than 100 by the end of the 1960s.[128] The popularity of this and the other international programmes was important for the Board's finances, which regularly benefited from a surplus arising from the summer courses' accounts.[129]

Courses for managers, supervisors and apprentices – and for members of the National Union of General and Municipal Workers – all continued through the 1960s. These were run very much on the same lines as before, and sometimes with the same teaching materials. The managers' course, running for the fifteenth time in 1967, had the same general purpose that it had always had: as course secretary Alan Stripp explained, it did not aim to 'teach management', but rather

> to help members to think systematically about those aspects of the national economy which primarily concern managers. It is expected that over the next five or ten years those attending the course will become increasingly concerned with the more general problems of management, and with the external relations of their company in the national or international economy. The course aims at throwing light on the economic, political, social and human background against which these problems should be seen.[130]

Thus the course 'members' studied topics in economics, industrial organisaton and social policy and, as before, were organised into 'syndicates' of seven or eight students to discuss 'The Basic Problems of the British Economy'. An innovation was the opportunity to play a 'business game' using the University of Cambridge 'electronic computer'.[131] Parallel courses for supervisors and for personnel officers had similar approaches: the latter, organised in collaboration with the Industrial Relations Branch of the Department for Employment, were 'concerned primarily with the general economic and industrial setting within which the Personnel Officer works, rather than with a detailed appraisal of the work itself'.[132] The willingness of companies in industry – as well as the civil service, banks and other organisations – to send their staff on these courses was testament to their perceived value, although numbers on the apprentices' courses were small in most years.

The 'most regularly successful' programme of this kind, though, was one that ran annually from 1967 with the technology firm IBM.[133] This was a seven-week course, running from mid-June to early August and based in Churchill College, which had opened in 1960. The course was initially led by Leslie James, although almost all the Board's teaching staff contributed. The course featured a long series of lectures on a remarkably diverse range of topics. In 1968, for example, there was a series by Leslie Wayper on 'The Theory of the Modern State', while James Mitchell spoke on 'European History', Leslie James himself on 'European Ideas', Christopher Lee on 'Modern Art' and Alan Stripp on 'Modern Music'. There were one-off lectures by J. T. B. Marshall on scientific topics, Jack Herbert on Bertholdt Brecht and Michael Allen on bird migration, and many others, along with English language classes – the participants were from IBM Europe, though this also included South Africa – and project work, as well as excursions to locations in Cambridge and beyond.[134] Michael Allen recalls that the programme

> was supposed to be academic in interest with a few extras added such as a tour of a Cambridge setting, or as far as Suffolk. We would take them to a play at Stratford; we would take them to a musical concert somewhere, or an opera at the Royal Opera House. There were usually 35 to 40 of these engineers and they became students, and we were allowed to teach them whatever we wanted but nothing to do with computing or management.[135]

The IBM course would run for decades, and although it was perhaps out of step with other developments in management education in this period, it embodied the ideas that Geoffrey Hickson had articulated in the late 1950s about the distinctive contribution that universities could make to professional and technical education. This company, at least, was willing and able to send around 30 of its staff to Cambridge for a whole term, and in retrospect Allen reflects that 'it was amazing that IBM was prepared to do this'.[136]

A more conventional strand of activity was started in 1965: magistrates' training. This was more directly related to 'vocational' concerns – albeit in an area of voluntary work – with courses addressing the specifics of bench chairmanship, sentencing and so on. The key figure here was Vivian Ramsbottom, himself a magistrate in Cambridge, who worked with the Magistrates' Council to organise, and sometimes to lead, the courses. These wey often aimed at magistrates who were starting out on the bench, but there were also successful conferences for senior magistrates – two of them in 1967-8, at Churchill College, with 53 and 49 delegates respectively. Training for clerks was also being introduced, with even more attending these courses.[137] Both residential and non-residential training was provided, with senior magistrates from all over the country in attendance, though unsurprisingly there was a more local clientele for the non-residential courses. New magistrates were asked to take part in sentencing exercises, and were presented with case studies of potential criminal activity that they would discuss in groups and report back to the course leader.[138] By the early 1970s there were fifteen courses or conferences for magistrates each year, for groups from the bench with different levels of seniority; the total attendance at these, most but not all at Churchill, amounted to almost 600.[139] Alongside these practical courses for magistrates were some on criminology, aimed at broader audiences but often attracting social workers and youth workers; and this paralleled the growing interest in sociological topics on the regional programme. These would evolve into social workers' courses on the juvenile court system and other topics, and for probation officers too, in due course.[140]

Provision for the armed forces, in decline during the 1950s, revived somewhat in the 1960s, aligned with the formal training programmes of the Army and RAF. Courses on international affairs, aimed at either junior or senior officers, were the staple element of this relatively small part of the Board's overall provision. In 1964-5 there were 29 one-off lectures to service personnel, 34 courses of lectures and six residential courses, with a total attendance of 217 officers. This was a tiny proportion of the overall provision for the services across the university adult education sector. Birmingham, Bristol, Leeds, Hull and Oxford, as well as Southampton and Exeter, were all doing more than Cambridge, as indeed was the University of London: Cambridge was responsible for just 3.4% of residential course attendance, for example.[141] There was, though, some acknowledgement, by the mid-1960s, of 'greater readiness' across the three services to take part in courses and conferences, and some pioneering efforts were made in this direction by Leslie Wayper, Alan Stripp and others. In 1967, for example, a discussion group on international affairs was convened by the Board, bringing together delegates from the Army, Royal Navy, Ministry of Defence, Foreign Office and the university itself.[142] Meanwhile, a wide range of the Board's staff contributed to residential courses that supported the RAF Staff College Qualifying Examination – not just Stripp and Wayper, but also, for example, Chris Barringer lecturing on developments in Nigeria. While this course was taking place, more senior officers – Colonels, Commanders and Group Captains – were discussing 'Britain and Europe', with delegates from the Foreign Office also in attendance.[143]

*

The 1960s closed, as had the 1950s, with a debate within and beyond the Board about its own functions and future, and about those of other university adult education departments. This reflected a series of critical assessments of ongoing developments in extramural education, many of which centred on the apparent moves made by departments – including the Cambridge Board – in the direction of 'vocational' education. It was clear to John Andrew, for example, as it was to most others, that demand was driving the provision of 'an increasing volume of teaching at a high academic level … in response to specific professional needs', bringing a 'reverse flow' of students – many of whom were already university graduates – into courses provided by Cambridge, often on a short-term, residential and specialist basis.[144] This *could* be seen as undermining the Board's mission to provide liberal adult education in the community – mainly through classes that conferred neither academic recognition nor obvious vocational advantage – although in fact these courses too, on the 'traditional pattern', had proved successful in many cases, and indeed had expanded considerably during the previous decade. For Andrew, though, this was not a helpful way of seeing what had happened in the 1960s, because 'a University characteristically both instructs and educates; blurs, indeed, the distinction between vocational and liberal forms of education by the very nature of its function'.[145] Like Geoffrey Hickson a decade earlier, Andrew was grappling with a distinction between two forms of education that was rigid, unhelpful and arguably meaningless; he would surely have concurred with Hickson that all university education was in some senses 'liberal', whether or not it also served a vocational purpose.[146] What had become clear by this time was that the demand for adult education was increasingly motivated not only by 'professional status' and 'occupational identity', but also by a desire to develop the 'role [that] an individual seeks for himself [or herself] in society'.[147] This would generate more complex educational needs in the future, and present greater challenges for those, including university adult education departments, who were trying to meet them.

Chapter 4
An active ferment: the 1970s

As extramural teaching from Cambridge neared its centenary in the early 1970s, the leadership of the Board of Extra-Mural Studies was reassessing its position within the field of adult education. The boundaries of the university's extramural region were now clearly set, but at the same time the Board's expanding activities beyond 'traditional' extramural teaching were gradually modifying the overall shape of its provision. The vocabulary of adult education continued to evolve during the 1970s: the phrase 'continuing education' was increasingly used to refer to the blend of vocational and 'liberal' studies that were becoming the mainstay of university provision.[1] Some extramural departments would become departments of 'adult (and) continuing education' or just 'continuing education', and in due course – though not until 1983 – the National Institute of Adult Education would become the National Institute of Adult Continuing Education.[2] At Cambridge, the diversity of provision made by the Board persisted through the 1970s, though the regional programme – underpinned by longstanding relationships with local centres and the WEA – remained the largest single area of activity, at least in terms of raw student numbers (see table 4.1). The most significant moment of change in the decade was the Board's departure from Stuart House, its base in the centre of Cambridge since 1927; in 1975 its headquarters would be transferred to Madingley Hall. This reflected the importance attached by the Board secretary – now also known as the 'director' of extramural studies – John Andrew, and others to residential courses, which were described in 1973 as 'the principal development in the extra-mural teaching of the University in the last twenty years'; they would remain a key priority for Andrew and his successor for the rest of the decade.[3]

The expected range of university involvement in adult education was set out in the Russell Report of 1973 which, although it did not mention Cambridge specifically, clearly reflected the priorities that Andrew had already anticipated during the previous decade. The report was produced by a committee appointed by the then secretary of state for education, Ted Short, in 1969, and chaired by Lionel Russell, a former chief education officer for Birmingham.[4] The remit of the committee was to consider 'non-vocational' adult education, but it took a fairly broad view of what this meant, and its report called for a funded expansion of adult education with both central and local government support. Russell praised the existing 'partnership of statutory and voluntary bodies' – including local education authorities, the universities and the WEA – and wanted this to continue.[5] Only a small minority of existing or future students would be involved in *university* adult education, but Russell recognised that the universities had 'an important and expanding contribution to make'.[6] In short, adult education was presented as a post-war success story, which should be continued and further enhanced:

> adult education is by any standards a mass activity. It is growing, has demonstrated its great adaptability to local conditions and proved its responsiveness to local demands. It is popular, voluntary education rooted in a profound sense of need. We believe that this area of education can no longer be denied the modest resources we claim for it and are certain that the time has come when the government should show its concern for one of the truly popular educational movements of our time.[7]

Russell outlined several areas in which universities should be financially supported in their work in adult education, beginning with 'liberal studies of the traditional kind, characterised by intellectual effort by the students ... and the customary freedom from externally imposed syllabuses and examinations'.[8] This neatly described the regional programme offered by Cambridge and other universities, but Russell also identified scope for 'role education' – 'of a liberal and academic nature ... for groups ... from industry and the professions', instancing doctors, clergymen, social workers and those with voluntary roles such as magistrates or councillors – and 'industrial education' focused on 'human relationships rather than technical processes'.[9]

These emphases were also found at Cambridge, specifically in the teaching of magistrates and on the IBM programme, and sat on the boundary of 'vocational' and 'non-vocational' adult education – although Russell insisted that there could be no 'sharp line of division'

Table 4.1
Student numbers, 1971 to 1980

Year	Tutorial classes			Sessional classes		
	Classes	Enrolled students	Effective students	Classes	Enrolled students	Effective students
1971-2	21	368	239	98	2022	1151
1972-3	16	312	201	117	2282	1235
1973-4	15	268	160	136	2788	1582
1974-5	13	199	149	139	2801	1711
1975-6	14	229	182	129	2896	1717
1976-7	13	300	210	134	2852	1855
1977-8	13	249	186	129	2769	1768
1978-9	15	312	195	120	2914	1682
1979-80	15	336	220	117	2492	1772

	University extension lectures		Miscellaneous classes, including terminals	
	Classes	Students	Classes	Students
1971-2	36	1297	36	352
1972-3	34	1222	31	348
1973-4	29	926	51	392
1974-5	27	941	11	n/a
1975-6	33	1061	26	n/a
1976-7	27	1104	23	n/a
1977-8	28	1028	31	n/a
1978-9	25	821	36	n/a
1979-80	34	1260	29	n/a

Year	'Foreign Students'	Residential courses at Madingley Hall		Other residential courses	
	Students	Courses	Students	Courses	Students
1971-2	557	25	617	55	1470
1972-3	441	29	647	64	1742
1973-4	507	29	616	78	2042
1974-5	460	36	788	58	1483
1975-6	549	78	1583	32	1123
1976-7	462	100	2047	20	517
1977-8	433	91	2125	16	436
1978-9	326	129	2687	12	307
1979-80	395	117	2764	10	281

Source: annual reports.

between these two things.[10] Other areas identified in the report included the training of adult educators, group 'project work' – such as the activities supported by Lionel Munby and others in local history – and 'pioneer work'. The latter was considered in light of the growing demand for part-time degrees and the wider need among an expanding group of adults for re-training in mid-career or before a career change.[11] Unsurprisingly, John Andrew felt that Russell's proposals 'conform to the present practice and future intentions of the Board, which are to maintain the provision of adult education at the highest possible academic level, and increasingly to concern themselves with the post-experience education of a wide variety of people in the professions'.[12]

However, by the time the Russell report was published in 1973 the political landscape had shifted: Margaret Thatcher was the Conservative secretary of state for education and the economic conditions were much less propitious in which to meet calls for what amounted to a real-terms doubling of the amount of public money spent on adult education.[13] Other political and administrative developments also raised barriers to the kinds of changes that Russell envisaged. The report seemed to point to more intensive collaborations with local authorities in the extramural region, but this was made more difficult by the local government reorganisation of 1974, which created six 'enlarged' local education authorities in East Anglia, undermining a number of pre-existing relationships that the Board had cultivated. The situation seemed to be one of 'no lack of goodwill but an acute lack of hard cash': just a year after Russell, for example, Norfolk County Council was charging its adult students the full cost of courses that had previously enjoyed a significant subsidy.[14] By this time there was already a 'sombre background' to the extramural work of the university, and in the following year the Board felt 'the sense of a siege economy'.[15] In 1976, with an unsteady income compounded by high inflation, it had already become clear, in Cambridge at least, that the Russell Report was to be 'a sad addition to the growing but unrealised aspirations in adult education, the demand for which remains undiminished'.[16]

Cambridge remained the dominant university provider of adult education in East Anglia in the 1970s. At this time there was still no sign of either of the new 'plateglass' universities at Colchester or Norwich starting its own extramural programme; and the Open University's arrival seemed to have 'widened the range of adults interested in education', which was 'positively helpful' in marketing the Board's courses.[17] In the early 1970s, though, the Board did lose two corners of its extramural region: the longstanding extension centre at Derby was 'surrendered' to the University of Nottingham, and the three remaining centres in Northamptonshire to the University of Leicester.[18] This made for another round of controversy at Wellingborough, as the threat of transfer had done a decade earlier: centre secretary Avies Platt again objected in the strongest terms to what she deemed nothing less than a 'tragedy'.[19] Wellingborough had by this time hosted Cambridge courses for some 80 years, and Platt melodramatically insisted that 'if Cambridge no longer wants us, no matter how much Leicester does, then we must die, because we cannot be "handed over"'.[20] Attempting to enlist students in another 'rebellion', Platt was headed off by the intervention of one of the Board's assistant secretaries, Michael Allen, who travelled to Wellingborough to 'have a word' with her. Platt was not easily appeased – she considered the transfer 'a very grievous thing, which should never have been, and need not were it not for this trend of uniformity' – but Cambridge duly withdrew its involvement from Wellingborough and the other remaining Northamptonshire centres.[21]

*

The core staff at the Board in the early 1970s comprised the director, the deputy secretary, three assistant secretaries and 15 staff tutors. The assistant secretaries and staff tutors were still initially appointed on two- or three-year temporary contracts, but these were often extended to permanent employment after one or two rounds.[22] Some staff tutors – such as Chris Barringer and David Dymond – were still based away from Cambridge, and all spent much of their time teaching on the regional programme, though they might also contribute to residential courses. The assistant secretaries did some teaching and managed the complex programmes and relationships with external organisations. In 1975, the Board advertised for a junior assistant secretary, for a term of three years with a possible two-year extension, to work specifically on armed forces education and residential courses: the appointee would be paid either on grade III (£2,475 to £3,495 – equivalent to around £22,000 to £31,000 today) or grade II, which went up to £5,022 (£45,000). In this case, the Board were looking for a graduate of a British university, aged between 23 and 30.[23] As could be the case elsewhere, academic employment in extramural studies was often precarious.[24] For those who were appointed and stayed, though, there was increasingly a career structure and some prospect of progression. Christine Yeomans, a specialist in European literature who joined the Board as a junior assistant secretary in 1971, gained her permanent contract in 1977 and was promoted to the post of deputy secretary in the same year, replacing Vivian Ramsbottom.[25] Yeomans, though, left Cambridge shortly afterwards.[26]

There were few new appointments to key academic positions at the Board in the 1970s, though Roland Randall – staff tutor in biological sciences from 1972 – was an important exception. Formerly a lecturer in biological and environmental sciences at the University of Ulster,

Randall remained as a staff tutor until 1995, and in 1977 was appointed a fellow of Girton College – one of the first male fellows when the college became co-educational.[27] Randall's arrival in Cambridge was shortly followed by that of Teresa Spens, appointed to a three-year staff tutor post in social sciences: a Cambridge PhD graduate, Spens stayed for three years.[28] Then in 1976 came the appointment of Jacqueline Leverson – a specialist in international politics – as a junior assistant secretary in 1976, again initially on a three-year contract.[29] These new members of staff were exceptions to what was otherwise a long-serving group of secretaries and staff tutors: in 1976, of the 19 individuals holding these posts, eight (Montagu Clifford, Colin Griffiths, Leslie James, Christopher Lee, James Mitchell, Lionel Munby, Vivian Ramsbottom and Leslie Wayper) dated their appointment to the 1940s, John Andrew to 1950 and Alan Stripp to 1958. (Ramsbottom had moved from a tutor to assistant secretary post in 1955.) Then there were Michael Allen, Chris Barringer, David Dymond, Jack Herbert, Graham Howes, Anthony Storey and David Trump from the 1960s – and just Yeomans, Randall and Leverson since then.[30] In the late 1970s – when Clifford and Lee retired – Susan Rawlings joined as an assistant secretary and Erica Towner as a staff tutor in biological sciences.[31] From 1977 until his retirement in 1980, Leslie Wayper was director of extramural studies, following Andrew's departure to take up the post of senior tutor at St Catharine's College. Meanwhile, Stripp moved from his role as assistant secretary in 1976, to become staff tutor in music.

Staff workloads could still be quite high, and often involved a lot of travelling. Lionel Munby, for example, still lived in Cambridge and travelled to west Hertfordshire – Hemel Hempstead, St Albans and Kings Langley, among many other places – to do much of his teaching.[32] In 1972-3 Chris Barringer taught 97 two-hour sessions in local centres – noting that '[t]eaching is the lowest for three years' – and a further 112 hours leading 'in-service training', and estimated that he spent a further 244 hours on 'organising'. As a residential tutor in Norfolk, he was responsible for much of the administrative work in local centres, and noted that there were some particularly heavy times of year: '[o]rganising occupies particular blocks of time: May and June are periods of many meetings with tutors; September is another month when many organising questions arise'. Barringer added a further 160 hours for letter-writing, 50 for time spent on research committees, and 16 for staff meetings at the Board of Extra-Mural Studies itself.[33] By the 1970s all staff tutors used cars, and John Andrew insisted in 1973 that 'it is of first importance that our cars should be in first-rate trim in order that we may never fail in our teaching commitments'; the Board made regular car loans to staff tutors.[34] Not all staff had modern vehicles: Michael Allen recalls that Leslie Wayper 'drove an incredibly ancient car' with a running board, and that

> One day he was stopped … in his battered car by a policeman, who said 'your running board is producing sparks from the road, sir'. 'Oh', said Leslie, 'I'm sorry for that', and he went to the boot and got out an axe and slashed off his running board and put it in the boot.[35]

As in earlier decades, the established teaching staff was augmented by a much larger group of 'panel tutors', paid on a part-time basis. Many of these had college affiliations at Cambridge, including doctoral students such as Mike Brearley, later captain of the England cricket team, who ran a 21-week course on 'Philosophy' at Barnfield College in Luton in 1973-4.[36] Some of the panel tutors, though, had no university affiliation, and the Board relied heavily on this workforce: at the beginning of the 1970s, some 44% of its tutors were non-members of the university, compared with just 9% at Sheffield and 20% at Leeds, though at Bristol the figure was as high as 74%.[37] Many of the panel tutors – internal and external – worked for a long time; one example is Gillian Sheail, who taught her first course in 1970, at Swavesey Village College. A young graduate of University College London, where she had spent an additional two years on research for a higher degree, she was appointed as a lecturer in environmental science at the University of Lancaster in 1967, also joining the panel of part-time tutors for the University of Liverpool Board of Extra-Mural Studies. When she moved to Cambridgeshire she immediately applied to the Cambridge Board and remained on the part-time tutor panel for many years, before taking up an established appointment in 1996. Although the teaching was enjoyable, she recalls that the role of panel tutor – particularly for those without a Cambridge degree or a college affiliation – could be challenging:

> I think it is quite fair to say that I was considered to be inferior because I didn't have Cambridge qualifications ... I could not become a member of Regent House. There were various other limitations, the most annoying of which was that I was not granted full use of the Cambridge University Library. One of the more serious problems facing part-time panel tutors was the fact that you didn't have immediate access to a photocopying machine. At some of the local centres – for example Bedford and Letchworth – it was possible to request copies to be prepared for the following week, or, later in time, you could use the machines yourself before or after the teaching session. But if you were teaching at a school or in a village hall ... or museum there were no facilities for photocopying.[38]

Many tutors had to go to the Board's headquarters to do their photocopying; this was relatively easy for those who lived nearby, but of course many did not.

The range of panel tutors was impressive. For example, in addition to staff tutors Lionel Munby, Chris Barringer and David Dymond, local history was taught by 'secondary school teachers, lecturers in technical and training colleges, archivists, librarians, museum directors, members of the staff of the Royal Commission on Historical Monuments and of the Ministry of Works, archaeologists, architects, geographers, sociologists and free-lance writers'.[39] Other subjects brought a comparable mixture of non-university specialisms to the extramural audience, and recruitment seems to have been somewhat easier than in earlier decades. Tutors often had to be 'persuaded to travel on winter evenings into remote places and to teach students who var[ied] in age and ability', but many were willing and able to do so.[40] From within Cambridge, the Board was able to recruit Jean Holm, author of religious studies textbooks for children, to teach theology, for example, and other well-known tutors included Noel Odell, who had now been teaching for the Board for several decades.[41] In the face of the panel's size and diversity, maintaining quality was not always easy, but because the

Board was so dependent on student and local centre demand, it was always possible for students to 'vote with their feet' if a tutor proved unpopular, unintelligible or uninteresting. For the most part – perhaps as a result of this – the quality of teaching seems to have been high.[42]

*

The Board continued to place great emphasis on its 'traditional' work in the region – it often used that word in its annual reports and elsewhere – and student demand seemed to accord with this emphasis.[43] Although tutorial class numbers were not as high as some would have liked, sessional classes and extension lecture courses continued to flourish (see table 4.1). Many of the 'traditional' subjects of study remained popular, particularly history, art and architecture, and English literature, and these continued to feature heavily on the programme, as they did on those of other university adult education departments. An essential feature of all courses, as always, was their openness 'to all over 18 who wish to study a subject for its own sake', and the aspiration was that students would 'come from every walk of life, drawn together by a common educational challenge'.[44] The fees charged to students remained modest: £1.75 (the equivalent of around £22 today) per term was the 'typical' amount in 1973-4.[45] In that year, courses were held in 80 towns and villages across the region, in Norfolk, Suffolk, Cambridgeshire, Bedfordshire, Essex and Hertfordshire. These ranged from large cities such as Norwich, where 20 separate courses took place across five separate locations, to villages such as Great Shelford, four miles south of Cambridge, where a single course on 'European Painting of the 18th and 19th Centuries' ran for 21 weeks on Wednesday evenings.[46]

Student numbers on the regional programme remained healthy through the 1970s; indeed, 1973-4 saw 'the largest programme of courses ever arranged', despite the loss of the last Northamptonshire centres at the end of the previous year.[47] This momentum continued: in 1975-6, there were courses in 71 local centres, with local and regional history, literature and art and music appreciation in the ascendancy. The largest number of courses that year were in Cambridge itself, held at several different locations: 22 courses ranged from 'New Approaches to the Study of Religions' to 'Music at the Courts of Europe'. In Essex, Colchester was the most important centre, with nine courses, and in Suffolk Ipswich hosted seven. Sixteen were held in Norwich, three of them – on landscape history and archaeology – taught by resident tutor Chris Barringer. There was a steady stream of religious courses, including 'What the Spirit Says to the Churches Today' (Ipswich) and 'The Holy Spirit' (King's Lynn). Small villages continued to feature on the programme: at Boxford in Suffolk, there was a twenty-week 'Introduction to Bird-Watching', and at Gunthorpe in north Norfolk Colin Griffiths taught a twelve-week course on 'The Making of Modern China'.[48] Gunthorpe was a revived centre, having struggled to recruit students in the 1960s, and it does not seem to have flourished for long, but its inclusion on the 1975-6 programme is indicative, from a supply point of view, of a desire to extend the Board's coverage, and of what its annual report called 'the importance to the adult population of the extra-mural provision of the university'.[49]

The relationship with the WEA remained important to the Board through the 1970s and indeed beyond. The key figure was still Frank Jacques, district secretary and also a member of the Board. Michael Allen remembers that, in the 1970s, 'the WEA centres were very powerful, because Frank … was like a three-line whip in his own right'.[50] Elsewhere, too, the WEA had exercised a strong influence on the culture of university extramural teaching: the Russell Report argued that the 'self-governing' nature of its courses had become a 'prototype' for both local authority and university provision, and that such an arrangement was 'singularly appropriate to adult education'.[51] The relationship was an integral element of the 'tradition' to which the Board repeatedly returned in its reports and publicity. The annual course prospectus reminded readers that the University had 'been providing this form of adult education since 1873', and that the collaborative organisational arrangements with the WEA and others were long-standing.[52] Reports issued by the Board usually listed its 'field work' first,[53] and great pleasure was expressed whenever the regional programme offered signs of buoyancy. Despite ongoing financial challenges, the annual report for 1978-9 expressed 'a modest satisfaction that [the] field work is in good heart and ready to take full advantage [of] new opportunities when these present themselves'; and in the following year the Board declared its pleasure that the work in East Anglia had been 'as widespread and as vigorous as ever'.[54] Numbers taking the courses were certainly impressive: in 1978-9, for example, 'there was an unusually high level of enrolment and an above average attendance', and in 1980-1 some 4,000 students attended courses in the region.[55]

The regional programme was also supported by the Local Centres Union, on which many – if not most – of the centres were represented. Given the range of collaborators across the region and the complexity of the programme and its partnerships, the Union was considered to perform a useful service, and in the mid-1970s its meetings were attended by several members of the Board's staff, including deputy and assistant secretaries and staff tutors, and sometimes John Andrew himself.[56] The Union provided small bursaries to help students with course fees, including for residential courses, although students were not always aware of this. Gillian Sheail remembers 'a widow living by herself, who always said "I'd love to go to Madingley for a course". And in the end, someone pointed out that she could apply for a grant from the Local Centres Union which allowed her to do just that.'[57] The Union also supported the Board's library; on occasions it made a one-off contribution, such as £50 for a television in 1976 and £100 for record players to support Alan Stripp's music classes in 1979.[58] The Union staged an annual residential weekend, on a different theme each year, at the same time as its annual general meeting; this proved relatively popular, albeit with students from a fairly limited range of centres. In 1977, the weekend course on 'William Morris', mostly led by Lionel Munby, was attended by 38 members from 12 centres, with 17 of these also attending the annual general meeting.[59]

Local centres were the lifeblood of the regional programme. Many had been associated with the Board for decades or more, something that was celebrated in various ways: in 1977, for example, Chris Barringer wrote a short historical account to mark the centenary of Cambridge courses in Norwich.[60] Here, the Board had for some time used Wensum Lodge, a well-appointed adult education centre housed in a former brewery, that had been taken over by the county council in 1961.[61] Other centres were less suitable: at March, for example, the courses took place in a museum, which meant that furniture had to be moved around and coffee cups placed carefully on top of display cabinets.[62] Many centres did not have their own slide projectors, so tutors would need to take them, and David Dymond always took a spare blackout sheet in his car. Extension leads, plug adaptors and a torch were other useful accessories that were also sometimes needed.[63] Elsewhere, there remained the problem of caretakers finishing their evening's work at a set time, which could mean the 'abrupt and often rather early ending of class meetings'.[64] However, the hospitality provided at some centres more than made up for the deficiencies of equipment and lack of comfort. At Downham Market, for example, there was a long tradition of feeding the tutor before an evening class: Gillian Sheail remembers that

> when we got there we were presented with a basket containing a filled Thermos flask, sandwiches, rolls and cakes, because we were supposed to be having our supper 'on the house' before we had to give the lecture .... The food was very good because each week a student had to volunteer to do it and there was some competitiveness in what they produced.[65]

Not all centres provided such frequent meals, but others had traditions of a Christmas dinner, to which tutors were invited, and at Letchworth the end of a three-year tutorial class was marked with a buffet lunch provided by the Settlement.[66]

Both Letchworth and Downham Market were strong and efficiently organised local centres, with engaged leaders and active students who participated in their governance. The Letchworth Settlement was extensively refurbished in the mid-1970s, with support from Hertfordshire County Council and the local district council; and it had a strong management committee and governing council to oversee the work of its dedicated and effective warden, although its finances were often precarious.[67] At Downham Market, the Board worked with a local lecture society that was 'well established, well organised and thriving' by the early 1970s, and provided courses ranging from local history and archaeology to music, literature and botany. According to one recollection, 'the subject and proposed tutor for each session was chosen by vote at each [annual general meeting], resulting in good attendances at lectures given by known tutors'.[68] Such organisational arrangements were not to everyone's taste, and could certainly cause difficulties for those who did the detailed work of liaison with the local centres. David Dymond, who as resident tutor dealt with the Suffolk centres, declared that 'I increasingly doubt the value of permanent, self-perpetuating groups who think up each spring what they want for next autumn, and so on year after year'.[69]

There was a related concern – raised repeatedly through the 1970s – about the level of student engagement with courses in the local centres. Attendance, which was directly linked to the amount of funding received, could be too low, and where written work was done by students the number 'satisfying their tutors' was also low.[70] In 1979, it was reported that attendance was 'good', but it was still the case that 'student effort had been a little disappointing'.[71] The broader context for this was the declining participation in three-year tutorial classes: these were described as 'the first flowering of the traditional kind of adult education', but they were in a 'parlous state' by the end of the 1970s.[72] For Jack Herbert and Lionel Munby, who articulated a belief shared by them with many in the WEA, the tutorial class was 'a unique creation, [which] represents a close partnership between the voluntary student movement following its own educational path and the university striving to make learning of the highest quality an active ferment in the community'.[73] There was a strong possibility that the tutorial class would be allowed to 'die out completely', but this, for Herbert and Munby, 'would be a serious educational loss and a reproach to our seriousness of purpose'.[74] As with all courses, however, the tutorial class was dependent on student demand, and this was diminishing in favour of sessional and even shorter classes. A proposal to create a series of 'linked sessionals', which could partly replace the tutorial class, was entertained in the early 1980s, and was judged to have had some success.[75]

Another development that could fill the space vacated by demand for tutorial classes was the accredited Certificate programme, which had existed for local history since the 1960s and which required a similar level of commitment among the students. The problem with these courses, though, was that a high proportion of students did not complete them: for example, on a three-year Certificate in Local History in Norwich that started in 1978 with 22 students, just nine completed the first-year examination, with six leaving early because they 'had clearly not understood from the publicity the level at which the course was being pitched'.[76] These issues made the Board reluctant to expand its provision of Certificate courses to other subject areas in the 1970s, though there were some discussions of how this might be done: a new Certificate in Landscape History and Field Archaeology, taught by David Trump and David Dymond, was introduced at the start of the 1980s.[77] Nevertheless, even the long-standing local history Certificates seem to have been under some threat in the late 1970s.[78]

Local history, though, remained one of the most enduringly popular subjects on the regional programme in the 1970s. David Dymond later recalled that, '[w]hen a new centre or branch was being formed, or when a group needed to be revived, we invariably thought of providing Local History because it always had a good chance of recruiting good numbers'.[79] In Hertfordshire, Lionel Munby led tutorial classes in St Albans, Harpenden, Bishop's Stortford, Stevenage, Hunsdon, King's Langley, Braughing, Therfield and Bricket Wood in the 1970s, as well as one at Bottisham in Cambridgeshire, in addition to numerous sessional and short courses.[80] Both Munby and Dymond had a profound influence on the development of local history in England, and on their own students. Michael Allen recalls that 'local history was very remarkable because of these men who were teaching and developing the next generation of people who would lecture, and sometimes students in their classes would become lecturers later, in their speciality. It was like a family offering, really.'[81]

Munby, in particular, continued to inspire and support research groups in various Hertfordshire towns and villages, who published their work and in many cases managed to sell it widely and profitably. His courses in Bricket Wood, Hunsdon and Kings Langley all resulted in publications, and from 1973 to 1980 a series of pamphlets on the parishes of Harpenden and Wheathampstead were issued by members of a class taught by Munby and the architectural historian Tony Baggs.[82] As in previous decades, self-sustaining research groups emerged from the courses, including the Harpenden and District Local History Society and the North Hertfordshire Villages Research Group.[83] While all this was going on, Munby was finishing his own book, *The Hertfordshire*

Landscape, and completing his long stint as editor of the *Local Historian*.[84] In the preface to his book, Munby acknowledged that his

> debt to the many people who have been in my extramural classes on local history during the past twenty-seven years is immeasurable. Almost every page of the book contains for me the memory of some apt comment or idea contributed in discussion, for any worthwhile adult education is always a partnership in learning.[85]

It was a commonplace among adult education tutors, at Cambridge and elsewhere, to feel that they learned as much from their students as the students did from them: other historians, for example, also acknowledged the contributions their adult students had made to their understanding.[86] Munby even dedicated one of his books 'to all those people who, over many years, have joined me in studying Hertfordshire history in adult education classes'.[87]

Field trips were a growing part of the programme, not least in local history, landscape studies and archaeology. The value of outdoor educational activities had been endorsed in the Russell Report, which noted that 'a simple walk over a hill might precipitate a desire to take up sketching or photography, geology, botany, meteorology, ecology, local history, romantic poetry, map-making, orienteering [or] mountaineering'.[88] Residential field study courses took students to locations across the UK and abroad: in 1979 David Trump took students to Sicily for two weeks, at a fee of £348 (equivalent to around £1,600 today), while Michael Allen and Roland Randall ran a week-long trip to Islay and Jura, in the Inner Hebrides, for botany and bird-watching. Chris Barringer led a course on 'The Making of the Lakeland Landscape' at Brathay Field Studies Centre; this was relatively affordable at £65 for a week, but students had to sleep in dormitories and were 'asked to do a small amount of washing up'. There was also a 'How to Write Local History' week at Flatford Mill in Suffolk taught by David Dymond, and a month-long practical archaeological excavation in Cambridge, again led by Trump.[89] Archaeological opportunities like this in the UK, however, were diminishing, as accommodation became more expensive and excavation, as Trump later described it, more 'professionalised'. Apart from a brief attempt in the mid-1980s to revive them, residential excavations did not continue.[90]

Pedagogical innovations continued through the 1970s, benefiting – according to John Andrew and Lionel Munby – from the 'unique distinction' of working in an extramural department, enabled by the absence of entry criteria and formal assessment requirements.[91] Although a plan for each course, and a reading list, would be provided in advance, the 'syllabus' itself would evolve according to the 'particular learning group', and 'the ground actually "covered" may only approximate to the early aspirations'.[92] In psychology, for example, a course in Cambridge evolved into a three-year 'experimental learning group', in which the students spent their time studying each others' behaviour in an approach derived from psychotherapy.[93]

At this stage, though, the accumulated experience of the staff tutors and others at Cambridge did not evolve into a substantial programme of research into adult education itself, as it did in some other universities, and as the Russell Report had recommended. The Board felt that a move in this direction would not be possible, at least not without a significant change in its staffing. Research was largely carried out within subject specialisms, and apart from a two-week training course for adult education tutors, the programme at Cambridge did not include any significant interventions to support pedagogical innovation or development.[94] Sabbatical leave to pursue this research was permitted, albeit infrequently, and could last a whole academic year: most staff tutors availed themselves of this opportunity at one time or another.[95]

*

Developments in vocational education persisted into the 1970s, although expansion was limited by the funding available from partner organisations. Courses for magistrates, the armed forces and others were mostly residential, and their development was linked closely by John Andrew to the expansion and wider use of residential accommodation. In 1971-2 he emphasised that

> The Board's most immediate need is to extend its accommodation for residential teaching .... But this need is itself only an index of

> the increasing demand that universities should continue to respond to the needs of the adult student, not merely for traditional adult education, but also for a wide range of post-experience education which is urgently needed in many sectors of the adult population. The need is obvious, and it is only the universities which can answer it.[96]

By the mid-1970s, the Board was working with court staff as well as magistrates, and also ran courses for probation officers and social workers, mainly using Cambridge colleges for both residential and one-day courses.[97] The range of these courses, and the attendance across them, was impressive: 70 attended a one-day event on 'The needs of social workers for the deaf and partially deaf' in November 1973, and attendance at weekend or week-long professional courses was usually above 20.[98] Other groups were also catered for: there were courses for A-level business studies teachers, for candidates taking University of London external degrees in law and economics, for university managers and for trade unionists (run in collaboration with the Trades Union Congress). Management studies were offered in collaboration with the National Dock Labour Board, and the IBM course, which had commenced in 1967, continued to take more than 30 students each year to Churchill College.[99] Newer developments included 'courses in economics for young graduate scientists' who worked for British Petroleum.[100]

Another element of 'post-experience' teaching was the Board's work with members of the Army and RAF, particularly candidates for promotion and for admission to the Staff College. The forces 'looked to the University to contribute the latest thinking to their own discussion on major issues of defence policy and strategy, and to complement their own programmes of officer education with an intensive examination of the constantly changing political, economic, and social context within which the armed services operate'.[101] In practice, this meant a varied programme of courses on international relations and politics, military strategy and social subjects: in 1973-4, for example, there was a one-week course on 'Society and Social Change in Britain Today', taught for the RAF and attended by 19 officers. This emphasises the bridges between 'liberal' and 'continuing' education that John Andrew had been keen to build in the 1960s.[102] Alan Stripp, a man with a wide range of interests, was a key figure in the Board's work with the armed forces: widely respected for his code-breaking work in the Second World War, he contributed heavily to these courses, along with members of other university departments.[103] Stripp helped to establish a 'Defence Study Group' in the early 1970s, bringing together participants from the Foreign and Commonwealth Office, the Ministry of Defence and the university.[104] Tutors like Stripp ranged across both the regional and professional courses, and thus although the different branches of activity were in many ways quite separate, the involvement of key individuals linked them together.

Meanwhile, the Board was grappling with the problem of space in Stuart House, and it was finally in the mid-1970s that a significant change in the use of Madingley Hall took place. The Hall itself, with its mixture of functions, was struggling financially by the early 1970s: it was running significant annual deficits, amounting to £1,380 (almost £20,000 today) in 1971-2 alone.[105] As a residence for graduate students and visiting researchers, its appeal was limited by its distance from Cambridge and by poor transport facilities. Buses ran to Cambridge along the main road from Bedford, but stopped a mile away from the Hall; and cyclists were deterred by the heavy traffic.[106] In turn, the deficits meant that repairs and refurbishment were unaffordable, and the appeal of the Hall was further reduced: the kitchen, for one thing, was 'badly planned and difficult to keep clean', and significant rewiring work was also needed.[107] In December 1972, the Board proposed a wholesale takeover of the Hall, along with substantial renovation and additional building works to make it suitable as a replacement for Stuart House: not least, the library of some 8,000 books would need to move to Madingley. This was something of a leap in the dark, but the Board managed to persuade an initially sceptical committee, established by the University Senate, to endorse its proposal.[108]

The committee was encouraged by a large bequest offered to the Board from the Dart Foundation, a philanthropic organisation established by the American industrialist Justin W. Dart, owner of the United Drug Company. Dart had promised a donation of £47,000, on the condition that a small number of students from universities in California could spend a year at a time in Cambridge, and this – along with a fairly substantial sum from the Board's own resources – was used to expand and improve the facilities at Madingley. These improvements would include the construction of an 'appropriately modest' office building, and the conversion of the stable block into a suitable library.[109] An added advantage for the university, of course, was that Stuart House could be turned to different uses. Nevertheless, the university was clearly worried about the plans: it wanted to preserve 'the residential character of the Hall' in some way, and was therefore keen to maintain a small 'permanent community' on the site. The latter would take the form of around 15 graduate students and visiting researchers. The Senate committee had reservations about the assurances made by the Board that it could make the plans work, but they came 'to the conclusion that there is no way of being certain … except by experience', and so the Board was given permission to move in.[110]

The Board's plans for Madingley were remarkably ambitious. The aim was to use it for 51 weeks each year for residential courses, and that it would become 'a focus for the aspirations of adults in the eastern region and elsewhere who are committed to their continued education'.[111] In the short period of optimism following the Russell Report, there was perhaps some justification for this level of ambition, and in the early years at Madingley the Board succeeded in using it effectively, achieving a room occupation rate of 79% for the accommodation in 1975-6. In that year there were 78 residential courses at the Hall (see table 4.1), 29 of which took place at a weekend and a further 42 lasting from five to seven days; and there were 13 'permanent' inhabitants.[112] By the late 1970s the Hall was making a substantial annual profit – £35,000 in 1977-8 (more than £200,000 today) – of which most was set aside for further improvements to the buildings. It soon became clear that the lecture room was not big enough, and security became something of a concern: these problems can in part be attributed to the early successes of the Board in its new home.[113] The premises at Madingley were overseen by Vivian Ramsbottom, who was appointed as warden, serving until his retirement in 1983.[114]

In the following years, Madingley Hall would become emblematic of the Board of Extra-Mural Studies and its successors. The move would have a profound impact on the Board's sense of identity. As a historic building with a distinctive appearance and remarkable gardens – laid out by 'Capability' Brown in the eighteenth century – it was a resource that gave the Board grade-1-listed accommodation that could compare in grandeur, if not in size, with many of the university's oldest and most prestigious colleges. Within a year of taking possession, the Board had reissued Lionel Munby's revised version of an earlier book by Jean Salter, *Madingley Hall*, originally published in 1961.[115] As in earlier decades, the Hall mimicked the college experience for students who attended courses there; its catering and bar were reliably popular. Room service was carried out by au pairs who worked on short-term contracts and lived on the upper floor, an arrangement that lasted until the end of the century. Alongside the televisions that were purchased for the Hall, a colour set was hired for the au pairs' use in 1978.[116] The new office buildings provided space for both administrative and academic staff, although by the mid-1980s the expanding administrative workforce had already outgrown the office accommodation provided by the new Dart Building.[117]

The 'saloon' at the Hall was ideal for concerts, and the Board acquired a 'quartet-in-residence' – the Alberni String Quartet – who became an important annual feature of the residential course programme. A regular week-long residential 'string masterclass' led by the Alberni quartet proved to be enduringly popular, and culminated in a concert in the saloon, which was 'acoustically wonderful, ideal for quartet music … the Wigmore Hall of Cambridge'.[118] The quartet reported that 'they have never played in a more perfect setting'.[119] Michael Allen recalls that

> The final concerts were … popular and most seats in the saloon were taken. With upwards of 50 seats for students on the courses, a good turnout by administrative and teaching staff (and often guests of theirs from Cambridge), the concerts were well attended and the Alberni, who loved playing in full evening dress in the saloon, were aware that their programmes at the Hall were much appreciated.[120]

Members of the public paid for tickets – £2 a head, including a glass of wine, in 1978 – and this helped the Board to retain some of its contact with Cambridge following the move to Madingley.[121]

The early experience of teaching and working at Madingley presented various challenges, most of which were fairly easily solved – the need for expanded telephone connections, poor acoustics in the dining hall, unsuitable carpets, and so on.[122] Some of the fittings were old: Ramsbottom noted in 1979 that most of the mattresses and blankets dated from 1950, and although the former were 'still satisfactory', the latter were in need of replacement after almost 30 years of continuous use.[123] A little over £2,000 was spent on replacing such items, and further expenditure was incurred on the purchase of televisions, electronic typewriters, cassette recorders and other equipment for teaching, administrative and recreational use.[124] There was also a ping-pong table and dartboard, though it was noted that these two items 'appear to be used by the staff more frequently than course members'![125] Meanwhile, Madingley attracted a large number of visitors – from both the university itself and beyond – and while this could hardly be begrudged by John Andrew and his staff, there were some concerns about their intrusion into its core activities. On one occasion Andrew pleaded with the university to allow the Board to close off some areas of the Hall, arguing that

> Madingley Hall … is now a teaching institution providing courses seven days a week for 51 weeks of the year, to people who pay to enjoy both the courses they attend and the amenities offered to them …. We suffer considerable distraction already because one of our main lecture rooms gives onto the terrace across which people tramp on their way to the lawns and lower grounds, We do not complain of this even when faces are pressed against the windows and children play on the terrace while we are trying to teach.[126]

If National Trust properties could set areas aside for private use, Andrew reasoned, then the same should be possible for an institution belonging to the University of Cambridge.

*

The acquisition of Madingley Hall enabled a year-round programme of residential courses to be provided, and this became the key 'growing point' for the Board.[127] Table 4.1 shows the extent of the increase, with student numbers on residential courses at Madingley alone increasing almost fourfold in the second half of the 1970s. Some of the residential courses took a more intensive approach to the study of subjects that featured prominently in the regional programme. In 1973-4, for example, there were week-long courses on palaeography, eighteenth-century literature – run from 28 December to 4 January – 'history and society' and a whole series of summer schools on archaeology, among many others. Residential courses were particularly liable to be over-subscribed, even at a cost of between £25 and £30 (around £320 to £390 in today's values) – and in some cases students were obliged to share rooms – although in the case of courses for particular professional groups the fees would often be covered, in whole or in part, by employers.[128]

Courses run over the new year were a particular feature of the programme that did not survive the twentieth century: 'it was very cold', according to one student, a young teacher, who attended a new-year residential course on Shakespeare in the 1970s. For this student, Madingley itself was an important attraction. 'I remember vividly the sense of almost being overawed by the building', he recalls, although he found Leo Salingar and John Andrew, who taught the course, 'very genial'. Madingley gave this student 'a sense that everybody was worth respect, whatever their background, whatever their experience, and whatever their intellectual develop thus far'. This, he felt, was the epitome of an ideal that could be traced back to James Stuart, although the residential component was perhaps a little different from that which Stuart might have envisaged.[129]

Some, though, felt that the focus on residential courses undermined the academic standards of extramural provision, and that – at the very least – considerable care needed to be taken in planning them. Lionel Munby admitted that residential courses were 'a success story' and had 'much glamour', but also insisted that

> Madingley weekends cannot be compared as educational exercises with a good Sessional or Tutorial Class, except where a series of linked weekends is planned … or where they supplement traditional field classes, making possible intensive study of a particular problem or learning a new technique (as palaeography).[130]

Nevertheless, the residential weeks and weekends at Madingley were popular, and by the end of the 1970s there were usually more than 100 courses there in any year, attracting 2,764 students in 1979-80. Most of these were attending courses for Army officers or magistrates or some other specific professional group – and these courses often lasted longer – but others were studying 'The Enlightenment' (37 students), 'Art and Society in Hardy's England' (23) or 'Tudor England' (26). Courses such as 'The World of Wine' (18 students) may have fuelled Munby's concerns, but the weekend courses had undoubtedly become an important element of the programme in a short space of time.[131] Supporting the regional programme, such courses elicited a 'good response', and Michael Allen told the Local Centres Union that there 'could be greater benefit in a single weekend at Madingley than in an entire term's work based on one evening in the week'.[132] It was possible for centres themselves to apply to run residential weekends at Madingley – as long as at least 15 students attended – and there was some modest financial support to foster this development.[133]

The largest element of the Board's residential provision, though, was the international summer programme, which had a long history going back to the 1920s. The longstanding 'Vacation Course for Foreign Students' had moved to the new Sidgwick Site in Cambridge in 1967, and in 1969-70 it attracted 338 students from 38 countries. It consisted of a general 'survey of contemporary Britain', and students could choose to specialise – within the relatively narrow confines of a four-week programme – on specific disciplinary or thematic approaches, including 'Britain in the World Economy' and 'Twentieth-Century Poetry'. Running from early July to early August and using accommodation in various Cambridge colleges, the vacation course had more than 300 students in most years in the 1970s, with a significant and growing number recruited through formal or informal partnerships with overseas universities, particularly in the United States. The University of Southern California (USC) had been sending students since 1963 – and this was a particular aspect of the Dart bequest that supported the move to Madingley Hall. The USC connection remained unbroken through the 1970s and beyond.[134] Alongside the main summer programme was the four-week ‘Linguistics and the English Language’ course that had started in the 1960s and was directed by John Trim. It recruited 137 students in 1969-70 and would continue for a further quarter-century thereafter.[135]

There was some disquiet about the growing profile and popularity of the summer schools. Although there was no suggestion that they might displace the regional year-round work, they did form a substantial proportion of the Board’s activity, and this generated some discussion. Lionel Munby submitted a paper to a staff meeting at the beginning of the 1980s, noting that

> The recent expansion of residential work in the summer … has largely been for overseas students. This is an acceptable form of University activity, common to many British and foreign universities, and it can be profitable both in prestige and financially. However, it is necessary to ask whether a university department specifically concerned with adult education can be justified merely by such activity.[136]

It was true, of course, that the summer courses attracted a very different student body from the regional programme: they were mostly younger and of course more diverse in origins given the international remit of the vacation course, and their association with Cambridge was more transient, although many did return for second or subsequent visits. In contrast with many students in the East Anglian region, though, these visitors did actually spend their time *in* Cambridge, and it was often the Cambridge ‘experience’ that formed the basis of their later memories of the summer programmes. Living, eating and socialising in a college environment was clearly a significant attraction for many of those who attended, and it was in connection with the summer schools that the Board’s annual report for 1971-2 announced that ‘Cambridge is a magnet to the adult student at home and abroad’.[137] Indeed, some such students returned to Cambridge as affiliate or graduate students in due course.[138] By the end of the 1970s there was increasing demand from American universities wanting to organise summer schools in Cambridge, and more structured collaborations with some of these institutions – including USC – would emerge in the early 1980s.[139]

*

At the beginning of the 1980s Alan Rogers – Professor of Continuing Education at the New University of Ulster – wrote that '[m]ost universities in [Britain] have turned their back upon the local region because they believe they are part of a national system and indeed an international system'.[140] This did not quite adequately describe Cambridge, where the Board retained a strong commitment to a programme of courses in its established region, and was making increasing use of its new base at Madingley Hall to support that programme. Indeed, the 'local region' remained important even in much of the 'continuing education' provision: Cambridgeshire County Council often sent its social workers to courses at Madingley, for example. With several members of the early post-war generation of staff tutors still working for the Board, the sense of identification with an educational tradition remained very strong at Madingley and across the wider region. In 1982, the Board insisted that, along with the WEA, it was 'helping to maintain the tradition of liberal adult education' in East Anglia.[141] There was as yet, though, no concrete proposal to replace the 'Extra-Mural Studies' in its name with 'Continuing Education' – Leslie Wayper, as director, was resistant to the idea, and it would not happen for another decade – whereas Rogers, at Ulster, was leading an 'Institute of Continuing Education'.[142]

Despite the changes in university adult education, there were more cautious voices in the sector urging the maintenance of its 'traditional' mission. Harold Wiltshire, for example – who had named and lauded the 'Great Tradition' in the 1950s – continued to to defend it robustly into the 1980s, arguing that at extramural department would best succeed and flourish 'by being itself and by going about its own business'. This, in fact, is largely what the Cambridge Board did in the 1970s.[143] Some of its 'business', perhaps most notably the international summer programme, was somewhat different from that of most other extramural departments, but on the whole – and despite the financial and political upheavals of the decade, the move to Madingley Hall and the gradual expansion of its role in continuing education – the profile of the Board's work at the end of the 1970s would have been recognisable a decade earlier. The 1980s would see more profound challenges to the status and mission of university adult education, and these are the subject of the next chapter.

The ‘unfinished’ portrait of James Stuart by Hubert von Herkomer, dating to 1881. This is a black-and-white photograph of the portrait, which currently hangs in Madingley Hall.

IMAGE COURTESY OF THE UNIVERSITY OF CAMBRIDGE INSTITUTE OF CONTINUING EDUCATION. ALL OTHER IMAGES ARE FROM THE SAME SOURCE UNLESS STATED.

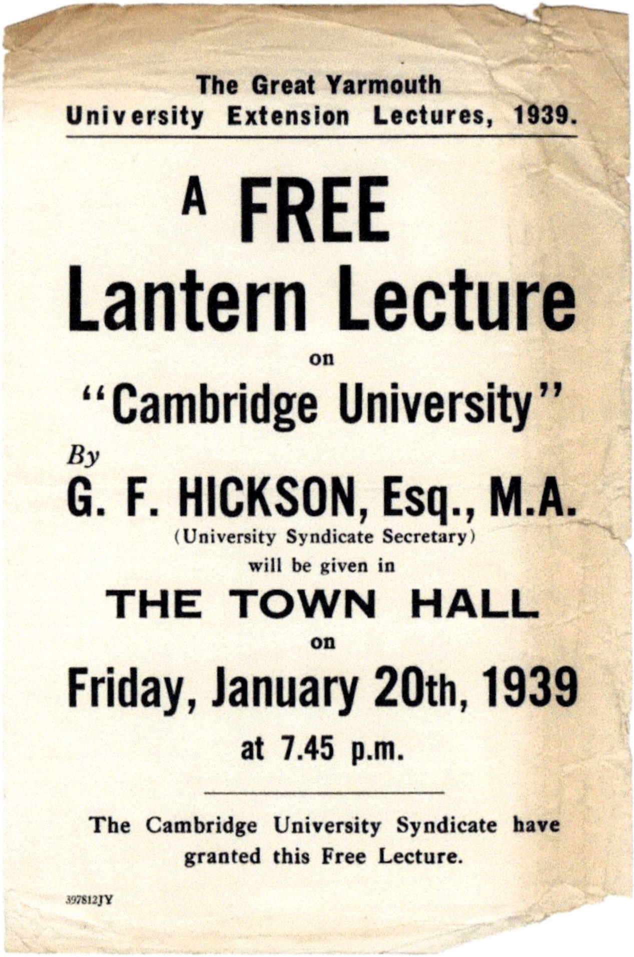

Above: flyer for a lecture in Cambridge by Geoffrey Hickson in 1939.

Right, above: cover and sample inside page of a syllabus by W. P. Baker, the first full-time staff tutor for the Board of Extra-Mural Studies.

Right, below: portrait of Geoffrey Hickson, secretary of the Board of Extra-Mural Studies from 1928 to 1967. The picture, by Patrick George, hangs in the Board Room at Madingley Hall.

PHOTOGRAPH: AUTHOR, FROM A PORTRAIT IN THE POSSESSION OF THE UNIVERSITY OF CAMBRIDGE INSTITUTE OF CONTINUING EDUCATION.

CAMBRIDGE UNIVERSITY LOCAL LECTURES

SYLLABUS

OF A COURSE OF TWELVE LECTURES ON

THE HISTORY OF RURAL ENGLAND

BY

W. PEARSON BAKER, B.A.

Jesus College

Cambridge: Printed at the University Press

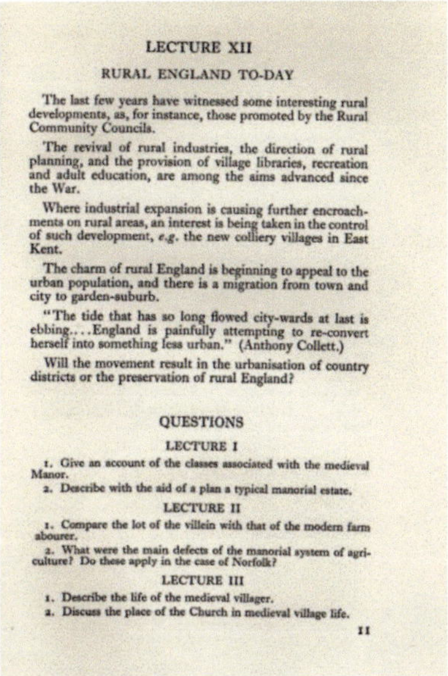

LECTURE XII

RURAL ENGLAND TO-DAY

The last few years have witnessed some interesting rural developments, as, for instance, those promoted by the Rural Community Councils.

The revival of rural industries, the direction of rural planning, and the provision of village libraries, recreation and adult education, are among the aims advanced since the War.

Where industrial expansion is causing further encroachments on rural areas, an interest is being taken in the control of such development, *e.g.* the new colliery villages in East Kent.

The charm of rural England is beginning to appeal to the urban population, and there is a migration from town and city to garden-suburb.

"The tide that has so long flowed city-wards at last is ebbing....England is painfully attempting to re-convert herself into something less urban." (Anthony Collett.)

Will the movement result in the urbanisation of country districts or the preservation of rural England?

QUESTIONS

LECTURE I

1. Give an account of the classes associated with the medieval Manor.

2. Describe with the aid of a plan a typical manorial estate.

LECTURE II

1. Compare the lot of the villein with that of the modern farm abourer.

2. What were the main defects of the manorial system of agriculture? Do these apply in the case of Norfolk?

LECTURE III

1. Describe the life of the medieval villager.

2. Discuss the place of the Church in medieval village life.

11

Left: Stuart House, north elevation, picture of unknown date. The Board of Extra-Mural Studies moved into the new Stuart House in 1927, and was based there until 1975.

Below: one of the early Vacation Courses for Foreign students, 1923.

1920s SUMMER SCHOOLS GROUP, © INTERNATIONAL SUMMER PROGRAMMES.

APPENDIX II

UNIVERSITY TUTORIAL AND SESSIONAL CLASSES

Centre	Year	Subject	Tutor	Number of Students: Men	Number of Students: Women	No. of effective Students
University Tutorial Classes						
Bedford	2	Art and Civilization	Miss H. O. Lowenthal, B.A.	2	17	13
Braintree	3	Sociology	L. M. Munby, M.A.	5	3	5
Cambridge	1	International Affairs	J. Hampden Jackson, M.A.	5	17	20
Desborough	2	19th-Century History	C. L. Wayper, M.A.	11	8	16
Gorleston	1	Philosophy	H. H. Daisley, M.A.	10	5	12
Hertford	3	English Literature	J. Stewart Collis, M.A.	2	10	9
Ipswich	1	Psychology	E. J. D. Radclyffe, M.A.	4	11	14
Kettering	4	Science	M. H. Clifford, M.A., Ph.D.	5	7	9
Kettering	1	English Literature	A. E. Douglas-Smith, M.A.	8	16	4
Leighton Buzzard	2	Art	Miss M. Kay	4	15	12
Luton	3	Social History	L. M. Munby, M.A.	7	5	8
Northampton	3	Economics	F. Lee, B.A., B.Sc. (Econ.)	11	9	15
Norwich	1	International Affairs	J. Hampden Jackson, M.A.	8	18	20
Norwich	1	Local History	Miss R. M. Young, B.A.	20	11	23
Norwich	1	Philosophy	P. Roubiczek	9	9	7
Peterborough	1	International Problems	J. R. Mitchell, M.A.	14	2	10
Peterborough	1	English Literature	A. E. Douglas-Smith, M.A.	4	13	7
Wellingborough	1	Science	M. H. Clifford, M.A., Ph.D.	6	12	10
				135	188	214
University Sessional Classes	No. of Meetings					
Aylsham	24	Economic Problems	C. H. Macgregor, B.A., B.Sc. (Econ.)	13	8	12
Bedford	24	Historical and Geographical Background to Western Europe	N. J. G. Pounds, M.A., Ph.D.	9	8	11
Cambridge	24	English Literature	A. E. Douglas-Smith, M.A.	5	20	3
Cambridge	24	Botany	E. A. George, M.A.	13	14	13
Colchester	22	Philosophy	H. H. Daisley, M.A.	10	4	11
Costessey	24	Social History	Miss R. M. Young, B.A.	9	7	9
Diss	24	Music	P. Burges, B.A., A.R.A.M.	6	24	7
Diss	24	Economic Problems	C. H. Macgregor, B.A., B.Sc. (Econ.)	12	20	22
Dunstable	24	Psychology	Miss R. B. Bassett, B.A.	7	11	13
Fakenham	24	English Literature	K. Cruise, B.A.	6	8	3
Halstead	24	Philosophy	H. H. Daisley, M.A.	4	10	7
Harleston	24	English Literature	Mrs D. E. A. Rash, M.A.	4	19	16
Harpenden	24	Philosophy	H. P. Rickman, B.A., D.Phil.	11	9	4
Hingham	24	Art	Miss H. O. Lowenthal, B.A.	9	16	9
Impington	20	International Affairs	H. Plaskitt, M.A.	9	21	14
Kettering	24	Economics	J. A. Knapp, M.A.	12	6	14
Kettering	24	Art	Miss P. Llewellyn Smith, M.A.	6	13	10
King's Lynn	24	English Literature	G. Garrod, M.A.	6	10	6
Knebworth	24	Present-day Economic Problems	F. V. H. Ramsbottom, M.A.	11	14	16
Leighton Buzzard	24	Economic Problems	F. Lee, B.A., B.Sc. (Econ.)	9	8	11
Linton	20	East Anglian Countryside	M. H. Clifford, M.A., Ph.D.	13	16	16
Luton	24	English Literature	J. Stewart Collis, M.A.	3	9	8
Luton	24	International Affairs	C. L. Wayper, M.A.	11	6	10
Martham	24	Economic Problems	C. H. Macgregor, B.A., B.Sc. (Econ.)	9	6	9
Mundford	24	Norfolk Village Life	Miss R. M. Young, B.A.	20	9	16
Northampton	24	Social History	C. P. Griffiths, B.A.	6	14	11
Northwold	24	Norfolk Village Life	Miss R. M. Young, B.A.	12	13	16
Norwich	24	Art	Miss H. O. Lowenthal, B.A.	10	21	22
Peterborough	24	Economics	F. Lee, B.A., B.Sc. (Econ.)	6	8	10
Rushden	24	Shakespeare to Shaw	A. E. Douglas-Smith, M.A.	4	10	5
St Neots	24	Science	M. H. Clifford, M.A., Ph.D.	10	11	12
Saxmundham	24	Local History	Miss L. M. Springall, B.A., Ph.D.	12	11	9
Sprowston	24	Introduction to Psychology	D. C. Fraser, M.A., B.Sc.	6	12	13
Stevenage	24	Problems of Peacemaking	J. Hampden Jackson, M.A.	18	6	10
Stowmarket	24	Economic and Political Geography	P. Marsden, B.A.	11	12	12
Sudbury	24	Music	P. Burges, B.A., A.R.A.M.	10	12	7
Thrapston	24	Social History	C. P. Griffiths, B.A.	9	5	5
Tittleshall	24	Europe Since the War	Mrs F. L. Ralphs, B.A.	9	15	18
			Carried forward	350	446	420

A page from the Board of Extra-Mural Studies annual report, 1948-9, listing tutorial and sessional classes run during the year.

Above: Madingley Hall, pictured in 2022.
PHOTOGRAPH: MARK FREEMAN.

Below: the dining hall at Madingley, c.1951.

John Andrew, assistant secretary from 1950, deputy secretary from 1955, and director of extramural studies from 1967 to 1977. This portrait hangs in the Board Room at Madingley Hall.

PHOTOGRAPH: AUTHOR, FROM A PORTRAIT IN THE POSSESSION OF THE UNIVERSITY OF CAMBRIDGE INSTITUTE OF CONTINUING EDUCATION.

THE SETTLEMENT
THE SETTLEMENT

Left, above: Letchworth Settlement, an adult education institute opened in 1920, and a venue for Cambridge extramural courses for several decades. The building opened as a temperance pub, the Skittles Inn, in 1907.

Left, below: Wensum Lodge, Norwich, a former brewery used for classes on the regional programme from the 1960s.

Right: plan of Madingley Hall, included in programmes for residential courses, 1979.

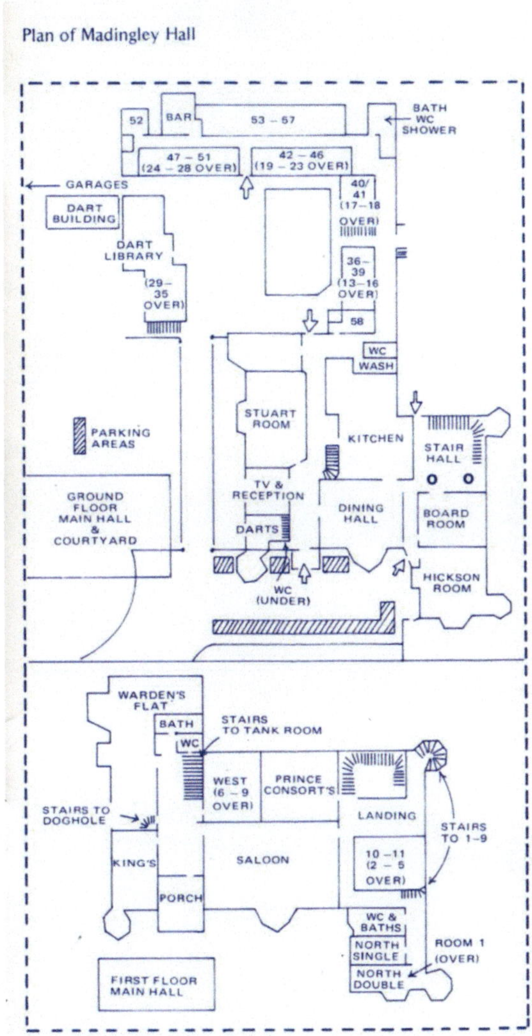

Above: students on the first IMB course, 1967.

Below: Lionel Munby's local history course at Harpenden in 1974.
IMAGE COURTESY OF DIANA MUNBY.

CAMBRIDGE
UNIVERSITY
Board of Extra-mural Studies

Adult
Courses
in East Anglia
1967-8

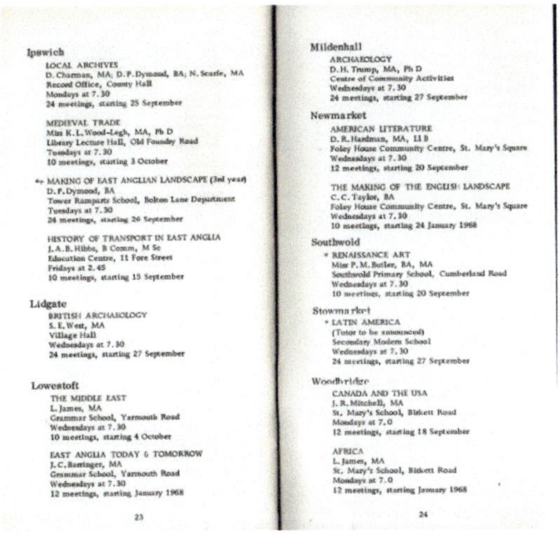

Ipswich

LOCAL ARCHIVES
D. Charman, MA; D. P. Dymond, BA; N. Scarfe, MA
Record Office, County Hall
Mondays at 7.30
24 meetings, starting 25 September

MEDIEVAL TRADE
Miss K. L. Wood-Legh, MA, Ph D
Library Lecture Hall, Old Foundry Road
Tuesdays at 7.30
10 meetings, starting 3 October

* MAKING OF EAST ANGLIAN LANDSCAPE (3rd year)
D. P. Dymond, BA
Tower Ramparts School, Bolton Lane Department
Tuesdays at 7.30
24 meetings, starting 26 September

HISTORY OF TRANSPORT IN EAST ANGLIA
J. A. B. Hibbs, B Comm, M Sc
Education Centre, 11 Fore Street
Fridays at 2.45
10 meetings, starting 15 September

Lidgate

BRITISH ARCHAEOLOGY
S. E. West, MA
Village Hall
Wednesdays at 7.30
24 meetings, starting 27 September

Lowestoft

THE MIDDLE EAST
L. James, MA
Grammar School, Yarmouth Road
Wednesdays at 7.30
10 meetings, starting 4 October

EAST ANGLIA TODAY & TOMORROW
J. C. Barringer, MA
Grammar School, Yarmouth Road
Wednesdays at 7.30
12 meetings, starting January 1968

23

Mildenhall

ARCHAEOLOGY
D. H. Trump, MA, Ph D
Centre of Community Activities
Wednesdays at 7.30
24 meetings, starting 27 September

Newmarket

AMERICAN LITERATURE
D. R. Hardman, MA, LL B
Foley House Community Centre, St. Mary's Square
Wednesdays at 7.30
12 meetings, starting 20 September

THE MAKING OF THE ENGLISH LANDSCAPE
C. C. Taylor, BA
Foley House Community Centre, St. Mary's Square
Wednesdays at 7.30
10 meetings, starting 24 January 1968

Southwold

* RENAISSANCE ART
Miss P. M. Butler, BA, MA
Southwold Primary School, Cumberland Road
Wednesdays at 7.30
10 meetings, starting 20 September

Stowmarket

* LATIN AMERICA
(Tutor to be announced)
Secondary Modern School
Wednesdays at 7.30
24 meetings, starting 27 September

Woodbridge

CANADA AND THE USA
J. R. Mitchell, MA
St. Mary's School, Birkett Road
Mondays at 7.0
12 meetings, starting 18 September

AFRICA
L. James, MA
St. Mary's School, Birkett Road
Mondays at 7.0
12 meetings, starting January 1968

24

Above: cover and sample inside pages of the first list of courses produced by the Board for prospective students, 1967-8.

Below: an Alberni 'masterclass' at Madingley Hall, probably in the early 1980s.

Right: Michael Allen (left) and Michael Richardson, directors of extramural studies at Cambridge from 1980 to 1990 and from 1990 to 2004 respectively.

Below: a plaque in the Madingley Hall garden marking the retirement of Leslie James, James Mitchell and Lionel Munby. The plant behind is Alstroemeria 'Indian Summer'.

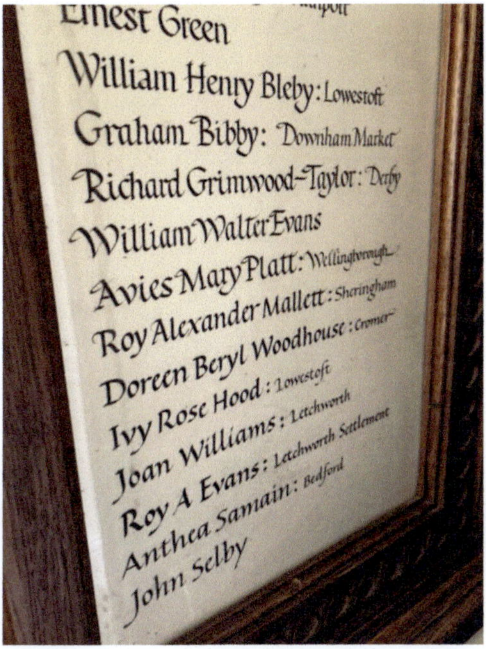

Left: part of the 'roll of honour', originally in Stuart House and now in Madingley Hall. This is the right-hand panel of the roll, containing names of people associated with local centres in the region.

Below: Lionel Munby's students from King's Langley on a 'Bunyan Trail' on Barton Hills in 1979.

IMAGE COURTESY OF DIANA MUNBY.

From the left: staff tutors Leslie James, James Mitchell and Lionel Munby, and chair of the Board of Extra-Mural Studies Peter Sykes, photograph of unknown date.

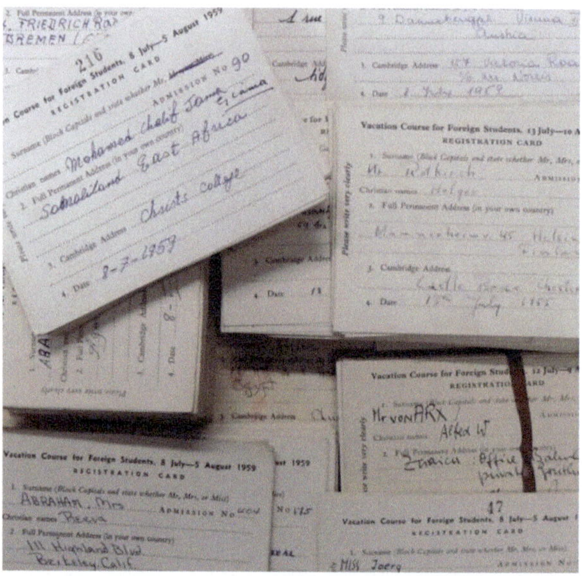

Left: student record cards from the Vacation Course for Foreign Students, 1959.

Right: examples of course publicity from the late 1970s and early 2000s

Above: Lady Mitchell Hall at the University of Cambridge Sidgwick site, the venue for plenary lectures on the International Summer Programmes.

PHOTOGRAPH: AUTHOR.

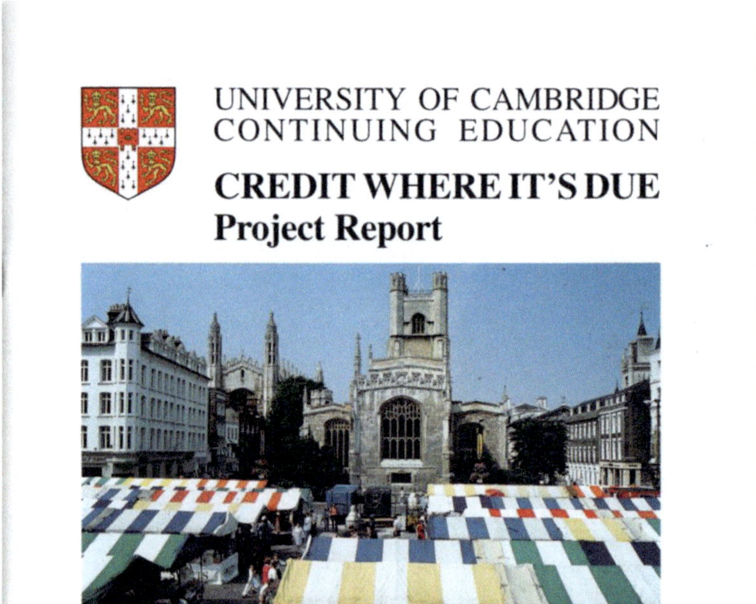
UNIVERSITY OF CAMBRIDGE
CONTINUING EDUCATION

CREDIT WHERE IT'S DUE
Project Report

Employment Department
Credit Frameworks and Learning Outcomes Programme

Credit Where It's Due: project report on the accreditation of courses on the public programmes, 1995.

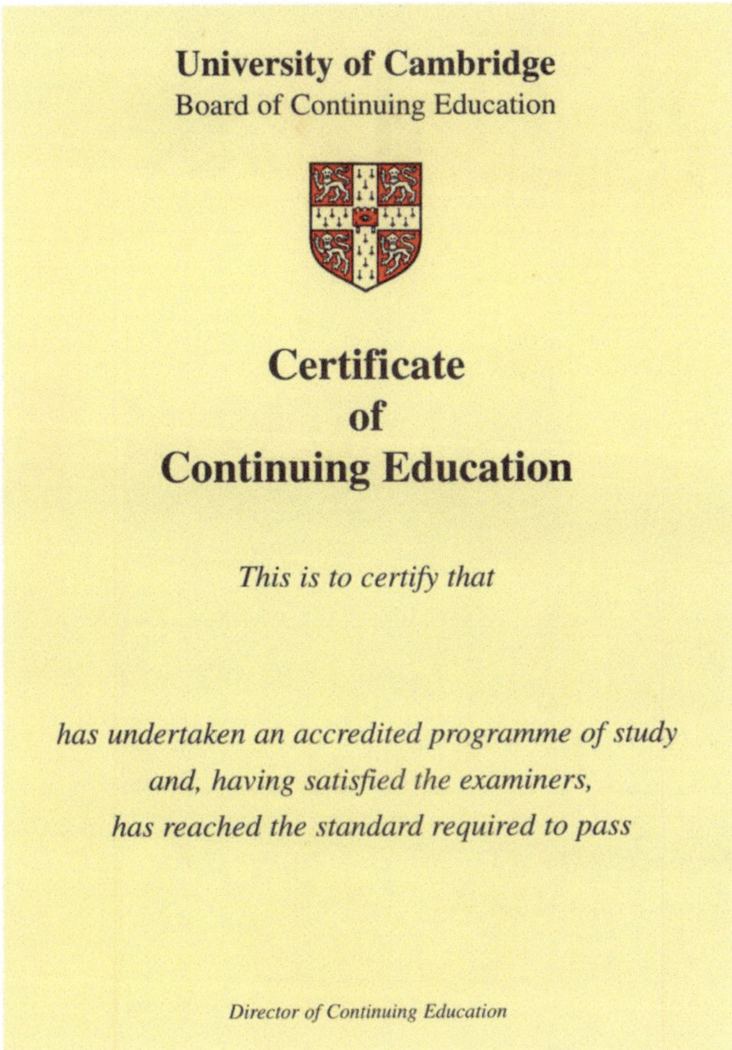

University of Cambridge
Board of Continuing Education

Certificate of Continuing Education

This is to certify that

has undertaken an accredited programme of study
and, having satisfied the examiners,
has reached the standard required to pass

Director of Continuing Education

Sample Certificate of Continuing Education, awarded from the mid-1990s to students on the public programmes.

IMAGE BY MARK FREEMAN FROM AN ORIGINAL DOCUMENT SUPPLIED BY DAVID DAVIES.

QUILL

THE MADINGLEY HALL IN-HOUSE STAFF NEWSLETTER

CONTENTS

NB THE OFFICE WILL BE CLOSED AT EASTER FROM FRIDAY 24 - MONDAY 27 MARCH INCLUSIVE

MADINGLEY HALL.
CAMBRIDGESHIRE.

MR· QUILL by sjo

Front page of an early issue of *Quill*, the Madingley Hall in-house staff magazine which ran from 1989 until the mid-1990s. The cartoons of 'Mr Quill' are by Sarah Ormrod.

IMAGE COURTESY OF THE UNIVERSITY OF CAMBRIDGE INSTITUTE OF CONTINUING EDUCATION, AND REPRODUCED WITH THE PERMISSION OF SARAH ORMROD.

Above: HRH the Prince of Wales and delegates at the 1994 meeting of the Prince of Wales Business and Environment Programme, at Madingley Hall

IMAGE COURTESY OF DAME POLLY COURTICE.

Right: English oak (Quercus robur) in the garden at Madingley Hall. The oak was given on 6 March 1992 by Mrs Cleo Garland, a student on the Certificate in Ecology at Thorpe-le-Soken, taught by Roland Randall. Her project was a study of germinating acorns, and the tree was in the walled garden from 1992 to 2000.

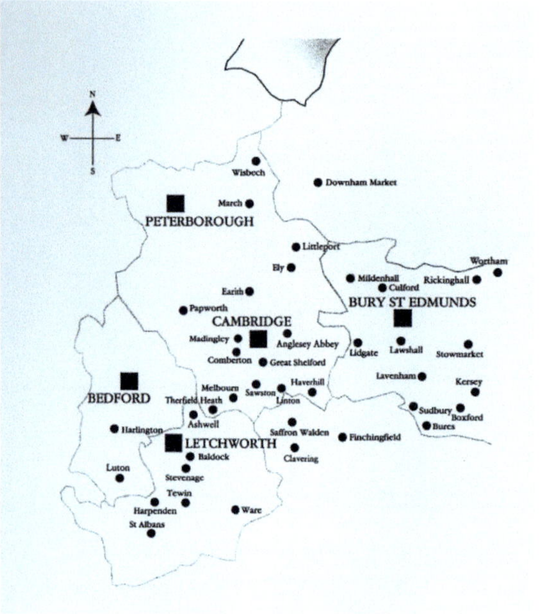

Left: map of Cambridge local centres, 2002-3. The region was much smaller at this time than in previous decades, with the loss of Northamptonshire, Norfolk and most of Essex to other universities.

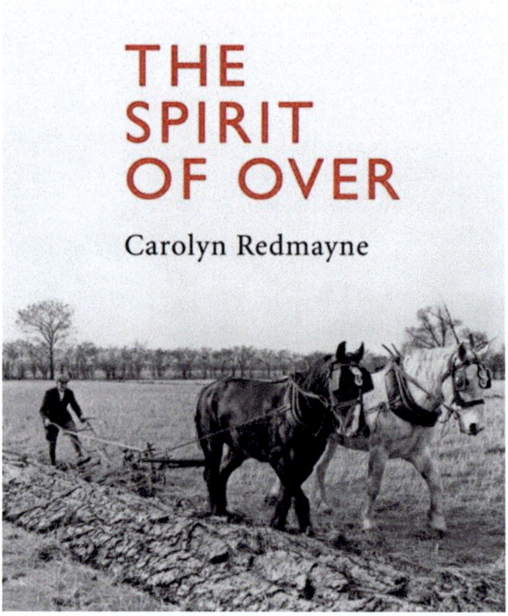

Right: front cover of *The Spirit of Over* by Carolyn Redmayne, published in 2021. The book was inspired by the author's work on local history courses at ICE.

IMAGE COURTESY OF CAROLYN REDMAYNE.

Chapter 5
Lifting the soul: the 1980s

For university adult education, the early 1980s marked the start of 'perhaps the most critical 25 year period in [its] history'.[1] During the following decade a complex series of pressures were felt across the sector: the beginning of the end of the separate stream of funding that university adult education had enjoyed since 1924; the rise of quality assurance and the beginnings of a sustained government focus on accreditation; the emergence of research assessment related to university funding; and the seemingly inexorable spread of a 'human capital' approach to education which many saw as undermining its 'social purpose'.[2] Most of these pressures were not new – as we have seen – but they accelerated in the 1980s, and it has been argued that they ultimately caused a 'change in the whole culture of university continuing education'.[3] Nevertheless, there were many continuities in the activities of the Cambridge Board through the 1980s; and, as this chapter will show, the traditional programme of courses maintained its presence in the East Anglian region, and remained comfortably the largest area of activity across the whole decade. Although some elements contracted, the regional programme as a whole continued to respond creatively and effectively to the demand that had driven its creation, expansion and survival in previous decades. Student numbers declined over the decade, but there were signs of strength in some subjects and centres, which consolidated their position, and residential courses in particular grew in importance and popularity. While other areas of work – particularly in continuing professional education – enhanced their profile, and while threats to the future of university 'liberal' education were certainly identified in the 1980s, at the end of the decade the regional programme, at the heart of the Board's activities for more than a century, would remain in a perhaps surprisingly strong position. In the 1980s, reflecting its origins, the regional programme was generally referred to as the 'extension programme', and that usage is adopted in this chapter.

At the heart of the issues faced by Michael Allen, who took over as director of extra-mural studies from Leslie Wayper in 1980, was the problem of funding. Allen inherited the complex financial system that had long characterised university adult education, in which Responsible Body grants direct from the Department of Education and Science were augmented by student fees, local education authority support and money from the central university – in

Cambridge's case, the University Chest. In 1981 the Universities Grants Committee announced a 14% cut in direct funding to higher education institutions, implemented over three years. This did not directly affect government funding of extramural departments, but it had the potential to reduce the element of income from the University Chest, and the Cambridge Board was well aware of 'the deteriorating economic climate with which adult education must contend in the immediate future'.[4] In due course, there was a three-year cut, amounting to 14.3%, in Responsible Body funding, which took effect in the last three years of the decade, and in 1989 – following the Education Reform Act of 1988 – the Responsible Body system was abolished, replaced with direct support from the short-lived Universities Funding Council, itself succeeded in 1992 by the Higher Education Funding Council for England.[5] These new direct grants were subject to a competitive bidding process, which reduced the number of universities that could get them, although Cambridge, with its strong and popular regional programme, was able retain its place in the system. In the early 1980s, Allen and his colleagues were aware that the 'encouraging' position in which the Board found itself could 'provide some protection' in a worsening financial climate.[6]

The 1980s would see significant changes in the profile of staffing at the Board. From a high point of 15 staff tutors in 1976, the complement was reduced to just eight by 1988. The early years of the decade saw the retirement of several tutors who had served since just after the Second World War: Colin Griffiths – appointed as resident tutor in Northamptonshire in 1946 – retired in 1981, and he was followed by Lionel Munby, Leslie James and James Mitchell the following year. Meanwhile, Erica Towner left in 1984, long-serving deputy secretary and latterly warden of Madingley Hall Vivian Ramsbottom retired in 1983, and Alan Stripp followed in 1988.[7] The post-war generation of resident and staff tutors, imbued with the 'Great Tradition' of university extramural education, had now departed the scene, and change was led by a group of teachers and administrators who had emerged in the 1960s and 1970s. There were some new members of staff in the 1980s: Gwythian (Gwyn) Prins was for several years a staff tutor in modern history and international relations, and art historian Nicholas Friend worked as an assistant staff tutor from 1981 to 1986.[8] By 1988, in addition to the director, there were three assistant secretaries: Martin Horrox, Richard Evans and Richard Mason. The Board itself was chaired at various times by Peter Sykes, a well-known chemist from Christ's College; the ancient historian and master of Corpus Christi Michael McCrum;

the economic historian and master of St Catharine's Barry Supple; and University Librarian Frederick Ratcliffe.[9]

Meanwhile, Susan Rawlings was both deputy secretary and warden of Madingley Hall; and there was also a finance officer, director of legal studies, publicity officer, director of continuing education for industry and four administrative assistants, as well as a large number of administrative and clerical employees who greatly outnumbered the small body of full-time teaching staff.[10] Key individuals such as the Board's librarian Barbara Pemberton, finance director Cyril Pritchett (appointed in 1986) and head of maintenance Ken Naylor made indispensable and often overlooked contributions its work. Naylor, for example, worked at Madingley Hall for 42 years, and lived in the lodge house at the bottom of the driveway; his wife was one of the cleaners at the Hall. He 'was the first awake in the morning, opening up the Hall and kitchen and switching on the ovens for the cook. He checked that the outside lights were turned off before there was an automatic system.' As Lionel Munby remembered,

> those of us who work in the rarified atmosphere of administration and teaching are often barely conscious of all the little things that are done for us. … Ken replaced light bulbs, dealt with curtains in lecture rooms that did not draw, and even leaks which damaged ceilings, [and his work] too easily went unnoticed.[11]

*

Across the country the number of student enrolments on university adult education courses increased rapidly during the 1980s: it stood at 272,795 in 1982-3 and reached 597,136 by 1989-90.[12] In Cambridge, too, the extension programme maintained its numbers and vitality despite the requirement to increase student fees in the face of retrenchment in funding from other sources. It was clear that, contrary to what may have been feared, the fee increase 'did not seem to have deterred student enrolment significantly', although in any case the cost of courses remained low, averaging £1.50 (£4.50 today) per class in 1987-8.[13] In 1989-90, a twenty-week class at Great Shelford on 'The Landscape and Natural History of East Anglia', meeting for two hours each time, was charged at £22 (about £58), or £15 for concessions. A course led by the same tutor, Roland Randall, at Letchworth in the same year cost a little more at £26, but had an even more competitive concession rate of £14.[14] During the 1980s the Board was 'under pressure' to increase the proportion of the fees that it took from local centres, which was not easy given the financial pressures on many of the centres themselves, particularly in rural areas.[15]

The 1980s saw an expansion of named Certificate programmes, following the lead of the existing Certificate in Local History, which had been developed in the late 1960s (see chapter 3). These led to named awards, and were in some respect the successors of the tutorial classes that had continued to decline through the 1970s and into the new decade. By 1989-90 there were just four tutorial classes running under the Board's auspices but, according to a report at one staff meeting, 'their values were still alive' on Certificate courses.[16] Certificates were not usually offered in conjunction with the WEA, but took the place of tutorial classes in supporting 'learning of the highest quality'. A new Certificate in Landscape History and Field Archaeology began in Impington in 1980-1, and recruited 29 students, though only 19 of these took the 'written test' at the end of their first year.[17] Others followed: by 1985-6 there were 24 tutorial and Certificate classes across 14 centres in the region, with a total of 317 'effective' students. There were named Certificates in 'The History of European Painting', in ecology and landscape, in criminology, and in counselling and groupwork, as well as local history, offered at various centres. These were mostly in the larger towns of the region – Cambridge, Norwich, Ipswich, King's Lynn, Bedford and Thetford – but some smaller centres were also used, such as Henham and Thorpe-le-Soken in Essex. Some attracted small numbers – only around eight each year for the counselling certificate at Cambridge – but others were usually quite buoyant, particularly those dealing with landscape studies.[18] Staffing levels made some programmes difficult to resource, and in the late 1980s the Certificates in European painting and criminology were 'in abeyance'.[19] Nevertheless, there was a strategic determination to provide more such programmes, with a standard three-year structure; they were seen to 'fill an important gap between other forms of adult education and full-time internal university study'.[20]

Students on Certificate programmes were encouraged to read very widely and to produce substantial amounts of written work, culminating in a long dissertation. For a third-year Certificate in Local History course taught by Chris Barringer and local historian Paul Richards at Thoresby College, King's Lynn, the reading list amounted to well over 30 items – delivered in the ubiquitous book-boxes – including 'broad-sweep' texts, histories of population, protest and the church, and a number of local studies of East Anglia.[21] Dissertations were to be 10,000 words, and the smaller numbers on the course – just nine in this particular case – allowed for individual supervision meetings as students worked on their own projects.[22]

The teaching of Certificates and tutorial classes was largely in the hands of full-time staff tutors, but most extension students took shorter courses: few were willing to commit to the assessment demands of a longer course. In 1985-6, as well as the 24 tutorial and Certificate courses there were a further 132 sessional courses – 29 of which were discontinued due to lack of students – and a further 21 extension lecture courses on the original nineteenth-century model. Total student numbers on the extension programme had fallen to 3,220 from a high of just over 5,000 at the start of the decade. The number of centres, too, had fallen to 51, well below its earlier peak.[23] Moreover, a larger number of courses were shorter, ten weeks in length, and these were proving more popular than the longer ones. This presented difficulties of scheduling: Michael Allen had earlier reminded the Local Centres Union of

> the problems in equating requests for courses with the availability of tutors. One difficult area was requests by centres for one term courses by a staff tutor. Unless this could be matched by an identical request from another centre for the second term, this type of request had a low priority in view of the need to make full use of teaching time for staff tutors.[24]

In 1985-6 the single best-attended course was in St Albans, where 64 'effective' students were taught 'Praying and Helping Others to Pray' by octogenarian retired bishop George Appleton. St Albans was a diocesan city with a Christian Study Centre, at which 11 of its 13 Board courses were taught, mostly by men of the cloth, although archaeologist Martin Biddle also contributed to a course on 'Archaeology and the Monastic Life'.[25] Across the region, local history and landscape studies remained predominant in the extension programme, alongside art and music appreciation, and a steady stream of courses on psychology and the natural sciences.

Although the extension courses continued to include some in small villages with a tradition of association with the Board, this element of the programme was in decline, and the presence in many places was not what it had been. Michael Allen recalls that

> We could see that the traditions of extension, the evening classes, were going to have to change. We were going to be focusing more completely on communities which actually existed in education, like the village colleges. So we would continue to build strong programmes around [Cambridge] and in places where there were educational institutions, such as Letchworth, which were very well run. But there is no doubt that the writing was on the wall, and that the government grants-in-aid were going to dry up.[26]

The process of contraction and consolidation was slow but steady for the remainder of the 1980s: in 1988-9, there were 16 tutorial and Certificate classes, 99 sessional courses and 55 'extension and short sessional' courses, together attracting around 3,000 students (see table 5.1).[27] In fact, the number of centres actually increased, as new courses were tried in the second half of the 1980s in villages such as Stanton in north-west Suffolk; but in Cambridgeshire there was indeed, as Allen pointed out, a growing focus on the village colleges as locations for courses: Bassingbourn and Comberton hosted two each, and Bottisham, Burwell, Cottenham, Gamlingay, Impington, Linton and Sawston one each.[28] The courses met with varying success, but in 1989-90 a remarkable 150 students attended a one-day course at Impington, on 'Walter Gropius and Impington Village College': the college was built by Gropius and Maxwell Fry, and was an important influence on post-war school architecture.[29] Where there was a strong local interest in a particular topic, it was possible to enlist large numbers for one-off courses like this.

Some places managed to maintain and strengthen their association with university extension over longer periods. One example was the small village of Boxford, in Suffolk, which provides a striking indication of the continuing demand for university adult education in the second half of the 1980s. One 20-week class ran each year, on a wide range of topics and each with a different tutor. In 1984-5 'Documentary Film 1900-1960', taught by Stuart Sillars – who worked both for the Board and the Open University and specialised in English – attracted 16 'effective' students. In the following year 29 attended the landscape historian Peter Warner's 'Archaeology of East Anglia', and in 1986-7 there were 24 for staff tutor Jack Herbert's 'Landscape into Literature'. Then in 1987-8 there was a more modest attendance of 10 students for 'The Growth of the Novel' (tutor not known), but in 1988-9 there were two courses: 18 attended 'English Literature at the Turn of the Century', taught by Janet

Bottoms on Monday evenings, and 30 'Suffolk Churches', led by Canon John Fitch, on Tuesdays. In 1989-90, there were no fewer than three courses: 20 weeks on 'English Literature: Waste Land or Brave New World' (Bottoms again; 14 students), and 10 weeks on each of 'China Yesterday and Tomorrow' (Keith Bradbury; 30 students) and 'The Treasures of Florence' (Stella Dodd; 35 students). Then a remarkable 69 students attended 'The Social History of Suffolk' in 1990-1, taught over 20 weeks by David Dymond himself.[30] Dymond's Tuesday class rather overshadowed an eighteenth-century literature course, taught on Monday evenings with only 10 students, but Boxford continued to run successful and popular extension courses into the mid-1990s. Of course, it is likely that many, if not most, of those who took part in the courses were repeat attenders – one recollection suggests that '60% of any course' were in this category[31] – but this record of success in a small village (2011 population: 1,221) is nevertheless really quite striking.

The great majority of students in the local centres attended out of interest and enjoyment. Boxford may have been exceptional, but many other centres succeeded regularly in attracting large numbers to Cambridge extension courses. This was often down to a single active individual who liaised with the Board: Vanessa Nedderman, who managed some elements of the extension programme in the early 1990s, recalls that 'a lot of those centres had someone who was really pivotal, who really made things happen'.[32] At Letchworth, for example, the key figure was Roy Evans, warden of the Settlement since the 1960s, who remained in the job until his retirement in 2001, and who worked closely with the Board to provide courses that attracted a reliable stream of students, particularly in local history. There was also a tradition at the Settlement of taking courses to nearby villages, where, as at Boxford, an enthusiastic group of regulars could keep adult education going for many years.[33] Nedderman remarks further that,

> living in a rural community now, I can see how that worked. If you have somebody who's really energetic, they can get things going. … It becomes a social activity as well as an educational one. I suspect that at a lot of local centres the social and community aspect was as important as anything else.[34]

Indeed, it is possible that this aspect limited the extent of pedagogical innovation in some subject areas: although local history students were used to working collaboratively on research projects under the direction of an involved staff tutor such as Lionel Munby or David Dymond, and geology students did the same with Gillian Sheail, some tutors encountered students who preferred to listen to 'chalk and talk', particularly when the 'talk' was lively and the lecturer charismatic. Nedderman suspects that, by the turn of the 1990s, 'in a lot of places, the courses had become much more entertainment' than education.[35]

Teaching on the extension programme could be 'quite a lonely job, in many ways'.[36] Nedderman recalls that 'every year when I was trying to put the programme together, I was trying to persuade tutors to drive off to Downham Market for ten or 20 weeks', and this was not always easy.[37] The more remote the locations to which a staff or panel tutor travelled, the more challenging the job could become. Two-hour classes sometimes began at 8pm, and some students would stay and talk with the tutor afterwards, which made for many late nights.[38] Even where a resident tutor was responsible for a smaller section of the region, such as Norfolk or Suffolk, the distances travelled in a term could still be significant. In the autumn term of 1989-90, for example, Chris Barringer taught on Wednesday evenings at Swaffham, Thursday mornings in Norwich and Thursday evenings in Aylsham.[39] Lionel Munby, too, travelled significant distances on a regular basis.[40] The schedule could make things particularly challenging for those with young families. Mark Bailey, who began work for the Board in the early 1990s, recalls a time when, in addition to having a young child and college responsibilities, he was teaching three or four evenings a week during term-time. 'I was dashing home for half an hour … and then I was off to Biddenham or driving down to Letchworth', he remembers, working the 'antisocial hours' that were often the lot of the extra-mural tutor: 'it was great fun, and I learned a huge amount, but it was unsustainable'.[41]

Acutely conscious of the changes in grant funding for extension courses, the Board was actively seeking to further diversify its activities, and with them its income streams, in the 1980s. One area of expansion within the extension programme was residential courses at Madingley Hall, of which there were more than 100 a year by the mid-1980s, mostly weekend courses but with a few lasting four or seven days. (Table 5.1 shows the numbers on these, and on other courses, in the late 1980s.) Some were organised as add-ons to weekly extension courses, and over 2,000 students attended these each year, with numbers varying from more than 50 for an Alberni 'string quartet masterclass' in 1985-6 to just 12 for medieval palaeography in the same year, although this small class was felt to be 'the optimum number' for such an intricate subject.

Table 5.1
Summary of courses and student numbers, 1988-9

	Courses (number)	**Students (number)**	**Students (% of total)**	**Students (% of regional programme students)**
Residential courses (2 to 7 days)	126	2,613	29.46	40.73
Foreign study tours (5 to 10 days)	3	77	0.87	1.20
Day schools	14	411	4.63	6.41
Total of residential and day schools	*143*	*3,101*	*35.00*	*48.33*
Tutorial and certificate classes (24 to 30 meetings per year for 3 years)	16	251	2.83	3.91
Sessional courses (20 meetings)	99	1,554	17.52	24.22
Extension and short sessional courses (10 to 12 meetings)	55	1,240	13.98	19.33
Total of courses for the public	**313**	**6,416**	**72.34**	**100.00**
Continuing education courses	53	1,312	14.79	--
International courses	17	1,411	15.91	--
Grand total	**383**	**8,869**	**100.00**	--

Source: annual report.

The disciplinary balance was again heavily slanted towards the arts and humanities, with rather fewer courses on natural sciences or psychology. An attempt was made to promote more science courses, and some evidence of student demand was identified.[42] Meanwhile, the residential programme, in particular, was designed in such as a way as to ‘provide a sequence of linked topics throughout the year', catering for the many students who returned to study at weekends again and again; a series of courses on classical languages and civilisation was one example of this.[43]

Residential courses were consistently popular: in the 1984-5 academic year, only one was cancelled due to low registrations, and some received twice as many applications as there were places.[44] Fees were low, just £44 for a typical weekend course in the same year (about £140 today) for seven sessions with food and accommodation at Madingley Hall, and some impressive external tutors were recruited to teach. Christopher P. Driver, for example, a former editor of the *Good Food Guide*, taught courses on seventeenth-century food and on the history of British restaurant cuisine since 1940, and Peter Luff – previously manager of Edward Heath's private office and later a government minister – taught 'Behind the Scenes in Parliament'.[45] According to one account, the residential students were around 60% female, with an average age in the forties and many retired people. The 'cosy bar' was a particular attraction, and the courses were 'definitely something people on their own [could] do happily, and not feel in any way conspicuous', according to a female student who was one of many repeat attenders. On this occasion she was taking a course on antique furniture, taught by a local antique dealer, Martin Beazor. This included an excursion to the Victoria and Albert Museum; and some other weekend courses, too, managed to squeeze a field trip of some sort into the already tight schedule.[46] Many of the long-serving staff tutors – including Lionel Munby, who had retired a few years before but still taught on some courses – continued to take part in the residential programme in the mid-1980s.[47]

Students clearly enjoyed the 'residentials', especially at Madingley Hall itself. A feature of weekends at the Hall was the mixing of students on different courses, as it was not unusual for two or three to run at once. Students would arrive late on Friday afternoon, perhaps have a drink in the bar, and would be given dinner in the hall: 'Latin grace and wonderful food by candlelight'.[48] A fairly typical account of a weekend course in 1989 – in this case 'Family History', taught by Joanna Martin – explained that '[t]he course members were a good normal mixed bag from as far away as Somerset and Yorkshire. We got on well and when the time came to leave on Sunday people were saying what a shame it was to meet for so short a time.'[49] Much of the time was spent eating, '[m]aking a pig of yourself with four huge meals in forty-eight hours', and a lot was packed into the seven sessions, before the course finished after lunch on the Sunday. Most students took part actively in the learning, although

> One little lady, a regular at Madingley by all accounts, fell soundly asleep through every class, only to wake up in time to ask intelligent questions. Yet she seemed to be enjoying her weekend and was planning another in a few weeks' time.[50]

Some tutors – and perhaps students, too – thought weekend courses were less focused and academically rigorous than regular weekly classes. One tutor, who worked for the Board in the 1990s, felt that sometimes 'this [was] just a country hotel holiday for people … with a bit of learning thrown in'.[51]

Nevertheless, it was residential courses that were expanding in the 1980s: the number doubled in the first half of the decade, and by its end (see table 5.1) they accounted for more than a third of overall student numbers on the extension programme – and, if one-day courses were included, nearly a half (48.33%).[52] In the following year numbers outstripped those on weekly courses for the first time (3,230 students against 2,978), although of course the teaching hours were fewer, given that most residential courses lasted only a single weekend.[53] This was itself an attraction, and the Board emphasised that, in contrast, '[t]he commitment of adults attending … longer term courses was considerable'; it amounted to a whole 'normal working week' over two terms.[54] Meanwhile, the one-day courses, introduced for the first time in 1981-2, remained a relatively minor element of the extension programme, but were seen as useful 'in testing potential interest in new subjects which might be included in the residential programme'.[55]

There was also a smaller programme of international study tours, some of which were very ambitious. Two three-week trips to China were planned for 1986, although only one of these appears to have taken place: this was 'Ancient China', led by Helen Espir, an expert on oriental porcelain. Priced at £1,659 (the equivalent of around £4,000 today), this was attended by ten students, and involved visits to the Great Wall, the Terracotta Army at Xi'an and the imperial tombs from the Song dynasty.[56] In the same year David Trump took 21 students to explore 'The Archaeology of Sardinia' (fee £495); architectural tours went to Venice, Tuscany and Transylvania; and 18 participants studied ornithology in southern Morocco; but a planned visit to Macchu Pichu and other sites in 'Ancient Peru' failed to attract enough students, and did not take place.[57] By the end of the decade, it was still proving difficult to enlist students on ambitious trips, for example to Russia or Swaziland, but 30 students went to Pompeii in February 1989, another 16 to study 'Natural History in Portugal' in April of the same year, and 29 on an archaeological visit to Cyprus in April and May.[58] Even in the mid-1980s it was clear that the international study tour programme would not be expanded, and by 1990 some were running with only two or three students. A handful of enthusiasts still went on the tours – all in Britain or Europe – into the 1990s, but the cost and administrative effort of organising them was becoming too great for both students and staff.[59]

Some of the regular extension courses – in geology, landscape studies or local history, for example – lent themselves to excursions, and these might take place at weekends. These field trips required meticulous planning, some of which was undertaken at the local centres: Roy Evans at Letchworth was a very effective organiser of buses and tea urns, for example. Gillian Sheail, too, was well aware of the importance of planning ahead for access to toilets. On one occasion she had arranged to meet members of a class at West Runton – between Sheringham and Cromer on the coast – and had told the group that there were public toilets in the car park. Fortunately, though, as she recalls,

> two weeks before, my husband and I went to reconnoitre … I always did this, though it wasn't paid for, but I couldn't take a group of 20 or more students without making sure that everything was OK. When we got to the car park, there was a big notice which said 'These toilets will be closed for the season from 30 September onwards'. And the date of the field trip to study the features of the cliff and beach (which depended on the tide) was on 3 October. So I thought, 'nothing ventured, nothing gained', and when I got back I rang the local authority and said 'do you think you could keep the toilets open for the group coming that day?' and to my surprise they said yes.[60]

Student demographics created additional challenges for outdoor field trips. Gillian Sheail worked with many elderly students from the Bedford Retirement Centre, for some of whom walking, 'especially on uneven ground', and climbing over stiles was difficult. Often detours had to be planned, and occasionally early coach pick-ups for some members of the group. In addition to day-long field trips, she took her Bedford students on a long weekend course in Yorkshire, where challenges included descending a 'long craggy drop' to the bottom of a valley, while on one occasion they were divided into 'shorter route' and 'longer route' groups. The students clearly enjoyed this course – the weather helped – but the distance from Bedford meant a 'tedious coach journey' in both directions.[61]

The 'project' work that had been emphasised in the Russell Report and had been an important element of Lionel Munby's local history teaching, in particular, continued in the 1980s, although it involved only a small proportion of students on the East Anglian programmes. Munby himself continued to work with some local history groups, and David Dymond extended this activity into Suffolk. According to one of his successors at Cambridge, Mark Bailey, Dymond 'conveyed a passion, excitement and infectious enthusiasm, which brought history to life and spawned various local research groups that outlived his courses and went on to produce some excellent research'. These included detailed studies of Lavenham in Suffolk, itself a strong centre of Cambridge extension teaching.[62] Similar things happened in other subjects, too. Popular courses generated self-sustaining groups, supported by staff and panel tutors, and in due course these groups produced publications and developed their own independent educational activities. When Gillian Sheail first taught at Bedford Retirement Centre, there was little demand for her subject, geology, and she ran a taster course which recruited only about 10 students. However, in the following year a 20-week course, to everyone's surprise, attracted 60 students, and had to be run twice. The course proved to be so popular that it became a three-year tutorial class, and eventually a research group that published a town trail booklet on the geology of the building stones in Bedford.[63]

Subjects taught in university adult education continued to generate interdisciplinary interests and to evolve somewhat independently from the disciplinary traditions of other university departments. Local history and 'local studies' have been mentioned in previous chapters, but landscape history also involved tutors from different disciplinary backgrounds, and was later described by one tutor as

> an excellent example of a multidisciplinary subject, allowing students to explore the physical past through a variety of interconnecting and fascinating fields. Incorporating at its core the discipline of landscape archaeology and history, the subject also touches significantly upon [other aspects of] local archaeology and history, geology and ecology, vernacular and church architecture, and place-name studies.[64]

The study of landscape also linked to art history and literature, as in Jack Herbert's 'Landscape into Literature' course, and it could be a way in to studying more explicitly 'scientific' subjects. Gillian Sheail remembers that, at March, where the Board had a long tradition of teaching local history, landscape studies was taught to an initially reluctant group who 'said "we've never done science before, we're not scientists"'. By the end of the course, 'one of the ladies came up to me and said "I thought this was going to be the most boring course I could take, and now I carry a magnifying glass in my handbag to look more closely at the rocks as I go round"'.[65]

It can be difficult to obtain detailed information about the demographic characteristics of students on the extension programme at this time. However, some was collected in a survey carried out in February 1986 as part of an examination of the 'nature and scope' of the Board's activity funded by a special grant from the Department of Education and Science (DES). Questionnaires were circulated to all students on extension courses at the time, and 62% of 'effective' students filled them out, an impressive response rate yielding 1,810 returns.[66] Of these students across the Cambridge extra-mural region, 31% were men – a little lower than the 36% observed in a similar study of the University of London's programme at around the same time – and 49% were retired. The high proportion of retired people was reflected in the age distribution of the students (see table 5.2): a majority were aged 60 and over, and there were only a handful of under-40s. Women predominated in most age groups, and 12% of the sample described themselves as housewives.[67] Differences in the age distribution by gender were not particularly significant, but there were more men than women in their thirties, the only age group where male students had a numerical preponderance.

None of this would have surprised the Board, which had already noted that the majority of students (in fact, it was the vast majority) were aged over 40 and that many were retired; but this did represent a change from earlier in the twentieth century.[68] The Cambridge students also had a different age profile from those in the London extension programme, of whom 28% were aged 60 or over and 38% (versus 20% in the Cambridge region) aged 30 to 49. This partly reflected the different demographics of London and East Anglia, but it did point to a possible untapped 'market' among younger age groups for Cambridge extension courses.[69] This point was reinforced by a comparison with national data from the early 1980s, covering *all* types of adult education,

Table 5.2
Percentage of regional programme students in each age group, total and by gender, February 1986

Age	All students	Women	Men
20-29	4	4	3
30-39	5	3	10
40-49	15	16	23
50-59	23	25	19
60-70 [*sic*]	35	36	32
70+	18	16	23
Total	100	100	100

N = 1,810 = 62% of 2,920 'effective students.

Source: adapted from 'Nature and Scope', pp. 30-2. The exact figures as presented are not given, and the percentages have been recalculated.

which showed that almost a third of men and more than a quarter of women on courses were aged under 25, and only 3% of men and 9% of women were 65 and over.[70] At Cambridge, the DES-funded inquiry identified a demographic that the Board might be able to attract, comprising people aged 20 to 50, and particularly those who wanted in due course to advance to higher levels of study, perhaps with the Open University.[71]

The occupational backgrounds of students were surveyed at the same time, and it was found that 40% were in – or had retired from – 'professional' occupations. Another 51% were in or from 'skilled' occupations, and just 9% were in the 'unskilled' category. (It is assumed that, since the percentages add up to 100, these figures excluded the 'housewives'.) This differed somewhat from the national picture: across the whole gamut of adult education, 19% of male participants and 17% of women were in social classes A and B, the professional and 'higher professional' classes, with a substantial majority in both genders (more than 60%) in the C1/C2 groupings, i.e. 'lower middle class' and 'skilled manual'.[72] Although the Cambridge student demographics were not so divergent in this respect as in relation to age, it was recognised that scope might exist to broaden the appeal of the extension programme in some respects. Again, the growing opportunities for mature students in other universities might in turn provide the Board with a role in supporting this transition.

In terms of their educational background, Cambridge extension students were 'unusually well-educated'. Thirty-four percent were university graduates, with 4% having higher degrees or doctorates; another 37% had completed post-secondary education of some kind – including secretarial, nursing and technical training – and only 1% had not finished a secondary school education.[73] (Universal and compulsory secondary education had been introduced following the Education Act of 1944.) Almost a half – 43% of students – were enrolled in another adult education course at the same time; these might be others provided by the Board or WEA, or local education authority courses on a very different subject, including 'yoga, slimnastics, arts or crafts'.[74] The relatively high levels of prior educational attainment are, again, not particularly surprising given the nature of the courses and the academic orientation of the extension programme. It was suggested that here, too, there was an opportunity, in this case to strengthen the academic rigour of the Board's courses:

> The social and educational backgrounds of Board students suggests [*sic*] that the student body have the capacity to respond favourably to greater academic challenge. The Board provide many courses which are 'introductory' by nature – introductions to particular periods of history, appreciation of particular cultures, familiarisation with aspects of the local environment, and so on. The [B]oard should place more emphasis on approaches which provide students with the opportunity to go beyond introduction, familiarisation and appreciation and to improve skills of critical analysis and systematic interpretation as well as promote the desire for new knowledge.[75]

In retrospect, this recommendation prefigured the near-universal accreditation of extension courses in the 1990s, but it is not clear that it was acted upon immediately, although the Board did continue to promote its existing Certificate courses, which had 271 students by the end of the decade, together with 76 taking the few remaining tutorial classes run in conjunction with the WEA.[76]

*

The summer vacation residential schools for 'foreign students' were 'continuing vigorously' in the early 1980s. The speed of expansion was such that 'the demands on the time of five administrators [were] almost too much', and by the end of the decade the size of the team had expanded to eight.[77] The main four-week course – attended by 331 students in 1983, 426 in 1984 and 425 in 1986 – was much the same as in the 1970s: an intensive programme, focusing on British topics, particularly English literature and history, with some international politics and relations included too.[78] Students could attend a series of plenary lectures given by Cambridge academics and others on a huge range of topics, and many undertook written assessment to gain credit at their home institutions.[79] Cambridge was developing partnerships with specific universities, particularly in the USA, but in 1982-3 the majority of students were from non-English-speaking countries.[80] The programme was directed by one of the Board's assistant secretaries: first Martin Horrox and later Richard Mason, a philosopher and former civil servant who left a prominent post in the Welsh Development Agency to move to Cambridge in the mid-1980s. Both made sustained efforts to strengthen the links that the Board already enjoyed with US universities.[81] Horrox and Michael Allen 'used to go … to the United States in the winter, and beat the drum': a particularly successful effort was with the University of Utah, which by the end of the decade was sending 65 students a year to the summer school.[82] An even stronger relationship was with Florida International University, which recruited students 'from universities and colleges throughout the state system', and was sending more than 100 students by 1990.[83]

The changing shape and size of the summer programme resulted in the development of more specialised content in the second half of the 1980s: a three-week course specifically on English literature was offered from 1986, and on art history from 1987. From 1983 the rather old-fashioned name 'Vacation Course for Foreign Students' was dropped in favour of 'International Summer Schools' – the plural was significant, given the expanding variety of provision and the rapid increase in student numbers.[84] A series of joint programmes, often developed on a bespoke basis for individual American universities, added to the complexity of the administration. In 1985-6, alongside the main four-week course, there was an 'International Summer School term 2' with 186 students, the new English literature course with 99, and two large three-week programmes taught with the University of California Los Angeles (UCLA) with 134 and 126 students respectively. Smaller programmes were run with the University of Florida at Gainesville, the University of Texas, the American Institute for Foreign Study, Villa Maria College and James Madison College.[85] Total student numbers amounted to 1,525, calculated as 23,324 student-days or 81,684 student-hours, all a significant increase on the previous year.[86]

The summer schools strengthened the Board's relationship with many Cambridge colleges: Newnham and Selwyn had been accommodating students since the 1920s, and in some years as many as ten colleges were involved.[87] Michael Allen recalls that 'we maximised the use of college accommodation in the long vacation … the colleges liked it, it was a good source of revenue, and it was reliable'. Accommodation was cheap – around £19 (equivalent to less than £50 today) a night, according to one recollection – but often basic: like Madingley Hall itself, en-suite rooms were a rarity in the colleges, which at this time had not developed their facilities to the standards that would be expected for conferences and other paying guests.[88] The summer school demographics – most students were much younger than those typically on the extension programme – meant that behavioural issues sometimes arose: Allen remembers that, on one occasion, 'the Master of Christ's College told me to get those French students out of his college before the morning. They had tipped some water out of a window and some of it had nearly hit the Master on his evening stroll.'[89]

The International Summer Schools were intended to be taught at first-year undergraduate level: again, this was similar to many of the Board's extension courses, and some of the staff tutors contributed to the summer programme. David Dymond, Chris Barringer and David Trump took part, as well as Alan Stripp, who spoke about his wartime code-breaking experiences to alumni groups from UCLA and the University of Texas.[90] As with the extension programme, tutors had a 'free rein' to teach in the way that they wanted, and to 'decide what they wanted to teach, within reason'. This freedom also applied to the planning of the programme as a whole: Sarah Ormrod, who joined the team in 1987, remembers that 'one thing that has been wonderful is the freedom to decide what we put on, what we have developed'.[91] On the other hand, it was also vital to match supply to demand, and some topics and individuals were more popular than others. Over time the British – and indeed local – interests of some of the more established staff tutors were increasingly out of step with the specific requirements of US universities and with a growing tendency for the programmes to cover more international topics. Tutors therefore needed to be drawn from a wider pool.[92]

Not everything that was attempted on the summer programmes was successful, at least not initially. The art history course did not meet its target in its first year, although 52 students attended, and in the following year numbers fell to a precarious 30. However, by 1989 numbers had recovered to 77, and it had 'a secure place in the programme'. Numbers rose still further in the following year.[93] Another new course, in 'legal and constitutional history' offered in conjunction with Duke University in 1987, ran with 23 students, but this was a one-off.[94] In the following years, similar joint programmes were also struggling: by 1990, the courses run with UCLA, the University of Texas and other American universities were attracting fewer students, and the Board was refocusing its efforts on its own programmes rather than those run in partnership with others.[95] It was becoming clear that many universities, including some in the USA, were running their own summer programmes, which put pressure on Cambridge and some other UK providers. All this meant that the summer programmes had to evolve, and to focus on areas of strength: as Sarah Ormrod has remarked, 'we are fully responsible for the consequences of changes, and miscalculations can be extremely expensive'.[96]

As this comment emphasises, the financial contribution that the International Summer Schools made to the Board was important but often uncertain. As much as three-quarters of the revenue from the schools was handed over to the colleges in return for accommodation, and in the mid-1980s the full cost of increases in accommodation charges was not passed on to the students. Moreover, the 'surplus' that the summer programmes usually made came from a small number of the courses in each year. A report in the mid-1980s declared that '[t]he volume of international work would need to increase two- or three-fold before it could provide an income on which the Board could rely from year to year', and such an increase would be limited by the availability of college rooms and the size of the university's teaching estate.[97] Student numbers did in fact expand significantly in the second half of the 1980s, reaching a total of 1,573 in 1989, of whom 688 (43.7%) were on joint programmes with other universities. More than a third of these joint-programme students were from UCLA, but this relationship would end in the next few years, as would the partnership with the University of Texas.[98] Overall numbers would not be sustainable through the 1990s – for reasons explored in the next chapter – but the summer programmes remained an important element in Cambridge's extramural provision.

Pedagogical approaches on the summer schools were the subject of debate, negotiation and experimentation in the 1980s. The sheer size of the programmes meant that they could not replicate the traditional college supervision system, which involved one-to-one or very small-group teaching, but American universities in the early part of the decade were asking for an experience that mirrored the 'pattern of study' followed by full-time Cambridge undergraduates. The 'older universities in England' were seen as embodying '"traditional" education values' and supporting high standards of learning and attainment, and there was an experiment with individual supervisions on two of the summer courses in 1983. The outcome of this, though, was that

> The Board will continue ... to offer lecture classes as the staple of any short course for foreign students, as this is the best means of providing the broader view of a subject (and a characteristically English view) which students from abroad cannot hope to achieve from their own reading.[99]

This view may have underestimated the capacities of some 'foreign students', and it certainly reflected the Anglo-centric content of the courses, which would come under increasing challenge in the later 1980s and into the 1990s. Given the substantial student numbers, however, any replication of college-style teaching across the board would clearly have been impracticable. There was a small 'honours option' that did involve weekly supervisions, but this did not have large numbers of students.[100]

*

The industrial and 'vocational' sides of the Board's activities were also expanding and changing in the 1980s. The summer programme for IBM Europe, based at Churchill College but organised by the Board and dating back to the 1960s, continued to draw around 36 students each year, although its duration was reduced for cost reasons from seven weeks to five in the mid-1980s.[101] Members of the core Board staff – including Michael Allen, Leslie James and Alan Stripp – were all involved in the IBM programme in various ways, ensuring a link with other areas of extramural activity, and the programme retained its unusual and deliberate focus on 'non-vocational' content. In 1987, for example, the theme of the course was 'Understanding the Future'; it was led by Leslie James and Richard Mason, and involved 33 lecturers from across Cambridge and beyond.[102] These included Michael Allen and staff tutors Chris Barringer, Jack Herbert, Anthony Storey and Alan Stripp, as well as fellows of numerous colleges and some external contributors ranging from a superintendent in the Northamptonshire Police and a consultant cardiothoracic surgeon from Sheffield. The heavily timetabled programme opened with introductory tours of the colleges led by Barringer, and featured a series of 12 lectures on international politics by James, six on social psychology by Storey and another half-dozen on 'Exploring the Universe' by Dr S. A. Mitton, a fellow of St Edmund's. Stripp and others covered music, and there were visits to the Royal Opera House, the Aldeburgh Festival concert at St Edmundsbury Cathedral and a production of *Twelfth Night* at the Royal Shakespeare Theatre in Stratford. One-off lectures were as varied as 'Population' – by E. A. Wrigley, founder of the Cambridge Group for the History of Population and Social Structure – 'China Today' by R. P. Sloss of Darwin College, and 'An Introduction to New Towns' by Mac Dowdy, a Wolfson historian whose lecture was followed by an afternoon visit to Peterborough. The students – from 19 different countries – were given meals at Madingley Hall, Corpus Christi College and Churchill.

This approach was not entirely suitable to the emerging economic environment of the 1980s, when global, national and local developments all influenced the relationship between the University of Cambridge and the business world. The publication in 1985 of *The Cambridge Phenomenon*, a report by Segal Quince and Partners – a new 'research and analysis company' based in Cambridge – drew attention to ongoing developments in and around Cambridge itself, and to the potential of partnerships between universities and industries. The Cambridge science park had been established in the mid-1970s, and the Cambridge Technology Association in 1979, and there was a fast-growing high-technology sector in and around the city.[103] These developments presented the university with opportunities to work with industry in both scientific and managerial research and education, although Segal Quince did not discuss the work of the Board of Extra-Mural Studies in this context.[104] There was a brief mention of continuing education as an 'initiative' that universities might take in this area – the University of Salford was the preferred example – but the scale and scope of the Cambridge Board's existing activities was below the radar of the report.[105] The Board, though, did respond to *The*

Cambridge Phenomenon, noting that it had 'aroused national interest in the transfer of technology between universities and industry in general',[106] and it responded in new ways that involved further collaboration with other parts of the parent university.

Whereas it was clear that the IBM course fitted 'more readily into the provision of courses in the liberal arts than into a programme of professional management training', there were also some cautious attempts to move into what was generally referred to as 'post-experience vocational education' in the mid-1980s.[107] Some of these were not successful: an attempt in 1985 to run a senior managers' seminar did not attract enough participants, and in the following year a three-day residential course on 'finance, marketing and other practical business topics' had only 12 students, and was not run again. Two intensive two-day courses for 'industrialists' on robotics and automated manufacturing had been staged in 1984, and in 1987 the Board worked with the University of Virginia Graduate Business School to run 'a typical, middle-level American practical business course'.[108] Response to this within the university was 'disappointing', although it was scheduled to run again in 1988 and 1989. Assistant secretary Richard Mason commissioned some market research, which identified a possible 'corner of the market' for one-day non-residential courses on 'high level' issues in finance and marketing, but this would involve entering a competitive market and was not expected to be a significant generator of income.[109] For Mason, the key issue was that the Board had 'no staff competent in business or management studies: a field where a knowledge of supply and demand in the market can be unusually crucial', and the bottom line was that 'financial returns can only be expected as a consequence of investments in money and staff time at a much higher level than in the past'.[110]

The opportunity to make these investments was provided by a new government 'pump-priming initiative', established in 1983 by a diversion of a proportion of the Responsible Body grant. The PICKUP (Professional, Industrial and Commercial Updating) scheme – from 1985 onwards – gave contracts to universities on a short-term and 'extremely interventionist' basis to promote post-experience vocational education. It was a clear and deliberate attempt to encourage universities to support a stronger focus on human capital development.[111] Some obtained funding to appoint a 'PICKUP Officer', who would identify opportunities to expand work in the continuing vocational area; this could, and did, include both established extramural departments and specific disciplinary areas within universities. Such activity, in some universities, was seen as a threat to existing traditions of adult education, and in some cases the PICKUP staff were seen as a 'threat' or even a 'pest'. As one historian has explained,

> negativity arose … from the view of some traditional, subject-based adult educators, that the content of [continuing vocational education] programmes was superficial, not at university level, and not demanding enough given the brevity of many [such] courses. In short, [continuing vocational education] was seen as alien to the 'great tradition' of liberal adult education, and little more than the narrow and plodding industrial training inflicted on generations of workers and working-class young people by unenlightened employers and colleges.[112]

Cambridge was initially reluctant to apply for PICKUP funding,[113] but in due course an officer, Eve Williamson, was appointed. There is little record of 'negativity' towards her work, which identified various opportunities for extending post-experience vocational courses. These included a new open-access learning exchange centre at the Cambridge science park, 'science and technology updating' for teachers and college lecturers, and more advanced training in robotics and biotechnology for industrial companies.[114]

The most significant outcome, in the longer term, from PICKUP was the establishment of the Cambridge Advanced Programme for Industry, later the Cambridge Programme for Industry (CPI). This was established in 1988 and run under the Board's auspices for the next decade. Its first director, Christopher Padfield, had worked in industry and held a PhD in engineering from Cambridge, and he was joined by a marketing manager, Polly Courtice, a Cambridge history graduate with a marketing background. The CPI was based in the Faculty of Engineering – initially in 'one room and a broom cupboard' – and its aim, according to Padfield, was 'to integrate management with technical and professional matters, as an aside to competitive development in business and industry'.[115] This was done through collaboration with other University of Cambridge departments, and involved a range of external experts. Early courses included some in advanced technologies such as air flow in jet engines and the mathematical modelling of risk, and by 1990 there were 32 scheduled courses, ranging from computing to metallurgy and superconductivity, as well as data evaluation, human genome mapping and food technology.[116] Courtice remembers that identifying the market for courses was difficult: 'we had to spend an awful lot of time working out precisely what it was that industry wanted and that Cambridge could provide'.[117] Padfield emphasised to the Board that the positioning of the CPI was 'an extremely time-consuming process', but he expressed optimism that the Programme would be a success: 'the provision of vocational continuing education represents no pot of gold, but … it should be possible to develop a substantial programme that will, taken overall, be self-financing'.[118] The CPI aimed that *all* its courses should be self-financing by their second year.

In its early years the CPI aligned itself with the emerging regional needs identified in *The Cambridge Phenomenon*. Padfield and Courtice recall that the Cambridge technology sector was finding it difficult to 'maintain the learning' of its staff, and as a result the CPI 'was expected to have a relationship with local companies'. This was in part a matter of 'helping [them] to stay current with the latest thinking', but also of supporting relationships between them, which *The Cambridge Phenomenon* had identified as an important element that could be developed: '[t]here is … a strong interest in learning from the experiences of others'.[119] As a result a key early priority, as Padfield recalls, for the CPI was the provision of places and opportunities for leaders in local companies to meet:

> our products represented quite a spectrum – from very advanced technological courses, of which there were not many (and proved a difficult area to operate in), through to dinner seminars for local business leaders, which we set up randomly and chaired in such a way that it was possible for anyone of any level of seniority to speak. That was I think just as much appreciated as some of the more technological enterprises.[120]

For the most part, though, the main 'clients' for post-experience vocational education would be large national and multinational companies, and the CPI worked with external organisations, notably the Foundation for Management Education – a pioneering institution that had supported the development of business schools in the UK – and by the mid-1990s it was running 45 courses a year for 1,100 students, and had 13 members of staff, half of whom worked on the administrative side.[121] Like the IBM programme, the CPI drew in historians, philosophers and some from other disciplines 'which, on the face of it, have little to do with industry'; however, it moved in different directions from the broad 'liberal' approach of the older course, trying to be 'dynamic and responsive' to the needs of the external organisations on which it relied for much of its income.[122] As with local companies, it became clear that many of the problems to which businesses looked to Cambridge for solutions were not technological – and in any case, such problems were perhaps most suitably addressed directly by research and collaboration rather than by training courses. What did emerge as a key concern were 'what we now call sustainability challenges', in Courtice's words 'things for which they were totally unprepared by their education, their experience and certainly by the business schools'. By the early 1990s the challenges faced by industry in light of the emergence of human rights, environmental destruction and climate change issues generated substantial opportunities for the CPI: companies 'were increasingly being held to account by civil society organisations, campaigning organisations, who were rightly accusing them of trashing the planet in the pursuit of profit'. This tension between profitability and sustainability would shape what the CPI did in the next decade and beyond.[123]

Institutionally, the CPI had to tread a fine line: in a 'highly decentralised' university, it had to be built up through a series of departmental and individual relationships, rather than via any particular centrally driven strategic initiatives. The Cambridge University 'aura' or brand was important in attracting delegates to the programme, but a measure of independence was also necessary to ensure its responsiveness to demand.[124] In this sense the extramural nature of the Board made it the most suitable place for the CPI; and indeed the experiences of the CPI echoed those of the much older extension programme. Courtice, by then director of the CPI's professional development programme – noted that

> Many providers of continuing education from within higher education institutes have to perform a delicate balancing act. They have to operate in a complex environment, in competitive markets, adapting and applying commercial principles. At the same time they also have to operate within the framework of a wider institution which may have a different primary mission, where market forces may be less clearly defined or perceived, and where continuing education is not necessarily central on its agenda.[125]

The extension programme had been operating in such an environment for more than a century by this time, although its longevity and success had given it a much stronger institutional framework than newer initiatives such as the CPI, which in its physical location was somewhat marginalised from the Board itself, just as the activities at Madingley were from the rest of the university.

The 1980s also saw an evolution of the training programmes for magistrates and court staff, which used both Churchill College and Madingley Hall itself. This was a small area of activity compared with others in which the Board was engaged (for data on all 'continuing education' courses, see table 5.1), and its success was by no means certain. No internal staffing was available, and there were some difficulties in obtaining qualified tutors in the mid-1980s. Reviewing this strand of work, Mason briefly considered that the Board might 'get out' of magistrates' training, but this was quickly rejected given its importance to the financing of Madingley Hall, where the courses 'ma[d]e up so much of the business'.[126] In due course a new position of director of legal studies was created, to which John Stanford was appointed, but the teaching of the courses remained heavily dependent on the participation of justices' clerks, who – it was admitted – were not paid particularly well for the work.[127] Nevertheless, magistrates' and clerks' training was a stable element of activity, with 23 courses taught, ranging from introductory to advanced levels, in 1984-5.[128] This legal work was 'the largest single activity' under the broad heading of 'continuing education', with 583 students attending 29 courses in 1985-6.[129]

Perhaps the most significant development on this side of the Board's work was the launch in 1984 of a series of 'training packages' for magistrates.[130] The packages were prepared under the direction of John Murrell, director of postgraduate studies at Homerton College, who had considerable experience of developing training courses for members of the legal and medical professions. Just as the teaching of local history, landscape archaeology and geology on the extension programme often, and increasingly, involved hands-on work and active learning among participants, so the magistrates' training was 'based on certain principles of learning' and 'assume[d] a specific approach to teaching'.[131] As Murrell explained in his foreword to one training package,

> Learning becomes meaningful when it involves *activity* on the part of the learner. True understanding comes from doing exercises, solving problems, answering questions and practising skills, and making errors which are identified and corrected. Whilst information may be conveyed from a Training Officer to a Justice in the form of a talk or lecture, such passive learning will only become meaningful when linked to practical experience.[132]

Students were given a handbook in which there was space for their own notes, sometimes under given headings, and worked in groups through sample cases to make decisions on bail and sentencing.[133] One case involved an imaginary defendant named 'Ivor Notion', while the solicitors in other cases were 'John Committem' for the prosecution and 'Roland Rodent' for the defence (the children's television character 'Roland Rat' had first appeared on screen in 1983).[134] Trainee magistrates were, of course, required to take the courses seriously, and were introduced to key issues in practice, procedure, sentencing and a range of decisions in juvenile and domestic courts. The importance of active learning was hammered home to the tutors:

> Justices are volunteers and eager to learn. The enthusiasm should be reinforced by enlightened, lively teaching methods rather than exploited by requiring them to listen passively. Not only is passive learning ineffective, it is also boring and demotivating.[135]

The Board's experience of work in magistrates' training led to further involvement in the training of probation officers, solicitors – in collaboration with the university's Faculty of Law – and social workers.[136] Cambridgeshire Social Services used Madingley Hall for non-residential training in the mid-1980s, although the arrangement did not become a long-term relationship at that stage.[137] There were also smaller interventions in ministerial training for the Church of England – hence the large attendances at the courses run in St Albans – but this was a short-lived experiment in which the Board's role was mainly 'pump-priming'.[138] Work with the armed forces, too, continued through the 1980s, with all three services involved, although some of the Army education was moved away from Cambridge later in the decade. In 1985-6 there were 288 students across 12 military residential courses, including one for Army education tutors.[139] Yet another group of professionals who visited Madingley or one of the Cambridge colleges for in-service training were lawyers from overseas. The biennial residential course introducing English law to legal professionals from overseas, which had begun in the 1940s and was taught in conjunction with the Faculty of Law, attracted 128 students at the end of the 1980s.[140] Again, though, this 'market' would not easily survive the growing demands for the internationalisation of course content, which intensified in the following decade.

*

Given the popularity of Madingley Hall as a location for residential and day courses, and for external bookings, it was clear by the mid- to late 1980s that the premises were in need of improvement. The bedrooms by this time were 40 years old, and 'the facilities and furnishings [were] falling below the expectations of the general public'.[141] In particular, there were no en-suite rooms, and in the courtyard block the occupants of some 45 rooms had to share three or four bathrooms; all the rooms needed new beds, curtains, carpets and other fitted furnishings. The amount of accommodation, too, was inadequate: 55 single bedrooms and 12 doubles was not enough for weekend courses, but at the same time the capacity of the dining hall made it impractical to provide more than 30 additional rooms. Such an increase, in any case, was not affordable, particularly given that office space, in particular, was also in need of improvement and expansion.[142] In terms of teaching space, there was probably enough given the numbers who could be accommodated, although there were issues with acoustics and lighting; large bedrooms could quite easily be converted into small seminar rooms for up to about 12 people. A small enhancement to the teaching space had been made with the construction of an out-building – the Leslie Wayper Room – in 1984-5, but this was 'very unattractive to almost all users'. The Wayper Room was variously used as a classroom and as an extension to the bar, which at this point was just opposite it; it has since been used as a café. The saloon could comfortably hold 80 people, effectively the whole population of the Hall at any one time, and was regularly used for public events, particularly concerts performed by the Alberni String Quartet during their regular 'masterclasses'.[143]

There was an extensive refurbishment of the kitchens in 1988-9, but apart from this and the new Wayper Room – and an extension to the car parking area – there were only modest changes to the buildings in the 1980s. An old ice house in the grounds was excavated in 1985, with a view to potentially restoring it, but this resulted in an accident: a 'terrifying fireball of exploding gas' injured two men, Paul King and John Fredericks, who were working there at the time.[144] Later in the decade, the refuse store was relocated and there were improvements to allow for wheelchair access, but developments were limited.[145] Toilets and bathrooms were at the ends of corridors, and en-suite facilities would not be installed until the 1990s, although new furniture and tea-

and-coffee-making equipment was installed in the bedrooms at the end of the 1980s. The lack of improvements, especially to the bedrooms, meant that the facilities were 'becoming increasingly inadequate to meet the needs and expectations of the business and professional community the Board wish to attract in the future and upon whom the Board's hopes for increased revenue in large part depend'.[146] By 1990 the residential accommodation had become an even more pressing issue: there was an identified need for at least 75 bedrooms, as well as extra library and office space, and more teaching rooms that could hold 50 or more people. By this time new technologies had also generated demands for improvements to the office space: more power lines for computers, and more telephones, were required, and a new bar, potentially in the Wayper Room, was 'desirable'.[147] The funding for these extensive redevelopment works would have to come from the Board's own resources: it had asked the Dart Foundation, which had provided funding in the 1970s, for money in 1987, but this had been declined.[148] A substantial sum – £1.5 million – had already been set aside for the work, which would be carried out in the 1990s, resulting in significant changes to the buildings, although not quite as initially envisaged.

The garden was an important attraction of Madingley Hall, and when the Board initially took it over it was managed and overseen by the university estate management service. In 1979, though, a head gardener was appointed, and there was a staff of two further full-time gardeners and part-time garden mechanic.[149] The walled garden on the south side of the Hall was developed in the mid-1980s – a haven of 'peace and tranquility with its enclosed format' – and in 1988 Richard Gant was appointed as the new head gardener, a post that he still occupies at the time of writing.[150] He explains that 'we have always tried to keep the garden, although it belongs to a big educational institution, so that it retains the *feel* that it belongs to a private family home' – as, of course, it did until 1948.[151] The garden suffered in the 1980s and early 1990s from a series of wind damage, most notably the hurricane of 16 October 1987 but also significant storms in 1985 and 1990. The latter caused 'devastating and demoralising' damage to several trees, but freed up space for new plantings; as Gant reminded readers of the in-house staff magazine, 'no garden stands still and motionless'.[152] He has recently added that 'it is a plantsperson's garden, growing unusual plants amongst the more familiar for interest, education and stimulation', and in this sense its 'intimacy and naturalness' supports the aims and atmosphere of Madingley Hall.[153]

Madingley generated a sense of community, and this is fondly remembered by many who worked there or visited in the 1980s. According to one recollection, longstanding members of staff, most of whom had spent the majority of their careers based in Stuart House, developed 'an affinity with Madingley', and this was shared with newer colleagues. 'There was a sense of belonging, of unity, of togetherness in a common goal', and 'it was a wonderful place to be part of.'[154] New members of staff, who knew no other home for the Board, also found it an inspiring place to work: one comments that 'Madingley … lifts the soul; it makes you feel good going up the drive in the morning'.[155] Students, too, many of whom returned for residential courses several times in a year, 'had a sense of belonging, that this was their home'.[156] The warden, Susan Rawlings, would emphasise the 'home' elements of Madingley in her welcome speech to students at the beginning of residential courses on a Friday night.[157] Interaction between staff and students was easy: one former member of staff recalls that 'one of the things that I found out straight away about Madingley … [was] that there was very little sense of "we are more important than you"; it was very much a place where people met on equal terms'.[158] There was 'a solid core of regular courses, which gave it a sort of solidity and resonance': repeated visits by trainee magistrates, Army officers and social workers, among others, supported this, and staff would eat lunch – always served from 1pm to 1.30pm at this time – alongside the students.[159] There were ongoing security issues throughout the 1980s, ranging from 'petty pilfering' to a burglary to 16 cars being broken into on one night in 1987 – and on one occasion two sculptures were stolen from the garden – but on the whole the environment was experienced happily and is fondly remembered.[160]

*

The evolution of the Board's work in the 1980s had implications for staffing, particularly on the administrative and managerial side. In the mid-1980s there were 11 members of 'clerical/secretarial staff', including a chief clerk, finance clerk and librarian, but it was apparent that this would not be enough in the future. Some regrading of administrative posts was considered to be important, as it was becoming difficult to attract and retain good staff.[161] Meanwhile, changes in the wider environment generated new staffing demands. For example, publicity became increasingly important in the late 1980s, and this was reflected in the appointment – in 1988 – of Janet Keystone as publicity officer. With a varied background in art, teaching, research and administration, Keystone had a remit across the range of the Board's activity, and made a significant contribution to the development of successful programmes into the 1990s. She attended the annual week-long 'community education fair' in Cambridge, which showcased provision across the county and facilitated contact with other providers of adult education.[162] At this time the printed publicity for extension and residential courses was undergoing significant improvement, and the Board was linked to the 'Taplink' terminal, a computer that contained details of courses across Cambridgeshire.[163] Meanwhile, computers were gradually being introduced at Madingley – there was an internal debate as to whether PCs or Macs should be bought – and this would in due course, though not immediately, lead to fundamental changes not just in publicity but also in the administration of the programmes.[164]

Meanwhile, in addition to the gardening team, Madingley Hall itself occupied two chefs and a kitchen assistant, a 'housekeeper' and six 'dining hall assistants', a barman, two 'maintenance assistants' and nine part-time cleaners, all funded from the income earned by the Hall itself and some resident on the premises.[165] The Board was content with the 'quality and level' of these employees, whose contribution was supplemented by casual workers from time to time. There was 'a high standard of catering: waitress service at lunch and dinner; varied and imaginative menus; attractively presented meals; considerable use of fresh foodstuffs; alternative menus for special diets and the high standard of cleanliness in the kitchens which is essential for health in a catering establishment'.[166] Some dishes are particularly well remembered: a cut of salmon with lemon and parsley sauce, for example, and banana fritters with syrup and cream.[167] Others from this period were mushroom 'tartlets' served as starters, steak with Guinness sauce, moussaka and, for pudding, crème caramels decorated with cream, cherries and angelica.[168] A new catering and conference manager, Ian Willis, was appointed in 1988, with overall responsibility for housekeeping, laundry and portering, as well as the kitchens.[169] In many cases, though, it was difficult to recruit and retain domestic staff, given Madingley's 'relatively isolated position'.[170]

The administrative, garden and domestic staff worked hard, and made a vital, though perhaps sometimes unrecognised, contribution to the success of the Board's activities and to the smooth running of Madingley Hall. In 1990 one account of garden work reminded readers that, '[w]hen sitting in the comfort of the Saloon, or gazing out of the office or library windows at the delightful flowerbeds, lawns, pools and courtyards of the Hall, it is salutary to remember the all-weather efforts of … all the gardeners who help to produce such a magnificant environment'.[171] The chefs, too, put in long hours, including at weekends. Mark Walker and Tony Marrone worked on a shift system, with one in charge in the morning and one in the afternoon and evening, but when one was on holiday, the other would cover both shifts in a working day that ran from 7.15am to 8.20pm.[172] Meanwhile, in a largely un-computerised finance office, staff were dealing with cheque and credit payments from students, and with invoices of all sorts, and also had to manage three 'pay runs'. Casual staff were paid weekly; there was a fortnightly pay run for panel tutors – usually between 50 and 100 each time – and the established staff were paid monthly salaries. As one financial administrator explained ruefully, '[w]e could cope quite easily with all this if it was not for the telephone and the door'.[173] Meanwhile, administrators on the extension programmes processed tutor review forms and expense claims, typed acceptance letters for students onto Certificate courses, made telephone calls to local centres, and took dictation from assistant secretary Richard Evans, who directed this area of the Board's work.[174] Most of this, of course, was invisible to students, though some understood the administrative complexities. According to Sarah Ormrod, 'it is a huge effort to get the programmes running, and a handful of the students recognise that. A lot of them don't, but that's fine: if you go to a ballet, you don't need to know how much the ballerina's feet are hurting, you just need to see something that is beautiful.'[175] In any case, most of those who worked at Madingley in the late 1980s seem to have enjoyed it: one of the au pair waitresses, Veronique Jenny, declared that '[w]e have a great time even when we are working'.[176]

*

The Cambridge Board of Extra-Mural Studies was in better shape at the end of the 1980s than many other university departments of adult and continuing education. It had faced the challenges associated with the changes in government funding more successfully than some, and retained a strength in the East Anglian region that would stand it in good stead for the further changes that were to come in the 1990s. In 1989-90 the annual report referred to 'the steady progress that has characterized [the] work in recent years', and in particular noted the importance of the CPI as a 'significant contributor' to the growth in student numbers.[177] In terms of full-time equivalent students, the figure of 844 was a 6.6% increase on the previous year alone, making the Board at least equivalent in size to a large Cambridge college. With the exception of the CPI, though, the Board was doing little that was completely new, with much of the expanded activity resting on older foundations. The key change over the previous decade had been in staffing: the increase and growing specialisation of administrative staff, and the reduction of staff tutor numbers, made a significant difference to the Board's self-perception as an academic unit. Eight staff tutors remained in post at the end of the 1980s, all but one of whom had been appointed to the Board in the 1960s, and it was these men – they were all, at this time, men – who carried the 'Great Tradition' of university extension forward. The extension programme itself was renamed 'public courses' and then the 'public programmes', a name that was used through the next decade and beyond. Other areas of work were increasingly distinct, and operated in different 'markets' and with very different groups of students. This was a matter of concern to some: at the start of the 1980s, for example, Lionel Munby had called for more 'integration' of the Board's activities, but if anything the opposite had happened.[178] From the mid-1980s a new divisional structure had been adopted, with the administration of the Board divided into sections: the Extension Division, the Continuing Education Division, the International Division, the 'Admin Division' and the 'Madingley Division'; and a version of this structure was retained into the 1990s.[179] The separate divisions of work would move in very different directions in the 1990s, when new funding pressures and opportunities would generate new educational and administrative imperatives, and when the 'Great Tradition' of university adult education – and much else – would be substantially reshaped.

Chapter 6
Credit where it's due: the 1990s

At the beginning of the 1990s it was clear that fundamental changes in the culture of British universities were on their way. Many of these would centre on 'access' to higher education and 'widening participation', and this posed some profound questions for university extramural departments. The incorporation of polytechnics into the university sector in 1992 was especially significant: with a different student demographic and a stronger tradition of part-time study, the 'post-92s' would pose a challenge to traditional conceptions of a university education.[1] According to one account in 1990, 'the very distinction between initial and continuing education means less and less', and this was both 'disturbing and enticing' for existing continuing education departments.[2] On the one hand, 'it seems to threaten the organizational identity of adult and continuing education'; but, on the other, it presented potential opportunities:

> As higher education moves towards mass access the experience and skills of adult educators, once seen as honourable but peripheral, will become more and more relevant. A tradition that seemed to look backwards – to the earnestness and enthusiasm of evening class students and the celebration of 'culture' ... will be redirected forwards – to open access, lifelong learning, professional updating, social education and the rest. Extramural no longer but outreach, a rewritten project.[3]

The 1990s would see a rapid increase in the 'age participation rate' – the proportion of young people entering higher education – from around 15% to almost 35%.[4] Although this was accompanied by a drive to 'widening access', and did indeed result in a modest expansion in the proportion of working-class young people who went on to study in universities, there remained a persistent gap between them and young people from higher social status backgrounds in terms of access to higher education.[5] Moreover, there were clear and peristent inequalities in access to elite universities, including Cambridge, whose resident student body remained overwhelmingly middle-class, and almost entirely young.[6] Less than half of one percent of full-time Cambridge undergraduates were mature students in the mid-1990s.[7]

On some levels, these developments were not particularly significant to the Board of Extra-Mural Studies, which would in 1991 become the Board of Continuing Education. Its public programmes, summer schools and growing industrial partnerships educated very different student constituencies and served different educational needs. In 1993, an article in *Varsity* magazine by Janet Keystone drew attention to 'the other 11,000': the number of students taking courses run by the Board, which was about the same as the total Cambridge undergraduate student population. Continuing education students, Keystone noted, had 'access to the knowledge, teaching and values of Cambridge' but did not 'go to the societies fair or stock up with mugs from the Reject Shop'.[8] These students

> come from all walks of life. For some, university education is a totally new experience and can often transform their lives. Many others are former students of this and other universities, with considerable educational experience, as well as academic expertise and ability, who are seeking to expand or up-date their existing knowledge, or explore new areas of interest. All are taking part in the lifelong learning experience which this University offers to all who wish to make use of it.[9]

Although largely invisible to the rest of the university, these students were an important part of what Cambridge did in the community. In the same year the Board itself – rather vaguely but expansively – expressed its purpose as being

> to secure the provision and development of Continuing Education across a wide range of subjects in order to meet the educational needs of the wider community after the first formal stages of education. The wider community served by Continuing Education is made up of individuals and organisations, including industry, the professions and the public service and it is seen as local, regional, national and international.[10]

In practical terms, the early 1990s saw more changes in the funding arrangements for higher education, and these in turn had an impact on the evolving work of the Board. The abolition of the direct Responsible Body funding stream in 1989 and its replacement by a system of competitive bidding for Universities Funding Council (UFC) grants was just the first in a series of reforms that created new challenges for university adult education departments. Cambridge was reasonably successful in meeting the standards required by the bidding system, but this in turn was replaced in 1992 when the UFC was replaced by the Higher Education Funding Council for England (HEFCE) as part of a wider series of changes that ended the 'binary' system of universities and polytechnics that had been at the heart of higher education since the 1960s.

The new funding system brought continuing education students into the same orbit as full- and part-time students in other university departments, which in turn meant an increased emphasis on the importance of accredited courses that led to named university awards. Although HEFCE recognised, at least rhetorically, the value of non-award-bearing adult education provision, from 1995 onwards funding for continuing education was largely contingent on the number of students who achieved credit.[11] This effectively amounted to the 'mainstreaming' of university continuing education, at least in funding terms, and precipitated, at Cambridge and elsewhere, a widespread review of the kinds of work that extramural departments did.[12] This often took place in anticipation of the expected 'mainstreaming', and while it did not always lead to fundamental changes in the nature of the courses provided, it was argued that it must have significant implications for the ways in which university adult education defined itself. No longer would it be so easy to sustain 'an "open" tradition within an otherwise "closed" system': continuing education had been a corner of the university sector that had no admissions pre-requisites and often no particular expectations of the students who attended, but the latter at least was expected to change.[13] It was very clear that '[t]he new link between funding and credit sent shock waves through the world of adult and continuing education'.[14]

The emergence of accreditation could be seen as an opportunity to review the academic quality of some university adult education courses, particularly on public programmes like the one that Cambridge ran in East Anglia. There had been a long-standing concern, at the level of individual universities and the funding bodies, that three-year tutorial class enrolments had been in long-term decline relative to shorter, term-long courses that lacked the academic rigour associated with longer periods of study. Accreditation meant that these courses would have to be strengthened to ensure that they led to outcomes that could be externally scrutinised. It also had potential implications for the composition of the student body. 'There was', for example, 'a considerable number of students – particularly the elderly – who were not particularly interested in further qualifications and progression routes', while younger students might be more attracted to the prospect of a university qualification, particularly one that was 'portable' within a nationwide system of credit acculumation and transfer.[15] As the last chapter showed, the majority of students on the Cambridge extension programme were older and already 'unusually well educated'. Other universities found that accreditation altered the balance of their continuing education intake, and HEFCE also made some additional funding available for 'widening provision' courses aimed at preparing students for degree-level study.

This chapter examines how the Board responded to these and other developments, evolving its work under the shadow of significant changes in its external relationships and internal priorities. It also explores how students negotiated the changes, particularly the expectations that were increasingly required of them on accredited courses. The 1990s were a time of transition in the public programmes and in the other areas of the Board's extensive adult and continuing education activity. It saw the Board move to a fully computerised student records system, the normalisation of computer use across the University and the routine use of email for correspondence, and a fresh series of developments to the buildings and facilities at Madingley Hall. Yet some features of life in adult and continuing education did not change: well into the 2000s, for example, book-boxes were still sent out to courses from the library at Madingley, put together by the librarian for tutors and taken in the back of their cars to local centres, for the books to be issued in turn to students.[16] And despite the increases in staff and student numbers that took place across the range of the Board's provision, there was no completely new area that had not already emerged in the 1980s or even earlier.

Partly as a result of this, the Board and its leaders – when they wanted to – were still able to represent what they did as part of a 'tradition' of adult and continuing education that had its roots in the nineteenth-century origins of university extension. Thus when the Labour government issued its Green Paper on *The Learning Age: A Renaissance for a New Britain* in 1998, the Board's annual report announced confidently that

> The importance of 'The Learning Age' is that it gives welcome recognition at the highest national level to the value of learning throughout life and to the benefits it can bring to the state as a whole as well as to the individual citizen. Since the extension of university education to the wider community began in Cambridge in the 1870s, the University has been engaged, primarily through the Board of Continuing Education and its predecesors, in providing and fostering opportunities for lifelong learning.[17]

During the 1990s this mission had been substantially expanded and in some ways renewed, but there was usually scope for challenge to be presented as opportunity and change as continuity.

*

The changing shape of both the Board's work and the wider landscape of adult and continuing education resulted in significant organisational changes at the beginning of the 1990s. During the previous decade there had been a 'small but increasing' amount of 'extra-mural work' done by other University departments at Cambridge, and the new UFC funding mechanism – requiring the submission of tenders – meant that more sustained cross-departmental collaboration was required. Ad hoc arrangements had been made between the Board and University departments to consider 'funding requirements', but these were not acceptable as a long-term basis for coordination on 'matters of mutual concern'. As a result the Council of Senate proposed, in 1990, the 'reconstitution' of the Board as a Board of Continuing Education, with representation from across the University and a clearly defined remit for 'extra-mural' work across the faculties and departments, with the important exceptions of medical and in-service teacher training, which were already significant areas of activity for which the Faculties of Clinical Medicine and Education were responsible.[18] The new Board itself was to comprise up to 21 members, including representatives from the Senate and from the relevant faculties, and the existing staff would continue to be employed by the new Board. It was envisaged that the existing course provision would be retained and managed by the Board, albeit perhaps delegated to substantial sub-committees; but there was nervousness about this among some of the Board's staff, who were concerned about the implications of being accountable to a new institution, which they feared may not have an evolved understanding of their work.[19]

In the event, the new Board of Continuing Education was duly constituted in 1991, and it had a new director, who took office in the previous year. This was Michael Richardson, a Cambridge theology graduate who had begun his career teaching adults in Derbyshire before moving to the Open University in 1970 and becoming a pro-vice-chancellor.[20] At Cambridge, Richardson would be 'warmly remembered as a highly able, astute and personable leader', qualities that would be needed in abundance during his time as director.[21] One colleague from the time describes him as 'an extremely nice man … clever and perceptive … adroit at negotiating personal relationships and managing people'.[22] Richardson was committed to strengthening the vocational elements of the Board's work, and was careful to emphasise the historical foundations of this ambition. Quoted in the educational press in 1991, he reminded readers that 'continuing education at Cambridge was started by James [Stuart], who was an engineer … You had the central institution in the university and an extremely practical, vocational orientation in the man's mind. We are picking up the strands of that tradition.'[23] Richardson embarked on a strategic review of the Board's work, looking at other universities' provision alongside Cambridge's own, with a view to submitting a 'corporate plan' that would rebalance the focus of work without compromising its 'commitment to quality of provision'.[24] What this meant in practical terms was, on the one hand, the continuation and expansion of existing activity, and on the other, a shift of focus towards accreditation.

Developments in the 1990s were underpinned by further alterations to the full- and part-time staffing at the Board. The number of staff tutors continued to fall, standing at just five by 1996: Graham Howes, David Trump, Mike Sewell (modern history), Mara Kalnins (English Literature) and former assistant secretary Richard Mason.[25] Jack Herbert had retired in 1991, and Anthony Storey followed in the mid-1990s, as did Roland Randall and David Trump, who was replaced by Caroline Malone, recruited from the University of Bristol.[26] Other members of the teaching staff included Mark Bailey, who spent a few years teaching local history in the early 1990s and would later become Professor of Late Medieval History at the University of East Anglia. Bailey was later replaced by Evelyn Lord, who joined the staff at the same time as Carola Hicks and Frank Woodman, who taught history of art and architecture.[27] Academic staff were now known as academic development officers rather than staff tutors; from the mid-1990s they would include Susan Oosthuizen, who had worked for several years as a part-time tutor in archaeology and landscape history, and Lynne Harrison and Gillian Sheail, who both focused on science.[28]

In 1991 a new director was appointed for the public programmes, to replace Richard Evans: this was David Davies, who – like Richardson – had previously worked for the Open University. Davies was assisted by three academic programme managers – Vanessa Nedderman, Linda Fisher and Shelley Lockwood – and Susan Rawlings remained deputy secretary to the Board as well as warden of Madingley Hall, and also took over from Davies as director of the public programmes when he left for the University of Surrey in 1996. Sarah Ormrod, who had worked for the Board since the 1980s, was by this time head of the International division, with responsibility for the International Summer Schools, assisted by six members of administrative staff. The Cambridge Programme for Industry had 15 members of staff, four of whom were part-time; and 'Legal Studies', led by Philip Brown, comprised four full- and two part-time employees.[29] There was also a large central administrative department and a growing body of domestic staff at Madingley Hall itself.

The new leadership and organisational arrangements did not mean any immediate changes in the public programmes in East Anglia, which continued much as before, except in one significant respect: in the early 1990s Cambridge lost parts of its 'extramural empire' to two other universities. The University of East Anglia (UEA), established in 1961, had opened some of its undergraduate courses to the public in 1976, and later established a Department of Extra-Mural Studies, which took over university adult education provision in local centres in Norfolk and some of Suffolk in 1991-2. The University of Essex took responsibility for most of its county in the following year.[30] Among other things, the Norfolk transfer meant that Chris Barringer, staff tutor in the county for 25 years, moved to be director of extramural studies at UEA. Yet the Cambridge public programmes as a whole continued to grow in the early 1990s, attracting 3,321 students in 1993-4, an increase of more than a quarter on the previous year.[31] There were significant developments in the scale and scope of the public programmes in the early 1990s. In 1992, for example, the Board began using the facilities of the university's Sidgwick Site, on the west side of Cambridge city centre, for the public programmes (it was already used for summer courses). Meanwhile, in the mid-1990s new local centres were established or revived in Sawtry, March and Ashwell (Hertfordshire).[32] The Sidgwick Site – where the Board used the Classics faculty building – had the advantage of a central Cambridge location with ample car parking, but one student complained that it 'has to be, apart from the car park, one of the most unsuitable and uncomfortable [venues] that the Board could have chosen'.[33]

At other centres, the public programmes were fairly buoyant in the early 1990s. The Board emphasised the longstanding arrangements that it had in some places: for example, in 1990-1 Downham Market marked 80 years of association with Cambridge, and Michael Richardson visited Lowestoft, 'whose records of University of Cambridge Extension classes go back to 1892'.[34] On this occasion Richardson presented a framed address to the Lowestoft Literary and Scientific Association referring to its 'long and fruitful association in bringing university adult education to the people of Lowestoft'.[35] This was one of the centres that were 'lost' to UEA, but Downham Market continued as a Cambridge centre, running a successful course on the history of theatre in 1993-4, for example.[36] Meanwhile, newer centres also flourished: the Suffolk village of Boxford continued its record of attracting significant numbers of students – 33 for 'Europe Yesterday, Today and Tomorrow' in 1993-4 – and collaboration continued with the Cambridgeshire village colleges, the WEA and successful centres such as Letchworth and Bedford. The Local Centres Union, now representing around 70 centres, continued in operation, and provided small bursaries and grants for research projects. Attendance at its meetings, however, was in decline by the mid-1990s, and relatively few centres were making the required contributions to its funds.[37] It operated on a shoestring budget, and some delegates to its meetings were concerned about the amount of 'waffle'; essentially its role in a changing climate was uncertain, but it survived thanks largely to the leadership of Roy Evans, the long-serving director of the Letchworth Settlement.[38]

Certificate courses, which had been expanding in the 1980s, continued to develop, and in retrospect can be seen as pioneering the wider accreditation of the public programmes in the mid-1990s. The Certificates were linked to the system of credit accumulation and transfer (CATS), derived from the Council for National Academic Awards, and by 1993-4 there were 21 programmes, taught over two or three years, with a total of 377 students, almost half of whom were studying counselling or related subjects; the number increased to 439 in the following year.[39] A typical Certificate course would involve 160 hours of study over two years, made up of a series of two-hour seminars as well as Saturday workshops and field trips. In 1993-4, fifty-four students were working towards a Certificate in Local History, taught by David Dymond and Mark Bailey. The fee for this Certificate was £195 (about £420 today) per year, although other Certificates – in Legal Studies and in Historic Building Conservation – came at a considerably higher cost of £345 (around £750).[40] Local history had the longest record of awarding Certificates to students, and therefore of developing suitable instruments by which they could be assessed. It had long involved an element of negotiation with students over course content – a key element of the WEA tradition – and this could conflict with both the content and spirit of stipulated 'learning outcomes'. However, the fact that students usually came with a pre-existing interest in a particular place or theme enabled them to shape their own studies within the architecture of the Certificate programme, and to focus on the place and period that most interested them.

Local history was also at the forefront of part-time Master of Studies degrees, which began on the public programmes in the mid-1990s. At Oxford, a part-time Master's in the subject had already started, and it became a 'key strategic objective' at Cambridge to move in the same direction.[41] The first cohort of 11 students on the new Master of Studies in English Local History started in 1995.[42] They covered an impressive chronological range – from c.1100 to c.1900 – and, like study at other levels, encountered 'seminar-style' teaching using primary sources, as well as palaeography training and the requirement to write a 10,000-word dissertation.[43] Organised jointly with the university's Faculty of History, it was led by David Dymond and Mark Bailey, and was followed by a Master of Studies in Modernism in English Literature: this began with nine students.[44] The development of part-time postgraduate degrees, though, encountered some opposition within the university. When proposed in 1993, one contributor to the *Varsity* student magazine considered it a 'radical idea', which 'could change the face of Cambridge', and explained with some concern that '[e]ntry could be open to people in industry, or without qualifications'.[45] This account opined:

> Cambridge is seen as an elite university. We ought to safeguard our reputation by trying to attract the most able candidates and specialising in academic elitism, not selling courses. … I felt like screaming. Cambridge doesn't have to and shouldn't try to cater for everyone.[46]

Notwithstanding such sniffy responses, recruitment to part-time Master's degrees 'remained steady' for the rest of the 1990s.[47]

With Certificates and Master's degrees in place, but no part-time undergraduate degree at Cambridge, it was not possible to follow a traditional route into postgraduate study. Some students entered the Master of Studies with undergraduate degrees from elsewhere, but the Board also created Diplomas and, later, Advanced Diplomas, which allowed students to continue on its courses beyond the Certificates. Again, local history was in the vanguard here, along with field archaeology, literature and ecology.[48] One student who followed this route – and became one of the earliest students on the Master of Studies degree – was Peter Bysouth, a manager in the pharmaceutical industry who began studying on the Board's courses in the early 1990s. Following successful completion of a Certificate in Local History at Letchworth, Bysouth proceeded to an Advanced Diploma, taught at Cambridge, and then to the Master of Studies programme. For students like him, though, there was no opportunity for part-time doctoral study at Cambridge: to work at this level, students generally proceeded to a different institution. Bysouth went to the University of Warwick, where he completed a part-time PhD; and in due course he taught on some programmes at Madingley, and on the Diploma in Local History at Homerton College, in the 2000s.[49]

The existence of part-time Master's students caused some difficulties within Cambridge itself. Evelyn Lord, who joined the staff in 1996-7, recalls that 'people [on the Master's programmes] had other things to do ... a lot of them were still working, and they had to have extensions [for coursework]. And then there was a period when [the University] would not give *everyone* the degree because there was someone still working through an extension.' Moreover, when the first cohort of Master's students graduated, they found that they did not have the usual Cambridge graduate access to the University Library; this, too, had to be negotiated before they could become 'proper alumni'.[50] These students had to have a college affiliation, and some colleges simply would not take part-time students, while others did not offer them the same privileges as other postgraduates, or indeed undergraduates. Corpus Christi, though, treated the Board's students well, and invited them to feasts and other events alongside the other members of the college; Wolfson and Darwin also embraced the new part-time students.[51] Bysouth remembers that, at Corpus Christi, 'we were just accepted – nobody made any distinctions because we were part-time students'.[52] They 'went dining in each others' colleges', and appreciated the facilities that were available. For many, like Bysouth, such experiences were unexpected: 'I left school with one A-level', he explains, and took his first degree as a day-release student at the University of London: 'the fact that I finished up at Corpus, in Cambridge, was absolutely amazing. And I revelled in it, and took full advantage.'[53]

Through its well evolved structure of accredited programmes, local history teaching at Cambridge and beyond continued to support research activity across the extramural region, sustaining a tradition that had been pioneered by Lionel Munby and others in the post-war period. The courses attracted some students who were already working in local history, helping them to develop a critical approach that enhanced the research that they were already doing. Shirley Wittering, a housewife with two children from Thriplow in Cambridgeshire, whose husband Bill had started a local history group in the village, enrolled on a Certificate in Local History in 1992, and progressed through to a Master of Studies. Taught almost throughout her time at Cambridge by David Dymond – as well as others including Mark Bailey – she recalls Dymond as 'a wonderful tutor, with a great sense of humour, [and] very knowledgeable, especially about East Anglia'.[54] Covering a wide range of themes in local history including architecture, the poor laws, economic history, landscape and church politics, students were exposed to a chronological range that would be unusual in most history degree courses, and Wittering even studied medieval Latin to support her local history research. She feels that the courses taught her 'how to be analytical', particularly in relation to historical primary sources: 'how to look at a document and see how it connected with another document or with another bit of research'.[55] This professional approach helped her, and other local historians, to move beyond an antiquarian approach to their subject, and in Wittering's case led to doctoral research at the University of East Anglia, and in due course to a book on the impact of enclosure on society, farming and the environment in south Cambridgeshire.[56] She also credits her study with supporting the development of Thriplow Society, which remains very active today, producing a long-running journal and occasional books.[57]

*

Residential courses at Madingley Hall were reliably popular in the early 1990s, not least because of the competitive fees – inclusive of accommodation and meals – that remained a feature of the Board's provision across the public programmes. They were advertised in a smartly produced brochure, issued twice in each academic year; by the time the second was available, many of the courses were already full. In 1991-2 there were 142 residential courses, mostly run over a weekend, with a total attendance of 2,654 (many students attended more than one course); this was an average of 18.7 students per course. The largest weekend course, with 44 students, involved an intensive study of Wagner's *Parsifal*, 'illustrated on the piano and with recordings', led by Ian Beresford Gleaves, some time editor of *Wagner News* and a 'wonderful music lecturer', according to one recollection.[58] Slightly more – 48 students – attended a week-long Alberni 'masterclass' at the end of July 1992; one of four such courses run in that year by the Alberni String Quartet, this featured evening concerts and opportunities for one-to-one work. Students often attended in groups, each person paying £280 for the course, and another 34 attended the same course in the week immediately following. Other musical weekends were also popular: Alan Stripp's 'Rachmaninov and His Contemporaries' and 'Monteverdi's *Vespers*' attracted 21 and 29 students respectively, although his course 'New Paths in Music 1900-1940' – featuring the atonalities of Schoenberg and others – was rather less popular, with only eight students in attendance.[59] The American-born saxophonist and composer Kevin Flanagan taught 'The Evolution of Jazz' to 25 students in August 1992.[60]

Students clearly enjoyed residential courses at Madingley, not least the convivial hospitality that they encountered at the Hall. Indeed, both students and tutors sometimes found it difficult to focus on the work, which ran across seven separate sessions and was interspersed with meals, walks around the gardens and other informal activities.[61] According to one account, a student on one course 'knitted with impunity throughout the seminars', and an '[e]xcess of food and wine on Saturday night ... inhibited serious after-dinner discussion'.[62] Meals were served in the hall, commenced in the evenings with a Latin grace, which was one of the 'trappings of collegiate ritual' that some students 'could have done with a little less of'.[63] On this occasion around 80 students were in residence for the weekend, including 22 on 'Stars of the Fifties' and others working on 'Reading Latin', family history and 'African empires'. Many of the students were retired people – including a former TV production assistant and an ex-electronic engineer – but not all of them: one taking 'Reading Latin' was a middle-aged single mother, another a young Latin graduate who wanted a 'refresher course'.[64] Some students went back again and again: a married couple from Girton, Janice and Ray Adams, featured in the *Cambridge Evening News* in 1996, had been taking the Board's courses for five and three years respectively. They focused particularly on Latin, the classics, poetry and ancient history, and Janice was also studying at the Open University.[65]

*

Although some subjects had already made the transition, at least in part, to accredited provision, the integration into the CATS system of all 350 or so courses in the public programmes would be an enormous task, albeit one shared by many other continuing education departments in British universities. At Cambridge, the process would be overseen by David Davies, alongside two new managers, Lynne Caley and Vanessa Nedderman.[66] With Richard Wheeler – a research and development officer

– and Shelley Lockwood, Davies, Caley and Nedderman formed a 'project team' whose work fundamentally changed the ways in which the public programmes were organised. They realised that the process of accreditation was 'fraught with structural, philosophical and cultural problems', an enterprise that was 'distinctly problematic to many adult educators and to many students who represent the traditional clientele of university extra-mural classes'.[67] For Davies, though, accreditation presented university extramural departments with an opportunity to contribute to developments resulting from 'the emergence of mass higher education', and in particular to shape a widening participation agenda that was unlikely to be adopted elsewhere in the University of Cambridge.[68]

The accreditation process began with a pilot scheme or 'feasibility study', funded by the Department for Education and Science and involving around 40 courses.[69] This resulted in a key report that paved the way for the accreditation of most of the rest of the public programmes, published in 1995 as *Credit Where It's Due*. The report was written by Davies and Wheeler, with contributions from Caley and Nedderman. As well as setting out the processes and instruments that would be associated with accreditation, *Credit Where It's Due* presented them as embodiments of a significant 'cultural change' that reflected a shift in emphasis within the higher education sector. This entailed a change in focus, away from 'knowledge for its own sake' and towards a situation in which 'learning had to be demonstrated by reference to outcomes and products'.[70] For Davies and Wheeler, this did 'not seem altogether unreasonable where publicly funded provision is involved'; indeed, it was a clearly justified development that presented an opportunity to draw together the 'liberal' and vocational sides of adult learning in universities and therefore 'to develop a cohesive and genuinely open culture of lifelong learning', with an emphasis on the 'learning'. Indeed, accreditation and the credit transfer framework entailed an 'empowerment' of the learner that could have profound educational and social significance:

> The recognition of individual achievement through credits and qualifications actually empowers the person by offering a currency which can be traded in for opportunities for furthering learning or for employment. Learners in adult and continuing education now have the opportunity to have their achievements acknowledged. … The

> [*Credit Where It's Due*] Project was therefore conceived as an opportunity to recognise learning as it currently takes place in diverse settings and to enlarge educational opportunity by creating a framework within which … students can achieve and progress.[71]

In practice, this would mean two routes that could be taken through the Board's courses. As was already the case, some students would take a named Certificate in a particular theme or discipline such as local history or archaeology. Others would accumulate credits through taking a series of one-off courses, each with a different weighting depending on its length, and if successful would obtain credits that could be used towards a generic Certificate in Continuing Education. A 20-week course was worth 20 credits, a ten-week course ten credits, and five credits were available for a weekend course. Once a student had obtained 60 credits, they could write to the director of public programmes to claim their award.[72] The credits were transferable, which enabled students to move between universities, or other course-providing bodies as appropriate, to follow a self-shaped programme of study. This was presented as having benefits for staff, students and the institution itself: it could be seen as the latest example of university adult education's adaptation to 'student needs', and also as 'liberating talent and energy in new and modern ways',[73] just as James Stuart had attempted to do in the late nineteenth century. It could also be a way of maintaining – and demonstrating the maintenance of – the academic standards that had been central to the mission of the Cambridge Board across its history:

> The award of credit is the start of a cycle of quality assurance which includes moderation yet allows tutors a high degree of autonomy. The standards to be reached by students must have regard to the mission of the teaching institution, to comparable provision elsewhere and to the available resources. To enable university continuing education to be responsive to student needs and to link effectively with its community of learners, there must be clear procedures for the award and recording of credit and institutional involvement in advisory and guidance services.[74]

Seen as a way of demonstrating the learning that was already, and had always been, happening in extension courses, accreditation could have been an unthreatening development, albeit one with implications for the administration, teaching and oversight of the Board's courses.

Nevertheless, some of those who taught on the Board's programmes were concerned about the new credit system; in Mark Bailey's words, it amounted to 'such a profound cultural change that it was bound to trigger emotive responses and cause tensions'.[75] The very idea of assessment – which 'interferes in the staff/student relationship' – was anathema to some, while others were concerned about their inability to give the kind of 'guidance' that might be needed to support students' negotiations of the wider credit framework.[76] One tutor felt that 'the shadow of assessment … threatens to sour the fun of the [class] meetings and the wonder of the subject', and this sentiment may well have been shared by many others.[77] Most had no experience of the rather alien notion of 'intended learning outcomes', which was relatively new in any case and was not used elsewhere in the University of Cambridge at this time. There were very real concerns about the workload associated with the assessment of students' work and 'verifying' their attainment of the learning outcomes – not to mention the extra demands on administrators and on library resources that might result.[78] Tutors recognised, and sympathised with, the 'diffidence' that students felt about their writing skills, a long-standing feature of extramural work in the 'older tradition', in which written work had been expected of students and had been necessary for them to be deemed 'effective'.[79]

Davies argues that opposition to the credit system betrayed a deeper conservatism at Cambridge: 'accreditation was contentious and awarding recognition to non-traditional students was regarded by many in the University and on the Board itself with deep suspicion'.[80] The changes of the period certainly disrupted what remained of the 'Great Tradition', which had long eschewed examinations and awards. For Davies, the staff at the Board 'had been forged in the heat' of that tradition, 'over many years', and as a result 'had acquired the skills and expertise that made them good tutors'.[81] Their courses were popular and their services in demand at the local centres. However, 'many … refused to acknowledge the social revolution that mass higher education had produced since 1960 and especially in the 1990s', from which – as Davies argues – 'there was no going back'.[82] Indeed, as it turned out, the breadth of assessment methods introduced across the public programmes, in a relatively short space of time, suggests that the Board was well-equipped to produce an interesting and innovative set of courses with assignments effectively tailored to the learning outcomes. Davies and some of his colleagues expressed a hope that 'as credit issues become more familiar there will be greater recognition of the benefits and opportunities' that might arise from them.[83]

Davies and his colleagues recognised that the accreditation of the public programmes would require a significant investment in staff development. This consisted of an 'induction morning' for new tutors, and training for both new and existing tutors on assessment and 'classroom management and effective teaching'; and a series of 'evaluation visits' was undertaken in the 1996-7 academic year, providing opportunities for both staff development and 'quality control'. Further training was provided in 1997-8 on audio-visual aids and on 'interactive teaching and evaluation'.[84] The annual 'tutors' handbook' included hefty sections on the credit framework, with detail on such arcane topics as 'keeping credits alive' and 'award of partial credit'.[85] Such explanations of the complexities around the edges of the credit system were important, but were more technical than pedagogical, and the Cambridge Board – unlike similar departments at some other universities – did not participate heavily in professional training for adult educators.

One innovation was made in this area: a one-year part-time Professional Certificate in Adult and Continuing Education, which in 1993-4 ran at both Cambridge and Bedford, attracting 12 and 16 students respectively. This aimed at supporting both the development of adult pedagogies and the promotion of professional development in the post-compulsory sector. The course required a commitment among participants to 'active' or 'self-generated' learning, and aimed to 'share and develop ideas, knowledge and theories of adult learning and teaching'. The course was team-taught, featuring Davies himself among others, and strongly reflected the evolving contexts of adult education, stressing as Davies had elsewhere the importance of both 'tradition' and change. The latter was expressed mainly in the language of 'professionalisation':

> The field of adult and continuing education itself is becoming more tightly organised, structured and constrained by national policy. The

> spread of adult learning opportunities is taking place within more tightly organised systems of accountability. More and more teachers are required to gain professionally recognised qualifications. All of these factors must gain recognition in this course; in short we all must be sensitive to the need to be effective as managers of learning.[86]

The Certificate comprised three elements: a 'foundation unit' and a course called 'Learning Outside the Institution', both assessed by a 2,000-word essay, and then a 5,000-word dissertation. It ran for a second year in 1994-5; at Bedford the Certificate had a large team comprising staff from the Further Education Funding Council, the WEA, colleges of further education and various 'community education providers and training partners', offering what the course publicity called 'expertise from the widest possible range of post-school education currently on offer'.[87] Despite the impressive staff profile, however, and despite the apparent need for staff development in the continuing education sector, by 1995-6 the Certificate was running only in Cambridge, and had just eight students.[88]

Student responses to the new credit framework ranged from enthusiasm through 'reservations' to outright 'hostility'; some saw credits as 'foreign goods imported into the liberal adult tradition'.[89] Accreditation did not necessarily suit the demographics of the public programmes, which attracted an older student body, many of whom already had higher qualifications and did not view their learning primarily in developmental terms. One commented: 'you cannot leave your [credits] to your grandchildren … so what use [are] they to a third age student?'[90] Some students, too, did not appreciate the pedagogical implications of accreditation, preferring a more didactic method of teaching: quite happy to attend, and pay for, a simple series of lectures, these students had little interest in active participation in seminars or workshops.[91] Among other students – perhaps especially those with less prior educational attainment – there were fears associated with assessment, which could be seen as 'external, imposed and threatening'. It formed 'a major psychological barrier' for some, 'associated … with memories of compulsory, formal education … and with the failures of the past'.[92] Others, though, enjoyed the challenges of producing assignments: one felt that 'writing at home kept senility at bay', while others expressed a clear ambition to take their learning further, perhaps by pursuing an Open University degree or making an independent in-depth study of some kind.[93]

One account – from a student in Great Shelford, a few miles south of Cambridge – perhaps typifies the impact of accreditation in the local centres. There, initially, the students had ‘many reservations’. Some were concerned about the impact on the tutor – noting ‘the toll it took on a tutor’s time reading and commenting upon some quite lengthy pieces of work’ – and others were simply unused to doing written work: some had been attending the Board’s courses at Great Shelford for 30 years. It was found that, as they took part in the accreditation pilot, ‘heavier use’ was being made of the book-boxes, and many students felt that they benefited from the requirement to demonstrate their learning, in this case on a course in medieval history. ‘The majority attending courses for enjoyment over many years’, it was reported, ‘felt that attempting assignments gave them a greater depth of understanding and appreciation of the subject through their research into extra background.’[94] Ultimately, though, there was some dissatisfaction with the *requirement* to produce work: ‘[t]here are many benefits from the accreditation system but we must be vigilant in urging that it remains voluntary and that access to courses remains open to all, thus preserving the ideal of liberal education as a lifetime experience’.[95]

All tutors and students had to grapple with the new demands that accreditation made on assessment: as *Credit Where It’s Due* explained, a key objective was to devise ‘assessments which are compatible and commensurate with the traditions and standards of extra-mural education’.[96] These would vary significantly across the public programmes. Students on history courses, for example, were asked to produce essays and primary source analyses; music courses used multiple-choice questions; and architecture students were assessed by an in-class ‘quiz’, among other things. In botany, students developed frameworks for the study of wild flowers; in literature, they gave oral presentations and kept personal journals, as well as writing more traditional essays; and in local history, they collected files of material on a particular area over time and created a series of ‘exemplar questions’ for use in the analysis of parish churches.[97] These new activities presented significant pedagogical challenges, which were particularly acute for subjects that typically attracted student numbers in the thirties, forties or fifties, and which had often relied on didactic lectures with a relatively modest element of student participation. In field archaeology, the ten-week class based on lectures was replaced by group-work to support the new system of assessment, and other subjects had to shift their focus too. Of all subjects taught on the public programmes, local history was perhaps the best placed to meet the challenges of accreditation, given its long-standing use of active methods of learning, with problem-solving at their heart, and a tradition of co-production of research outputs involving both tutor and students.[98]

The central instrument of assessment, which was used across most of the public programmes, was a new 'personal statement of learning' (PSL), which students were expected to complete at the end of the course, and which formed 'the key to the "contract" between the learner and the University'.[99] The PSL was developed at Cambridge and also adopted by the University of Oxford and others who were grappling with the accreditation of extramural courses. It stemmed from Davies's previous involvement with key figures in the Access and widening participation movement, and became a key device in helping the public programmes to transfer to the accredited framework. It had three sections. The first was entitled 'Personal Learning and Progress', in which students were asked to reflect on the course itself and their participation in it; and the second was headed 'Progression … Where Now?' In this section students outlined where they might take their learning next: this may have been useful for many students, and perhaps also to the Board itself in formulating its programme of courses and marketing strategies. The final section asked students to rate – on a scale of one to five – their attainment of the intended learning outcomes. The whole PSL was 'verified' by the tutor and, along with an attendance requirement (two-thirds of the sessions) and satisfactory completion of the assessment, then entitled the student to receive the appropriate credit for the course.[100] The PSL could be, and often was, a useful opportunity for students to reflect – as some did enthusiastically – on their academic and personal development. Some did not appreciate the purpose: one wrote angrily on the PSL that 'I feel no need to justify myself. I didn't join the class to prove anything to anybody. I joined because it sounded interesting – which it was.'[101] Others, though, wrote

> considered, reflective and highly positive comments about the knowledge and self-knowledge gained from both the formal tuition and the informal discussion and social interaction on the course. Confidence, inspiration, rekindled enthusiasm and a desire to go on with learning recurred as the most common 'gains', together with the development of a more critical stance, greater appreciation of different interpretations of a subject and the benefits of an encouraging and stimulating environment.[102]

The PSL remained a key element of the public programmes through the rest of the 1990s and 2000s.

In its course publicity the Board attempted to reassure students who were worried about accreditation. In the residential course brochure for 1994-5, for example, Davies explained that '[w]hen we talk about assessment we do not mean timed examinations'.[103] Most importantly, though,

> the fees we charge are subsidised. If we passed on the full cost to the students the courses would be way out of many people's reach. It is true that from Autumn 1995 the money necessary to subsidise all our courses … is going to depend on a grant for each student who is registered for assessment. The funding body is insisting that if subsidies are to be awarded then individual students should demonstrate the fact that some learning has taken place.[104]

A leaflet was produced explaining the details of the credit framework, and in due course the information was included in the annual 'students' handbook': by the turn of the twenty-first century the section entitled 'Credit Accumulation and Transfer' amounted to nine A5 pages of rather small print.[105] During the implementation phase, Davies urged, the credit framework 'will make very little difference to you as a student', but at the same time he admitted that *some* courses might be affected:

> the tutors will need your help for they will have rather more responsibility than in the past and will be bearing the brunt of the changes … [T]hey would appreciate your forbearance if things do not always work out quite as planned at first. Some of you will have the

> privilege of being in designated pilot courses … [and, if so,] we hope you will tell us about your experience and we will ensure you have the opportunity to do so.[106]

In the next course brochure, Davies again drew on tradition to support his explanation of accreditation, opening his introductory remarks with a reference to James Stuart and to the model of the 20-week course with a written examination, after which successful students were awarded certificates. He continued, '[a]lthough we at the Board like to think that we are in the vanguard of change, it is chastening to find that credit for adult learning is an old concept', but added: 'certificates are not new, [but] the way in which they can be earned is certainly modern and innovative'. Again, he made it clear that few courses would have traditional written examinations, but rather a range of assessment methods, 'limited only by the imagination of the Board's tutors'.[107]

*

Named Certificate and Diploma programmes proliferated from the mid-1990s onwards, but most attracted only relatively modest numbers of students. In the 1995-6 academic year, there were 425 students pursuing Certificates, a small increase on the 377 two years earlier; but these students were spread across 31 different groups and a wider range of subjects than before.[108] By 1998-9 there were Certificates in Archaeology, Art History, Drama and Society, English Local History, Film Studies, Medieval Studies, Modern English Literature, Science, Historic Building Conservation, Town Planning and Management, and Counselling and Groupwork, alongside Diplomas in Archaeology, Landscape History and Field Archaeology, and Religious Studies, as well as the Advanced Diploma in English Local History. More students were taking these, still a minority of total numbers on the public programmes, but a substantial body of enrolments none the less.[109] The counselling Certificates were often among the most popular, recruiting 15, 20 or even 30 students; and a two-year Diploma in Educational and Vocational Guidance also ran, with a cohort of 16 students in Cambridge, in 1994-5 and 1995-6, for which a counselling or social science Certificate was a pre-requisite. Designed as an explicit 'in-service professional training course', this

Certificate was studied by members of the Board's own staff as well as the public, and Vanessa Nedderman credits it with helping her to find employment on the guidance side of adult education when she left Cambridge in 1997.[110] Certificates had by now almost entirely supplanted tutorial classes, although there was *one* tutorial class running at this time, on 'Twentieth Century Literature' in Saffron Walden, with 28 students.[111] As the examples of town planning and counselling show, there was in some cases a more explicit 'vocational' element to the Certificate courses.

Whatever the merits of the Certificates and Diplomas, it was still impossible to obtain a Cambridge undergraduate degree through the accumulation of credits on the public programmes. The university would not countenance the award of a part-time undergraduate degree; hence the advice to students to take their credits elsewhere in order to complete the required programme. David Davies puts it more forcefully: 'a certificate could be gained and undergraduate credit used elsewhere in higher education, but not within the sacred precincts of the Cambridge colleges'.[112] This was a matter of contention in the late 1990s and into the 2000s: one former member of staff recalled that a student from one of the local centres, with enough credits to qualify, attempted to claim a Cambridge degree, though without success. More widely, the relationship between the Board and University could be 'very difficult', because the latter 'didn't really understand about part-time students'.[113] Davies, though, feels that stronger claims could have been made on behalf of part-time undergraduate study:

> The elite system which Cambridge embodied and its 'contract' with social groups and the public was being re-shaped by wider and more pervasive forces but in the main the academic staff at Madingley resorted to the dominant ideology of the day – which was to accept and adapt and thrive (in its own terms) around the conscious *exclusion* of the mass of adult learners from accessing degree-level courses for part-time adult students. The development of part-time degree-level studies should have been the meat and drink of the Cambridge Extra-Mural Department. … Across the University there was little formal institutional appetite for widening participation … [and as a result] a class-bound, elitist and hierarchical system was eventually reinforced, and the reformist and democratic impulse of

> mass participation was deemed incommensurate with the wider Cambridge mission.[114]

The result of the failure to establish a part-time undergraduate degree was that many students took their Cambridge credits elsewhere to pursue degree-level courses. The Board had a 'credit agreement' with the Open University, and with the extramural departments at the Universities of Essex and East Anglia; and students could also go on to the newly designated Anglia Polytechnic (now Anglia Ruskin) University or the University of Hertfordshire.[115]

These were also the eventual destinations of many students who participated in a Access to Higher Education course, pioneered by Davies and offered in 1993-4 at Cambridge, Ely and Bedford. With 47 students, this was reasonably successful in its first year.[116] In Cambridge, the course was offered in collaboration with Hills Road and Long Road Sixth Form Colleges, but the initiative was not widely supported within the university. Davies felt that the newer Universities of Essex and East Anglia, as well as the former polytechnics in the region, were much more open to the Access movement, and that 'Cambridge had set its face against that concept of higher education'.[117] Indeed, Cambridge had not participated in the Access 'movement' when it first emerged in the 1970s and 1980s, despite the potential that it had to transform university admissions and to address social inequalities across the education system.[118] Nevertheless, Davies had the strong support of Colin Greenhalgh, principal at Hills Road, who was 'particularly helpful' in developing Access provision, and whose legacy can still be seen in a 'significant adult education programme' at the college today.[119] Davies argued that Access could give 'further practical expression to the University's existing commitment to widening access' as well as extending 'the role and obligations of the University to adults in the wider community'.[120] Access could present an opportunity to increase the very small proportion of Cambridge undergraduates who were mature entrants, as well as supporting a diversification of the student body in terms of gender, ethnicity and social background.[121] However, HEFCE funding for the initiative was soon withdrawn, and the Board's involvement in Access courses did not survive for long, though the initiative would be restarted, again briefly, in the 2000s (see chapter 7).

A further, and rather different, example of widening participation activity in the 1990s – and running into the 2000s – was the Fenland Oral History Project, which drew on the Cambridge tradition of local history and – like many other courses – resulted in students publishing work based on their research.[122] Directed by Susan Oosthuizen, the project had funding – intended to support widening participation – from HEFCE, and addressed what Oosthuizen described as 'a major local barrier to participation in [higher education]: a defensive regional culture, the result of a long history of a mistaken perception of Fenland "backwardness"'.[123] A largely agricultural region, comprising villages often poorly connected to each other and to larger centres of population, the Fens had high unemployment, a high proportion of older people, and low levels of car ownership; and they were culturally distinct from other parts of Cambridgeshire (and the ancient county of Huntingdonshire).[124] Communities were approached through existing local branches of organisations such as Age Concern, the British Legion and Women's Institutes, with specially trained oral history tutors employed to carry out the teaching.[125] The oral history groups that met under the Project's auspices included both Fenlanders and 'incomers', and involved recorded group discussions, individual interviews and walking tours of particular villages.[126] The resulting publications, it was claimed, 'form part of the social history of Britain in the twentieth century', and 'make an essential, if minor, contribution to this history'.[127]

*

In the short term at least, accreditation did not cause a significant change to the content and popularity of the public programmes. Excluding those run at the Sidgwick Site, there were 133 'successful' courses in 1995-6, with student numbers falling by 13.7% from 2,444 to 2,110. The drop, though, was attributed mainly to a sharp decline in the joint provision of courses with the WEA (from 45 courses with 1,132 students down to 17 with just 338 students), without which the overall numbers would show a significant increase.[128] The picture regarding credit was more mixed: 47% of students on 20-week courses and 33% of those on ten-week courses gained credit, while among courses taught at the Sidgwick Site the proportion was even lower at 26%. The latter had increased to 40% by the turn of the millennium. For residential courses, there was again little difference in overall student numbers in the first year of full accreditation, and a much higher proportion – 87% – gained credit.[129] Student numbers fell slightly towards the end of the 1990s, although there were two new local centres at Rickinghall (Suffolk) and Dunstable (Bedfordshire) in 1998-9.[130] In the same year eight separate courses ran with more than 40 students, including 'English Cathedrals' at Lavenham, attended by 75; this Suffolk village, with one course each year on a different theme, was reliably successful at attracting students.

Meanwhile, a concerted attempt was made to provide courses on popular science subjects: this was successful at Tewin, where 46 students enrolled for 'Astronomy: An Introduction to the Night Sky' in 1998-9. The same course attracted 19 students at Ashwell, and only eight at Sharnbrook, near Bedford, though there it still out-recruited 'Identifying Wild Flowers', which had just five enrolments. Meanwhile, 'Observational Astronomy' was taught to 21 students at Stowmarket, and 'The Science behind the News' to 12 at the Letchworth settlement.[131] National Science Week was used to publicise courses, through displays and leaflets, and in both 1997 and 1998 the Week was co-ordinated by Lynne Harrison, one of the Board's academic development officers for science.[132] The other, Gillian Sheail, recalls that National Science Week 'was an important way of publicising the work of the public programmes'. However, it was still an uphill struggle to persuade some local centres to take science courses:

> When Lynne and I were appointed as academic development officers for Science we tried to broaden both the range and the variety of topics covered by our courses. While Lynne's interest was in biochemistry and mine in geology and landform studies we had some very good panel tutors for astronomy, genetics, ornithology, ecology and marine biology. However hard we tried to interest local centres in these topics, there were still some who said 'No, we don't want science'.[133]

As these comments suggest, in terms of overall student numbers on the Board's courses, science was much smaller than the arts and humanities. Of 648 student enrolments across the Certificate programmes in 1998-9, just 27 were on astronomy courses, 25 in geology and another 27 on either or both of 'Birds in Autumn and Winter' or 'Birds in Spring and Summer'.[134] All these Certificates were based at the Sidgwick Site. For comparison, the most popular single subject at Certificate and Diploma level – archaeology – had 162 enrolled students, across centres in Cambridge, Peterborough, Letchworth and Fulbourn (Cambridgeshire).[135]

Day-schools and residential courses at Madingley remained popular throughout the 1990s, and the attractions of the place remained the same: the collegiate atmosphere, the food and the gardens were all important elements of a stay at the Hall. The gardens were used as a resource in some teaching, while the history of the Hall and village were also covered. In 1993 Lionel Munby contributed heavily to a weekend course on 'Madingley: Hall, Church, Estate and Village', which included a two-hour 'walk about'; and Patrick Harding – a long-serving panel tutor – led a course in the following year entitled 'Of Trees and Woods'. This featured the Hall's head gardener, Richard Gant, leading a session 'looking at the importance of trees in the landscape'. Harding later led an accredited weekend course on 'The Medicinal Properties of Plants', again based at Madingley, while college gardens and the university's Botanic Garden also featured in courses of this kind.[136] By the time they were accredited after the mid-1990s, the academic content of residential courses, even at weekends, was more reliably rigorous: Peter Bysouth remembers that 'it was not just a three-day break in the Cambridgeshire countryside'. Although he recalls that some of those who attended 'were less academically inclined' than those who had taken Certificate and Diploma courses, nevertheless 'we were expected to produce some written work at the end' of a residential course. Bysouth, at least, found it easy enough to concentrate on the work: 'we were there to learn, and the tutors were there to make sure we learned'. He adds, though, that with the excellent catering and lively bar, 'we had great fun too'.[137]

*

The Cambridge Programme for Industry became increasingly vigorous and successful in the 1990s, although usually somewhat independent of, and isolated from, the remainder of the Board's activities. It moved in the early 1990s from the the Faculty of Engineering to its own premises at 1

Trumpington Street, and had 30 members of staff by the end of the decade.[138] It was scheduling 32 courses year in the early 1990s, and more than 60 a few years later, ranging from short focused meetings for business leaders to two-year part-time Master's programmes that provided Cambridge postgraduate degrees for post-experience students.[139] Some early courses had to be cancelled owing to low enrolments, and not all ventures were successful. It was difficult to ensure that provision was both 'cutting edge' and self-financing – once the PICKUP and other pump-priming funding had come to an end (see chapter 5) – given the constantly changing demands of the CPI's customer base.[140] Some elements of the work were more successful than others: a 'senior managers' programme' enjoyed only a 'slow start', and an 'executive management programme' failed to get off the ground, although a 'professional development programme', led by Polly Courtice, attracted more students, despite the effects of the recession of the early 1990s. By October 1993 the CPI was working with more than 20 academic departments at Cambridge, and expecting to run courses in that academic year for around 1,800 people, amounting to 89 full-time equivalent students.[141]

The main impetus for growth was a successful application by Courtice to run the Prince of Wales's Business and Environment Programme; this was won in the face of widespread competition and, according to the CPI's director Christopher Padfield, became 'the foundation for everything else that we did'.[142] Awarded in spring 1993, sponsorship funding was raised that enabled the CPI to establish a week-long summer school programme at Madingley Hall in the following year, which would form the basis for a long-term series of initiatives in sustainability training and leadership. The context was shaped by the Brundtland Report, *Our Common Future*, in 1987, and the Earth Summit, the United Nations Conference on Environment and Development in Rio de Janeiro in 1992, both of which shone a light on the crucial role of business, and paved the way for many subsequent developments in multinational and corporate action on sustainability.[143] The then Prince of Wales himself visited Cambridge to discuss the arrangements in 1993, and attended the first and second meetings in September 1994 and April 1995. His active support was pivotal in encouraging very senior business leaders to attend at a time when the very concept of sustainable development was still emerging in the corporate sector.[144] According to Courtice, the programme was 'transformational' for both the CPI and those who attended: delegates learned about the systems pressures and trends that were posing risks to society, the environment and their own businesses. They heard from academics and practitioners alike: biodiversity experts talking about ecosystems decline; climate scientists explaining starkly how the planet was warming; and a visit to the British Antarctic Survey powerfully demonstrating the correlation between greenhouse gas emissions and temperature rise, a fact that was critical at a time when climate change denial was still a powerful force in business and policy-making.

The programme drew on an extraordinary range of academic disciplines, including technologists, natural scientists, economists, anthropologists, historians, philosophers and even the Astronomer-Royal, to help delegates get a better understanding of the whole system within which they were operating. For Courtice, this was teaching, of a kind, 'but we never saw it as teaching' – the aim was 'to work with these business leaders to help them understand and solve these problems'.[145] The initiative gained a strong momentum, attracting sponsorship amounting to some £200,000 from ten 'major companies' in its first year.[146] Thereafter the programme went from strength to strength, and was developed internationally in the following years, developing an alumni network that today numbers around 3,500. The programme later went on to spawn the Prince of Wales's Corporate Leaders' Group on Climate Change, as well as numerous other leaders' groups and executive programmes. Courtice explains that 'we were on a roll because we were tapping into a problem that companies were beginning to recognise and for which they had no ready-made solutions'. She argues that business schools – even the new Judge Business School at Cambridge – did not cater, at least at this period of their development, for this kind of wider contextualised approach to solving a society-wide problem that had major implications for businesses' licence to operate.[147]

It is clear from this account that what the CPI was doing in the 1990s was very different from the main focus of the Board of Continuing Education. The Board had been a useful, and perhaps critical, vehicle for the early development of a new initiative in the late 1980s, but the CPI became something very distinct that involved few of the long-standing members of staff and catered for a very different kind of student. Courtice explains that, although the Board itself occupied a somewhat marginal position in relation to the university, it was 'staffed by people who were more interested in academic subject-matter than in entrepreneurial activities', and as such, 'as long as we weren't too disruptive, we were out-of-sight-and-out-of-mind' for much of the time. 'We were', she says, 'effectively a spin-out company.'[148] Moreover, the CPI was effectively financially independent of the rest of the Board's activities by the mid-1990s, and by the end of the decade 'almost entirely focused' on the core issue of sustainability that had formed the most significant area of growth following the intervention of the then Prince of Wales.[149] By the turn of the new millennium, the work was loosely organised around four themes: 'the management of diversity', 'corporate social responsibility', 'business sustainability' and 'innovation and futures thinking', and there were accredited initiatives in sustainability learning, social inclusion management, inter-cultural management and various other areas.[150]

For much of the CPI's activity, the accreditation process through which the Board was passing in the mid-1990s was considered 'not relevant to the corporate market': Courtice recalls that companies 'wanted content and they wanted it fast', and this could not be supported by the usual complex academic quality assurance process.[151] Nevertheless, some elements of the CATS framework were useful, and the CPI developed various initiatives at Diploma and Master's level during the 1990s, in collaboration with other Cambridge departments and some external organisations. There were eventually four Master's programmes under CPI auspices, including a Diploma/Master's in Manufacturing, directed by professor of engineering Mike Gregory.[152] Perhaps the most significant was a part-time Master's in Interdisciplinary Design for the Built Environment, which arose from a conference as early as 1991 sponsored by the Ove Arup Foundation. This allowed practising architects and civil engineers to study part-time, with some intensive residential components, working on a range of projects from – as the involvement of both the engineering and architecture faculties suggested – an interdisciplinary perspective. It also had an identifiable relationship with the wider focus of the CPI on sustainability issues: for example, one of the projects on the course considered 'the task of inserting bridges into a sensitive natural environment incorporating sites of special scientific interest'.[153] According to one account, the project, 'supported by an eminent structural engineer and landscape architect, also queried the nature of the natural environment as the drained fenlands which provided the site for the project were themselves the product of large-scale engineering intervention'.[154] Although numbers on the programme were relatively small, it was considered a leading example of 'current initiatives', and today it is a flagship programme of the Institute for Sustainability Leadership (as CPI became), running annually at full capacity in terms of student numbers.[155]

Underpinning these longer-term educational initiatives under CPI auspices were two key principles: the importance of practice-based learning and the need for 'systems'-level investigation. Practice-based learning was at the heart of industrial, commercial and management education, and could bring some tension to the relationship with the academic content of post-experience courses. The CPI's director Christopher Padfield recognised that companies 'may be broadly well disposed' to its initiatives, 'but want to see a set of relevant (in their terms) products which are not predominantly "academic"'.[156] This in turn involved working closely with those who were buying the CPI's 'product', a complex set of relationships that could sometime cause unease within the university. For example, a proposed Certificate of Professional Development, in collaboration with a large multi-national company, generated a 'wide-ranging discussion' at the Board, at which 'concern was expressed that [it] could be seen to be endorsing the products or trading tactics of a particular company'.[157] There were suspicions on the other side too: could universities, particularly Cambridge, provide what companies needed, or wanted? Lynne Caley later explained that 'we spend an inordinate amount of time demonstrating that, as an institution, we are no more or less flexible than the majority of higher education institutions … that "traditional" does not necessarily mean "hidebound"'.[158]

The practice-based element was central to creating the synergies between academia and industry that the CPI sought and achieved. As Courtice explains, 'there was an appetite from people who wanted to do a Cambridge degree with a more practice-based approach', and this underpinned the pedagogical aims of the CPI. For Courtice, 'learning from what you have been doing in your professional capacity is difficult and messy, but every bit as stuffed with possibility as learning from the classroom'.[159] It was, though, also difficult, especially for graduates in scientific and technical disciplines, whose first-degree education, according to Padfield, often 'fails to prepare students to find out for themselves'. Universities could help such mature professionals to reflect on their own experiences, and to provide 'the linking context between isolated bits of experiential knowledge'.[160] It was widely recognised across the continuing education sector that 'short injections of "expertise"' were no longer the most suitable model, and that 'training' was giving way to 'managing learning' and providing support for professional development.[161] The CPI's programme development managers, Elaine Hendry and Mark Waltham, insisted that 'individual professionals' should be seen 'as the creators of their own specialist knowledge', and that this could broaden the traditional notion of the university as a 'community of students' to many who were not associated with it on a full-time basis.[162]

Within all these developments, there was a sense that universities still had a role to play, but that this was evolving. One side of universities' contribution to industry was in subject-specific research, and in many cases specific technological problems clearly required a research 'solution' rather than a short bespoke training course.[163] For Padfield, though, the link between research and teaching – a traditional feature of universities – epitomised what Cambridge could do in and for the professional world; and at the heart of this lay the process of learning, rather than teaching:

> The *process* of learning through research, reflection and scholarship is … transferable in its own right. It has potential application in the facilitation of high-level professional development. If it is useful for professors, it can be useful for professionals too. If professors can learn by research, scholarship and reflection, then so too can professionals. Who teaches the professors? What would professionals need to be taught, but not professors?[164]

Learning by reflection could be difficult to achieve for people working, for example, in the field of engineering; and as such continuing education, tied into the practice of industry or management, could support professional development through the injection not only of subject expertise but also pedagogical practice. The aim, then, was for professionals to 'strive to become capable of self-motivated reflection on their own learning and experience, and to become researchers into the professional concerns of their day, so that they can play a role in the building and development of themselves, their profession, and importantly also, the competitiveness of their companies'.[165]

From the academic side, this endeavour was necessarily of an interdisciplinary kind. For Padfield and others in the CPI, the contribution that the university could make to the business world was in the support and development of 'systems'-level learning and understanding. For Polly Courtice, the aim of the CPI's programmes was to 'make sure that people *really* understand what's going on', to think in a 'whole-system' rather than a 'deep-dive' way. The CPI held formal sessions on 'systems thinking', which was seen as a very different educational strategy from those favoured by business schools, or indeed from the research-led solutions to specific problems that could be generated by external funded projects within subject-based university departments.[166] Like the early focus on sustainability, this emphasised the fundamentally interdisciplinary character of the CPI's work, a feature that distinguished it from the subject-based research and teaching of most of the rest of the university. Courtice explained that 'companies don't think about problems by department names', and that 'we helped [them] to access the [university's] knowledge in cross-cutting disciplinary ways'. The Board itself *was* offering interdisciplinarity of various kinds, but at the CPI it 'was applied in a different ways to a different audience'.[167] Sometimes this even meant a return to the principles of the long-running course for IBM managers: in the mid-1990s, the CPI provided a course for around 400 senior leaders at BP, for which they were instructed to teach 'anything that's not related to this business'. Like the IBM course, this would – in theory, at least – help people to 'hold their own at any meeting or any dinner table in the world, because they understood the world in which they were operating'.[168]

In practical terms, by the end of the 1990s the CPI was catering for more than 2,500 students – representing 123 full-time equivalents – on programmes ranging from small focused activities with a handful of participants to huge events such as the Millennium Conference on Passive and Low Energy, with 299 delegates amounting to 17.9 full-time equivalents.[169] It was concluding its project with funding from the Department for Education and Employment to create a series of guidelines for workplace learning, and was trialling various online learning initiatives.[170] In student number terms it remained a fairly small part of the

Board of Continuing Education's overall activity, but the CPI was clearly establishing a strong profile in the sectors where its work was focused. It remained somewhat marginal to the core concerns of the Board, and there were clear signs that it could become an independent institution in the future.

The IBM Cambridge programme ran for its 30th successive year in 1996, and was based on much the same principles as had underpinned its origins in 1967. Like the public programmes, it had long-standing members of staff who returned year-on-year: Jonathan Steinberg of Trinity Hall taught in 1996, as he had done every year since the programme began, and Richard Mason was in his eleventh year as the course leader.[171] In the face of an expanding range of alternatives in the form of business schools and management programmes, IBM continued to insist on the non-vocational, or 'work-irrelevant', nature of the five-week Cambridge residential experience: '[t]he only ground-rule from IBM to the University was that the teaching should contain nothing on computers and nothing on business management'.[172] By this time around half the content comprised international politics and economics, with the rest ranging from drama to astronomy to religious studies; and there were 'alarming amounts of free time' for the students, at least compared with their normal working lives. With the aim of preparing engineers for management roles, the course sought to achieve a 'wider perspective' that could support them in making complex decisions. According to Mason,

> Maybe one way to encourage such understanding is with teaching on the theory of change, or with the type of inspirational psychology offered by many business schools. Another way might be to take people completely from their normal settings, to remove them from their normal pressures and to stimulate their thinking on subjects wholly outside their normal fields of work. This is not some form of brainwashing: more a rare chance, for excessively overburdened people, to *stop* and think about what they are doing in an academic framework.[173]

This could be challenging for both students and tutors – not all participants took easily to Mason's own subject, philosophy, for example – but the overall success of this course emphasises the potential vocationality of 'work-irrelevant' learning.[174]

The long-standing role of the Board in armed forces' training persisted through the 1990s, along with other areas of work in legal education. The successful Summer School in English Legal Methods continued to run – with scholarships available for students from eastern Europe – as well as the annual revision course for LLB students at the University of London.[175] Newer developments included the introduction of part-time Master of Studies degrees in Applied Criminology and Police Studies and in Applied Criminology and Management, the latter aimed at prison officers.[176] Vocational education in the public service was further developed in 1999, when a new training course was developed in association with Cambridgeshire Constabulary: an ambitious 11-module programme, overseen by a Metropolitan Police commander, resulted in a Certificate of Community Policing for 'beat bobbies'.[177] By this time, though, the involvement of the Board in magistrates' training was in decline, with the last residential programme for this group run in 1998-9; from then onwards the Board focused on the creation of training material rather than direct course provision.[178]

*

The International Summer Schools maintained their profile in the 1990s, but numbers fluctuated and the peak attendance – 1,573 students in 1989 – was never challenged. In 1992 numbers fell below 1,000, but the average across the 1990s was 1,151.[179] Several of the programmes run jointly with other universities were discontinued, or moved to other locations, by their home institutions as a result of staff or policy changes. Arrangements with some American universities persisted through the decade, notably Florida International University, the University of Southern California, UCLA and the University of Utah, and new specialist summer schools were added to the mix – history in 1990, Shakespeare in 1994 and medieval studies in 1996.[180] Student recruitment was challenging in the face of international politics and domestic crises: both the first Gulf War and the outbreak of 'mad cow disease' in Britain seem to have deterred registrations. Moreover, other universities were increasing their summer school provision, including Oxford, Amsterdam and several universities in the

USA. Sarah Ormrod, who took over as director of the International Summer Schools in 1995, spoke at various international events in Europe and the USA, representing the programmes regularly at the North American Association of Summer Schools and the European Association of International Educators conferences. This raised the profile of the Cambridge schools but may also have inspired other universities to enhance their own summer offerings.[181] Meanwhile, quality assurance considerations increasingly encroached into the summer schools, as they were doing on the public programmes: student feedback was shared directly with tutors from 1995, and tutors sometimes had to work quickly to amend courses to match the expectations and academic levels of the students who had signed up.[182]

As with the public programmes, there was a sustained attempt to increase the coverage of science in the summer schools. In 1998 Ormrod reported on a

> deliberate attempt … to broaden the offering given to our International Summer School students, which in 1996 and 1997 still retained strong leanings towards the liberal arts – a legacy of the programme's 74-year history. This, in a University which is known world-wide for its contribution to the sciences, clearly needed attention, and so the history of scientific ideas, scientific illustration, history of medicine, history of mathematics, environmental studies, philosophy of science and current perspectives on genetic engineering have now been added to our Summer School course lists.[183]

These efforts culminated in the establishment of a specialist interdisciplinary science programme in 1999, led by Lynne Harrison. This attracted 59 students in its first year and continued at roughly the same size into the early 2000s.[184] Ormrod had hoped for a larger expansion into the sciences: 'I never planned to have just a science programme – I was hoping that we would expand enough to have a botany programme, a zoology programme and a physics programme'. These hopes did not materialise, although the interdisciplinary science programme expanded from two to four weeks.[185] Meanwhile, the linguistics summer school was dropped in the mid-1990s, and did not return.[186]

The breadth of the summer schools led to an increase in the complexity of the organisational arrangements, and in the number of staff who taught on them. This stood at 75 in 1995 and 118 in 1999,[187] and was augmented each year by a series of high-profile Cambridge and other academics who gave one-off plenary lectures, intended to 'stimulate [the] audience for an hour each morning and encourage its members to think about things beyond their immediate course of study'.[188] In many years these were planned according to a specific theme, and selections were published by Cambridge University Press. Some of the lectures from 1993 were published in the following year as *Cambridge Minds*, edited by Richard Mason. With contributors including Colin Renfrew, Mark Goldie, Ernest Gellner and Gillian Sutherland – the only woman among the 16 authors – the book was mostly about Cambridge and some of the key individuals who had worked there. One chapter covered James Stuart, written by Paul McHugh, a historian of social reform based at Anglia Polytechnic University.[189] Mason offered an 'embarrassed apology' for the male-centredness of the book; and although another volume on *Cambridge Women*, edited by Edward Shils and Carmen Blacker, redressed the balance somewhat, this was not based on summer school lectures.[190]

A further collection of published summer school plenaries, *Cambridge Contributions*, appeared in 1998; this was edited by Sarah Ormrod, and its profits went to the scholarship fund.[191] Contributors to this volume included Gillian Sutherland (again), Madeleine Arnot, Martin Rees – who had recently been appointed as Astronomer Royal – and Stefan Collini, whose lecture was on 'Cambridge and the Study of English'.[192] Collini lectured, then and since, for the summer schools on many occasions, and has 'always enjoyed' the experience, despite the fact that most are delivered in the Sidgwick Site's Lady Mitchell Hall – a 'great sounding cavern … not, it has to be said, a venue that makes for intimacy or encourages a sense of occasion'. Nevertheless, he reports a 'lively and responsive (and always large) audience' whose members ask interesting, challenging and often 'unexpected' questions.[193]

The international character of the summer schools was maintained through the 1990s, and supported by an evolving programme of scholarships that focused on specific countries and regions of the world. In 1995, 40% of the 1,147 students were from the USA, with a further 28% from continental Europe and 12% from Japan. By the end of the decade the proportion from the USA had increased to 50%, and the scholarship programme was being directed towards students from eastern Europe and the former Soviet republics. From 1995 invitations were sent to specific institutions to nominate individuals to receive scholarships, but with only thirteen available by the end of the 1990s, the extent of support was limited.[194] As had always been the case, the age profile of students was rather different from the public programmes: in 1995, 44% of students were current undergraduates or postgraduates at other universities, a figure that rose to 62% by 1999, and around 40% usually held a university degree. Between a tenth and a fifth were teachers. Efforts were made to attract local students, too: the summer schools could be a 'way in' to the public programmes, or indeed vice-versa, and there was always a significant number of the older students who tended to predominate in the public programmes. One woman is remembered to have attended annually into her nineties.[195] In one respect, at least, the profile was similar: in 1999, more than two-thirds of summer school students were women.[196]

Accreditation affected the summer programmes, as it did other areas of the Board's activity. Assessment was not a novelty for many of the students, but the proportion submitting written work increased significantly, with 714 papers being marked in 1999. There was also a small intensive 'honours option', requiring students to produce a weekly assignment, although, given the intensity of study that it involved, this did not appeal to so many students.[197] Those who took the 'honours option' stayed for six weeks, and had weekly supervisions with their tutor on the Cambridge model. (The provision of supervisions was replicated in the twenty-first century, for the ten years of the International Association of Research Universities Global Summer Programme.)[198] As with the public programmes, the growth of assessment meant a greater need for staff development and a significantly expanded administrative workload for Sarah Ormrod and her staff of around eight people.[199] This was intensified by the collection of student feedback – on paper, prior to the widespread use of computers and the Internet. Although 'satisfaction rates' were usually very high, and some of the individual tributes paid by students to the teaching staff were effusive, the organisational efforts required to plan the summer schools were 'huge': Ormrod compares the requirements in terms of planning, publicity, liaison with colleges and dealing with student inquiries to organising 'a large festival'.[200]

*

The profile of activity in the Board of Continuing Education at the end of the 1990s was not dissimilar in some respects to that which faced Michael Richardson on his arrival at Madingley a decade earlier. However, profound changes in some aspects of this activity had brought the Board and its students into a 'learning age' that is recognisable today. There had also been significant changes in the profile of the students and 'clients' of the Board: it was still catering for an often older population in the extramural region who wanted to study subjects such as local history and English literature, but the accreditation of the public programmes had drawn some new students into their orbit; the growth of the CPI, in particular, brought different cohorts into an association with Cambridge; and the International Summer Schools continued to serve a rather different constituency – they were 'spectacularly successful', according to David Davies.[201] It is clear that all areas were affected in some way by the issue of accreditation that formed the central challenge of the 1990s, for other continuing education departments as well as Cambridge's. However, the challenge was successfully met, and overall student numbers continued to expand. The Board's student body, described as 'the other 11,000' in 1993, stood at a remarkable 13,337 in 1998-9.[202] All these students had different reasons for taking part, but the benefits of doing so were much the same as always. As Peter Bysouth explained, among them were 'the high quality of teaching'; 'the tremendous enthusiasm, varied backgrounds, expertise and interests of one's fellow adult students'; and 'the relief from the stress of my workday environment that escaping into the totally different world of an adult evening class provides'.[203] Whatever else may have changed, the desire to learn, among a large body of adult students, remained at the centre of the educational needs addressed by the Board of Continuing Education.

Chapter 7
The learning curve: into a new millennium

University adult education departments had, in many cases, been 'radically restructured' in the 1990s, and by the turn of the new millennium many had been closed completely. Others would be under threat in the early 2000s, and even in the more successful ones there was 'a lack of stability, staff demoralisation and planning blight'.[1] The reasons for this were complex, but many stemmed from the rapid developments of the 1990s and the 'mainstreaming' of university adult education funding. Alongside this, an intensifying culture of research assessment in the university sector made the existence of multidisciplinary departments – as most extramural departments were – more difficult to justify in research terms. Meanwhile, a growing focus at government level on 'lifelong learning' and continuing vocational education had a profound impact on conceptions of university adult education, on its staffing profile, and on the range of activities in which departments were involved. Even by the mid-2000s, further challenges had to be faced in the funding environment, and it was clear to most observers that '[t]he whole landscape is utterly altered':

> In the era of lifelong learning the idea of continuing education as the responsibility of a small department seems anachronistic; similarly, in an era of the politicising of higher education for the service of employment and global competitiveness, liberal education appears quaint in the curriculum of the new vocationalism; [and] the old extra-mural map – each region with a single providing university – is a curiosity in a sector with well over 100 universities.[2]

In the 2000s, all these developments would profoundly affect the Board of Continuing Education, although it was not until the very end of the decade – as this chapter will show – that the Cambridge extramural map was put away. In a rapidly evolving environment, some of the changes that took place were unpredictable, and it is perhaps surprising that so many aspects of the Cambridge programme survived largely intact for most of the decade. This chapter traces the changes and continuities in the activities of the Board, or the Institute of Continuing Education as it became in 2001.

*

Less than two years before the turn of the new millennium, the Labour government had issued its Green Paper *The Learning Age*, which put forward a set of bold proposals for educational renewal and reform. The secretary of state for education and employment, David Blunkett, wrote a foreword that reflected his commitment to lifelong learning, emphasising its potential contribution to both 'learning for its own sake' and 'the equality of opportunity it brings'.[3] *The Learning Age* was framed by the context of 'human capital' formation, but also embodied a broader sense of what lifelong learning should be able to achieve for individuals, businesses, communities and the nation – in that order. The opening statement of the paper made clear that

> Our vision of the Learning Age is about more than employment. The development of a culture of learning will help to build a united society, assist in the creation of personal independence, and encourage our creativity and innovation. … We learn in many different ways, through formal study, reading, watching television, going on a training course, taking an evening class, at work, from family and friends.[4]

The paper's vision for the benefits of learning to the individual obliterated the distinction between vocational and non-vocational education:

> learning offers excitement and the opportunity for discovery. It stimulates enquiring minds and nourishes our souls. It takes us in directions we never expected, sometimes changing our lives. Learning helps create and sustain our culture. It helps all of us to improve our chances of getting a job and of getting on. Learning increases our earning power, helps older people to stay healthy and active, strengthens families and the wider community, and encourages independence. There are many people for whom learning has opened up, for the first time in their lives, the chance to explore art, music, literature, film, and the theatre, or to become creative themselves. Learning has enabled many people to help others to experience these joys too.[5]

It is not surprising that universities responded enthusiastically to *The Learning Age*: the Committee of Vice-Chancellors and Principals produced their own document, *The Learning Curve*, in the same year. This contained little about adult education departments *per se*, but some of the teaching carried out by the Cambridge Board – and some at other universities – at this time was mentioned favourably in the document.[6]

In Cambridge itself, the Board responded enthusiastically to the message of *The Learning Age*, welcoming 'the emphasis placed in it on widening participation in, and access to, learning'.[7] It was recognised, though, that 'issues of funding remained unclear', even though the Green Paper had praised the 'vital contribution to lifelong learning' that was made by university adult education departments. *The Learning Age* insisted that higher education institutions should 'attach high priority' to this work, but did not explain how this might be funded; and it was not clear how aspects of the provision at Cambridge might be incorporated into the government's proposed 'individual learning accounts'.[8] In the event, that new funding stream lasted only a couple of years, and much of the optimism generated by the *The Learning Age* in university adult education petered out in the face of subsequent government policy.

In the same year, 1998, the University of Cambridge established a Committee on Continuing Education and Lifelong Learning, chaired by Anne Lonsdale. This comprised 'a comprehensive, positive and forward-looking review of the totality of the University's commitment to Continuing Education'.[9] The main focus of the committee's report, which appeared in 2000, was on governance: it was proposed that the university establish a Council for Lifelong Learning, with oversight of continuing education across Cambridge, rather than just the Board of Continuing Education itself. This was envisaged as the main quality assurance body for continuing education, regardless of whether it took place under the Board's auspices or elsewhere. Meanwhile, the Board should be reconstituted as an Institute of Continuing Education, with its 'supervision' transferred to the university's General Board from the Council of the Senate, and a management board appointed for this purpose. At the same time the Cambridge Programme for Industry could be separated from the Board of Continuing Education, and itself become a General Board institution.[10] In due course the Board did indeed become an Institute from 1 January 2001, and the CPI became independent of it a year later. Although this may not have had significant implications, at least in the short term, for the experience of teaching and learning across the various programmes, it was hoped that the new governance structures would enhance both the quality and organisation of continuing education under the university's auspices. The Institute of Continuing Education (ICE) is still in existence today.

The separation of the CPI from ICE was welcomed by Polly Courtice and Christopher Padfield, who had done so much to establish and develop the programme. Courtice feels that 'we were being held back … and we were a distraction from [ICE's] core purpose'.[11] There was little opposition within ICE to the move, given that the CPI was financially self-contained and self-sufficient, and both ICE and the CPI felt that 'the interests of the University and external bodies' would be served by independence.[12] There were, though, some concerns within the university itself. One member of the Senate remarked that independence as a General Board institution would 'bring the CPI into a new and *closer* relationship to the University', and although this could be 'a sensible plan to meet a need and perhaps do a bit of good',

> On a hostile construction, this could look like our bid to be like the British Aerospace University and provide classes for in-post businessmen seconded to us or prepared to pay. … [I]t is important to keep the 'clients' and 'partners' conceptually distinct …. If we are in 'partnership' with hundreds of businesses through the [CPI], and it is proposed to bring the CPI further inside our 'tent', these 'partnerships' need clarifying extremely sharply.[13]

For this speaker, the issue at stake was one that – although he did not mention it – had arisen in extramural education for a long time, and concerned the status of the *students* on these courses within the university. The question was

> whether those who 'enrol' on the CPI's courses could become members of the University (when non-business students have to apply and compete to get in); [and] whether they are, in the long term, to be given degrees or diplomas of the University of Cambridge as distinct from awards clearly under the umbrella of 'Continuing Education'[.][14]

As we have seen (in chapter 6), similar questions had arisen in relation to the accreditation of the public programmes, and in particular the institution of new Master's degrees. These comments reflect a certain ongoing ambivalence about both continuing education and business studies within the university, despite the long-standing existence of the former and the successful establishment of the latter through the Judge Business School and CPI itself. In any case, the decision was indeed taken to separate CPI from ICE, and their ways fairly quickly parted, although the director of ICE did sit on the CPI's management board.[15] The CPI celebrated its twentieth anniversary in 2008, by which time it had 45 members of staff and 'operated' on four continents; in due course it became the Cambridge Institute for Sustainability Leadership, with Polly Courtice serving as director until 2021.[16]

Although this element of ICE's activity was separated out, the ongoing diversity of the work still made for some organisational complexity. This was reflected in the broad separation of courses into three areas: 'Lifelong learning in the community', which comprised the public programmes; 'Lifelong learning worldwide', representing the international summer schools; and 'Lifelong learning for the workplace: legal and professional studies'.[17] This separation was not particularly neat, as the public programmes included courses and Certificates that could certainly be described as 'continuing professional development'. Examples included, in 1999-2000, the ongoing courses for the armed forces, the annual IBM course and Certificate programmes in town planning and management.[18] For reporting purposes, though, the tripartite division of courses remained in place through the remainder of the 2000s, and this emphasised the very different elements of the teaching undertaken by ICE. Even after the departure of CPI, the range of activities at ICE was such that it would be difficult to draw out from the three main areas of teaching a single coherent idea of what ICE might be. This was not necessarily detrimental, since the regional, continuing professional and international programmes all had – or appeared to have – a secure place in the ongoing activities of the university, and nothing seemed under particular threat at this point. However, diversity could make 'branding' somewhat difficult, and some felt there was a lack of 'common purpose' across the Institute.[19]

*

The public programmes remained comfortably the largest area of activity in the early 2000s, however this might be measured. In terms of full-time equivalents, they formed around half the total student numbers, and over two-thirds in some years on a 'headcount' (see table 7.1). For much of the decade, they were led by Susan Rawlings, who also continued as warden of Madingley Hall and was titled deputy director of continuing education, but from 2006 onwards the public programmes were the responsibility of Adrian Barlow, who had been a panel tutor since the 1990s and had subsequently joined the full-time staff. A former school teacher, Barlow's subject was English literature, but he also ran courses on architecture and stained glass. He taught at Downham Market, Saffron Walden and other centres, and comments that he 'was very peripatetic and enjoyed that'; he liked moving around the extramural region.[20] Like many others before him, Barlow appreciated 'the freedom to create your own syllabus' on the public programmes, and valued the breadth of opportunities that this gave to both staff and students. There was, of course, full oversight of the process of providing courses: for non-Certificate courses offered at local centres, tutors would submit their proposed syllabi to the academic development officer in charge of their subject, and for Certificate, Diploma and Advanced Diploma courses the draft syllabus would be devised in collaboration with the academic development officer and then reviewed and approved by the subject moderation panel, which included a university moderator and an external examiner.[21]

The region served by the Institute was now smaller than before, but there were still some 60 local centres across Cambridgeshire, Bedfordshire, Hertfordshire and Suffolk, and a handful of places in Norfolk and Essex. In some of the local centres, a substantial number of courses, with good attendances, continued to take place, and through the subject-specific Certificate, Diploma and Master's programmes many students built up long-lasting relationships with ICE. These accredited programmes were concentrated in the larger centres, at Cambridge, Letchworth, Peterborough, Bury St Edmunds and, in a handful of cases, Saffron Walden and Bedford.[22] Many of the smaller centres, though, continued to offer courses year on year, which could in due course be used to build up credits towards a generic Certificate of Continuing Education (60 credits) or Certificate of Higher Education (120 credits). At Bures in Suffolk, for example, Mike Sewell ran a course on 'The Cold War' in autumn 2002, and this was followed by 'Understanding the World's Religions', taught by Graham Howes, in spring 2003: these were attended by 14 and 23 students respectively. In the still-flourishing local centre at Boxford, 42 students enrolled for 'Tudor Suffolk', taught by local historian Clive Paine, and the same number for 'The Viking Age in East Anglia and Beyond', for which the tutor was Sam Newton, a historian of the Anglo-Saxon

Table 7.1
Summary of courses and enrolments, 2002-3

Type of course	Number of courses	Number of enrolments	Full-time equivalents
Regional	171	2847	261.9
Day schools	32	530	10.7
Certificates and Diplomas	82	1078	163.1
Master's	2	20	10.0
Residential	207	3737	164.0
Total regional and residential	**494**	**8212**	**609.8**
Armed forces	8	127	7.8
Legal	31	1385	311.0
Master's (continuing professional)	5	103	51.5
Other	1	32	16.6
Total continuing professional	**45**	**1647**	**386.9**
International programmes	**143**	**2464**	**205.6**
GRAND TOTAL	**682**	**12323**	**1202.2**

Note: the total number of *students* on the international summer programmes was 1,048 (see p. 222), but many enrolled for more than one part of the programmes.

Source: annual report, 2002-3.

era who has appeared on *Time Team* and other television programmes, and written various books on the topic. As had often been the case before, in 2002-3 Lavenham attracted the largest number (86) to a single course: ‘East Anglia in the Middle Ages’, taught by the architectural historian Leigh Alston.[23] Some courses in the region ran with fewer than 10 students, but these were a minority. New centres were still emerging, while others were revived: in autumn 2003 the small village of Wortham in Suffolk hosted a class on the history of landed houses and estates in the county, taught by Clive Paine, and in the spring Paine was the tutor at Rickinghall for a course on seventeeth-century Suffolk and the civil wars. These attracted 55 and 56 students respectively, demonstrating both the strength of local demand and the ongoing capacity of ICE to respond to it; and meanwhile, a centre was established close by at Burgate.[24] Even on the edge of the extramural region, near the border of Norfolk, the public programmes were flourishing, especially when it came to ten-week courses.

Some local centres were held up as worthy examples of community education and the part that the University of Cambridge could play in it. One such was Downham Market Lecture Society, which had a relationship with ICE going back to 1920 and which continued to attract good numbers of students to the courses offered each year. In 2004-5 nineteen students attended ‘English Education since the Late Middle Ages’, while 26 went to ‘An Introduction to Opera’, and the ICE annual report singled out the contribution made by the Society:

> Throughout its recent history its members have tackled such subjects as Genetics, Philosophy, Art History and Psychology. The Society continued to play a part in the local and regional community. It supported the school, whose premises it was able to use, by donating a prize for achievement in examinations. It welcomed the school’s older sixth-form students into its classes where the subject-matter complemented their studies, The vital message of lifelong learning was, therefore, seen by all to span the generations, and students’ acceptance and respect for a wider range of life experience was deepened.[25]

Downham Market was also a model centre in that it remained an active participant in the Local Centres Union, which was seen as ‘an imaginative and creative concept’ by many, despite the reluctance of most centres to pay their subscriptions to it.[26] It was not unknown for the Union’s annual general meetings to be postponed due to low attendance, but the body was nevertheless seen as a key channel of communication between ICE and the centres, which were themselves vital 'bridgeheads into the community'.[27] In the early 2000s, the annual general meeting was combined with a 'students' day' at Madingley Hall, featuring 'student success stories' shared in what one student called a 'civilised and refined atmosphere'.[28]

In Cambridge itself, the Adult and Continuing Education Centre was relocated in 2004 from the university's Sidgwick Site to Homerton College, where Kate Pretty – who now chaired the Institute's management board – was the principal. In practical terms, this meant better car parking facilities, catering and public transport access, as well as 'more flexible' teaching spaces.[29] Several courses were taught there, notably – among others – on garden history, to which tutors Twigs Way and Caroline Holmes were able to attract large numbers of students. A selection of these students' work – edited by Way – was published in 2003, on topics ranging from Chinese influences on eighteenth-century English garden design to the gardens at the Cambridgeshire Pauper Lunatic Asylum in Fulbourn.[30] Science Certificates – in astronomy and genetics – were also available at Homerton, while a substantial suite of accredited courses in theology and religious studies was taught at Wesley House, the Methodist Centre in Cambridge.[31] By 2004-5 there were 16 Certificate programmes across ICE's provision, including one in Town Planning taught at Madingley Hall, and others in Historic Building Conservation, Counselling, Film Studies, History of Art and Creative Writing; the Wesley House courses counted towards a Certificate in Orthodox Christian Studies; and eight subjects were offered at Diploma level. By this time more than 1,000 students were enrolled on named Certificate and Diploma courses.[32] Meanwhile, the part-time Master of Studies programmes that had been pioneered in the 1990s continued to draw in a small number of committed students and to provide opportunities for some to progress to PhD study, though usually not at Cambridge itself. In 2004-5, there were programmes in Local and Regional History, Modernism in English Literature, and International Relations; 40 places were offered on the latter for the following academic year.[33]

Studying on the public programmes could lead to second careers for some students. The system of credit accumulation allowed students to pursue the now well-worn pathway to a Certficate of Continuing Education, and although there was still no opportunity to obtain a Cambridge degree through part-time study, the Advanced Diploma provided a route into ICE's Master of Studies programmes. In the early and mid-2000s, one student who followed this path was Sean O'Dell, self-employed and in his early forties. O'Dell had left school after taking O-levels, but had a long-standing interest in history and archaeology. Travelling regularly from his home in Essex to Cambridge and nearby locations, he began with a Certificate course in the archaeology of ancient Egypt, and gained credits across a range of archaeology courses, which included field trips to locations in East Anglia and some practical excavation experience. This was followed by an Advanced Diploma in Local History, on which his dissertation was supervised by Peter Bysouth, by this time a tutor on some of the Institute's programmes. O'Dell's dissertation – on the history of the Stour Navigation in Essex and Suffolk – was eventually published as a book by the History Press in 2006.[34] Other students also published their work on local history, either as books or journal articles,[35] although by now this was more often an individual enterprise than had been the case on Lionel Munby's courses, when students in local centres worked collaboratively on projects specific to the area where courses were taught.

From the Advanced Diploma O'Dell proceeded to the Master of Studies, attending courses taught by David Dymond and Evelyn Lord, and again his dissertation – supervised by Dymond – made it into print. The subject-matter was completely different: the nineteenth-century 'skillingers' (offshore oyster-catchers) of Brightlingsea in Essex.[36] Students on the Master's programme were exposed to a wide range of historical periods and techniques, as well as studying the history of local history in its post-war development. There was also strong support for academic writing: O'Dell attributes much of his success as a writer to the careful feedback that Dymond provided on the drafts of his dissertation chapters, and the published version acknowledged the 'guidance, encouragement and enthusiasm' of both Dymond and Evelyn Lord.[37] As in Munby's time, local history had an interdisciplinary flavour even when taught at Master's level, drawing on architecture, law, archaeology, landscape studies and other influences to prepare students for addressing a wide range of historical questions in various local contexts and from different periods. O'Dell himself demonstrates the success of this approach: like his first supervisor Peter Bysouth, O'Dell went on to obtain a PhD, in his case from the University of Essex. As with his Master's dissertation, this was again on a topic unrelated to his previous work: the holiday caravan park in the twentieth century.[38] By this time – 'completely as a result of the work I'd done at Madingley on the Master's programme' – he was teaching 'key skills' to further education students at

Colchester Institute, and in due course became a Senior Lecturer in Contextual Studies and Social History, teaching higher education students in the same location. Not many ICE students had such a clear career trajectory, and few would have wanted one: as with most courses, many of those who studied at Master's level with O'Dell were retired, or simply doing it for general interest. Nevertheless, these programmes had the potential, at least, to transform the lives of those who studied on them.[39]

Many other students gained both tangible and intangible benefits from studying on ICE courses, though they did not lead to academic careers, or even to accredited awards. Carolyn Redmayne, who studied for a Certificate in English Local History in the early and mid-2000s, is a good example.[40] Born in 1957, Redmayne grew up in the Fenland village of Over, in Cambridgeshire, and was living there again as an adult, from 1994. Although she had no experience of studying history formally since school, she had always had a strong interest in local history, and as early as the late 1970s had considered writing about Over; she had a collection of primary sources obtained through her family, which could trace its presence in the village back through several centuries. Redmayne stumbled across ICE at an open evening at Homerton College in the early 2000s, at which she was encouraged to enrol on the Certificate, despite some misgivings on her own part. She enjoyed the course – 'it was my favourite part of the week, those two hours at Homerton on a Tuesday night; it was what I lived for at that time, I just loved it' – and found that she was able to participate in class discussions, usually basing her contributions on her knowledge of Over. She struggled at first with the assessed elements of the course: 'I was still learning – I didn't know how it was done, I didn't know about referencing'. However, with the support of Lord and some of the other students, Redmayne was able to flourish as a local historian and to succeed on the modules that she took.

Redmayne's progress through the Certificate programme was delayed because some modules did not run due to low numbers, and she had some breaks for family reasons. In the end she never completed the Certificate, but took various other residential and day courses, some with ICE and some with the WEA, and was part of an informal local historians' group, whose members she met through ICE courses. Like many other students and former students on the local history courses, Redmayne eventually produced a book, *The Spirit of Over*, published in 2021, an immensely detailed and lavishly illustrated account of the village's history.[41] The foreword was written by Evelyn Lord, who described the book as 'a model of how to capture the life and times of a village'.[42] Redmayne is clear that 'if it were not the Institute of Continuing Education, I would never have written a book', and it is likely that many other local historians would say the same thing.[43] As had been the case with students taught by Lionel Munby and David Dymond in earlier decades, the tangible outputs of local history courses transcended their accredited elements, and supported students in the process of historical research in their local communities.

Some students progressed from ICE courses to become full-time undergraduate students at the University of Cambridge, though this was still unusual, and it remained for many a source of frustration that part-time undergraduate study was not possible in the university, and was not likely to be introduced.[44] One mature student, writing in 2003, had studied on 'Reading Classical Greek' courses at Madingley Hall, and credited them with her ultimate destination as a classics student at Lucy Cavendish College:

> These [courses] provided not only superb teaching which I could not have obtained elsewhere, but also inspiration and encouragement from both my tutors and fellow students to continue studying. Furthermore they enabled me to have something of my own which was outside my accustomed role as working wife and mother. This was, of course, very much a gradual process, but Madingley – as with the other courses I attended – helped to focus my mind, and … gave me the confidence to take the major life changing step of applying to Lucy Cavendish.[45]

Support for students to progress to full- or part-time undergraduate study was also provided in the form of Access to Higher Education courses, which were restarted in the 2000s and paved the way for students to take up undergraduate places in a number of universities.[46] From 2007, a 'pre-sessional' course, for those about to begin undergraduate study, was established, intended 'to focus on key areas where those teaching and tutoring mature students have identified a need for more effort to bolster student confidence and improve readiness to embark on Cambridge courses'.[47] These were subsequently considered 'very successful', attracting positive student feedback.[48]

Residential courses provided under the auspices of the public programmes continued to flourish during the 2000s. In 2002-3 there were 207 courses attracting a total of 3,737 students, amounting to 164 full-time equivalents and therefore representing more than an eighth of total student numbers (see table 7.1). These numbers fluctuated in subsequent years, but in 2007-8 there were 3,542 students on 221 courses.[49] As with other courses on the public programmes, history, art and literature were strong features of the programme, with a small but secure place for the natural sciences, theology and philosophy; and there were language courses including classical Greek and Latin. The standard fee for the courses had increased in real terms, but in 2007 the director of public programmes, Adrian Barlow, reminded students that they were 'subsidised by the University' on the condition that students submitted written work at the end of the weekend, or full week in some cases.[50] The standard fee was £204 for a weekend course in the spring term of 2007-8, while non-residents could take the course for £127. Courses were advertised on posters in trains running between Cambridge and London, as well as local and national publications, and glossy brochures were widely circulated; there was a mailing list amounting to 11,000 addresses.[51] Students often came from a distance, but some courses addressed areas of local interest: in 2007-8, students could take 'Landscape History of the Cambridge Region' with Nicholas James, for example, or 'Fenland Perspectives: Architecture and Literature' with Barlow himself. The latter course was 'designed to appeal to those who already know and enjoy the Fenland and to those for whom it is literally another country'.[52] Meanwhile, the Alberni String Quartet continued to offer its popular 'masterclass' – four times in 2007-8, at a full-week residential fee of £508, or £270 for a weekend.[53]

Day schools continued as a feature of the programme, though they were fairly insignificant contributors to the full-time equivalent student numbers in terms of which the Institute's data were increasingly reported, and they experienced 'uneven popularity' around the turn of the new millennium.[54] Day schools, as we have seen, were difficult to embed into an accredited programme of study, but were considered a valuable service provided by ICE, and took place in various local centres, one-off locations and Madingley Hall itself. In 2002-3, there were 32 day schools, attracting a total of 530 students, but this amounted only to just over 10 full-time student equivalents, and did not receive separate funding. Day schools were an opportunity to test the ground for possible longer courses, and this was one motivation behind a somewhat expanded programme in 2003-4, taking them to 19 towns and villages in the extramural region.[55] These included Wortham, where clear demand was identified and 30 students attended a day school on 'Landscape Painters of East

Anglia', Therfield Heath in Hertfordshire (a walking tour taking in prehistoric sites, nearby caves and Royston Museum), and Paxton Pits near St Neots, where the course was on bird-watching.[56] The standard day school fee of £20 in 2002-3 – equivalent to about £35 today – or £15 for concessions, meant that this was never likely to be a profitable venture for ICE, but it did provide an opportunity to market other courses and to bring new students into more academically rigorous and, for ICE, lucrative areas of study.

Teaching on the public programmes was supported by an expanding emphasis on staff development, including visits to classes taught by new tutors and in new local centres, a set of detailed guidance on assessment, and a 'tutor's handbook' that emphasised the particular challenges presented by the nature of the student body. In 2006, the handbook set out the key expectations of tutors:

> Coming to a university course, students will expect their tutor to have a thorough knowledge of their subject, supported by up-to-date research, and to approach it with intellectual rigour and open-mindedness. They will also expect their tutor to be able to convert specialised academic knowledge into a form accessible to a non-specialist audience.[57]

This was the basic requirement, but then tutors would also face the challenges of teaching a broad range of students:

> Each group … has its own characteristics. Most groups will have a mixture of different types of student. The approach to teaching therefore needs to be varied, flexible and responsive to the nature of the particular group of students. Some students will be new to adult education and have a long gap between formal education and returning to study; some will have a good knowledge of a particular subject, while others will be beginners; some will be experts in their own field, but studying a different subject for the first time. All will need support and encouragement as individuals to feel included and to continue learning.[58]

On top of this, there were practical matters, not least the new importance of working with virtual learning environments. Older challenges included the assessment of student work, dealing with the cancellation of courses if low numbers required it, and managing book-boxes: 'it is easier to reclaim books while the course is still running than to try and chase them up at the end when the student in question may have moved house'.[59] (The cover of this book shows some book-boxes that were used in the 2000s.) Moreover, the job of a panel tutor remained quite precarious, subject to the vicissitudes of student demand, which itself was affected by the cost of courses and in some cases the alternatives available.

The public programmes were still presented to students as part of a long-standing Cambridge tradition, as of course they were. In 2002-3, the student handbook continued to emphasise the example set by James Stuart well over a century earlier:

> Stuart … passionately believed that access to education had a central part to play in bringing about a better and more equal society. As part of this mission, he pioneered and developed the idea of extending university education, with its emphasis on independent thought, critical reasoning and the development of the individual, to all members of society.[60]

Adrian Barlow, too, identified with the 'James Stuart tradition' of adult education, and wrote about Stuart and the history of university extension in his book *Extramural*, published in 2012.[61] Here he emphasised that 'Stuart's concept – of extension lectures providing continuing education for previously disenfranchised adult learners in the form of recognised Higher Education level Certificates which could become a passport to part-time or full-time university study leading to a degree – was visionary'.[62] Barlow appreciated Stuart's inheritance, and the opportunity it provided for himself and others to learn from students, as much as they learned from their tutors. Ultimately, 'no teaching has been as challenging nor – certainly – as rewarding as the classes I have taught which are still most accurately described by the single term, extramural'.[63]

*

In the mid-2000s, ICE adopted a new internal structure, with five separate 'divisions': Programmes for the Public; Continuing Vocational Education; International; Community Education and Outreach; and Research. The second of these was quickly changed to 'Professional Studies'.[64] The addition of a 'Research' division reflected the priorities of the new director, Richard Taylor, who replaced Michael Richardson in 2004. Taylor's aim of strengthening the 'research culture' was a key theme of his leadership, which lasted until 2009.

On arrival, he felt that, for some academics in the Institute, research was a minority activity or a 'sideline', and that this limited the capacity for ICE to 'see itself and be seen as an academic department', especially in the context of a world-leading university such as Cambridge.[65] Taylor's strategy had two elements – first, to expand the opportunities for the specialist research pursued by members of staff in their own fields; and second, to encourage research on lifelong learning itself. There was some opposition to the latter direction within ICE, and, while there were some potential collaborators within the Faculty of Education at Cambridge, most researchers there tended to focus on school-age education.[66] Taylor himself sustained an active publication profile during his five years at ICE, but for the most part the members of academic staff continued to pursue and publish research on their own subject specialisms, for which they were entered in the national Research Assessment Exercise in many cases.[67]

Research and publication, as Taylor comments, is not always considered a 'high priority' in university continuing education departments: 'in the extramural world, teaching adults from a wide range of backgrounds has always been seen as challenging and as the central professional task of the adult educator'.[68] Nevertheless, some of his colleagues developed impressive publication records within their own disciplines. Evelyn Lord remembers that 'publications didn't really matter' within ICE itself, but that time was made available to academics to conduct research, and Adrian Barlow remembers the introduction of a new study leave policy under Taylor's leadership.[69] The increasing profile of research assessment in the university sector gave added importance to publications in terms of career development.[70] However, with a relatively low turnover of academics in ICE, opportunities to develop a strong culture of educational research were limited. A residential seminar in partnership with the National Institute of Adult Continuing Education was established in 2007, taking as its first theme 'Developing policy and provision in lifelong learning with refugees and asylum seekers in the UK'; there was a termly reading group for staff at the Institute; and in 2008 Susan Oosthuizen and Richard Taylor contributed to a conference on the history of universities and community engagement, held in Cambridge to mark the octocentenary of the university.[71] This resulted in a book edited by Peter Cunningham from the Faculty of Education, with Oosthuizen and Taylor, which explored historical perspectives on continuing education in Britain and elsewhere in the English-speaking world, but there were no other contributors from ICE. Despite this, Taylor remembers developing 'very close' relations with the Faculty of

Education: he sat on their faculty board, and met regularly with members of staff who had similar research interests.[72] By the end of his tenure in 2009, however, a review of ICE conducted by the university had determined that research into lifelong learning could not be made a priority, a decision Taylor thought then – and continues to believe now – 'was a fundamental mistake'.[73]

The establishment of a 'Community Education and Outreach' division, directed by Susan Oosthuizen, also reflected one of Taylor's priorities as director, and he recalls that 'we got all kinds of courses off the ground … either with disadvantaged groups or people who worked with them'.[74] The division was involved in an ambitious programme of activity, with funding from various sources. For example, a new Certificate in Working with Voluntary Organisations and one in Teaching and Training in Voluntary and Community Contexts were followed by others in Voluntary or Community Business Development and Supporting Equality and Diversity through Social Enterprise Management, taught across the region in centres such as King's Lynn, Bury St Edmunds and Writtle in Essex.[75] These programmes expanded still further in the following years, but they were withdrawn from 2008-9 – and the Community Education and Outreach division closed down – after a strategic review of ICE 'questioned the appropriateness of some of the work'.[76] Taylor now feels that this, too, was a mistake, especially in relation to the 'Teaching and Training' programme: 'we recruited quite large numbers, and it was a good course … we shouldn't have closed it'.[77] Community education and outreach was dropped as a division of ICE, and subsumed back into the public programmes. Taylor has 'always seen adult education as driven by a social purpose ethic …. If university adult education does not have this social purpose – and, by implication, politically radical – dimension at its heart, then it is pretty worthless in my view.'[78] The failure to sustain this strand of community education and outreach work can be viewed as a missed opportunity for ICE to participate in ongoing, and perhaps more radical, developments in subsequent years.

*

The 'Professional Studies' division was – in Taylor's words – 'always a bit arms-length from the rest of the Institute', partly because, while ICE was responsible for the administration of the various courses provided under its auspices, its own staff did little of the actual teaching.[79] Nevertheless, in terms of size it was a substantial and vital element of ICE's profile, accounting for almost a third of its full-time equivalent students (see table 7.1). The vast bulk of these were on the legal programmes, with 103 students enrolling in a single year, 2002-3, onto a distance-learning Diploma in Notarial Practice, and even more onto the first year of a two-year Diploma in English and European Union Law taught in Warsaw.[80] New initiatives in the early 2000s included workshops on tax law, organised with Cambridge's Centre for Tax Law, and seminars on criminal injuries compensation. ICE continued to provide courses for police officers, IBM managers and students revising for the University of London LLB degree, as well as training for magistrates, which had by this time been taking place for almost 40 years.[81] When Taylor took over as director, he was well aware of the potential for development of legal and professional studies:

> Whilst it's not a specialism or particular interest of mine, I was very committed to seeing it as a growth area. It fitted in exactly with government policy; it was potentially a very good link with some of the departments across the university; it was also potentially an income generator; and it certainly shouldn't draw down subsidy. So it had an awful lot going for it.[82]

As a result, under Taylor's leadership the Institute invested heavily in the professional programmes, and a new programme director, Sharon Collins, was appointed in 2006.[83] The 'arms-length' nature of the division was emphasised by a physical move away from Madingley Hall, to a separate building closer to the centre of Cambridge.[84]

Under Collins's leadership, 'partnerships' were a key focus for the professional studies courses, both with university departments – most importantly the Faculty of Law – and with external bodies including branches of the armed forces, another long-standing relationship that persisted, albeit on a small scale, into the 2000s.[85] A wide range of new programmes was established, with still more 'under discussion' – notable examples were two Certificates in Alternative Dispute Resolution and Grief and Bereavement Studies, and a Postgraduate Diploma in Property Investment, the latter in partnership with the university's Department of Land Economy.[86] The Certificate in Grief and Bereavement Studies was aimed at healthcare workers, clergy, counsellors and funeral directors, among others.[87]

A successful venture in this period was a programme for senior secondary school teachers – with a particular focus on involving teachers from areas of social and economic disadvantage – funded by the Prince's Teaching Institute (PTI). This involved week-long residential courses, on which Cambridge academics – who participated free of charge – would present their research and discuss with teachers 'the current preoccupations and problems of teaching their particular subjects'.[88] Beginning with history and English, the programme subsequently embraced geography, the life sciences, modern languages and other subjects, and was initially directed by Bernice McCabe, head of North London Collegiate School and a key figure in the establishment of the PTI; Christopher Pope, a former Decca record producer, became co-director in 2006-7.[89] It was able to attract 'big-name' plenary speakers, again free of charge, including among others Stephen Fry, Melvyn Bragg, Susan Greenfield, Michael Morpurgo and Michael Palin. Taylor explains that 'its purpose was to rekindle enthusiasm for [teachers'] subject specialisms', through seminars that 'focused exclusively upon on the specialist academic subject disciplines, and emphatically involved no consideration of educational policy, bureaucracy … or the endless funding constraints upon the sector'. He sums up the PTI programme as one that, in the second half of the 2000s, 'enrolled several hundred senior teachers and did much to revivify the intellectual enthusiasm and informed research base of secondary school provision across a range of subject disciplines'.[90] As such, it can be seen as an evolution of the long-standing involvement of ICE and its predecessors in teacher development, going back to the early residential 'refresher' courses of the 1950s. With more than 100 teachers taking part each year, the programme evolved into a Master of Studies in Advanced Subject Teaching.[91] Aimed at teachers of English and history, the Master's programme commenced in 2012-13 with 20 students.[92]

Not everything undertaken by ICE in professional studies met with the same degree of funding, or ultimate success. Even the Diploma in Notarial Practice saw numbers fall off through the second half of the 2000s, and was eventually withdrawn in 2010-11, despite winning an award from an American-based lifelong learning association, LERN.[93] Overall, though, student numbers on the professional studies programmes increased steadily after 2005, rising from 14.8% of total enrolments in 2004-5 to 17.2% in 2008-9.[94] Subsequent developments included Master of Studies degrees in Construction Engineering, approved in 2010, and Sustainability Leadership, commencing in the same year with most of its students based overseas.[95] Meanwhile, the provision of courses for the armed forces declined: there were 141 students on nine courses in 2007-8, 112 on seven courses in 2008-9, and thereafter this strand of work disappeared.[96] In a sign of changing times and priorities, in 2010-11 ICE piloted two courses for 'high-ranking Chinese civil servants and institutional leaders' for the Shanghai Regional Government, focusing on 'financial innovation and risk control'.[97]

*

Madingley Hall itself remained a key focus for ICE, housing most of its staff and many of its residential courses, particularly those associated with the public programmes. The Hall continued to undergo some development – there was another kitchen refurbishment at the turn of the millennium – but there were no significant building projects in the next decade. In 2003-4 there were some charitably funded repairs to the external fabric, along with the installation of high-speed internet in the teaching rooms; and further upgrades to the IT infrastructure were needed towards the end of the decade, reflecting the 'increasing expectations of students and clients'. At the same time, accessibility was enhanced for people with disabilities – always a challenge when a building is listed.[98] The Hall continued to win praise for its atmosphere, its catering and its gardens, the latter overseen by the long-serving head gardener Richard Gant. In 2010, the deputy head gardener Faye Steer won the title Young Horticulturist of the Year, awarded at a national event held at Kew Gardens, which prompted Adrian Barlow to reflect on the qualities of the Madingley garden:

> Where else in Cambridge can you stand looking out across a landscape (the meadows and trees in front of the Hall) that is quintessentially Capability Brown: rolling grassland fringed with trees, glimpse of lake, raised bank beyond to obscure the road etc.? Then turn left and take the steps down to the north terrace and discover a garden that is formal, almost Italianate, with its croquet lawn, hedges and avenue of bushes manicured to within an inch of their lives? Or tread the gravel path that enfolds the whole meadow – still unmown at this time of year to allow the wild flowers full rein?[99]

To Barlow, one of the architectural features of the Hall itself also stands out: the ogee arch adjacent to the main entrance, topped with heraldic symbols and held together with iron staples. This arch formerly stood in the centre of Cambridge: it had once been the entrance to the west front of the Old Schools, facing Great St Mary's, before being dismantled and re-erected at Madingley in the 1750s. As such, it 'illustrates powerfully the links, seen and unseen, between the University and its Institute of Continuing Education, with its home at Madingley Hall'.[100]

Barlow acknowledges that to some colleagues Madingley – physically and in some ways culturally distant from the University of Cambridge and its colleges – may not have felt like an 'academic home'. However, to him it felt like a college, because of 'the whole experience of the building, and the fact that you would be there with students who were doing five or six different courses on different subjects, but all met together. It was much more like a college, and a lot of people used to say to me "Madingley is my college".'[101] On one occasion, Barlow recalled teaching a weekend course on Cambridge architecture, while six others were going on at the same time; here he saw the 'familiar faces' of people who might be attending their fourth weekend course of the year, as well as new and younger students. On this occasion, blessed with good weather, the gardens had been 'admired', the food 'its usual high standard' and 'the Bar well patronised'.[102] By this time the catering department – with its regular five-star hygiene and safety award from South Cambridgeshire District Council – was following a purchasing strategy based on 'ethical and environmental considerations', and also taking part in the Cambridge inter-college cooking competition.[103] There were discussions at a high level within the university about the possibility of making Madingley Hall a full college of the university – a direction that Homerton had taken in the 2000s, achieving the status in 2010 under Kate Pretty's leadership.[104]

In 2008, Madingley itself became the topic for a four-day residential course, held on the premises and involving several members of staff. The warden Susan Rawlings took part, along with Carola Hicks, Evelyn Lord, Richard Taylor, head gardener Richard Gant and former director Michael Richardson. There were also guest lecturers, and a special concert by the Alberni String Quartet. The course was badged as an 'anniversary celebration' marking 60 years since the University of Cambridge first acquired the Hall.[105] Rated at 10 Level 1 credits, the course required a personal statement of learning and completion of a tutor-assigned task, and was associated with two learning outcomes:

As a result of this course, students should be able to:

1. gain an appreciation of the history of Continuing Education at the University of Cambridge;
2. explore university architecture with increased knowledge and enjoyment.[106]

The course attracted 43 students, more than any other residential course at Madingley in the 2007-8 academic year, and contributions ranged from Gillian Sutherland on 'Women's Education at Cambridge' to Rosemary Horrox on 'The Early University' and Adrian Barlow on 'Madingley Church'.[107] Across that academic year, some 3,516 students took part in residential courses at Madingley, a clear demonstration of the attraction of what many felt to be a special place.

*

The International Summer Schools continued through the 2000s as a key element of ICE's activity: in their eightieth anniversary year, 2003, they attracted 1,048 students, comprising more than one sixth of ICE's total full-time equivalents (see table 7.1 and the note below it); between them, these students enrolled for 2,464 course places.[108] There were few significant changes, either in the profile of students or in the structure of the programmes, through the 2000s, though in 2008 a new course on English for Academic Purposes was introduced, followed by IELTS Preparation in 2010.[109] There was a gradual trend, already observed in earlier decades, for the content of courses, particularly the generic International Summer School, with its two four-week terms, to become more international in scope; this reflected growing international competition for summer school students.[110] Meanwhile, the long-standing collaborative arrangements with various universities – notably USC, Florida, Michigan State, Central Michigan and Utah – persisted through the decade, while other universities also worked with Cambridge to take students onto either generic or bespoke programmes. Key individuals participated again and again as tutors or course directors: one example was Nicholas Friend, who directed the Art History Summer School from 1987 to 2012.[111] In the range and style of teaching, the programmes were perhaps now less of a 'blending' with other ICE activity and more of a 'mirror', though some core ICE staff still took part in them and made substantial contributions to both the teaching and social side of the summer.[112]

One such tutor was Adrian Barlow, who taught 'every summer' from the early 2000s and 'enjoyed it very much'.[113] Barlow's account of a summer school course on 'E. M. Forster and Cambridge' in 2010 emphasises the diversity of origin, age and motivation among the 'great group' of students whom he taught:

> Their ages ranged from 20–80+ and they came from China, Pakistan, South Africa, Scandinavia, Italy, the Czech Republic, the United States and the UK: students, teachers, lawyers, scientists, journalists, the retired and the just beginning. Nina, a Norwegian, veteran of several summer schools, is about to start a full-time degree at Cambridge next term; Jason, a potential Gates Scholar, hopes to begin an MPhil here. Everyone has their reason for coming, or coming back, to Cambridge.[114]

For Barlow and others, including David Smith – who taught on and, from 2005, led the History Summer School – these experiences made teaching enormously enjoyable, as many also found in the different context of the regional public programmes. Smith recalled that

> The great pleasure of this [summer] work lies in the interest, commitment and infectious enthusiasm of the students. They bring so much energy and curiosity to their studies as well as a remarkable range of backgrounds and perspectives. They are also, for the most part, very willing to make comments and ask questions, and this interactive quality helps to make the Summer Schools a rewarding and stimulating teaching experience.[115]

The undoubted enthusiasm and commitment of these students certainly did not mean that teaching them was an easy job. A literature tutor, Simon Browne, noted in 2003 the challenges of dealing with English texts in the context of a class of international students: '[i]t … constantly reminds me of the signals a book or poem is giving me as a reader from England that I need to draw out for an audience from outside England'.[116] In many subjects, it was difficult to gauge in advance the level at which the students expected and needed to be studying: programme director Sarah Ormrod recalls occasions when the early parts of a course were pitched at too high a level, and others where lecturers 'came in after the first session and said "oh goodness, I've got through the first three sessions already – they're so hungry, I need to do more!"'.[117]

Although a significant proportion of students were submitting work for assessment – a feature that was important in terms of the relationship with some international universities – there was a curricular and pedagogical freedom on the summer programmes that many tutors valued. Moreover, ICE did not dictate any particular teaching style, preferring to make a virtue of the diversity of the large group of tutors who contributed to the summer programme.[118] Students praised the quality of traditional 'chalk and talk' lecturing, of seminar discussions, and the balance between the two approaches; and many chose a wide range of subject-matter within the large generic International Summer School, exposing them to diverse topics and disciplines in a short period.[119] The breadth of subject-matter taught in the two terms of the International Summer Schools was (and remains today) remarkable, ranging in 2003-4 from 'Architecture in Europe 1050–1530' through 'Britain and the European Community', 'The Rise of Civilisation' and 'The Philosophy of Zen Buddhism', to 'Four Brontë Novels' and 'A History of Science from the Ancients to the Nineteenth Century'.[120] Science was poorly represented on the generic programme, which tended to feature history of science rather than theoretical and practical topics, but the smaller (though growing) Science Summer School covered physics, biology and some topical courses on DNA and genetic modification, ensuring that students had the opportunity to explore multidisciplinary perspectives. Here, again, this meant that teaching was enjoyable but challenging, as course director Lynne Harrison explained:

> You cannot predict which course combinations students will select: they make some very eclectic choices, but this seems to enrich rather than detract from their learning. Each course is different, from the astronomy class where several students asked the meaning of the strange symbol P, to the engineering class where the tutor had to reintroduce all the mathematical treatments he had carefully eliminated, to appease a whole class of enthusiastic students hungry for more.[121]

The international student body had a fairly high proportion of younger participants, with a little over two-thirds being aged under 30, and many registered for an undergraduate or postgraduate degree at Cambridge or elsewhere. Many, though, were much older, with the oldest reputedly aged 94, and as with the regional public programmes many returned again and again to experience the Cambridge summer. A series of student recollections were published for the ninetieth anniversary of the summer schools in 2013, and some students reported that participation had been a life-changing experience.[122] As before, this was often explained in terms of the city and colleges, and the atmosphere, rather than the content of the courses themselves, though this also attracted comment. One student from Niger, who attended the first term of the International Summer School in 2008, wrote that

> I initially took the course because I wanted to be an outspoken lawyer and I dreaded public speaking, [but] by the second week of the course, I already had a confidence boost about public speaking because of the tutorial-based learning. The phrase 'outstanding teaching' is not one I use often but I have to hand it to the University of Cambridge.[123]

This student, Geoffrey Weli-Wosu, studied the team-taught course 'International Politics in a Global Age', from which he gained 'an in-depth knowledge of globalisation', and which he found 'intellectually challenging. I was constantly challenged to underpin opinions with sound arguments, to analyse critically the arguments in a debate, to develop original thoughts and to cross the boundaries among disciplines.'[124]

As one would expect, it is the positive and happy memories of summer schools that were collected and published in 2013, but overall 'student satisfaction' rates well above 90% suggest that these are not unrepresentative.[125] Student comments on the summer school environment and the inspiration gained from *being* in Cambridge clearly demonstrate the personal benefits gained by those who took part. The following were made by students from, respectively, Australia, China and Spain:

> I imbibed the infectious excitement of conversing with like-minded students from all corners of the world, and enriching my ideas in a stimulating forum of academic debate. The solidarity between all members of the summer school community – whether between fellow classmates, between teachers and students, or between academics across the different disciplines – generated an environment that was truly and beautifully cohesive.[126]

> My stay in Cambridge in summer 2010 belongs to my most cherished memories. … I loved every detail of its charming landscape as much as I

> enjoyed those wonderful lectures. The opportunity I got to share ideas, in class or over dinner, with people from across the globe was fantastic. I really appreciated the diversity it has to offer, which bettered my understanding of the world as a multicultural one.[127]

> Midsummer school's dream: imagine yourself, free from daily hassle, attending a broad variety of inspirational lectures on a topic of your choice. Imagine being granted access to the incredible resources of the University Library .... Imagine wondering while wandering: through hidden gates, open gardens and solemn halls, devoted to the advancement of learning.[128]

These happy memories were bought at a price: studying on the summer schools was not within reach of all, and was becoming more expensive in the 2000s. As in earlier decades, though, bursaries were still available for a small number of students, many of whom were based in eastern Europe or the former Soviet Union: in 2002 and 2003, for example, they were awarded to students from Armenia, Azerbaijan, Brazil, Colombia, Estonia, Hungary, Kazakhstan, Kyrgyzstan, Russia, Turkmenistan and Uzbekistan.[129] One of these, Artem Sadoyan from Armenia, reported that 'a month in Cambridge changed my life in a way that a year in any other university would not be able to do'.[130]

The evolution of the summer programmes was underpinned by technological and geopolitical change. Although virtual learning environments came a little later than they did to other parts of the university, they were in use by the mid-2000s, and online booking – as well, of course, as regular correspondence between ICE and its students by email – was introduced and enhanced.[131] However, there was no attempt to *teach* courses online or by correspondence, even in the 2010s, and the programme director Sarah Ormrod continued, in 2013, to emphasise the importance of its location-based elements, which she saw as being even more important in the context of technological developments: 'There will be a growing need to ensure we preserve the opportunity for people to take that step away from the screen, and from their everyday environment, to participate in learning activities which bring them in face-to-face contact'.[132] The numbers who chose to do this fluctuated, but there was a fairly high base of 1,000 or so students each year. Enrolments were affected by national and international political developments: for example, numbers fell in 2001, perhaps because of the UK outbreak of foot-and-mouth disease, and in 2003 on the outbreak of the second Iraq war.[133] Yet the overall health of the programmes was good: in 2009 there were 1,160 students across 163 courses, amounting to around 183 full-time equivalent students, and this was holding fairly steady as a proportion of the overall profile of ICE's work.

*

The first decade of the twenty-first century ended with the sudden, though not completely unanticipated, demise of the public programmes in the Cambridge extramural region. It had been clear for some years that the focus of government policy and funding was changing, with 'increasing concentration … upon the younger age cohorts', despite the emphasis at the end of the twentieth century on lifelong learning in the new 'learning age'.[134] A parallel shift of focus towards 'skills acquisition', alongside a promotion of widening access to mainstream higher education programmes, presented challenges for university continuing education.[135] However, the public programmes had proved remarkably resilient, despite the need to increase fees and in some cases pay more rent for premises within Cambridge. In 2006-7 the university's Learning and Teaching Review Committee presented a very favourable report on the public programmes, singling out the quality of the teaching and support for part-time students and of their publicity and documentation, as well as the collection of student feedback and the overall effectiveness of the programme management. The programmes continued to develop a strong culture of interdisciplinarity, and achieved a completion rate of 78%, supported by a programme of staff development designed to support tutors to work with students on assessment.[136] Student numbers remained relatively buoyant, and in 2006-7 the programmes generated £3 million, almost half the total income of ICE, and the annual report noted that this had 'underwritten most of the other activities of the Institute'.[137]

In autumn 2007, though, the announcement by HEFCE of a new funding policy spelled the beginning of the end of the 'extramural empire'. From 2008-9 no student would receive funding for studying any course that would lead to an equivalent or lower qualification than that which they had previously studied. The policy would be introduced in a 'staggered' way, and there were some exceptions for specific vocational areas of study, but – as Richard Taylor explained in ICE's annual report – 'the consequences … for adult learners and their providers were little short of catastrophic'.[138] In retrospect, he explains that 'government policy had a terrific impact, almost overnight', and affected

Cambridge more than most universities, because 'so many of our students on the public programmes were professional people with good qualifications already'.[139] It seemed that something like three-quarters of students on the public programmes would be affected by the new policy, and inevitably a new strategic review of provision was deemed necessary.[140] Unsurprisingly, the review cast doubt on the viability of work with the local centres, and recommended a substantial reduction of the number and range of courses. An immediate impact was the closure of the Certificate and Diploma courses for teachers in the lifelong learning sector, and it was clear that the regional provision – while it would continue in the short term – was under serious threat.[141] Other university departments and centres of continuing education almost immediately closed, but ICE was comparatively resilient due to the breadth of its profile in continuing education and the 'significant reserves' that it had built up.[142]

For many, the withdrawal of funding was tantamount to an assault on the principles that should lie behind continuing education and lifelong learning. There was a public campaign against the measure, supported by the Universities' Association for Lifelong Learning and by the newly constituted Campaigning Alliance for Lifelong Learning.[143] Many tutors and students in and around Cambridge shared in the anger and disappointment that resulted from the government's decision. Adrian Barlow

> hated it, because to me this was a fundamental part of what the Institute should be about. ... It flew in the face of what adult continuing education should be about, that you would only get credit for doing your work if you were actually applying to get a more advanced qualification than the ones you already had. That wasn't the ethos of the Institute as I'd come to know it. And I think a lot of the students – and these were retired people or people in serious mid-career, people in their 50s – saw this as a wrong step by the government.[144]

For the local centres, Evelyn Lord recalls, 'the atmosphere ... was sadness, really, because this was it – their lifeline had gone'.[145] The Local Centres Union was supportive of the Institute in the face of the unprecedented funding challenge, but some of the centres and their students – in Adrian Barlow's words – 'felt very strongly that the university was letting them down', echoing some of the complaints made by students about accreditation in the 1990s.[146]

Barlow, who was in the unenviable position of having to oversee the demise of the programmes and to explain the reasons to the local centres and their students, understood these frustrations:

> I think there was a feeling, and to an extent I shared it myself, that the university could and should have been more supportive or gone out of their way more strongly to support [the local centres]. There were people way outside of Cambridge like Richard Hoggart who felt very strongly that the universities themselves had been craven in simply giving in to this. But it was of course coming at a time when everything was dependent on funding deriving from research, and so it would have been be flying in the face of a much bigger concern in the university, than just the preservation of continuing education. And I have to say that one of the things I did discover, or become very much aware of, was that there was a feeling among many people in the university that continuing education was no longer something the university should be particularly concerned with.[147]

In light of the aims of government policy, some of the casualties amounted to 'unintended consequences': one example was the counselling programme, which clearly had a strong vocational orientation. Here, many of the students were graduates in their thirties or forties who were trying to pursue a second career; however, the implication of the funding change meant a sharp rise in fees which made the programme unviable.[148]

For the local centres in the region, it quickly became clear that the implications of the new funding regime would be profound. Richard Taylor felt pessmistic about the survival of the regional programme: 'my view', he explains, 'was that, if it was going to survive at all, it had to be very targeted, and with very specific objectives in view'.[149] In the short term, there was a reduction in the number of local centres: in 2009-10 courses were offered in 29 locations, with some concentrated into 'hubs' at Burghley House, just over the Lincolnshire border north-west of Peterborough, and Duxford in the south of Cambridgeshire.[150] Familiar places such as Bures, Burgate and Great Shelford continued in that year to run one or two courses each, but a substantial proportion of all courses were in Cambridge itself: of 167 advertised in the prospectus, 33 were at Homerton, and a further 39 elsewhere in Cambridge, including a few at Madingley Hall itself.[151] In some respects in the short term, the withdrawal of funding enabled a return to older ways of doing things. In 2009 Barlow was able to announce that

> from 2010 onwards an increasing number of our courses will no longer be credit-bearing. This will mean an easing of coursework requirements – welcome news for the large number of our students who prefer to study for the sheer pleasure of learning and intellectual stimulation. It also means that we shall have greater flexibility in the type and length of courses under offer.[152]

Also from 2010, residential courses on the public programmes became non-accredited: as the Institute's annual report explained, 'students will no longer be asked to undertake assessment and will be able to simply enjoy the unique opportunities which the residential programme at Madingley provides'.[153]

From June 2011, though, the regional programme was closed, and the Certificate and Diploma courses relocated to Madingley.[154] The end of the relationship with local centres prompted the reflection that

> The final year of the Regional Programme brought to an end an aspect of the Institute's work that dated back to the very earliest years of the University's engagement in extramural studies. However, demographic changes, the increasing age of the students mainly attending courses in the region, decreasing numbers of students and the inevitable rises in fees since 2008, have made the continuance of the courses run from Cambridge and taught mainly by part-time tutors in local (and sometimes very rural) centres from Peterborough to St Albans, Lavenham to Clacton, unsustainable.[155]

The programme of accredited Certificates, Diplomas, Advanced Diplomas and Master's-level qualifications survived, but from 2010 onwards these were awarded by the university rather than by ICE itself.[156] Barlow also saw the advantages of this 'closer collaboration': 'the University wants to see an increasing number of its own academic staff contribute to the Institute's teaching by sharing their research and expertise with our students and with the wider public'.[157] By this time there was also a small amount of online provision, notably a series of five linked courses on family history, running twice in the academic year.[158]

Many of the local centres survived independently of the Cambridge affiliation, not least because they had always themselves run a diverse range of activities. One example is the Settlement in Letchworth, which had hosted Cambridge courses since its inception after the First World War. There, 'most' of the Institute's panel tutors were re-employed by the Settlement itself, and the long tradition of adult education on the premises was able to continue.[159] A similar thing happened at other centres. Adrian Barlow recalls that 'there was almost a Madingley-in-exile group of tutors who went on teaching, and indeed I did so myself: I went back to run courses at Bedford Retirement Centre, even after I retired myself', which he did in 2011.[160] At Madingley itself, a new non-award-bearing 'Weekly Programme' was launched in January 2012, consisting of five classes spread over five weeks, and attracted 200 students in its first year.[161] The courses were designed to be multi-disciplinary, and included 'Legacies of War' and 'Humps, Bumps, Buildings and Hedges: Walking through History'.[162] The courses were charged at £100 in the first two years, rising to £150 in 2013-14, though this did not affect the fairly steady numbers who took them, which stood at 214 in that year.[163]

Organisationally, the changes at the end of the 2000s prompted further structural adjustment within ICE: the public and professional programmes were merged into a single division, offering a range of certificated courses. These were now organised on a yearly or two-yearly basis, without the modular complexity that had characterised earlier courses, and the provision concentrated on a smaller range of subject areas. By 2012-13 there were Certificates in Archaeology, Astronomy, Coaching, English Literature, Genetics, International Development and Principles and Practices of Assessment; Certificates of Higher Education in Historic Building Conservation and Practical Horticulture and Plantsmanship; Diplomas in Coaching, English Literature, History of Art and Local History; and Advanced Diplomas in English Literature, History of Art, Local History, Philosophy and the Study of Religion. In total, 213 students were enrolled on these programmes, together with a further 48 across two Postgraduate Certificates, in Medical Education and Architecture.[164] Still larger numbers, though, were taking the four 'Continuing Professional Education and Bespoke Courses': the English Legal Methods summer school had 66 students; there were 22 on 'Financial Innovation and Risk Prevention'; 111 were enrolled on the Investment Education Programme; and 167 were taking the long-standing LLB and Diploma in Law Revision Programme.[165]

Perhaps the most successful element of the public and professional programmes, however, were the part-time Master of Studies degrees, which had emerged in the 1990s and survived with substantial numbers of students into the early 2010s. Although local history, English literature and some other subjects from earlier decades had not survived at this level, by 2012-13 there were Master's programmes in Advanced Subject Teaching, Applied Criminology, Building History, Construction Engineering, International Relations, the Study of Jewish-Christian Relations and Sustainability Leadership, as well as the pioneering Interdisciplinary Design for the Built Environment. With 357 students across the two years of study, these Master's degrees would be further extended by the addition of a Creative Writing programme in the following year.[166] Between them, the surviving Master's degrees, Certficates and Diplomas epitomised much of the history of extramural education at Cambridge, engaging professionals and members of the public in developmental learning activities that drew widely on the expertise of academics across the university and within ICE itself.

The residential course programme, now referred to as the 'Weekend Programme', continued to thrive, and expanded in the early 2010s, with new courses in sciences and languages proving popular: Chinese language was offered for the first time in 2012-13.[167] Many of these weekend courses reflected long-standing areas of interest among students on the public programmes: landscape history, architecture, literature, music and theology all featured prominently. With 1,636 students attending 151 courses across 26 weekends in the year, this was a stable element of ICE's provision in a period of otherwise rapid and often uncomfortable change.[168] These numbers would not be sustained as quite such a high level to the end of the 2000s, but residential courses remain an important element of ICE's activity today. For 2023-4, plans are currently in hand to run courses across 13 weekends, on subjects including 'Art History, Business, Creative Writing, Global Challenges, History, Literature, Music and Science'.[169]

*

By the early 2010s, *The Learning Age* seemed a long time ago. For university continuing education, the fundamental changes in the funding environment had led most of the departments that remained – including Cambridge – to close the extramural activity with which they had been most strongly associated for more than a century. Some remnants did remain, not least at Cambridge the Certificate and other programmes in academic subjects across the social sciences and humanities, supplemented by creative writing, a reliably popular subject that met a substantial student demand. Science also gained in strength: in 2015-16 there were Certificates in Evolutionary Biology and in Astronomy, a Diploma in Astronomy, and an Advanced Diplomas in Ecological Monitoring and Conservation. Medical education was also covered with a Postgraduate Certificate; architecture featured on various courses, including another Postgraduate Certificate; and there were various programmes in coaching.[170] The umbrella term 'public and professional programmes' aptly captured the range of courses offered, although their modest scale meant that they focused on particular areas of activity in which ICE was able to specialise; they certainly did not cover the breadth of subjects taught across the university, as the pioneers of university extension may have once envisaged. With a small academic staff of its own, ICE continued to work closely with other academic departments in the University of Cambridge with which it had developed relationships over many years. Richard Taylor's aim of creating a 'research culture', focusing on adult education, had not succeeded, but there had been some recognition of the contribution of staff tutors and academic development officers when, under Taylor's leadership, they had the opportunity to become university lecturers or, in some cases, university senior lecturers. For Taylor, this was symbolically important, challenging the marginality that some in ICE felt from the rest of the university.[171]

The end of the regional progamme is an appropriate point at which to end this account of the history of extramural education at the post-war University of Cambridge. It marked the end of well over a century of 'extension' courses that covered first much of the country and later a fairly stable extramural region; and although it was never, by any means, the only activity of the Board of Extra-Mural Studies in its early years, it was the central purpose for which full-time teaching staff were initially appointed and retained, and it made contact with more students each year than anything else that ICE did until the end of the 2000s. It also marked a new set of governance arrangements for ICE, with a strategic committee replacing the management board and a 'much empowered' academic committee to run its day-to-day activities.[172] What this would mean for ICE at the time was unclear, though the number of students enrolled on its programmes fell sharply, from more than 12,000 in 2002-3 (see table 7.1) and over 11,000 in 2008-9 to 6,553 in 2010-11.[173] This did not necessarily mean a comparable reduction in full-time equivalent students, but it was a clear sign that ICE would need to reorientate its activities in the 2010s and beyond. It had lost its 'extramural empire', and would need to look elsewhere to secure its future.

Postscript

The end of the regional programme almost 15 years ago is just about far enough in the past to consider historically, but the impact of more recent developments, of which there have been many, are much harder to assess. Continuing education at the University of Cambridge looks very different now from a decade-and-a-half ago, and will no doubt evolve rapidly and in unpredictable ways in the coming years. Future historians will be able to write about it. I would, though, like to draw out some themes that have run through this book; these relate specifically to experiences at Cambridge, but may have a wider relevance too.

University extramural education has always had to respond to changing student demands for courses and subjects of study, and this has had an impact on staffing and on the shape of the programme. In chapter 2 of this book alone, the word 'demand' appears more than 30 times, often in quotations from documents from the period itself. University adult education is not unique in higher education in this respect, but it could be argued that the vicissitudes of student demand have had a more direct and immediate impact extramurally than on internal university departments. Today, when it is almost axiomatic to refer to students as 'consumers', it is striking to read John Andrew and Lionel Munby, writing in 1966, explaining that the organisational complexity of the Board of Extra-Mural Studies was the inevitable result of adult education that 'grows out of co-operation with consumers'.[1] Even in 1948, discussions of 'the changing demand for subjects' were an important element of staff meetings, and the development of residential courses for professional groups and others naturally brought a fresh dimension to the ways in which demands and 'educational needs' were met.[2]

Another theme that runs through the whole period is the distinctiveness of what universities could bring to adult education, compared with many other providers. In the mid-twentieth century this was often couched in the somewhat vague terms of ensuring 'university standards', both in teaching and in the expectations of students' written work; and the process of accreditation from the 1990s onwards yoked these 'standards' to a more formal framework of quality assurance and to a nationwide system of credit accumulation and transfer. This late twentieth-century development was certainly controversial, but in the long term it could be seen as meeting demands that were emerging from at least the 1960s, and probably earlier, for the formal certification of student achievement in extramural classes. These demands were by no means universal – and they were anathema to the 'Great Tradition' – but they were strengthened by the development of new universities and polytechnics in the 1960s, by the establishment and success of the Open University, and by the expansion of higher education thereafter, especially opportunities for part-time undergraduate study. Cambridge did not go down the route of part-time undergraduate degrees, though it did establish part-time Master's programmes; and through its Certficates, Diplomas and Advanced Diplomas a route to conventional academic recognition was created for its extramural students.

Adult education is often regarded, and often regards itself, as a marginal area of activity for universities, despite the large constituencies that it reaches and, in the cases of some departments, the substantial financial contribution that it can make. This has been a longstanding theme in the literature, both historical and contemporary, and much evidence has been given in this book to support it. The precarious and under-appreciated status of the Board's staff for much of the post-war period, the physical distance of Madingley Hall from Cambridge – increasingly significant after 1975 – and a rather dismissive attitude towards its work from some in the university itself all contributed to a sense that adult education was a peripheral activity of the parent institution. Its activities took place away from the university, or during vacations, and the openness of the 'Great Tradition' was set against the elitism of admissions to Cambridge colleges and its undergraduate degrees. Andrew and Munby felt the need to defend extramural education from charges that it was a 'charitable activity' or 'a kind of downtown intellectual slumming', and to insist that, '[i]n its own small way it is as vital to the health and development of the university as research and undergraduate teaching'.[3]

At the same time, the marginal position occupied by many in university adult education offered some freedom and opportunity: as Polly Courtice, quoted in chapter 6, noted, there were some benefits to being 'out-of-sight-and-out-of-mind'. Across its history, those who taught in university extension were able to create their own syllabuses, devise and deploy their own teaching methods, and – perhaps most importantly – move widely within and beyond their own areas of disciplinary expertise. Many post-war staff tutors covered a wide range of subjects – again, this was partly a function of demand – and others developed new multidisciplinary and interdisciplinary areas of teaching and research. Some areas of study gradually gained a measure of academic respectability through university adult education – local history was one such 'frontier' subject – and others, such as archaeology, reached new audiences through pioneering work, often literally in the field. Working closely with different subject specialists offered staff tutors the opportunity to collaborate across disciplines, and areas such as landscape history gained strength through interdisciplinary work in adult education departments. From a student perspective, too, the opportunity to study many different subjects at a local centre, or on the international summer schools, offered access to a breadth of learning that might not be available to a conventional undergraduate or postgraduate. Similarly, the Cambridge Programme for Industry in the 1990s demonstrated the potential uses of interdisciplinary approaches in courses for senior leaders and others.

As many observers have commented, feelings of marginality in university adult education departments have often existed alongside – and indeed enhanced – a strong sense of 'tradition'. This was most powerfully asserted by Harold Wiltshire in 1956, and his phrase 'the Great Tradition' encapsulated the sense that adult educators had a 'vital message' to deliver, and that their work had a long history. At Cambridge, the repeated invocations of James Stuart in both publicity material and internal debates – even during periods of rapid change – placed extramural education in the context of a history that validated its place in the landscape of learning. As the phrase 'the vital message' might suggest, the sense of tradition could lead university adult educators to seem self-regarding, or even pompous, in their insistence that the tradition was 'great'; this certainly coloured much of the historical writing on the subject in the second half of the twentieth century. Historians writing from within university extramural departments, as Malcolm Chase argued, 'acquiesced in the notion of the Great Tradition, or [were] read to that end; and … this version of history has shaped self-perception in adult education'.[4] It is clear that adult education histories, many focusing like this book on the story of a single institution, can be self-justifying in their approach; and it is similarly clear that university adult education, with 'tradition' as a refuge from marginality and uncertainty, could be 'suspicious' of change and defensive of its culture. As Chase suggested, 'tradition' could become 'a blunt instrument with which to strike at the unwelcome'.[5]

This relates to a further paradox that emerges in the story of extramural education at Cambridge, in particular: the existence of an open educational tradition in the context of an elite university. The challenges of operating in this context were revealed by some responses to the introduction of part-time Master's degrees, and more widely to some of the community education and outreach activities that were pursued in the 1990s and 2000s. Nevertheless, across the period covered by this book, Cambridge was at the forefront of progressive change in extramural education in many ways, and continuing education departments more widely – as David Davies argues – were 'significantly contributing to both the debate and the actual development and delivery of mass higher education'.[6] At the same time, though, there was a related mismatch between the regional role that was central to the Cambridge extramural programme on the one hand, and the university's national and increasingly global profile on the other. This was a matter of internal debate as the provision of residential courses expanded in the 1950s, and became more striking in the modern era of university league tables and research-driven 'excellence'. The Cambridge 'name' has always drawn attention, and students, to it – the enduring popularity of the international summer programmes are the most eloquent testament to this – but the tension between elite and open traditions of higher education are likely to remain, and to be highlighted by the continued participation of universities in extramural activity. It remains to be seen what the implications of an emerging emphasis on universities' non-academic 'impact' will be for continuing education in the longer term.

One virtue of an institutional history is that it can uncover the nature of internal debates about the aims, purpose and practices of education, and at the same time emphasise the diversity of approaches within a single institution. In post-war Britain, university extramural departments did a lot of different things, and one of the challenges of writing this book has been to attempt coverage of the sheer range of activities undertaken by just one of them. On the face of it the East Anglian regional programme, international summer schools, Cambridge Programme for Industry, magistrates' and armed forces' training, trade union and apprentices' education, the *Credit Where It's Due* project, the development of Access courses, and the Fenland Oral History Project – to take a few examples –

had little in common except that they were organised from the same small corner of the University of Cambridge. This fact in itself is striking to an outsider, and necessarily undermines the coherence of a single historical account of developments in a single decade, let alone the 65 years covered by this book.

What seems clear, though, is that all these activities arose from, and were sustained by, a sense of the social purpose of university adult education. This clearly ran through those who worked in it, across the whole period covered by this book. Maurice Bruce, writing of the late 1930s, recalled that many early university extension lecturers were 'fired with a sense of social purpose',[7] and this extended through the post-war generation of staff tutors – the first to have lifelong careers in extramural departments – to those who experienced the end of the Cambridge regional programmes in the 2000s. This sense of purpose has come across strongly in most of the interviews that I have undertaken, and from much of the archival material. When the ICE annual report for 2004-5 emphasised 'the vital message of lifelong learning', this was not merely a rhetorical flourish or a defensive insistence in the face of external challenges: it genuinely reflected a sense of mission that had animated earlier generations at Stuart House and in the local centres. Downham Market, to which this particular comment applied, may have taken the 'vital message' particularly to heart, but it was strong in most of the local centres, and across the other work that extramural education was trying to do. It endured through the upheavals of the 1990s: even while working through the challenges of accreditation, David Davies remembers a shared sense on all sides that 'we were doing progressive work'.[8] Most of those who worked for the Board of Extra-Mural Studies, for the Board of Continuing Education and for the Institute of Continuing Education enjoyed their teaching, and most of the students seem to have benefited. As one of the longest-serving tutors on the public programmes, Gillian Sheail, told me, 'working with adult students has been the most rewarding and valuable experience. They've been keen, enthusiastic and interested. They've been lovely.'[9] It is hard to think of a better note on which to end this book.

Notes and references

Preface

[1] Lawrence Goldman, *Dons and Workers: Oxford and Adult Education since 1850* (Oxford: Oxford University Press, 1995), p. 248.
[2] Joanna Bourke, *Birkbeck: 200 Years of Radical Learning for Working People* (Oxford: Oxford University Press, 2022), p. xiii.

Chapter 1

[1] Adrian Barlow, *Extramural: Literature and Lifelong Learning* (Cambridge: Lutterworth Press, 2012), p. 13.
[2] Thomas Kelly, *A History of Adult Education in Great Britain* (Liverpool: Liverpool University Press, 1970 [1st ed. И]), p. 229; Roger Fieldhouse et al, *A History of Modern British Adult Education* (Leicester: NIACE, 1996), pp. 40-1, 200-1; B. H. Tolley, *The History of the University of Nottingham* (2 vols, Nottingham: Nottingham University Press, 2001), vol. 1, pp. 10-19.
[3] See for example G. R. Evans, *The University of Oxford: A New History* (London: I. B. Tauris, 2010), pp. 36-7, 54-5; Michael Moss, J. Forbes Munro and R. H. Trainor, *University, City and State: The University of Glasgow since 1850* (Edinburgh: Edinburgh University Press, 2000), pp. 81-2; Sam Blaxland, *Swansea University* (Cardiff: University of Wales Press, 2020), pp. 60-2; G. R. Evans, *The University of Cambridge: A New History* (London: I. B. Tauris, 2010), p. 29; Christopher N. L. Brooke, *The History of the University of Cambridge, Volume 4: 1870-1990* (Cambridge: Cambridge University Press, 1993). For an exception, see Tolley, *History of the University of Nottingham*, vol. 2, pp. 207-31.
[4] Thomas Kelly, *For Advancement of Learning: The University of Liverpool 1881-1981* (Liverpool: Liverpool University Press, 1981), pp. 258-60, 441-4.
[5] Malcolm Chase, '"Mythmaking and Mortmain": The Uses of Adult Education History?', *Studies in the Education of Adults*, vol. 27 (1993), p. 53. See also, in particular, Stuart Marriott, *Extramural Empires: Service and Self-Interest in English University Adult Education 1873-1983* (Nottingham: University of Nottingham Department of Adult Education, 1984), pp. 10-13.
[6] Chase, '"Mythmaking and Mortmain"', pp. 56-7.
[7] Marriott, *Extramural Empires*, esp. p. 122; Goldman, *Dons and Workers*, p. 254.
[8] Barlow, *Extramural*, p. 13.
[9] Edwin Welch, *The Peripatetic University: Cambridge Local Lectures 1873-1973* (Cambridge: Cambridge University Press, 1973).
[10] Kelly, *History of Adult Education*, pp. 217-18.
[11] Ibid., p. 218; J. A. Secord, 'Sedgwick, Adam (1785-1873)', *Oxford Dictionary of National Biography* (Oxford: Oxford University Press, 2004). All references to the *Oxford Dictionary of National Biography* in this book are to the online edition.
[12] Kelly, *History of Adult Education*, pp. 219-21.
[13] Fieldhouse et al, *History of Modern British Adult Education*, p. 37; Welch, *Peripatetic University*, pp. 38-44.
[14] Welch, *Peripatetic University*, p. 43.
[15] Ibid., pp. 75-6; Kelly, *History of Adult Education*, p. 222.
[16] Welch, *Peripatetic University*, p. 178.
[17] Ibid., pp. 124-5, 127.

[18] Ibid., chapter 2; Roy Church, 'Colman Family (per. 1814-1898)', *Oxford Dictionary of National Biography*; H. C. G. Matthew, 'Stuart, James (1843-1913)', *Oxford Dictionary of National Biography*.
[19] Welch, *Peripatetic University*, p. 24. All translations of money values in this book use the Bank of England historical inflation calculator.
[20] Welch, *Peripatetic University*, pp. 178-9; Fieldhouse et al, *History of Modern British Adult Education*, p. 199.
[21] Kelly, *History of Adult Education*, p. 224.
[22] Ibid., p. 220.
[23] Welch, *Peripatetic University*, pp. 44, 64.
[24] Ibid., pp. 178-9.
[25] Ibid., p. 139.
[26] 'Second Revised Draft of Regulations for Courses and Classes', paper for Board meeting, 19 May 1950. Board meeting minutes from 1949 onwards are in the Madingley Hall (MH) archive, currently held in the Stuart Room.
[27] Welch, *Peripatetic University*, pp. 178-9.
[28] Kelly, *History of Adult Education*, pp. 231-3.
[29] Ibid., pp. 246-7; Welch, *Peripatetic University*, pp. 178-9.
[30] Fieldhouse et al, *History of Modern British Adult Education*, p. 38.
[31] Kelly, *History of Adult Education*, p. 229; Tolley, *History of the University of Nottingham*, vol. 1, pp. 10-19.
[32] Fieldhouse et al, *History of Modern British Adult Education*, p. 199.
[33] Goldman, *Dons and Workers*, pp. 107-8.
[34] Quoted in ibid., p. 106.
[35] Ibid., chapter 5; Kelly, *History of Modern British Adult Education*, pp. 248ff.
[36] Welch, *Peripatetic University*, pp 111-12.
[37] Ibid., p. 112.
[38] Ibid., p. 113.
[39] See esp. W. H. Draper, *University Extension: A Survey of Fifty Years 1873-1923* (Cambridge: Cambridge University Press, 1923), pp. 64-75. For earlier accounts see for example R. D. Roberts, *Eighteen Years of University Extension* (Cambridge: Cambridge University Press, 1891).
[40] Draper, *University Extension*, pp. 71, 74, 137-8. The London certificates were awarded after four years of continuous study.
[41] Marriott, *Extramural Empires*, pp. 91-2; Welch, *Peripatetic University*, pp. 142-3; John Holford, 'The University of Nottingham and Adult Education', *Andragoške Studije*, vol. 2 (2014), pp. 85-94.
[42] Fieldhouse et al, *History of Modern British Adult Education*, pp. 48-9, 206-8.
[43] Ibid., pp. 207-8.
[44] Ibid.; see, for a later period, K. T. Elsdon and others, *An Education for the People? A History of HMI and Lifelong Learning 1944-1992* (Leicester: NIACE, 2001), pp. 45-8.
[45] Marriott, *Extramural Empires*, pp. 89, 92-7.
[46] Welch, *Peripatetic University*, pp. 144-5.
[47] The front cover of this book features some book-boxes of more recent origin.
[48] Kelly, *History of Adult Education*, p. 224.
[49] 'Cranage, Very Rev. David Herbert Somerset', *Who Was Who* (online edition); Welch, *Peripatetic University*, chapter 7.
[50] Welch, *Peripatetic University*, p. 145.
[51] 'Mr G. F. Hickson', *The Times*, 2 November 1978, p. 19.

[52] Lionel M. Munby, 'Introduction', in Lionel M. Munby (ed.), *East Anglian Studies* (Cambridge: W. Heffer and Sons, 1968), p. xiii.
[53] *Local Lectures: Lists of Lecturers and Subjects 1937-38*, pp. 22-3: Cambridge University Library (CUL) UA/BEMS/53/18 (all subsequent lists of lecturers referenced in these notes are at the same location); 'Mr G. F. Hickson'; Maurice Bruce, 'Reminiscences Extra-Mural 1932-1941 and Reminiscences in Retrospect 1976', p. 20: typescript in CUL UA/BEMS/38/3.
[54] Board of Extra-Mural Studies, annual report, 1977-8, p. 2. Subsequent references are simply to 'annual report'. Reports before 1945-6 are in CUL UA/BEMS/22/8-10. There is a full run thereafter in the MH archive. Reports were also published in the *Cambridge University Reporter* (hereafter *CUR*).
[55] Annual report, 1935-6.
[56] Marriott, *Extramural Empires*, pp. 82-3, 104-5.
[57] Ibid., p. 106 and *passim.*
[58] Welch, *Peripatetic University*, pp. 148-50.
[59] Ibid., p. 150; annual report, 1936-7.
[60] Welch, *Peripatetic University*, pp. 180, 183; annual report, 1937-8.
[61] Welch, *Peripatetic University*, p. 189.
[62] Annual report, 1937-8.
[63] Welch, *Peripatetic University*, p. 189.
[64] Ibid., p. 183.
[65] Bruce, 'Reminiscences', p. 11.
[66] UCAE, *The Universities and Adult Education: A Report Prepared by a Working Party of the Universities Council for Adult Education* (London: UCAE, 1961), p. 8.
[67] Ibid.
[68] 'Second Revised Draft of Regulations for Courses and Classes'.
[69] WEA leaflet, 'The Tutorial Class', in Board meeting papers for 20 July 1950.
[70] Ibid.
[71] Annual report, 1937-8; 1944-5.
[72] Annual report, 1944-5; Welch, *Peripatetic University*, p. 150.
[73] 'Second Revised Draft of Regulations for Courses and Classes'.
[74] Welch, *Peripatetic University*, p. 180.
[75] Ibid., pp. 138-9; Geoffrey Hickson, 'Diplomas in Adult Education: Notes by the Secretary', paper for Local Centres Committee, 23 November 1951, filed with staff meeting papers. All staff meeting papers and minutes cited in this book are in the MH archive.
[76] Welch, *Peripatetic University*, p. 139.
[77] Ibid., pp. 115-16; *International Summer Programmes: 100th Anniversary 1923-2023* (Cambridge: University of Cambridge Institute of Continuing Education, 2023), p. 7. See also Draper, *University Extension*, p. 114.
[78] Summer meeting course papers, 1893-1938 in CUL UA/BEMS/2/16.
[79] Welch, *Peripatetic University*, pp. 112-13; Draper, *University Extension*, pp. 73-4.
[80] *International Summer Programmes: 100th Anniversary*, p. 7.
[81] Annual report, 1922-3.
[82] Quoted in *International Summer Programmes: 100th Anniversary*, p. 7.
[83] Quoted in ibid., p. 11.
[84] George Band, rev., 'Odell, Noel Ewart (1890-1987)', *Oxford Dictionary of National Biography*.
[85] *Local Lectures: List of Lecturers and Subjects 1937-38*, pp. 12-13, 24-5, 26-7.

[86] Ibid., pp. 28-9; Georgina Brewis, 'Matheson, (Marie) Cécile (1874-1950)', *Oxford Dictionary of National Biography*; Cécile Matheson, *Citizenship: An Introductory Handbook* (London: Student Christian Movement, 1917).
[87] *Local Lectures: List of Lecturers and Subjects 1937-38*, pp. 30-1; W. C. Atkinson, rev. John D. Haigh, 'Peers, Edgar Allison (1891-1952)', *Oxford Dictionary of National Biography*.
[88] Bruce, 'Reminiscences', p. 2.
[89] Annual report, 1934-5.
[90] Ibid.
[91] See for example Harold Plaskitt, *Synopsis of European History 476-1914* (London: University Tutorial Press, 1938); H. C. Shearman and H. Plaskitt, *Matriculation History of England, Part 3: 1688-1815* (London: University Tutorial Press, 1930).
[92] 'Shearman, Sir Harold (Charles)', *Who Was Who*.
[93] *Local Lectures: List of Lecturers and Subjects 1938-9*, pp. 24-5: CUL UA/BEMS/53/18; 'Mr J. Hampden Jackson', *The Times*, 3 December 1966, p. 10; annual report, 1957-8, p. 3.
[94] J. Hampden Jackson, *Marx, Proudhon and European Socialism* (London: English Universities Press, 1957); J. Hampden Jackson, *The Post-War Decade: A Short History of the World* (London: Victor Gollancz, 1955); J. Hampden Jackson, *Europe since the War* (London: Victor Gollancz, 1933); Charles Carrington with J. Hampden Jackson, *A History of England* (Cambridge: Cambridge University Press, 1932).
[95] Bruce, 'Reminiscences', p. 22.
[96] Ibid., p. 2.
[97] Ibid., pp. 22, 19.
[98] Ibid., p. 11.
[99] Ibid., p. 20; 'Darvall, Frank Ongley', *Who Was Who* (online edition); Michael J. Walsh, 'Ward [*married name* Jackson], Barbara Mary, Baroness Jackson of Lodsworth (1914-1981)', *Oxford Dictionary of National Biography*.
[100] 'Prof. Maurice Bruce', *The Times*, 25 May 1988, p. 16; Maurice Bruce, *The Coming of the Welfare State* (4th ed., London: Batsford, 1968 [1st ed. 1961]).
[101] Welch, *Peripatetic University*, p. 113.
[102] Ibid., p. 158.
[103] Annual report, 1937-8.

Chapter 2

[1] S. G. Raybould, *The English Universities and Adult Education* (London: WEA, 1951), p. xv.
[2] Marriott, *Extramural Empires*, chapter 5.
[3] Kelly, *History of Adult Education* (Liverpool: Liverpool University Press, 1970 [1st ed. 1962]), pp. 337-9.
[4] Ibid., ch. 20, fig. 4 (after p. 339).
[5] Raybould, *English Universities and Adult Education*, p. xvii.
[6] Ibid., p. 51.
[7] Ibid., pp. 20-2.
[8] H. C. Wiltshire, 'The Great Tradition in University Adult Education', *Adult Education*, vol. 29 (1956), pp. 88-97, esp. pp. 90-1.
[9] Fieldhouse et al, *History of Modern British Adult Education*, p. 218.
[10] John A. Blyth, *English University Adult Education 1908-1958: A Unique Tradition* (Manchester: Manchester University Press, 1983), pp. 317-21; *Liberal Education in a Technical Age: A Survey of*

the Relationship of Vocational and Non-Vocational Further Education and Training (London: National Institute of Adult Education, 1955).
[11] See for example annual report, 1950-1, pp. 5-6.
[12] See the minutes in CUL UA/BEMS/6/4 and 5/8.
[13] Fred Inglis, *Raymond Williams* (London: Routledge, 2005), p. 109.
[14] List of Board members, in Board meeting papers for 17 February 1950. On the functioning of the Local Centres Union see for example John Andrew to L. B. Scott, 19 November 1950: CUL UA/BEMS/33/12; John Andrew to W. H. Bleby, 1 May 1958: CUL UA/BEMS/38/5.
[15] 'Mr F. R. Salter', *The Times*, 24 November 1967, p. 12; F. R. Salter, *Karl Marx and Modern Socialism* (London: Macmillan and Co., 1921); F. R. Salter, *Sir Thomas Gresham (1518-1979)* (London: Leonard Parsons, 1925).
[16] Welch, *Peripatetic University*, pp. 105, 141-2; 'An Honorary Degree for Ex-Clerk', *Cambridge Evening News*, 14 January 1970, press cutting in MH cupboard 8, folder 'Miscellaneous'.
[17] Finance and General Purposes Committee (FGPC) report, 'Appointments of Full-Time Staff', paper for Board meeting, 19 February 1937. Pre-1949 Board meeting minutes and papers are in CUL UA/BEMS/4/2.
[18] Welch, *Peripatetic University*, p. 175.
[19] Frank Bell, *Undercover University: Artes in Arduis* (Cambridge: Elisabeth Bell, 1990). Bell's account of the 'Kuching University' was written in 1946, and published after his death.
[20] John Mackie, *Surveyor and Engineer: Captain Jack, the Autobiography of John Mackie* (Wellington: New Zealand Institute of Surveyors, 2007), p. 289.
[21] Ibid., pp. 289-90; see also Bell, *Undercover University*, pp. 34-40.
[22] Quoted in Mackie, *Surveyor and Engineer*, pp. 290-1.
[23] Bell, *Undercover University*, p. 77.
[24] Welch, *Peripatetic University*, p.170; 'Frank Bell', *The Times*, 25 July 1989, p. 16.
[25] F. E. Bell, 'Report on German Prisoner of War Summer School, Cambridge, June 1947', paper for Board meeting, 10 October 1947.
[26] 'John Andrew: Senior Tutor of St Catharine's College', *The Times*, 15 March 2010, p. 62. There is a longer version of this obituary in *The Times* online.
[27] Welch, *Peripatetic University*, p. 175 n.; annual report, 1947-8, p. 5.
[28] 'John Andrew: Senior Tutor of St Catharine's College'.
[29] Board meeting, 25 May 1955.
[30] FGPC, 'Full-Time Teaching Appointments: Conditions and Terms', paper for staff meeting, 24 April 1948.
[31] FGPC, 'Full-Time Teaching Staff', paper for Board meeting, 12 November 1945; 'Leslie Wayper', *The Times*, 28 April 2006, p. 72.
[32] Annual reports, *passim*; C. L. Wayper, *Political Thought* (London: Teach Yourself Books, 1954).
[33] Annual report, 1948-9, p. 3.
[34] Board meeting, 19 July 1947.
[35] Annual report, 1950-1, esp. p. 10.
[36] FGPC, 'Full-Time Teaching Appointments'; *List of Tutors, Lecturers and Subjects 1952-3*, p. 14: CUL UA/BEMS/53/18.
[37] H. A. Clement, *The Story of the Ancient World: From the Earliest Times to the Fall of Rome* (London: George Harrap and Co., 1936); H. A. Clement, *The Story of Modern Europe* (London: George Harrap and Co., 1956); H. A. Clement, *The Story of Britain, Volume Three: From 1914 to 1945* (rev. ed., London: George Harrap and Co., 1953 [1st ed. 1943]). The first edition *The Story of Britain, Volume Three* went through seven reprints.
[38] See for example Clement, *The Story of Britain, Volume Three*, pp. 73, 133, and *passim*.

[39] FGCP, 'Full-Time Teaching Appointments'; *List of Tutors, Lecturers and Subjects 1952-1953*, p. 24.
[40] See for example annual report, 1950-1, appendices.
[41] FGPC, 'Full-Time Teaching Appointments'; Bruce, 'Reminscences'.
[42] FGPC, 'Full-Time Teaching Appointments'; L. Marion Springall, *Labouring Life in Norfolk Villages 1843-1914* (London: Allen and Unwin, 1936); George Ireland, 'Obituary: Helen Lowenthal', *Independent*, 14 April 1993, online.
[43] Ireland, 'Obituary'; FGPC, 'Full-Time Teaching Appointments'.
[44] FGPC, 'Full-Time Teaching Appointments'; Board meeting, 17 February 1950; 23 October 1953.
[45] Board meeting, 21 May 1954.
[46] Michael Pollitt, 'Rachel Young: Norwich's "Voice of Local History" Pioneered Children's Activities at City Museums', *Eastern Daily Press*, 21 January 2014, online.
[47] 'Full-Time Teaching Staff', report for Board meeting, 19 February 1954.
[48] See annual report, 1945-6, appendices; 1955-6, appendices. Young taught five different classes in 1955-6, but one ran twice in the same centre.
[49] Annual report, 1955-6, p. 8.
[50] Ibid., p. 3; 1961-2, p. 3.
[51] Pollitt, 'Rachel Young'.
[52] FGPC, 'Full-Time Teaching Staff'.
[53] Annual report, 1947-8, p. 8; 1955-6, p. 8; *List of Tutors, Lecturers and Subjects 1952-1953*, p. 22.
[54] FGPC, 'Full-Time Teaching Staff'.
[55] *List of Tutors, Lecturers and Subjects, 1952-1953*, p. 14.
[56] *The Pictorial Encyclopedia of Scientific Knowledge* (London: Sampson, Low, Marston and Co., [1956]), pp. 6-7.
[57] David Short, 'Other Lives: Lionel Munby', *Guardian*, 23 July 2009 (online).
[58] David Short, 'Lionel Munby 1918-2009: A Tribute', *Herts Past and Present*, 3rd series, vol. 14 (2009), pp. 3-4; Lionel M. Munby, *The Hertfordshire Landscape* (London: Hodder and Stoughton, 1977).
[59] Short, 'Lionel Munby'; see for example Lionel M. Munby, 'Tithe Apportionments and Maps', *History*, vol. 54, no. 180 (1969), pp. 68-71. Munby was editor of this section of the journal, entitled 'Short Guides to Records'. See also, for example, Lionel M. Munby, 'Founding Fathers: The Beginnings of some Adult Education Institutions in North Hertfordshire', *History of Education Society Bulletin*, vol. 23 (1979), pp. 40-51.
[60] Short, 'Lionel Munby'; Doris Jones-Baker, 'Introduction', in Doris Jones-Baker (ed.), *Hertfordshire in History: Papers Presented to Lionel Munby* (Hatfield: University of Hertfordshire Press, 2004 [1st ed. 1991]), pp. v-viii.
[61] Lionel Maxwell Munby, 'Early Years, May 1918 to January 1946', p. 39: typescript in the possession of Diana Munby; Lionel M. Munby, 'For Discussion at Cultural Committee, January 8th, 1965', Communist Party of Great Britain Archive, Labour History Archive and Study Centre, People's History Museum, Manchester, CP/CENT/CULT/3/9. I am grateful to Antonio F. Canales for drawing my attention to this document.
[62] Bill Schwarz, '"The people" in History: The Communist Party Historians' Group 1946-56', in Richard Johnson et al., eds, *Making Histories: Studies in History-Writing and Politics* (London: Hutchinson, 1982), pp. 73, 77.
[63] 'Full-Tine Staff', paper for Board meeting, 23 July 1948; Board meeting, 23 October 1953.
[64] Annual report, 1948-9, p. 3; staff meeting, 19-20 December 1955.
[65] Annual report, 1955-6, p. 6.

[66] Staff meeting, 23 May 1951; Adrian Poole, 'Leo Salingar', address to memorial gathering, 5 February 2005, online.
[67] Leo Salingar, *Shakespeare and the Traditons of Comedy* (Cambridge: Cambridge University Press, 1976); Leo Salingar, *Dramatic Form in Shakespeare and the Jacobeans* (Cambridge: Cambridge University Press, 1988).
[68] Poole, 'Leo Salingar'.
[69] Annual report 1954-5, p. 4.
[70] Board meeting, 19 May 1950; 23 October 1953; staff meeting, 19-20 December 1955.
[71] Lionel Maxwell Munby, 'Later Years 1946-2005: The Development of Local History in England', pp. 2-3: typescript in the possession of Diana Munby.
[72] Annual report, 1947-8, appendices.
[73] 'Full-Time Teaching Staff: Memorandum by the Secretary', 12 October 1955, paper for Board meeting, 21 May 1958 [*sic*], p. 4.
[74] Annual report, 1957-8, p. 3.
[75] Staff meeting, 22 December 1958.
[76] 'Full-Time Teaching Appointments: Conditions and Terms', paper for staff meeting, 24 April 1948.
[77] Annual report, 1947-8, appendix.
[78] Munby, 'Later Years', p. 2; see also staff meeting, 11 January 1947.
[79] For examples, see staff meeting, 28 April 1950; 9 May 1952; 2 January 1957.
[80] 'Analysis of Expenditure 1956-7', paper for Educational Advisory Committee, 23 April 1958: CUL UA/BEMS/10/3.
[81] Staff meeting, 5 October 1946; 11 January 1947; 23 May 1951.
[82] Staff meeting, 23 May 1951.
[83] Staff meeting, 11-12 January 1952.
[84] Staff meeting, 2 January 1957.
[85] Memorandum by Hickson to staff meeting, 22 November 1946; staff meeting, 2 January 1957.
[86] Annual report, 1963-4, p. 3; Board meeting, 11 February 1964. Lionel Munby attended Board meetings regularly from 20 November 1957, and in 1959 Salingar was elected by the staff to represent them on the Board: staff meeting, 21 December 1959.
[87] 'Dr R. F. Rattray', *The Times*, 20 November 1967, p. 10; *List of Tutors, Lecturers and Subjects 1952-1953*, p. 28; R. F. Rattray, *Bernard Shaw: A Chronicle and an Introduction* (London: Duckworth, 1934).
[88] Annual report, 1960-1, p. 3; Barbara Harvey and Peter Linehan, 'Edward Miller 1915-2000', *Proceedings of the British Academy*, vol. 138 (2006), pp. 238-9.
[89] Harvey and Linehan, 'Edward Miller 1915-2000', p. 235.
[90] Ibid., pp. 239-40; see below, pp. 61-3.
[91] Geoffrey Hickson, 'Extra-Mural Teaching by University Teaching Officers', paper for Board meeting, 1 November 1946.
[92] See for example Board/WEA joint committee (WEAJC) meeting, 1 December 1952; 6 February 1953. WEAJC minutes and papers are in CUL UA/BEMS/6/3-4.
[93] 'Allowances for Travelling Time for Part-Time Tutors', paper for JC meeting, 21 January 1959; WEAJC meeting 6 May 1959.
[94] 'Allowances for Travelling Time for Part-Time Tutors'.
[95] Geoffrey Hickson, 'Rates of Fees for Part-Time Lecturers and Tutors', paper for Board meeting, 25 May 1955.
[96] FPGC, 'Fees of Part-Time Lecturers and Tutors', paper for Board meeting, 21 May 1958.

[97] Local Centres Committee (LCC) meeting, 18 November 1959. LCC minutes and papers are in CUL UA/BEMS/5/8-9.
[98] Ibid.
[99] WEAJC meeting, 8 May 1953.
[100] Annual report, 1955-6, appendices. The figures for full-time staff include some who had retired, and are approximate, as in the case of extension classes some were taught by 'various' lecturers. Extension courses include short courses.
[101] Annual report, 1959-60, appendices. In that year full-time staff taught 28 of 33 terminal classes, 15 of 35 sessionals, 17 of 32 tutorials and 18 of 44 extension courses (including short courses).
[102] J. Hampden Jackson, 'Report to the Special Sub-Committee', paper for Board meeting, 23 July 1948.
[103] Training course for tutors in adult education, 24 July to 7 August 1948, course papers in BEMS/14/25; training course papers, 1957, in BEMS/14/30.
[104] See for example Board meeting, 27 July 1950.
[105] 'Report of Resident Tutor in Hertfordshire: F. V. H. Ramsbottom, 1948-9', in Board papers for 20 May 1949; John Andrew, 'Report on the Board's Library and the Provision of Books to Courses and Classes', paper for Board meeting, 23 October 1953, in staff meeting papers for 1953.
[106] Hampden Jackson, 'Report to the Special Sub-Committee'.
[107] LCC meeting, 17 February 1950. In fact, the course did not run that year (LCC meeting, 8 May 1950).
[108] See for example WEAJC meeting, 4 November 1949.
[109] 'Statement on Written Work', paper for LCC meeting, 21 May 1958. On class logs, see Pushpa Kumbhat, 'The Experience of Adult Education: Workers' Educational Association Tutorial Class Logbooks as Sources', *History of Education*, vol. 50 (2021), pp. 257-78.
[110] 'Statement on Written Work'.
[111] Raybould, *English Universities and Adult Education*, pp. 1-18.
[112] Michael Allen interview with author, 14 April 2022.
[113] Gillian Sheail interview with author, 13 April 2022.
[114] Andrew, 'Report on the Board's Library'.
[115] J. R. Mitchell, syllabus for year 2 tutorial class on 'International Affairs' at Peterborough: CUL UA/BEMS/17/11.
[116] Leslie Wayper, syllabus for year 2 tutorial class on 'International Affairs', Peterborough: CUL UA/BEMS/17/14.
[117] See for example notes on a tutorial class led by Dr C. A. Smith, n.d.: Colchester University Extension Society papers, CUL UA/BEMS/33/12.
[118] Annual report, 1947-8, p. 8. This was year 2 of the course, which had by this time only seven effective students. See also Lionel Munby, syllabus for 'Sociology' lectures: CUL UA/BEMS/17/11.
[119] W. P. Baker, syllabuses in CUL UA/BEMS/17/7; W. Pearson Baker, *The English Village* (London: Oxford University Press, 1953).
[120] 'A List of the Books Added to the Library in Stuart House May 1945–April 1949': CUL UA/BEMS/53/21.
[121] Annual report, 1947-8, p. 9; syllabus for 'The Family and Social Change': CUL UA/BEMS/17/14; Marie C. Nutter, syllabus for 'The Peoples of the World': CUL UA/BEMS/17/11.
[122] H. F. Redlich, 'How the New Regulations Affect the Subject of Music', paper for LCC meeting, 20 November 1950.
[123] Anne Pimlott Baker, 'Redlich, Hans Ferdinand (1903-1968)', *Oxford Dictionary of National Biography*.
[124] Annual report, 1947-8, appendices; 1955-6, appendices.

[125] H.O. Lowenthal, 'Statement on the Value of the Teaching of Art History in Adult Education', paper for Board meeting, 24 November 1950.
[126] See for example Tom Steele, *The Emergence of Cultural Studies 1945-65: Cultural Politics, Adult Education and the English Question* (London: Lawrence and Wishart, 1997).
[127] Notes on tutorial class led by C. A. Smith; John Andrew and Lionel Munby, 'The Extra-Mural Work of the University', *Cambridge Review*, 19 November 1966, p. 121.
[128] F. E. Bell, 'The Board and Residential Courses', paper for Board meeting, 24 October 1952.
[129] WEAJC meeting, 15 July 1949
[130] Ibid.; report on 'Regency England' course, 1949: CUL UA/BEMS/14/25.
[131] Syllabus in CUL UA/BEMS/14/25.
[132] Report on 'Regency England'.
[133] Ibid.
[134] See discussions in WEAJC minutes, and in course reports in CUL UA/BEMS/14/25 and subsequent files.
[135] WEAJC meeting, 18 May 1951; 13 July 1951; report on 'The Age of Dickens', 1957: CUL UA/BEMS/14/30.
[136] Report on 'The Age of Dickens'.
[137] Report on 'Regency England'.
[138] Ibid.
[139] Report on 'The Age of Pericles': paper for WEAJC meeting, 16 November 1960.
[140] WEAJC meeting, 19 November 1962; 19 November 1963.
[141] Report on WEA summer school and tutors' training course, for WEAJC meeting, 6 November 1957.
[142] Annual report, 1950-1, p. 7.
[143] Annual report, 1955-6, p. 7.
[144] Summer school in natural history (taught jointly with the University of Glasgow), 18 to 31 July 1959, syllabus: CUL UA/BEMS/14/30; annual report, 1958-9, p. 7.
[145] 'The Changing Demand for Subjects', paper for Board meeting, 23 May 1956.
[146] Geoffrey Hickson, 'Full-Time Teaching Staff: Memorandum by the Secretary', 12 October 1957, paper for Board meeting, 21 May 1958; Jacquetta Hawkes, *Mortimer Wheeler: Adventurer in Archaeology* (London: Weidenfeld and Nicolson, 1982), chapter 11.
[147] Annual report, 1956-7, p. 3; 1963-4, p. 3; see for example John Alexander, 'Greeks, Italians and the Earliest Balkan Iron Age', *Antiquity*, vol. 36 (1962), pp. 123-30.
[148] Annual report, 1961-2, p. 4; John Alexander, 'The History of Cambridge: Excavations on Castle Hill 1956-1964', *History Today*, vol. 15 (1965), pp. 800-2..
[149] WEA summer school prospectus, 1958, in course papers: CUL UA/BEMS/14/30.
[150] John Alexander, 'Early Cambridge: An Interim Report on the Excavations at Castle Hill, Cambridge, 1956-1962', *Archaeological News Letter*, vol. 7 (1964), p. 226.
[151] Annual report, 1959-60, appendices.
[152] On Clement, see Lionel Munby, 'The Teaching of Local History', memorandum for staff meeting, 26 May 1965. Clement's local history syllabuses are in CUL UA/BEMS/17/8.
[153] Munby, 'The Teaching of Local History'.
[154] Ibid.
[155] Munby, 'Later Years', pp. 2-3.
[156] Munby, 'The Teaching of Local History'.
[157] 'Local History', tutorial class year 2 syllabus, Swavesey: CUL UA/BEMS/17/11.
[158] Munby, 'Later Years', pp. 36-7.

[159] Ibid., pp. 22-3; John Beckett, *Writing Local History* (Manchester: Manchester University Press, 2007), p. 113.
[160] John Andrew and Lionel Munby, 'New Developments in University Adult Education', *Cambridge Review*, 26 November 1966, p. 142.
[161] *Report by HM Inspectors on Classes in Local History Provided by Responsible Bodies in the Cambridge University Extra-Mural Area, Inspected during the Michaelmas Term 1954* (London: MoE, 1955), pp. 9-10, in Board meeting papers, 19 October 1955.
[162] Ibid., pp. 10, 5.
[163] *Knebworth: The Story of Our Village* (3rd ed., Knebworth: Workers' Educational Association, 1967 [1st ed. 1953]).
[164] Fieldhouse et al, *History of Modern British Adult Education*, pp. 239-52.
[165] Ibid., p. 255.
[166] Ibid., p. 256; Raybould, *English Universities and Adult Education*, pp. 43-5.
[167] For a study of one example, see Sharon Clancy, *Sir George Trevelyan, Residential Adult Education and the New Age: To Open the Immortal Eye* (Basingstoke: Palgrave Macmillan, 2023).
[168] Fieldhouse et al, *History of Modern British Adult Education*, p. 257.
[169] Staff meeting, 28 April 1950.
[170] Staff meeting, 5 October 1946; 'Report to Council on the Establishment of a Residential College for Extra-Mural Studies at Madingley Hall', 14 May 1948 (bound with Board minutes, 15 January 1959 [*sic*]). Welch, *Peripatetic University*, p. 167.
[171] Annual report, 1951-2, p. 3.
[172] Welch, *Peripatetic University*, p. 167.
[173] Draft brochure, 'Madingley Hall: A Residential College for Adult Education', in Madingley Hall Committee papers, CUL UA/BEMS/9/1.
[174] Welch, *Peripatetic University*, p. 168; 'Mr F. R. Salter'.
[175] 'Report of the Staff Sub-Committee on the Use of Madingley Hall', paper for staff meeting, 28 April 1950.
[176] Ibid.
[177] Bell, 'The Board and Residential Courses'.
[178] Ibid., p. 11.
[179] Ibid., pp. 8-9.
[180] 'Report of the Staff Sub-Committee on the Use of Madingley Hall'.
[181] Staff meeting 11-12 January 1952; Bell, 'The Board and Residential Courses', p. 8.
[182] Residential Courses Committee, 14 November 1955: CUL UA/BEMS/9/2; annual report, 1956-7, p. 4.
[183] Residential Courses Committee, 14 November 1955.
[184] 'The Music of Mozart' syllabus, paper for LCC meeting, 12 February 1958.
[185] Anne Karminski and nine others, letter in *Cambridge Review*, 20 February 1954, p. 322, responding to 'Senator', 'White Elephant for Sale', *Cambridge Review*, 13 February 1954, pp. 290-1.
[186] Welch, *Peripatetic University*, pp. 112-18; *International Summer Programmes: 100th Anniversary*, pp. 7-8.
[187] Annual report, 1946-7, p. 3.
[188] Bell, 'The Board and Residential Courses'.
[189] Ibid.
[190] 'Residential Courses 1957-58: Report by the Secretary', paper for Residential Courses Committee, 29 October 1958: CUL UA/BEMS/9/2.
[191] Vacation Course for Foreign Students (VCFS), prospectus, 1957: CUL UA/BEMS/14/30.

[192] VCFS prospectus, 1948: CUL UA/BEMS/14/25.
[193] Ibid.
[194] VCFS, 1957, course papers: CUL UA/BEMS/14/30.
[195] VCFS, 1958, course papers: CUL UA/BEMS/14/30.
[196] Bell, 'The Board and Residential Courses'.
[197] Ibid.
[198] 'Residential Courses 1957-58: Report by the Secretary'.
[199] 'Foreign Lawyers' course papers, 1948: CUL UA/BEMS/14/25.
[200] Course papers in CUL UA/BEMS/14/25; annual report, 1948-9, p. 3.
[201] Bell, 'The Board and Residential Courses'; Residential Courses Committee meeting, 14 November 1955: CUL UA/BEMS/9/1. Other papers from this committee are in the same archival folder.
[202] 'Vacation Courses 1955-56: Report by the Secretary', paper for Resident Courses Committee, 14 November 1956.
[203] Phrase used in Blyth, *English University Adult Education*, p. 328.
[204] Ibid., p. 334.
[205] Ibid.
[206] Ibid., pp. 337-8.
[207] Bell, 'The Board and Residential Courses', p. 5.
[208] Annual report, 1953-4, p. 4; 1955-6, p. 4. For Lee's course, see LCC meeting, 21 June 1950.
[209] See annual reports, and course papers in e.g. CUL UA/BEMS/14/30.
[210] Welch, *Peripatetic University*, p. 168.
[211] Annual report, 1955-6, p. 10.
[212] Geoffrey Hickson and Leslie James, 'Course for Managers in Madingley Hall, Lent Term 1957', report for Board meeting, 22 May 1957.
[213] Ibid.
[214] Vivian Ramsbottom, 'Residential Course for Apprentices in the Engineering Industry 13–27 August 1955', report for Board meeting, 7 December 1955.
[215] Ibid.
[216] Frank Lee, report on NUGMW residential course, paper for staff meeting, [17-18 December 1954?].
[217] Blyth, *English University Adult Education*, p. 318; Wiltshire, 'Great Tradition', pp. 90-2.
[218] G. F. Hickson, 'Extra-Mural Education and Industry', reprint from *Cambridge Review*, 14 November 1959: CUL UA/BEMS/50/42.
[219] Ibid.
[220] Ibid.
[221] LCC meeting, 22 May 1957.
[222] Hickson, 'Extra-Mural Education and Industry'.
[223] Report on seventh course for managers in industry, 1959: CUL UA/BEMS/14/31.
[224] Ibid.
[225] Fieldhouse et al, *History of Modern British Adult Education* pp. 55-7, 211; Welch, *Peripatetic University*, p. 163.
[226] Welch, *Peripatetic University*, p. 163.
[227] Ibid.; N. Scarlyn Wilson, *A United People Goes to War* (London: Hodder and Stoughton, 1939); N. Scarlyn Wilson, *Punch and Judy* (London and New York: Samuel French Ltd, [1934]).
[228] Annual report, 1947-8, p. 6.
[229] Fieldhouse et al, *History of Modern British Adult Education*, p. 55.
[230] Welch, *Peripatetic University*, p. 164.

[231] W. H. Moberly, 'Preface', in N. Scarlyn Wilson, *Education in the Forces 1936-46: The Civilian Contribution* (London: Institute of Education, 1948), p. v. See also Fieldhouse et al, *History of Modern British Adult Education*, p. 57.
[232] Board meeting, 18 November 1949.
[233] Education in HM Forces Committee, 9 December 1949: CUL UA/BEMS/9/1.
[234] Board meeting, 19 May 1950; 27 July 1950.
[235] FGPC, 'Full-Time Staff', paper for Board meeting, 23 July 1948; Scarlyn Wilson, *Education in the Forces*.
[236] Informal conference with RAF education officers, 11 April 1949: CUL UA/BEMS/9/1.
[237] Report on HM Forces education, April 1951–March 1952, paper for Board meeting, 23 May 1952.
[238] Ibid.
[239] Staff meeting, 21 July 1950.
[240] Report on HM Forces education, April 1951–March 1952.
[241] Ibid.
[242] Annual report, 1956-7, p. 4; 1957-8, p. 4; 1958-9, p. 4; 1961-2, p. 5.
[243] Informal conference with RAF education officers, 27 June 1950: CUL UA/BEMS/9/1.
[244] Annual report, 1960-1, p. 4.
[245] Report on courses at Madingley Hall, 1955-6, paper for Residential Courses Committee, 14 November 1956; annual report, 1955-6, p. 10.
[246] Calculated from annual report, 1960-1, p. 9.
[247] 'Courses in Madingley Hall 1953-54: Report by the Secretary', paper for staff meeting. 17-18 December 1954.
[248] International affairs for the RAF, 20-7 June 1959, course papers in CUL UA/BEMS/14/31.
[249] Ibid.
[250] 'The Commonwealth', 10-17 December 1960, course papers in CUL UA/BEMS/14/31.
[251] 'Report by the Educational Advisory Committee on the Work of the Board', in Board papers, 15 January 1959.
[252] Educational Advisory Committee, 11 March 1958: CUL UA/BEMS/10/3. All Educational Advisory Committee papers cited below are in this folder in CUL.
[253] Geoffrey Hickson, 'The Work of the Board', memorandum for Educational Advisory Committee, 18 July 1958, p. 1; Wilshire, 'Great Tradition', p. 89.
[254] Hickson, 'The Work of the Board', p. 2; Raybould, *English Universities and Adult Education*, esp. pp. 8-10.
[255] Hickson, 'The Work of the Board', p. 2.
[256] Ibid., pp. 2-3.
[257] Ibid., pp. 3-5.
[258] Ibid.
[259] Ibid., pp. 5-6.
[260] Ibid., p. 6.
[261] Hickson, 'Full-Time Teaching Staff'.
[262] See above, pp. 25-6, 28-9.
[263] Hickson, 'The Work of the Board', p. 6.
[264] Ibid.
[265] Rachel Young, Edward Miller and John Hampden Jackson, 'The Work and Organisation of the Board of Extra-Mural Studies', memorandum for Educational Advisory Committee, 18 July 1958, p. 1.
[266] Ibid.

[267] Ibid., pp. 3-4.
[268] Lionel Munby, 'The Work and Organisation of the Board of Extra-Mural Studies', memorandum for Educational Advisory Committee, 18 July 1958.
[269] Leslie James and Leslie Wayper, 'The Work and Organisation of the Board of Extra-Mural Studies', memorandum for Educational Advisory Committee, 18 July 1958.
[270] Ibid.
[271] Young, Miller and Hampden Jackson, 'Work and Organisation', p. 2.
[272] Ibid.
[273] James and Wayper, 'Work and Organisation'.
[274] Young, Miller and Hampden Jackson, 'Work and Organisation', p. 1.
[275] See above, pp. 59-60.
[276] Munby, 'Work and Organisation'.
[277] Annual report, 1950-1, p. 11.
[278] Hickson, 'Diplomas in Adult Education'.
[279] Ibid.
[280] Ibid.; staff meeting, 9 May 1952.
[281] Staff meeting, 11-12 January 1952.
[282] Ibid.; Blyth, *English University Adult Education*, p. 328.
[283] LCC meeting, 13 May 1959.
[284] Board meeting, 15 January 1959; staff meeting, 22 December 1958.
[285] Walter Evans to Geoffrey Hickson, 9 December 1958, in Board papers for 15 January 1959.
[286] Board meeting, 15 January 1959.
[287] Board meeting, 14 October 1959; 'Report to the Council of the Senate of the Committee on the Extra-Mural Activities of the University', paper for Board meeting, 19 October 1960.
[288] Claire Wallace, 'Ray Pahl Obituary: Sociologist Known for His Influential Studies of Work and Friendship', *Guardian*, 26 July 2011, online; and see for example R. E. Pahl, *Urbs in Rure: The Metropolitan Fringe in Hertfordshire* (London: London School of Economics, 1965); J. M. Pahl and R. E. Pahl, *Managers and Their Wives: A Study of Career and Family Relationships in the Middle Class* (London: Allen Lane, 1971); R. E. Pahl, *Divisions of Labour* (Oxford: Blackwell, 1984); Ray Pahl, *On Friendship* (Cambridge: Polity, 2000).
[289] Marriott, *Extramural Empires*, p. 115.
[290] Ibid., p. 116.

Chapter 3

[1] Robert Anderson, *British Universities Past and Present* (London: Hambledon Continuum, 2006), p. 182, quoting the Robbins report (emphasis added); S. G. Raybould, *University Extramural Education in England 1945-62: A Study in Finance and Policy* (London: Michael Joseph, 1964), pp. 143, 146.
[2] Calculated from Fieldhouse et al, *History of Modern British Adult Education*, p. 219; Raybould, *English Universities and Adult Education*, p. xv.
[3] Fieldhouse et al, *History of Modern British Adult Education*, p. 219.
[4] Geoffrey Hickson, 'The Finance of University Extra-Mural Departments', paper for Board meeting, 11 November 1964.
[5] Fieldhouse et al, *History of Modern British Adult Education*, pp. 219-20; Marriott, *Extramural Empires*, pp. 120-1. The University of Keele had also taken over provision in North Staffordshire from Oxford: Raybould, *University Extramural Education*, pp. 159-60.

[6] Geoffrey Hickson, 'Notes on the Possibility of Co-operation between University Extra-Mural Departments', 1967: CUL UA/BEMS/48/40A.
[7] Quoted in Raybould, *University Extramural Education*, p. 165.
[8] Raybould, *University Extramural Education*, p. 165.
[9] Fieldhouse et al, *History of Modern British Adult Education*, pp. 78, 87, 102.
[10] A Google Ngram of the phrase 'continuing education' shows a more than fivefold increase in the incidence of the phrase (28 August 2023; 1959 = 0.000042%, 1970 = 0.000214%).
[11] Universities Council for Adult Education and WEA, 'Proposals for the Expansion of Provision for Liberal Adult Education of the Industrial Community', paper in CUL UA/BEMS/48/40A.
[12] Welch, *Peripatetic University*, pp. 161, 171; Board meeting, 17 February 1950.
[13] Report of Bursaries Committee to Board meeting, 19 May 1950.
[14] Welch, *Peripatetic University*, p. 171.
[15] 'Bursaries for Adult Students, Academical Year 1950-51', paper for Board meeting 14 October 1949.
[16] Ibid.
[17] Ibid.
[18] Quoted in Welch, *Peripatetic University*, p. 158.
[19] Ibid., p. 159.
[20] Ibid., pp. 158-9.
[21] 'Report of the Bursaries Committee', paper for Board meeting, 19 May 1950.
[22] Board meeting, 15 May 1962.
[23] 'Award of Bursaries for 1952-3: Candidates Selected for Interview', paper for Board meeting, 7 March 1952.
[24] Board meeting, 15 May 1962.
[25] Annual report, 1952-3, p. 4; Welch, *Peripatetic University*, p. 171.
[26] Annual report, 1959-60, p. 3; Welch, *Peripatetic University*, p. 171.
[27] Francis Warner obituary, 2021, St Peter's College, Oxford, online.
[28] Annual report, 1976-7, p. 2.
[29] 'John Andrew: Senior Tutor of St Catharine's College'.
[30] Dan van der Vat, 'Alan Stripp: Breaker of Japanese Wartime Codes', *Guardian*, 7 May 2009, online; 'Alan Stripp', *The Times*, 25 February 2009, p. 55; Alan Stripp, *Codebreaker in the Far East* (London: Frank Cass, 1989).
[31] Michael Allen interview.
[32] Jack Herbert, *The German Tradition – Uniting the Opposites: Goethe, Jung and Rilke* (London: Temenos Academy, 2001); Jack Herbert, *Yeats and Jung: Similar Visions* (London: Guild of Pastoral Psychology, 1998).
[33] *List of Lecturers, Tutors and Subjects 1967-68*: CUL UA/BEMS/48/40A.
[34] Jay L. Halio, 'Anthony Storey, 1928–', *Dictionary of Literary Biography* (Gale, online); Board meeting, 24 May 1966; John Andrew to [?], 11 April 1967: CUL UA/BEMS/48/40A.
[35] 'David Trump FSA UOM (1931-2016)', University of Cambridge Department of Archaeology obituary, online; 'David Trump: Eccentric Archaeologist Who Undertook Extensive Work on Sites in Malta and Even Found a 2,000-Year-Old Bread Roll', *The Times*, 15 December 2016, online.
[36] D. H. Trump, *Skorba: Excavations Carried out on Behalf of the National Museum of Malta 1961-1963* (London: Society of Antiquaries, 1966).
[37] L. M. Munby, 'The Teaching of Local History', paper for Board meeting, 17 May 1965.
[38] Susan Dymond, 'Other Lives: David Dymond', *Guardian*, 26 November 2021 (online).

[39] Ibid.; David Dymond, *Writing Local History: A Practical Guide* (London: British Association for Local History/Bedford Square Press, 1982 [1st ed. 1981]); David Dymond, *Writing a Church Guide* (London: Church House, 1986 [1st ed. 1977]).
[40] See for example Chris Barringer, *Exploring the Norfolk Market Town* (Cromer: Poppyland, 2011).
[41] *List of Lecturers, Tutors and Subjects 1967-68*; Michael Pollitt, 'Chris Barringer: Author, Norfolk Historian and UEA's Director of Extra Mural Studies', *Eastern Daily Press*, 5 July 2013, online.
[42] Geoffrey Hickson, 'Teaching Staff of the Board: Appointment to the Retiring Age', paper for Board meeting, 24 May 1966; staff meeting, 26 May 1965; 29 October 1965.
[43] FGPC meeting, 28 January 1966.
[44] Geoffrey Hickson, 'Full-Time Teaching Staff: Memorandum by the Secretary', paper for Board meeting, 10 January 1967.
[45] Staff meeting, 2 May 1962.
[46] See for example staff meeting, 8 May 1969.
[47] Accounts presented to Board meeting, 9 November 1965.
[48] See for example FGPC meeting, 28 January 1966.
[49] List of Board members, for Board meeting, 3 February 1965.
[50] See Alan Burges and Richard J. Eden, 'Ashby, Eric, Baron Ashby (1904-1992)', *Oxford Dictionary of National Biography*.
[51] Annual report, 1979-80, n.p.
[52] Board meeting, 11 March 1965.
[53] Welch, *Peripatetic University*, pp. 105, 141-2; 'An Honorary Degree for Ex-Clerk'; see above, p. 22.
[54] Annual report for 1977-8, p. 3; Local Centres Union (LCU) minutes, 25 June 1977: MH archive, cupboard 5.
[55] Staff meeting, 21 December 1960.
[56] Jack Herbert and Lionel Munby, 'The Tutorial Class – Can We Prevent Its Further Decline as a Vital Part of Our District Programme?', October 1980, in staff meeting minutes folder.
[57] Ibid.
[58] Geoffrey Hickson, 'Publicity', paper for Board meeting, 14 February 1967; 'Adult Courses in East Anglia 1967-8', in MH archive, cupboard 3.
[59] Quoted in Deryck Harvey, 'Policeman's Wife Helps to Promote Goodwill', press cutting, n.d. [1969]: CUL UA/BEMS/38/26.
[60] Annual report, 1972-3, p. 5; Welch, *Peripatetic University*, p. 176n.
[61] LCU committee meeting, 10 February 1962: CUL UA/BEMS/38/5. Subsequent references in this chapter to LCU meetings are to documents in this folder. On Essex and East Anglia see staff meeting, 4 May 1965; 22 December 1967.
[62] LCU annual general meeting, 27 July 1957. Platt had an interesting, though at the time unheralded, personal story: in 1946 – when in her early 50s – she wrote a remarkable account of an encounter, at an open meeting of the Sex Education Society, with W. B. Yeats. See Avies Platt, 'A Lazarus Beside Me' (1946), *London Review of Books*, 27 August 2015.
[63] Avies Platt to John Andrew, 14 January 1961: CUL UA/BEMS/33/20.
[64] Ibid.
[65] Annual report, 1967-8, appendices; Michael Allen interview. On village colleges, see David Rooney, *Henry Morris, the Cambridgeshire Village Colleges and Community Education* (Sawston: Henry Morris Memorial Trust, 2013); Neil Hopkins, 'Creating Sites of Community Education and Democracy: Henry Morris and the Cambridgeshire Village Colleges, a Reflection 90 Years on from Their Inception', *British Educational Research Journal*, vol. 46 (2020), pp. 1099-1100.
[66] Papers in CUL UA/BEMS/48/40A; staff meeting, 4 May 1959.

[67] Annual report, 1960-1, p. 6; 1967-8, p. 6.
[68] 'Future Developments of the Board's Work: Report from the Staff Meeting', in Board meeting papers for 15 February 1966; see above, pp. 61-2.
[69] Kate Thompson, *A Century of Creative Learning: Letchworth Settlement 1920-2020* (Hatfield: University of Hertfordshire Press, 2020), p. 103.
[70] Ray Pahl, interview with Michele Abendstern, July 1998, 'Pioneers of Social Research', UK Data Archive, 6226. See '50 Years of Sociology at the University of Cambridge', conference at Clare College, 12-13 November 2018, website.
[71] Pahl, *Urbs in Rure*.
[72] See Mark Freeman, *St Albans: A History* (rev. ed., Hatfield: University of Hertfordshire Press, 2023), pp. 259, 311.
[73] R. E. Pahl, 'On the Teaching of Sociology in Hertfordshire', paper for Board meeting, 17 May 1965.
[74] Ibid.; annual report, 1960-1, pp. 6, 7.
[75] See annual reports for the early 1960s, appendices.
[76] Annual report, 1962-3, p. 7.
[77] Pahl, 'On the Teaching of Sociology in Hertfordshire'.
[78] Ibid.
[79] Ioan Davies, 'Adult Education and Social Change in Norfolk', paper for Board meeting, 17 May 1965.
[80] Annual report, 1963-4, pp. 7, 10.
[81] James Stourton, *Kenneth Clark: Life, Art and Civilisation* (London: William Collins, 2016), chapters 27, 28, 31-3.
[82] Annual report, 1965-6, appendices.
[83] Christopher Lee, 'Written Work and Class Work in the Study of Art', paper for staff meeting, 19 December 1969.
[84] Ibid.
[85] Alan Stripp, 'Class Work and Written Work in Music', December 1968, paper for staff meeting.
[86] Hickson, 'Full-Time Teaching Staff: Memorandum by the Secretary' (1967).
[87] Lionel Munby, 'Local History Studies in England', in Lionel Munby, D. Huw Owen and James Scannell, *Local History since 1945: England, Wales and Ireland* (n.p.: Socialist History Society, 2005), p. 4.
[88] Andrew and Munby, 'New Developments in University Adult Education', p. 142.
[89] Beckett, *Writing Local History*, 91-4, 195-7.
[90] Ibid.; Jones-Baker, 'Introduction', pp. vi-viii.
[91] *Hatfield and Its People: The Story of a New Town, a Garden City, an Old Village, a Historic House, the Farms and Countryside in a Hertfordshire Parish* (new ed., Hatfield: Hatfield Local History Society, 2014-15). The original volumes were published by the WEA's Hatfield branch.
[92] 'Report from the Sub-Committee on Practical Work' [probably written by Munby], paper for staff meeting, 21 December 1968.
[93] Short, 'Lionel Munby', p. 3.
[94] Andrew and Munby, 'New Developments in University Adult Education', pp. 141-2.
[95] Ibid., p. 142.
[96] Ibid., p. 141; Paul Fordham, 'The Humanities Curriculum Project in an Adult Class', *Studies in Adult Education*, vol. 6, no. 1 (1974), p. 3.
[97] Fordham, 'Humanities Curriculum Project', p. 3.
[98] Andrew and Munby, 'New Developments in University Adult Education', p. 142.
[99] E. R. Steiner to Michael Allen, n.d. [1970?]: MH archive, cupboard 8, folder 'Wellingborough'.

[100] Ibid.
[101] Ibid.
[102] See for example, the course papers for 1968, in CUL UA/BEMS/14/40.
[103] Annual report, 1961-2, p. 10.
[104] Pahl, 'On the Teaching of Sociology in Hertfordshire'.
[105] Staff meeting, 3 May 1967.
[106] Lionel Munby, 'Local History Certificate Classes', paper for Board meeting, 13 November 1979.
[107] Staff meeting, 9 February 1968.
[108] Staff meeting, 21 December 1968.
[109] Hickson, 'Notes on the Possibility of Co-operation'.
[110] John Andrew, 'Memorandum by the Secretary, Board of Extra-Mural Studies, University of Cambridge', p. 2: MH archive, cupboard 5.
[111] Munby, 'Introduction', pp. xi-xii; 'Preliminary Notice of Residential Courses in the Easter and Summer Vacations, 1954', paper for staff meeting, 29 April 1953.
[112] Staff meeting, 6 May 1957; 26 May 1965.
[113] Annual report, 1967-8, p. 12; Belstead course and 'Teaching Local Studies' papers, 1967: CUL UA/BEMS/48/40A.
[114] Andrew and Munby, 'The Extra-Mural Work of the University', p. 122.
[115] R. E. Pahl, 'Newcomers in Town and Country', in Munby, *East Anglian Studies*, esp. pp. 176, 177-82.
[116] Andrew and Munby, 'New Developments in University Adult Education', p. 142.
[117] Munby, *East Anglian Studies*.
[118] Andrew and Munby, 'New Developments in University Adult Education', p. 141.
[119] Quoted in Harvey, 'Policeman's Wife Helps to Promote Goodwill'.
[120] Andrew, 'Memorandum by the Secretary'.
[121] 'Report to the Council of the Senate of the Committee on the Extra-Mural Activities of the University', 18 July 1960, in Board papers for 19 October 1960. For Hickson's view, see above, p. 60.
[122] 'Residential Courses in English Literature Held in Madingley Hall, Christmas Vacation, 1955-56 to 1965-66', in Board papers for 3 February 1965; see above, p. 48.
[123] Welch, *Peripatetic University*, p. 168; 'Future Developments of the Board's Work: Report from the Staff Meeting'. Churchill and Fitzwilliam became colleges in 1966; Hughes Hall was a 'recognised institution' of the university from 1949, though it did not become a full college until the twenty-first century.
[124] VCFS, 1963, course papers: CUL UA/BEMS/14/34.
[125] Ibid.
[126] Michael Allen interview.
[127] 'Obituary: John Trim, 1924-2013', *TES Magazine*, 15 February 2013, online.
[128] Annual report, 1963-4, p. 4; 1969-70, p. 11.
[129] See for example, financial statement for Board meeting, 29 October 1963.
[130] Managers' course, 1967, course papers: CUL UA/BEMS/48/40A.
[131] Ibid.
[132] 'Personnel Management', 1969, course papers: CUL UA/BEMS/14/41.
[133] Michael Allen interview.
[134] IBM course papers, 1968: CUL UA/BEMS/14/40.
[135] Michael Allen interview.
[136] Ibid.
[137] Annual report, 1967-8, pp. 11-12.

[138] Residential conference for magistrates, 1968, papers in CUL UA/BEMS/14/41.
[139] Annual report, 1972-3, pp. 3-4.
[140] See for example annual report, 1972-3, pp. 3, 4.
[141] Committee for University Assistance to Adult Education in HM Forces, report for 1964-5, in Board papers for 9 November 1965.
[142] 'Discussion Group on International Affairs', 21 July 1967: CUL UA/BEMS/48/40A; annual report, 1967-8, p. 4.
[143] RAF course papers, 18 to 25 March 1967, and Course for Senior Officers papers, 20 to 24 March 1967: CUL UA/BEMS/48/40A
[144] Andrew, 'Memorandum by the Secretary', p. 2.
[145] Ibid., p. 2
[146] See above, p. 61.
[147] Andrew, 'Memorandum by the Secretary', p. 3.

Chapter 4

[1] A Google Ngram for 'continuing education' shows the incidence of the phrase almost doubling between 1970 and 1977 (28 August 2023; 1970 = 0.000214, 1977 = 0.000415). See above, p. 254 n.10. For a contemporaneous discussion of terminology, see Brian O'Hare, 'Local Education Authority Provision for Adult Education in the United Kingdom', *Irish Journal of Education*, vol. 15, no. 2 (1981), pp. 53-69.
[2] See for example Bill Jones, 'University of Glasgow, Department of Adult Continuing Education', in Bill Jones, Russell Moseley and Geoffrey Thomas (eds), *University Continuing Education 1981-2006: Twenty-Five Turbulent Years* (Leicester: NIACE, 2010) pp. 117-18; Janet Coles, 'Adult and Continuing Education at the University of Leeds', in Jones et al, *University Continuing Education*, pp. 126-7.
[3] Annual report, 1972-3, p. 2.
[4] *Adult Education: A Plan for Development, Report by a Committee of Inquiry Appointed by the Secretary of State for Education and Science under the Chairmanship of Sir Lionel Russell CBE* (London: HMSO, 1973; hereafter Russell Report); Richard Taylor, 'Russell, Sir (Edward) Lionel (1903-1983)', *Oxford Dictionary of National Biography*.
[5] Russell Report, pp. ix-xi.
[6] Ibid., p. x.
[7] Ibid., p. ix.
[8] Ibid., p. 72.
[9] Ibid.
[10] Ibid., p. 1.
[11] Ibid., p. 73.
[12] Annual report, 1972-3, p. 2.
[13] Russell Report, p. x; Taylor, 'Russell, Sir (Edward) Lionel'; Fieldhouse et al, *History of Modern British Adult Education*, esp. pp. 93-6, 222-4.
[14] Annual report, 1973-4, p. 2.
[15] Ibid., p. 2; 1974-5, p. 2.
[16] Annual report, 1975-6, p. 2.
[17] Annual report, 1971-2, p. 2.
[18] Welch, *Peripatetic University*, p. 176n.
[19] Avies M. Platt to Michael Allen, 1 December 1970: MH archive, cupboard 8, folder 'Wellingborough'.

[20] Ibid. See also above, pp. 78-9.
[21] Platt to Allen, 1 January 1971.
[22] *CUR*, 19 February 1975, p. 730
[23] *CUR*, 8 October 1975, pp. 86-7.
[24] See for example FGPC minutes, 19 October 1971; 26 January 1972; 28 April 1972.
[25] *CUR*, 20 October 1971, p. 213; 26 January 1977, p. 372; 20 July 1977, p. 935.
[26] Annual report, 1977-8, p. 2.
[27] *CUR*, 24 May 1972, p. 906; Roland Randall, staff webpage, Girton College.
[28] FGPC minutes, 21 June 1972; 29 July 1975; Mary Teresa Spens, 'Family Structure in a Dominican Village' (PhD thesis, University of Cambridge, 1969).
[29] Annual report, 1977-8, p. 2; *CUR*, 22 November 1978, p. 173; LCU minutes, 16 June 1979: MH archive, cupboard 5. Other LCU papers cited in this chapter are in this cupboard, in a folder labelled 'BEMS Not Madingley'.
[30] List of staff with dates of appointment, with FGPC minutes, 1 October 1976.
[31] Staff meeting minutes, 14 December 1978.
[32] 'Classes in Local History Taken by L. M. H.', typed list in the possession of Diana Munby.
[33] J. C. Barringer, 'An Estimate of a Resident Tutor's Year 1972-3', FGPC paper for 19 October 1973.
[34] Andrew to T. C. Gardner, 16 February 1973, 23 February 1973, FGCP papers; for loans see FGCP papers, *passim.*
[35] Michael Allen interview.
[36] 'Adult Courses in East Anglia 1973-74', p. 6: MH archive, cupboard 3. All subsequent course lists and advertising material are in this location unless otherwise stated.
[37] Sarah Speight, 'Teachers of Adult Education in British Universities 1948-1998', *Studies in the Education of Adults*, vol. 36 (2004), p. 117.
[38] Gillian Sheail interview.
[39] Andrew and Munby, 'The Extra-Mural Work of the University', p. 121.
[40] Ibid.
[41] Michael Allen interview.
[42] Ibid.
[43] See for example annual report, 1971-2, p. 3.
[44] 'Adult Courses in East Anglia 1973-74', p. 1.
[45] Ibid. In the previous year, the 'typical' fee had been £1.50. Inflation from 1972 to 1973 was 9.1%, and the increase was 16.7%.
[46] 'Adult Courses in East Anglia 1973-74', pp. 11, 22-4.
[47] LCU minutes, 15 June 1974.
[48] 'Adult Courses in East Anglia 1975-76'.
[49] Annual report 1975-6, p. 2; see above, pp. 82-3.
[50] Michael Allen interview.
[51] Russell Report, p. 38.
[52] 'Adult Courses in East Anglia 1973-74', p. 1.
[53] See for example annual report, 1971-2, p. 2; Andrew, 'Memorandum by the Secretary', pp. 4-5.
[54] Annual report, 1978-9, p. 3; 1979-80, p. 2.
[55] Annual report, 1978-9, p. 3; 1981-2, p. 4.
[56] For Andrew's attendance, see for example LCU minutes, 15 June 1974.
[57] Gillian Sheail interview.
[58] LCU statement of accounts, June 1976, and minutes, 13 October 1979.
[59] LCU, list of delegates, 25-6 June 1977, and 1977 summer weekend programme.

[60] J. C. Barringer, 'A Hundred Years of Cambridge Lectures in Norwich 1877-1977', typescript in CUL, Cam.a.977.4.
[61] Janet Keystone, 'Impressions of King Street, Norwich', *Quill*, issue 3 (June 1989), p. 11. *Quill* was the in-house staff magazine at Madingley Hall. There is a full run of issues in the MH archive, cupboard 3.
[62] Gillian Sheail interview.
[63] Ibid.
[64] Staff meeting, 2 May 1973.
[65] Gillian Sheail interview.
[66] Ibid.
[67] Thompson, *Century of Creative Learning*, pp. 59-61.
[68] Margaret J. Walshe, 'An Active Brain and a Contented Mind', *Ad Lib*, issue 11 (February 1999), p. 8.
[69] Memorandum by David Dymond for staff meeting, 3 May 1976.
[70] See for example staff meeting, 3 May 1972.
[71] Board meeting, 8 May 1975.
[72] Annual report, 1978-9, p. 3; Herbert and Munby, 'The Tutorial Class'.
[73] Herbert and Munby, 'The Tutorial Class'.
[74] Ibid.
[75] Lionel Munby, 'Linked Sessionals', n.d. [1980?], in staff meeting minutes; staff meeting, 4 November 1983.
[76] J. C Barringer and R. Virgoe, report on local history certificate at Norwich, 1978-81, in Board papers for 1979.
[77] Staff meeting, 23 January 1980.
[78] Staff meetings, 13 December 1974, 1 May 1974; Lionel Munby, 'Local History Certificate Classes', paper for Board meeting, 13 November 1979.
[79] David Dymond, 'Local History in Lionel's Time', *Ad Lib*, issue 4 (October 1996), p. 3.
[80] 'Classes in Local History Taken by L. M. M.'.
[81] Michael Allen interview.
[82] List of publications compiled by Munby, in the possession of Diana Munby. See for example L. M. Munby (ed.), *Life and Death in Kings Langley: Wills and Inventories 1498-1659* (King's Langley: Kings Langley Local History and Museum Society, in association with Kings Langley WEA, 1981); L. M. Munby (ed.), *Hunsdon and Widford: A Local History* (Hunsdon: Hunsdon Local History Society, 1979); *Wheathampstead and Harpenden, I: The Settlement of Wheathampstead and Harpenden* (n.p.: Harpenden and St Albans Branches of the Workers' Educational Association, 1973); *The Story of Harpenden and Wheathampstead, VI: The Schools* (n.p.: Harpenden and St Albans Branches of the Workers' Educational Association, 1976).
[83] List of publications compiled by Munby.
[84] Munby, *Hertfordshire Landscape*, p. 9.
[85] Ibid., p. 7.
[86] See for example E. P. Thompson, *The Making of the English Working Class* (Harmondsworth: Penguin, 1991 [1st ed. 1963]), p. 13.
[87] Lionel M. Munby, *The Common People are Not Nothing: Conflict in Religion and Politics in Hertfordshire 1575-1780* (Hatfield: Hertfordshire Publications, 1995), p. v.
[88] Russell Report, p. 12; Sarah Speight, 'Digging for History: Archaeological Fieldwork and the Adult Student 1943-1975', *Studies in the Education of Adults*, vol. 34 (2002), pp. 79-80.
[89] 'Residential Field Study Courses Programme: 1979'.

[90] David Trump, 'The Board and Archaeology', *Ad Lib*, issue 1 (November 1995), p. 4; Speight, 'Digging for History', pp. 79-80.
[91] Andrew and Munby, 'The Extra-Mural Work of the University', p. 121.
[92] Fordham, 'Humanities Curriculum Project', p. 9.
[93] 'On Not Teaching Pscyhology: An Experiment in Adult Education', April 1984, MH archive, cupboard 3.
[94] 'Comments by the Council of the Senate on the Report of the Joint Working Party of the Committee of Vice-Chancellors and Principals and the Universities Council for Adult Education on Adult Education', 20 March 1975, MH archive, cupboard 5 (box: 'Historical Development of Madingley Hall'); Russell Report, pp. xiv, 74-5.
[95] See for example, FGPC minutes, 19 October 1973, 31 January 1977, 26 January 1979.
[96] Annual report, 1971-2, p. 3.
[97] Annual report, 1973-4, pp. 3-5.
[98] Ibid., pp. 4-5.
[99] Ibid.
[100] Ibid., p. 3.
[101] University of Cambridge Board of Extra-Mural Studies, Extraordinary Report to Council of the Senate [1984-5] (hereafter Extraordinary Report), p. 17: MH archive, cupboard 5.
[102] Annual report, 1973-4, p. 5.
[103] Michael Allen interview
[104] Extraordinary Report, p. 18.
[105] 'Report of the Council of the Senate on the Future Use of Madingley Hall', *CUR* 14 November 1973, p. 279.
[106] Ibid., p. 281.
[107] Ibid., p. 286; annual report, 1977-8, p. 2.
[108] 'Report of the Council of the Senate', pp. 279-86.
[109] Ibid., pp. 282, 283-4, 287; annual report, 1974-5, p. 2.
[110] 'Report of the Council of the Senate', p. 281.
[111] Annual report, 1975-6, p. 2; 1974-5, p. 2.
[112] Annual report, 1975-6, p. 2. One residential course lasted for three weeks, and three for six weeks.
[113] Annual report, 1977-8, p. 2; 1981-2, p. 6.
[114] Annual report, 1982-3, p. 6-7.
[115] *Madingley Hall: A Short History and Description of the Hall and Estate, Their Owners and Occupiers* (4th ed., Cambridge: University of Cambridge, 1976 [1st ed. 1961]).
[116] Michael Allen interview; anonymous interview; FGPC minutes, 3 November 1978.
[117] 'Building and Development at Madingley Hall: Draft Note for Working Party', October 1987: MH archive, cupboard 5.
[118] Michael Allen interview.
[119] Annual report, 1978-9, p. 3.
[120] Michael Allen, correspondence with author, June 2023.
[121] *CUR*, 28 June 1978, p. 768; annual report, 1978-9, p. 3.
[122] See various meetings of the FGPC, 1975-8.
[123] 'Madingley Hall Equipment: Mattresses and Blankets', 22 January 1979, memorandum by Vivian Ramsbottom, in FGCP papers.
[124] FGPC minutes, *passim*.
[125] FGPC meeting, 30 January 1978.
[126] Andrew to R. E. Macpherson, 13 April 1977, in FGPC papers.

[127] 'John Andrew: Senior Tutor of St Catharine's College'.
[128] 'Adult Courses in East Anglia 1973-4', pp. 32-3; 'Residential Field Study Courses: Programme, 1978'.
[129] Adrian Barlow interview with author, 4 July 2022.
[130] Lionel Munby, 'Discussion Document', [1981], in staff meeting papers.
[131] Annual report, 1979-80, appendices.
[132] LCU minutes, 12 June 1976.
[133] LCU minutes, 25 June 1977.
[134] See *University of Cambridge International Summer Schools* (Cambridge: Institute of Continuing Education, 2003),pp. 6, 26.
[135] Annual report, 1969-70, p. 11.
[136] Munby, 'Discussion Document'.
[137] Annual report 1971-2, p. 3; *University of Cambridge International Summer Schools*, p. 6.
[138] 'Report of the Committee to Consider the Extra Ordinary Report (May 1985) of the Board of Extra-Mural Studies', FGPC papers, 30 April 1986.
[139] Annual report, 1978-9, p. 4.
[140] Alan Rogers, 'A University of the 1990s?', in Brian Groombridge, Alan Rogers and others, *The Universities and Continuing Education into the 1990s* (Londonderry: New University of Ulster Institute of Continuing Education, 1981), p. 13.
[141] Annual report, 1981-2, p. 4.
[142] C. L. Wayper, 'Extra-Mural Studies', *Cambridge: The Magazine of the Cambridge Society*, no. 4 (1979), p. 32.
[143] Harold Wiltshire, 'The Role of the University Adult Education Department', *Studies in Adult Education*, vol. 15 (1983), p. 8.

Chapter 5

[1] Richard Taylor and Bill Jones, 'Introduction: University Continuing Education 1981-2006', in Jones et al, *University Continuing Education*, p. 1.
[2] Ibid., p. 3.
[3] Bill Jones and Geoffrey Thomas, 'University Continuing Education: Changing Concepts and Prescriptions', in Jones et al, *University Continuing Education*, pp. 81-2.
[4] Annual report, 1980-1, p. 4.
[5] Jones and Thomas, 'University Continuing Education', pp. 82-3; Fieldhouse et al, *History of Modern British Adult Education*, pp. 227-9.
[6] Annual report, 1980-1, p. 4.
[7] Staff meetings, 15 September 1981, 2 April 1982, 13 April 1984; annual report, 1982-3, p. 6; 1983-4, pp. 6-7; 1987-8, p. 3.
[8] *CUR*, 8 July 1981, p. 739; annual report, 1982-3, p. 7; 1985-6, p. 6.
[9] See annual reports for various years.
[10] Departmental plan June 1988 to May 1989, June 1989 to 1990, FGPC papers, 19 October 1988.
[11] Lionel Munby, memories of Ken Naylor in a photograph album in Madingley Hall archive, cupboard 5.
[12] Universities Council for Adult and Continuing Education (UCACE), annual reports, 1982-3, tables 5(a) and 5(b); 1989-90, tables 1 and 6(b).
[13] Annual report, 1987-8, p. 1.

[14] 'Courses for the Public: The Landscape and Natural History of East Anglia' (1989), and 'Courses for the Public: Regional Ecology of the British Isles', both in MH archive, cupboard 3. Subsequent course guides and reading lists cited in this chapter are at the same location.
[15] Annual report, 1985-6, p. 2.
[16] Annual report, 1989-90, p. 9; staff meeting, 4 November 1983.
[17] D. H. Trump, report on year 1, Certificate in Landscape History and Field Archaeology, paper for staff meeting, 6 November 1981.
[18] Annual report, 1988-9, p. 9.
[19] 'Certificate Courses', paper for Board meeting, 9 February 1988.
[20] Ibid.
[21] 'Courses for the Public: Certificate in Local History, Year 3', schedule and reading list, 1989-90.
[22] Annual report, 1989-90, p. 9.
[23] Annual report, 1985-6, pp. 2, 11-16.
[24] LCU minutes, 17 June 1978.
[25] 'Guide to Lifelong Learning: Hertfordshire', 1985-6.
[26] Michael Allen interview.
[27] Annual report, 1988-9, p. 5.
[28] '1988-89 Guide to Lifelong Learning: Cambridgeshire'.
[29] Annual report, 1989-90, p. 13; Fiona MacCarthy, 'Walter Gropius in Britain', *Tate Etc.*, issue 45 (2019), online.
[30] See annual reports and Suffolk course lists for each year.
[31] Michael Allen interview.
[32] Vanessa Nedderman interview with author, 9 May 2022.
[33] Thompson, *Century of Creative Learning*, pp. 50-7, 103.
[34] Vanessa Nedderman interview.
[35] Ibid.
[36] Ibid.
[37] Ibid.
[38] Anonymous interview.
[39] '1989-90 Guide to Lifelong Learning: Norfolk'.
[40] List of courses taught by Lionel Munby.
[41] Mark Bailey interview with author, 27 May 2022.
[42] Annual report, 1985-6, p. 3; 'Nature and Scope', p. 34.
[43] Annual report, 1986-7, p. 4.
[44] Annual report, 1984-5, p. 2.
[45] Pauline Hunt, 'Learning to Brighten up Your Leisure Time', *Cambridge Evening News*, 19 January 1985: press cutting in MH archive, cupboard 5; 'Obituary: Christopher Driver', *Independent*, 22 February 1997 (online); 'Residential Courses 1986-7'; annual report, 1986-7, appendix.
[46] Hunt, 'Learning to Brighten up Your Leisure Time'.
[47] See for example 'Residential Courses 1986-7'; annual report, 1986-7, appendix.
[48] Angela Parker, 'Weekend Course: Being on the Receiving End', *Quill*, issue 4 (September 1989), p. 8.
[49] Ibid.
[50] Ibid., p. 9.
[51] Evelyn Lord interview with author, 30 March 2022.
[52] Extraordinary Report, p. 8.
[53] Annual report, 1989-90, p. 5.

[54] Ibid., p. 1.
[55] Extraordinary Report, p. 9.
[56] 'Residential Courses 1986-7'.
[57] Ibid.; annual report 1985-6, p. 5 and appendix pp. 9-10.
[58] 'Residential Courses 1989-90'; annual report, 1988-9, p. 15.
[59] Annual report, 1989-90, p. 14; 1993-4, appendix; Extraordinary Report, p. 11.
[60] Gillian Sheail interview.
[61] Ibid.; 'The Making of the British Landscape', *Quill*, issue 5 (December 1989), pp. 6-7.
[62] Mark Bailey, 'David Dymond', Suffolk Institute of Archaeology and History, 28 August 2021, online; Alec Betterton and David Dymond, *Lavenham: 700 Years of Textile-Making* (Woodbridge: Boydell, 1982); Alec Betterton and David Dymond, *Lavenham: An Industrial Town* (Lavenham: Terence Dalton, 1989).
[63] Gillian Sheail interview; *Look at the Building Stones of Bedford: A Town Trail* (Bedford: Bedford Retirement Education Centre, 1991).
[64] Sue Oosthuizen, 'Landscape History and Field Archaeology', *Ad Lib*, issue 6 (June 1997), p. 9.
[65] Gillian Sheail interview.
[66] 'Nature and Scope', pp. 25-6. The report gives the number of 'effective students' as 2,920, the number of returns as 1,810, and the response rate as 62.4%. However, if the numbers are correct, the response rate to one decimal place was 62.0%.
[67] Ibid., pp. 30-2, 17-18.
[68] Annual report, 1985-6, p. 80 (this report was issued in June, whereas 'Nature and Scope' is dated November 1986). See Welch, *Peripatetic University*, p. 190.
[69] 'Nature and Scope', pp. 17-19.
[70] Ibid., pp. 19-21.
[71] Ibid., p. 44.
[72] Ibid., p. 21.
[73] Ibid., pp. 31-2.
[74] Ibid., p. 32.
[75] Ibid., p. 45.
[76] Annual report, 1989-90, p. 9.
[77] Annual report, 1982-3, pp. 5-6; Sarah Ormrod interview with author, 26 July 2022.
[78] Annual report, 1983-4, p. 3; 1985-6, p. 10; Sarah Ormrod interview.
[79] Sarah Ormrod interview.
[80] Annual report, 1982-3, p. 5.
[81] John Naughton, 'Richard Mason (1948-2006): A Unique Spinoza Scholar', *Wolfson College Magazine*, vol. 30 (2005-6), reproduced online.
[82] Michael Allen interview; *University of Cambridge International Summer Schools*, p. 27.
[83] Annual report, 1982-3, pp. 5-6; *University of Cambridge International Summer Schools*, p. 27.
[84] Annual report, 1982-3, pp. 5-6.
[85] Annual report, 1985-6, pp. 9-10.
[86] Annual report, 1985-6, p. 4.
[87] Sarah Ormrod interview.
[88] Michael Allen interview; Sarah Ormrod interview.
[89] Michael Allen interview.
[90] Sarah Ormrod interview.
[91] Ibid.
[92] Ibid.
[93] Annual report, 1988-9, p. 2; annual report 1989-90, p. 15.

[94] Anunal report, 1986-7, pp. 7, appendix.
[95] Annual report, 1989-90, p. 2.
[96] Sarah Ormrod interview.
[97] Extraordinary Report, pp. 11-12, 21.
[98] *University of Cambridge International Summer Schools*, pp. 27-8.
[99] Annual report, 1982-3, p. 5.
[100] Ibid.; Sarah Ormrod interview. On the 'honours option', see below, p. 195.
[101] Annual report, 1986-7, p. 6.
[102] The account below is based on University of Cambridge, 'IBM Course Programme 1987': MH archive, cupboard 3 (filed with IBM course photos).
[103] *The Cambridge Phenomenon: The Growth of High Technology Industry in a University Town* (Cambridge: Segal Quince and Partners, 1985), pp. 58-61.
[104] Ibid., pp. 52ff.
[105] Ibid., p. 79.
[106] Extraordinary Report, p. 19.
[107] R. V. Mason, 'Management and Business Studies', paper for Board meeting, 9 February 1988; Eve Williamson, 'The PICKUP Initiative at Cambridge University: Progress Report on DES-Funded Research Project', paper for Board meeting, 13 May 1986.
[108] Mason, 'Management and Business Studies'; flyers for two courses in staff meeting papers for 19 April 1985.
[109] Ibid.
[110] Ibid.
[111] Fieldhouse et al, *History of Modern British Adult Education*, pp. 229-30; Geoffrey Chivers, 'Vocationalism and the Rise of Continuing Vocational Education', in Jones et al, *University Continuing Education*, pp. 92-5.
[112] Chivers, 'Vocationalism', pp. 96, 96.
[113] Christopher Padfield and Polly Courtice interview with author, 9 February 2023.
[114] Williamson, 'The PICKUP Initiative'.
[115] Christopher Padfield and Polly Courtice interview; Christopher Padfield, 'The Cambridge Programme for Industry', *Ad Lib*, issue 3 (July 1996), p. 10.
[116] Christopher Padfield and Polly Courtice interview; University of Cambridge Advanced Programme for Industry, interim report to Board meeting, 15 May 1990.
[117] Christopher Padfield and Polly Courtice interview.
[118] Interim report to Board meeting, 15 May 1990.
[119] Christopher Padfield and Polly Courtice interview; *Cambridge Phenomenon*, p. 93.
[120] Christopher Padfield and Polly Courtice interview.
[121] Polly Courtice, 'Satisfying Your Owner as Your Customer: Case Study of the Cambridge Programme for Industry', *Quality in Continuing Education: Proceedings of the 7th EUCEN European Conference* (Helsinki University of Technology Lifelong Learning Series, no. 3, 1995), p. 34.
[122] Padfield, 'Cambridge Programme for Industry'; Courtice, 'Satisfying Your Owner', p. 37.
[123] Christopher Padfield and Polly Courtice interview.
[124] Courtice, 'Satisfying Your Owner', p. 37.
[125] Ibid., p. 33.
[126] R. V. Mason, 'Magistrates' and Court Clerks Courses', 18 December 1986, paper for FGOC, 21 January 1987.
[127] R. V. Mason, 'Courses for Magistrates 1987-88 at Madingley Hall', paper for Board meeting, 15 January 1988.

[128] Extraordinary Report, pp. 16-17
[129] Annual report, 1985-6, p. 5, appendix pp. 1-5.
[130] Annual report, 1983-4, p. 3.
[131] University of Cambridge Board of Extra-Mural Studies, 'Magistrates Basic Training, First Stage: Notes for the Tutor' (Cambridge: Board of Extra-Mural Studies, 1984), p. iii: typescript in CUL Ub.3.457.
[132] Ibid.; original emphasis.
[133] University of Cambridge Board of Extra-Mural Studies, 'Magistrates' Basic Training, First Stage: Notes for the Justice' (Cambridge: Board of Extra-Mural Studies, 1984): typescript in CUL Ub.3.458; University of Cambridge Board of Extra-Mural Studies, 'Magistrates' Basic Training, Second Stage: Practical Exercises, Notes for the Justices' (Cambridge: Board of Extra-Mural Studies, 1984): typescript in CUL Ub.3.442.
[134] 'Magistrates' Basic Training, Second Stage: Practical Exercises, Notes for the Justices', pp. 26, 33.
[135] 'Magistrates' Basic Training, First Stage: Notes for the Tutor', p. iv.
[136] Extraordinary Report, p. 17; annual report, 1988-9, pp. 2-3.
[137] Annual report, 1984-5, appendix, p. 2.
[138] Extraordinary Report, p. 19.
[139] Annual report, 1985-6, p. 5, appendix.
[140] Annual report, 1987-8, p. 2; Michael Allen interview.
[141] 'Building and Development at Madingley Hall: Draft Note for Working Party', November 1986: MH archive, cupboard 5.
[142] Ibid.
[143] Ibid.; *CUR*, e.g. 4 June 1980, p. 563; 8 July 1981, p. 741; 17 June 1987, p. 705.
[144] 'Two Escape Fireball', *Cambridge Evening News*, 29 August 1985, pp. 1, 7: press cutting, MH archive, cupboard 5.
[145] Susan Rawlings, 'Building Work at Madingley Hall', *Quill*, issue 1 (December 1988), p. 10.
[146] 'Building and Development at Madingley Hall', November 1986.
[147] 'Working Party on the Development of Madingley Hall', 30 October 1990: MH archive, cupboard 5.
[148] Correspondence with the Dart Foundation, 1987: MH archive, cupboard 5.
[149] Annual report, 1978-9, p. 3.
[150] Richard Gant, 'Garden Notes', *Quill*, issue 1 (December 1988), p. 7.
[151] Richard Gant, personal correspondence with author.
[152] Richard Gant, 'Garden Notes', *Quill*, issue 6 (March 1990), pp. 10-11; Gant, 'Garden Notes', *Quill*, issue 1.
[153] Richard Gant, personal correspondence with author.
[154] Anonymous interview.
[155] Sarah Ormrod interview.
[156] Anonymous interview.
[157] Parker, 'Weekend Course'.
[158] Adrian Barlow interview.
[159] Anonymous interview.
[160] FGPC minutes, 22 September 1980, 6 November 1980, 26 October 1980, 23 January 1985, 21 October 1987.
[161] Extraordinary Report, p. 25.
[162] Janet Keystone, 'Community Education Fair', *Quill*, issue 8 (September 1990), p. 9.
[163] Ibid.

[164] Michael Allen interview.
[165] Extraordinary Report, pp. 25-6.
[166] Ibid., p. 26.
[167] Anonymous interview.
[168] 'A Day in the Life of a Madingley Chef', *Quill*, issue 2 (March 1989), p. 2.
[169] 'Ian Willis', *Quill*, issue 1 (December 1988), p. 3.
[170] FGPC minutes, 23 January 1985.
[171] 'A Day (or Two) in the Life of Darren Sillett', *Quill*, issue 6 (March 1990), p. 7.
[172] 'A Day in the Life of a Madingley Chef', *Quill*, issue 2 (March 1989), p. 2.
[173] Paul Munnery and Keith Mann, 'A Day in the Life of the Finance Office', *Quill*, issue 4 (September 1989), p. 3.
[174] Annabel Thomas, 'A Day in the Life of the Extension Division', *Quill*, issue 5 (December 1989), p. 3.
[175] Sarah Ormrod interview.
[176] Veronique Jenny, 'Impressions of Madingley', *Quill*, issue 7 (June 1990), p. 7.
[177] Annual report, 1989-90, p. 1.
[178] Munby, 'Discussion Document'.
[179] 'Staff Matters', paper for FGPC meeting, 16 October 1985.

Chapter 6

[1] On this wider history, see for example Peter Scott, *The Meanings of Mass Higher Education* (Buckingham: Open University Press, 1995), chapter 2; Robert Anderson, *British Universities Past and Present* (London: Hambledon Continuum, 2006), pp. 172-5; Peter Scott, *Retreat or Resolution? Tackling the Crisis of Mass Higher Education* (Bristol: Policy Press, 2021), chapter 3.
[2] 'The Adult Tradition', *Times Higher Education Supplement*, 20 April 1990.
[3] Ibid.
[4] See for example Geoff Whitty, Annette Hayton and Sarah Tang, 'Who You Know, What You Know and Knowing the Ropes: A Review of Evidence about Access to Higher Education Institutions in England', *Review of Education* 3 (2015), pp. 28-30.
[5] Kathryn Kelly and Stephen Cook, *Full-Time Young Participation by Socio-Economic Class: A New Widening Participation Measure in Higher Education* (London: Department for Education and Skills, 2007), esp. pp. 9-12.
[6] At the end of the 1990s more than half of Cambridge undergraduates were from private schools: see Famke Veenstra-Ashmore and Harry Hult, 'Widening Participation since 1999', *Varsity*, 17 February 2023, online. On the figures for the proportion of students from 'low participation neighbourhoods' in 2015-16, see Annabelle Allouch, trans. Lucy Garnier, 'Oxford University, Widening Participation, and the Education Market: Channeling Working-Class Students to an Elite Institution', *Revue française de sociologie*, vol. 58, no. 2 (2017), pp. 233-65, esp. table 1.
[7] David Davies, lecture slides, 'Access – What Is It?' (1993), in the possession of David Davies.
[8] Janet Keystone, 'The Other 11,000', *Varsity*, no. 394, 29 October 1993, p. 9.
[9] Ibid.
[10] Annual report, 1992-3, p. 1.
[11] Jones and Thomas, 'University Continuing Education', pp. 82-3; Fieldhouse et al, *History of Modern British Adult Education*, pp. 232-5.
[12] Fieldhouse et al, *History of Modern British Adult Education*, pp. 234-7.
[13] Ibid., pp. 237-8.

[14] *Credit Where It's Due: Project Report, Employment Department Credit Frameworks and Learning Outcomes Programmes* (Cambridge: Board of Continuing Education, n.d. [1994-5]), p. 11: MH archive, cupboard 3.
[15] Fieldhouse et al, *History of Modern British Adult Education*, p. 236.
[16] 'Credit Accumulation and Transfer (CATS): Informaton for Students, September 1995', p. 6; *Student's Handbook*, 2000-2001, p. 20: MH archive, cupboard 8; Evelyn Lord interview.
[17] Annual report, 1997-8, p. 1. See *The Learning Age: A Renaissance for a New Britain* (London: Department for Education and Employment, 1998).
[18] 'Draft Report of the Council of the Senate on the Reconstitution of the Board of Extra-Mural Studies as a Board of Continuing Education': MH archive, cupboard 5.
[19] Correspondence filed under 'Staff Comments': MH archive, cupboard 5.
[20] Helen Nisbet, 'Michael Richardson Obituary', *Guardian*, 18 December 2020, online.
[21] ICE obituary, quoted in obituary by Richard Taylor. I am grateful to Richard Taylor for supplying me with a copy of his obituary of Richardson.
[22] David Davies interview with author, 21 September 2022.
[23] Quoted in Tony Tysome, 'Cambridge Enters a New Age', *Times Higher Education Supplement*, 17 May 1991, p. 8.
[24] Annual report, 1991-2, p. 1.
[25] Staff list, in Board papers for 1 July 1996.
[26] Annual report, 1990-1, p. 5; 1994-5, p. 1; 1995-6, p. 1.
[27] Annual report, 1996-7, p. 1.
[28] Staff list, in Board papers for 1 July 1996; annual report, 1995-6, p. 2.
[29] Staff list, in Board papers for 1 July 1996.
[30] Annual report, 1991-2, p. 1; 1992-3, p. 2; 1993-4, p. 1; Barringer, 'A Hundred Years of Cambridge Lectures', p. 4.
[31] Annual report, 1993-4, p. 1.
[32] Pauline Hunt, 'University Courses Are Open to All', *Evening News*, 30 August 1996, p. 8.
[33] Peter Bysouth, 'A Local History Perspective', *Ad Lib*, issue 11 (February 1999), p. 2.
[34] Annual report, 1990-1, p. 1.
[35] Copy of address dated 15 March 1991: MH archive, cupboard 5. Richardson also presented a similar address to the Ipswich Co-operative Society, with the same date.
[36] Annual report, 1993-4, n.p.
[37] Documents in box labelled 'BEMS, Not Madingley': MH archive, cupboard 5.
[38] [?] to Julie Parrott, 28 December 1996: MH archive, cupboard 5. See other documents, including LCU financial statements, in this folder, and also Thompson, *Century of Creative Learning*.
[39] Annual report, 1993-4, n.p.; 1994-5, p. 2.
[40] 'Learning for Life: ACE Centre Courses for the Public 1993-1994', course list for the Sidgwick Site, Cambridge: MH archive, cupboard 3. Subsequent references to course lists, flyers and similar documents in this chapter are in the same location.
[41] Mark Bailey interview.
[42] Annual report, 1994-5, p. 4.
[43] Mark Bailey, 'MSt Part-Time Degree Course', *Ad Lib*, no. 1 (November 1995), p. 5.
[44] Annual report, 1995-6, p. 3; 1996-7, p. 2.
[45] Jennifer Whyte, 'Rubbish the University', *Varsity*, 8 October 1993, p. 9.
[46] Ibid.
[47] Annual report, 1998-9, p. 6.
[48] See for example annual report, 1994-5, p. 2.
[49] Peter Bysouth interview with author, 24 May 2022.

[50] Evelyn Lord interview.
[51] Peter Bysouth interview.
[52] Ibid.
[53] Ibid.
[54] Shirley Wittering interview with author, 27 October 2022.
[55] Ibid.
[56] Shirley Wittering, *Ecology and Enclosure: The Effect of Enclosure on Society, Farming and the Environment in South Cambridgeshire 1798-1850* (Bollington: Windgather Press, 2013).
[57] Shirley Wittering interview; *Thriplow Journal* (since 1992); Peter Speak and Shirley Wittering, *About Thriplow* (Thriplow: Thriplow Society, 1995). A book on the history of Thriplow Daffodil Weekend was completed in 2023 and a copy sent to every household in Thriplow. See also Chris Elliott, 'Journey Through Time', *Royston Weekly News*, 3 November 2004, press cutting in MH archive, cupboard 5.
[58] Annual report, 1991-2, appendix; 'Residential Courses: Madingley Hall, October 1991 – December 1992', p. 12; Andrea Bullock, 'Ian Beresford Gleaves', *Wagner News*, no. 219 (October 2015), p. 46.
[59] Annual report, 1991-2, appendix; 'Residential Courses at Madingley Hall October 1991 – December 1992', pp. 12-13.
[60] Ibid., p. 13; annual report, 1991-2, appendix; Kevin Flanagan website. The information in the following paragraph comes from these sources unless stated.
[61] Evelyn Lord interview.
[62] Martin Thompson, 'A Weekend Work-Out for the Mind', n.d. [1990s], press cutting in MH archive, cupboard 5.
[63] Ibid.; 'Education', *Travel and Leisure*, June 1994, p. 62: press cutting in MH archive, cupboard 5.
[64] Thompson, 'Weekend Work-Out'.
[65] *Evening News*, 30 August 1996, p. 8.
[66] Annual report, 1991-2, p. 6.
[67] *Credit Where It's Due*, p. 11.
[68] David Davies, personal correspondence with author.
[69] Annual report, 1993-4, p. 2; *Credit Where It's Due*, p. 12; annual report, 1994-5, p. 2. The number of courses given in these different documents varies from 30 to 50.
[70] *Credit Where It's Due*, p. 13.
[71] Ibid.
[72] 'Credit Accumulation and Transfer (CATS): Information for Students', pp. 3-4, 6.
[73] *Credit Where It's Due*, p. 10.
[74] Ibid., p. 8.
[75] Mark Bailey interview.
[76] *Credit Where It's Due*, pp. 30-1, 17.
[77] Ibid., p. 52.
[78] Ibid., pp. 52-3; annual report, 1994-5, p. 2.
[79] *Credit Where It's Due*, pp. 24-5, 52, 14-15.
[80] David Davies, personal correspondence with author.
[81] David Davies interview.
[82] David Davies, personal correspondence with author.
[83] *Credit Where It's Due*, p. 21.
[84] Annual report, 1996-7, p. 2; 1997-8, p. 3.
[85] *Tutor's Handbook*, 2002, pp. 11, 13, 25-7: MH archive, cupboard 3.
[86] Professional Certificate in Adult and Continuing Education, course handbook, 1993-4.

[87] Professional Certificate in Adult and Continuing Education, course flyer, 1994-5.
[88] Annual report, 1995-6, p. 19.
[89] *Credit Where It's Due*, pp. 29, 21.
[90] Ibid., p. 14.
[91] Ibid., pp. 30-1, 51.
[92] Ibid., pp. 29, 11.
[93] Ibid., pp. 50-1.
[94] Mrs Joan Lintot, 'Accreditation: The Students' Point of View', *Ad Lib*, issue 5 (February 1997), p. 2.
[95] Ibid.
[96] *Credit Where It's Due*, p. 7.
[97] Ibid., pp. 33-4.
[98] Ibid., pp. 30-1, 34.
[99] Ibid., p. 17.
[100] Ibid., pp. 17-18, 50-1.
[101] Ibid., pp. 15-16, 51-3.
[102] Ibid., p. 50.
[103] 'Residential Courses: Madingley Hall, 1994/95', p. 2.
[104] Ibid.
[105] 'Credit Accumulation and Transfer (CATS): Informaton for Students, September 1995'; *Student's Handbook* 2000-2001, pp. 8-17.
[106] 'Residential Courses: Madingley Hall, 1994/95', p. 2.
[107] 'Residential Courses at Madingley Hall, 1995', p. 2.
[108] Annual report, 1995-6, p. 3, appendix
[109] Annual report, 1998-9, appendix.
[110] 'Diploma in Educational and Vocational Guidance, 1994-1996', course flyer: MH archive, cupboard 3; annual report, 1994-5, p. 15; 1995-6, p. 20; Anon., 'Teaching Adults and the Staff Development Programme', *Ad Lib*, issue 6 (June 1997), p. 10; Vanessa Nedderman interview.
[111] Annual report, 1995-6, pp. 19-20.
[112] David Davies, personal correspondence with author.
[113] Evelyn Lord interview.
[114] David Davies, personal correspondence with author.
[115] 'Credit Accumulation and Transfer (CATS): Informaton for Students', p. 7.
[116] Annual report, 1993-4, n.p.; David Davies interview.
[117] David Davies interview.
[118] David Davies, *Turning the Tide: Access and Educational Disadvantage: The Social Purpose of Higher Education* (UK: Amazon, 2023). I am grateful to David Davies for showing me some of this book in draft form. See also Fieldhouse et al, *History of Modern British Adult Education*, pp. 73-4, 230-1.
[119] David Davies, personal correspondence with author.
[120] Davies, lecture slides, 'Access – What Is It?'.
[121] Ibid.
[122] Susan Oosthuizen, 'The Fenland Oral History Project', in Fred Gray (ed.), *Landscapes of Learning: Lifelong Learning in Rural Communities* (Leicester: NIACE, 2002), pp. 143-57; Liz Carter (ed.), *Keeping Time by the Crows: Oral History from Earith, Bluntisham and Colne* (Cambridge: ICE, 2002); Sue Edgington and Marie Askham (eds), *The Way of Things Here at the Time: Oral History from Isleham and Soham* (Cambridge: ICE, 2002).
[123] Oosthuizen, 'Fenland Oral History Project', p. 143.

[124] Ibid., pp. 143-5.
[125] Ibid., pp. 148, 154.
[126] Carter, *Keeping Time by the Crows*, p. 3.
[127] Ibid.
[128] Annual report, 1995-6, p. 2.
[129] Ibid.; annual report, 1999-2000, p. 3.
[130] Annual report, 1998-9, p. 3, supplement pp. 2, 3.
[131] Ibid., supplement.
[132] 'National Science Week', University of Cambridge *Newsletter*, April/May 1997, p. 8; Lynne Harrison and Gillian Sheail, 'Science – A Year On', *Ad Lib*, issue 6 (June 1997), p. 4; Lynne Harrison and Gillian Sheail, 'Science Gains Ground', *Ad Lib*, issue 9 (June 1998), p. 2.
[133] Gillian Sheail interview.
[134] Annual report, 1998-9, supplement.
[135] Ibid., supplement pp. 7-9. The figures for archaeology include landscape history and field archaeology courses, which are listed separately.
[136] Course programmes in the possession of Richard Gant.
[137] Peter Bysouth interview.
[138] Polly Courtice and Christopher Padfield interview; Board meeting minutes, 12 November 1991; annual report, 2001-2, p. 11.
[139] CPI, interim report to Board meeting, 1 May 1990; annual report, 1997-8, p. 7.
[140] CPI, 'Report for the Board of Continuing Education, 1995-6'.
[141] Christopher Padfield, 'Cambridge Programme for Industry: Half-Yearly Report to the Board of Continuing Education, October 1993', paper for Board meeting, 23 November 1993.
[142] Polly Courtice and Christopher Padfield interview.
[143] See Iris Borowy, *Defining Sustainable Development for Our Common Future: A History of the World Commission on Environment and Development (Brundtland Commission)* (London: Routledge, 2014); Felix Dodds and Michael Strauss with Maurice Strong, *Only One Earth: The Long Road via Rio to Sustainable Development* (London: Routledge, 2012).
[144] Polly Courtice and Christopher Padfield interview; Chris Elliott, 'Prince Calls in Wearing Different Kinds of Hat', *Cambridge Evening News*, 22 November 1993, p. 7.
[145] Polly Courtice and Christopher Padfield interview.
[146] CPI annual report 1993-4, paper for Board meeting, 22 November 1994.
[147] Polly Courtice and Christopher Padfield interview.
[148] Ibid.
[149] Ibid.
[150] Annual report, 1999-2000, p. 8, appendix K.
[151] Polly Courtice and Christopher Padfield interview.
[152] 'The Manufacturing Leaders' Programme', paper for Board meeting, 19 March 1993.
[153] Paul Kirby and Giles Oliver, 'Birth of the All-Round Construction Designer', *Proceedings of the Institution of Civil Engineers – Civil Engineering*, vol. 114, no. 1 (1996), p. 47.
[154] Ibid.
[155] Ibid.; 'MSt in Interdisciplinary Design for the Built Environment': ICE website (accessed 23 April 2023).
[156] Christopher Padfield, 'University of Cambridge Programme for Industry: Interim Report', Board papers for 23 February 1993.
[157] Board meeting minutes, 19 March 1996.

[158] Lynne Caley, 'The Possibilities in a Traditional University', in David Boud and Nicky Solomon (eds), *Work-Based Learning: A New Higher Education?* (Buckingham: SRHE and Open University Press, 2001), 117.
[159] Polly Courtice and Christopher Padfield interview.
[160] Christopher Padfield, 'Research and Reflection on Professional Practice as a Personal Goal in Continuing Education: Implications for Universities', paper for Board meeting, 15 October 1996.
[161] Elaine Hendry and Mark Waltham, 'New Shoots from Old Roots: Continuing Professional Development at the University of Cambridge', *Industry and Higher Education*, vol. 12, no. 3 (1998), pp. 173, 177.
[162] Ibid., 177.
[163] Polly Courtice and Christopher Padfield interview.
[164] Padfield, 'Research and Reflection'.
[165] Ibid.
[166] Polly Courtice and Christopher Padfield interview.
[167] Ibid.
[168] Ibid.
[169] Calculated from annual report, 1999-2000, appendix K.
[170] Ibid., p. 8.
[171] Richard Mason, 'The IBM Cambridge Programme: An Experiment in Adult Education', *Ad Lib*, issue 2 (March 1996), p. 3.
[172] Ibid.
[173] Ibid. Original emphasis.
[174] Ibid., p. 4; Michael Allen interview.
[175] Annual report, 1991-2, n.p.
[176] Annual report, 1997-8, p. 5; 1998-9, p. 9.
[177] *Cambridge Evening News*, 21 January 1998.
[178] Annual report, 1998-9, p. 4.
[179] Calculated from *University of Cambridge International Summer Schools*, p. 27.
[180] Ibid., pp. 7-8, 27-8; Sarah Ormrod interview; Ormrod, 'International Summer Schools', *Ad Lib*, issue 3 (July 1996), p. 11.
[181] Sarah Ormrod interview.
[182] Ibid.
[183] Sarah J. Ormrod, 'Preface', in Sarah J. Ormrod (ed.), *Cambridge Contributions* (Cambridge: Cambridge University Press, 1998), p. xv.
[184] Annual report, 1998-9, appendix C; annual reports for subsequent years.
[185] Sarah Ormrod interview.
[186] *University of Cambridge International Summer Schools*, p. 34.
[187] Annual report, 1994-5, p. 6; 1998-9, p. 118.
[188] Ormrod, 'Preface', p. xiii.
[189] Paul McHugh, 'James Stuart: Engineering, Philanthropy and Radical Politics', in Richard Mason (ed.), *Cambridge Minds* (Cambridge: Cambridge University Press, 1994), pp. 100-9.
[190] Richard Mason, 'Preface', in Mason, *Cambridge Minds*, p. xii; Edward Shils and Carmen Blacker (eds), *Cambridge Women: Twelve Portraits* (Cambridge: Cambridge University Press, 1992).
[191] Ormrod, 'Preface', p. xxi.
[192] Stefan Collini, 'Cambridge and the Study of English', in Ormrod, *Cambridge Contributions*, pp. 42-64.
[193] *International Summer Schools 90th Anniversary 1923-2013* (Cambridge: Institute of Continuing Education, 2013), p. 23.

[194] *University of Cambridge International Summer Schools*, p. 29; annual report, 1998-9, p. 8; Sarah Ormrod interview.
[195] *International Summer Schools 90th Anniversary*, p. 20.
[196] Ormrod, 'International Summer Schools', p. 11; annual report, 1998-9, p. 8.
[197] Sarah Ormrod interview; annual report, 1997-8, p. 4.
[198] Sarah Ormrod interview.
[199] Annual report, 1998-9, p. 8; Sarah Ormrod interview; *University of Cambridge International Summer Schools*, p. 26.
[200] Sarah Ormrod interview.
[201] David Davies interview.
[202] Annual report, 1998-9, appendix B.
[203] Bysouth, 'Local History Perspective', p. 2.

Chapter 7

[1] Russell Moseley, 'The Impact on University Continuing Education Departments', in Jones et al, *University Continuing Education*, pp. 48, 50-1.
[2] Jones and Thomas, 'University Continuing Education', p. 86.
[3] David Blunkett, foreword to *Learning Age*, p. 7.
[4] *Learning Age*, p. 10.
[5] Ibid.
[6] Committee of Vice-Chancellors and Principals, *The Learning Curve: Our Vision for a Learning Age* (London: Committee of Vice-Chancellors and Principals, 1998), pp. 18-19.
[7] Annual report, 1997-8, p. 1.
[8] Ibid.; *Learning Age*, p. 51.
[9] Annual report, 1999-2000, p. 1.
[10] 'Joint Report of the Council and the General Board on Continuing Education and Lifelong Learning, and the Cambridge Programme for Industry', *CUR*, 25 July 2001, pp. 1004-10.
[11] Polly Courtice and Christopher Padfield interview.
[12] Annual report, 1999-2000, p. 8.
[13] Discussion of reports at Senate House on 16 January 2001, *CUR*, 24 January 2001, pp. 386-7. Emphasis in the original.
[14] Ibid.
[15] Richard Taylor interview with author, 10 May 2023.
[16] 'University of Cambridge Programme for Industry Celebrates Its 20th Anniversary', University of Cambridge news website, 26 September 2008 (accessed 3 May 2023); Cambridge Institute for Sustainability Leadership website (accessed 3 May 2023).
[17] Annual report, 1998-9. The CPI, shortly to become independent of ICE, was in this report a fourth named area of activity.
[18] Public programmes division, annual report, 1999-2000, filed with a set of recent annual reports in MH archive, cupboard 8.
[19] Richard Taylor interview.
[20] Adrian Barlow interview.
[21] Ibid.
[22] 'Lifelong Learning in the Region: Institute of Continuing Education, Public Courses 2002-2003', pp. 14-20: course list, MH archive, cupboard 3. Subsequent references to course lists and handbooks in this chapter are in the same location.
[23] Ibid., pp. 30-1, 66; annual report, 2002-3, appendix E.

[24] Annual report, 2003-4, pp. 4, appendix C.
[25] Annual report, 2004-5, p. 5, appendix E.
[26] Ibid.; LCU minutes, 7 February 2001, 7 February 2002: MH archive, cupboard 8.
[27] LCU minutes, 13 October 1999, 7 February 2002.
[28] LCU agenda, 5 May 2001; feedback forms on Students' Day, 3 May 2002: MH archive, cupboard 8.
[29] Annual report, 2004-5, p. 6; LCU newsletter, 2004.
[30] Twigs Way (ed.), *Picturing Paradise: Studies in Eighteenth to Twentieth Century Gardens and Garden Design* (Cambridge: ICE, 2003).
[31] Annual report, 2004-5, appendix E.
[32] Ibid., pp. 5-6, appendix E; *Student's Handbook 2002-3*, pp. 10-11.
[33] Annual report, 2004-5, p. 12.
[34] Sean O'Dell interview with author, 23 May 2022; Sean O'Dell, *The Essex and Suffolk Stour: A History* (Stroud: History Press, 2006).
[35] See for example Heather Falvey, 'Crown Policy and Local Economic Context in the Berkhamsted Common Enclosure Dispute 1618-42', *Rural History*, vol. 12, no. 2 (2001), pp. 123-58.
[36] Sean O'Dell, *Skillingers of Brightlingsea: Essex's Offshore Oyster-Catchers* (Stroud: History Press, 2009).
[37] Ibid., acknowledgements; Sean O'Dell interview.
[38] Sean O'Dell, 'Post-War Tourism in the Tendring District and Beyond: The Rise of the Holiday Caravan Park c.1938-1989' (PhD thesis, University of Essex, 2015).
[39] Sean O'Dell interview.
[40] This paragraph is based on Carolyn Redmayne interview with author, 10 May 2022.
[41] Carolyn Redmayne, *The Spirit of Over* (n.p., 2021).
[42] Ibid., foreword by Evelyn Lord.
[43] Carolyn Redmayne interview.
[44] Richard Taylor interview.
[45] Mary Ann Coates, in LCU newsletter, 2004, p. 3.
[46] Richard Taylor interview.
[47] Annual report, 2005-6, p. 8.
[48] Richard Taylor interview.
[49] Annual report, 2007-8, p. 4
[50] 'Residential Courses at Madingley Hall 2007-8', p. 1.
[51] Ibid.; annual report, 2008-9, p. 7; 2007-8, p. 4.
[52] 'Residential Courses at Madingley Hall 2007-8', p. 19.
[53] Ibid., p. 31.
[54] Annual report, 2000-1, p. 6.
[55] Annual report, 2002-3, pp. 5, 7.
[56] Annual report, 2003-4, appendix C; 'Day Schools 2002-3': MH archive, cupboard 3.
[57] *Tutor's Handbook* (July 2006), p. 7.
[58] Ibid.
[59] Ibid., *passim* (quoted at p. 22).
[60] *Student's Handbook 2002-3*, p. 6.
[61] Adrian Barlow interview; Barlow, *Extramural*.
[62] Barlow, *Extramural*, p. 20.
[63] Ibid., p. 25.
[64] Annual report, 2004-5, pp. 3-4
[65] Richard Taylor interview.

[66] Ibid.
[67] Ibid. Among many examples of Taylor's publications in this period, see Tom Steele and Richard Taylor, 'R. H. Tawney and the Reform of the Universities', *History of Education*, vol. 31 (2008), pp. 1-22; Richard Taylor, 'Lifelong Learning under New Labour: An Orwellian Dystopia?', *Power and Education*, vol. 1 (2009), pp. 71-82.
[68] Richard Taylor interview.
[69] Evelyn Lord interview; Adrian Barlow interview.
[70] Adrian Barlow interview.
[71] Annual report 2005-6, p. 9; Peter Cunningham, Susan Oosthuizen and Richard Taylor (eds), *Beyond the Lecture Hall: Universities and Community Engagement from the Middle Ages to the Present Day* (Cambridge: Faculty of Education and Institute of Continuing Education, 2009).
[72] Richard Taylor interview.
[73] Ibid.
[74] Ibid.
[75] Annual report, 2006-7, p. 10.
[76] Annual report, 2008-9, p. 6.
[77] Richard Taylor interview.
[78] Ibid.
[79] Ibid.
[80] Annual report, 2002-3, p. 17, appendix E.
[81] Ibid., pp. 15-16; Welch, *Peripatetic University*, p. 168.
[82] Richard Taylor interview.
[83] Ibid.; annual report, 2005-6, p. 6.
[84] Richard Taylor interview.
[85] Annual report, 2006-7, pp. 7-8, 9; Welch, *Peripatetic University*, pp. 163-6.
[86] Annual report, 2006-7, pp. 8, 9.
[87] Ibid., p. 8.
[88] Richard Taylor, personal correspondence with author.
[89] Caroline Henshaw, '"The world has lost a bright light": Leading Head Bernice McCabe Dies', *TES Magazine*, 19 February 2019, online; 'Our History', PTI website.
[90] Richard Taylor, personal correspondence with author.
[91] Richard Taylor interview; annual report, 2005-6, p. 6; 2010-11, p. 3.
[92] Annual report, 2012-13, pp. 18, 63.
[93] Annual report, 2010-11, p. 8; 2007-8, p. 7.
[94] Calculated from annual reports, 2004-5, 2008-9, appendices.
[95] Annual report, 2010-11, pp. 3, 11.
[96] Annual report, 2007-8, p. 5; 2008-9, p. 13.
[97] Annual report, 2010-11, p. 9.
[98] Annual report, 2003-4, p. 16; 2008-9, p. 11.
[99] Barlow, *Extramural*, pp. 145-6.
[100] Ibid., pp. 149-51.
[101] Adrian Barlow interview.
[102] Barlow, *Extramural*, p. 153.
[103] Annual report, 2008-9, p. 11.
[104] Richard Taylor interview.
[105] 'Madingley and Cambridge: An Anniversary Celebration', 24-8 March 2008, course programme in the possession of Richard Gant.
[106] Ibid.

[107] Ibid.; annual report, 2007-8, pp. 4, 39.
[108] *University of Cambridge International Summer Schools*, p. 27. I am grateful to Sarah Ormrod for clarifying these figures.
[109] *International Summer Schools 90th Anniversary*, pp. 13, 27.
[110] *University of Cambridge International Summer Schools*, p. 8.
[111] *International Summer Schools 90th Anniversary*, p. 16; correspondence with Sarah Ormrod.
[112] Sarah Ormrod interview.
[113] Adrian Barlow interview.
[114] Barlow, *Extramural*, p. 179.
[115] Quoted in *International Summer Schools 90th Anniversary*, p. 17.
[116] *University of Cambridge International Summer Schools*, pp. 10-11.
[117] Sarah Ormrod interview.
[118] Ibid.
[119] Ibid.; *University of Cambridge International Summer Schools*, p. 12.
[120] Annual report, 2003-4, appendix D.
[121] Quoted in *University of Cambridge International Summer Schools*, p. 11.
[122] *International Summer Schools 90th Anniversary*, pp. 68, 69, 82-3 and *passim*.
[123] Quoted in ibid., p. 74.
[124] Ibid.; annual report, 2007-8, appendix G.
[125] Sarah Ormrod interview.
[126] Quoted in *International Summer Schools 90th Anniversary*, p. 67.
[127] Ibid., p. 65.
[128] Ibid., p. 71 (ellipsis in original).
[129] *University of Cambridge International Summer Schools*, p. 29.
[130] Quoted in *International Summer Programmes: 100th Anniversary*, p. 92.
[131] Sarah Ormrod interview.
[132] *International Summer Programmes: 100th Anniversary*, p. 100.
[133] Sarah Ormrod interview; *University of Cambridge International Summer Schools*, p. 8.
[134] Annual report, 2004-5, p. 2.
[135] Annual report, 2006-7, p. 2.
[136] Ibid., pp. 4-5.
[137] Ibid., p. 4, appendix H.
[138] Annual report, 2007-8, p. 2.
[139] Richard Taylor interview.
[140] Annual report, 2007-8, pp. 2, 3.
[141] Annual report, 2008-9, pp. 5-6, 7.
[142] Annual report, 2007-8, p. 3.
[143] Ibid., pp. 2-3; 2008-9, pp. 3-4.
[144] Adrian Barlow interview.
[145] Evelyn Lord interview.
[146] Annual report, 2008-9, p. 6; Adrian Barlow interview.
[147] Adrian Barlow interview.
[148] Richard Taylor interview.
[149] Ibid.
[150] 'Part-Time Courses for the Public, 2009-2010'.
[151] Ibid.
[152] Ibid., p. 3.
[153] Annual report, 2008-9, p. 10.

[154] Annual report, 2010-11, pp. 3, 7.
[155] Ibid., p. 7.
[156] Ibid., p. 8.
[157] 'Part-Time Courses for the Public, 2009-2010', p. 3.
[158] Ibid., pp. 36-7.
[159] Thompson, *Century of Creative Learning*, p. 86.
[160] Adrian Barlow interview.
[161] Annual report, 2011-12, pp. 3-4,16, 48.
[162] Ibid., p. 48.
[163] Annual report, 2013-14, pp. 12, 23, 62.
[164] Annual report, 2012-13, pp. 54-5.
[165] Ibid., pp. 19, 62.
[166] Ibid., p. 63.
[167] Ibid., p. 11.
[168] Ibid., pp. 11, 56-62.
[169] '2023-4 Weekend Course Dates', ICE website, accessed 2 June 2023.
[170] Annual report, 2015-16, pp. 4, 65-7.
[171] Richard Taylor interview.
[172] Annual report, 2008-9, p. 4.
[173] Annual report, 2010-11, p. 13.

Postscript

[1] Andrew and Munby, 'The Extra-Mural Work of the University', p. 121.
[2] 'The Changing Demand for Subjects', paper for Board meeting, 23 May 1956.
[3] Andrew and Munby, 'The Extra-Mural Work of the University', p. 122.
[4] Chase, '"Mythmaking and Mortmain"', p. 57.
[5] Ibid., pp. 56-7.
[6] David Davies, personal correspondence with author.
[7] Bruce, 'Reminiscences', p. 10.
[8] David Davies interview.
[9] Gillian Sheail interview.

Index